Amanda Foreman, *Georgiana, Duchess of Devonshire*

'Anita Leslie's dispassionate account of her own extraordinary role in World War II is a rediscovered gem, and her harrowing description of the fighting in Alsace particularly stands out as one of the finest pieces of war reporting to come ou... ...book'

Corre... ...w Foreign
...rld War II

'As a front line Red Cross ambulance driver to the 1st French Armored division and later as a war correspondent in Africa and the Middle East during WWII, Anita Leslie was a lionhearted heroine of the first order, whose extraordinary bravery and sangfroid knew no bounds. She seems to have been too busy providing vital service to country, and relishing life's more perilous adventures to have entertained a moment's trepidation. An astonishing life and a fascinating book'

Anjelica Huston

'A vivid reminder that a woman can experience and write about a war, and seventy years on, her words stand the test of time: precise and compelling'

Kate Adie, BBC broadcaster

'It's glorious! Had me utterly gripped, I couldn't put it down. I wish I'd been able to meet her and ask her a thousand questions about the war'

Caroline Wyatt, BBC war correspondent

'The emotional truths of front-line war revealed – a charming writer, bold, female and brave'

Fay Weldon, *Death of a She Devil*

'A sharply observed account of one woman's unique war. Surreal, funny, dark, and profoundly moving. Gold dust'

Rick Stroud, *Lonely Courage*

'I loved *Train to Nowhere*. Anita Leslie's voice is highly distinctive - arch, witty, sometimes detached and utterly of her era. As the extraordinary and often appalling scenes of war progress, she draws you in with eagle-eyed observations and her astonishing bravery - always mentioned with modesty. Gripping'

Sofka Zinovieff, *The Mad Boy, Lord Berners, My Grandmother and Me*

'For every distressing episode there is the leavening effect of Anita Leslie's indomitable spirit, her canny observations and wry sense of humour in the face of unimaginable adversity, all of which turned the book into something quite unexpected and extraordinary'

Lynne Hatwell, *Dove Grey Reader*

TRAIN TO NOWHERE

ONE WOMAN'S WAR
AMBULANCE DRIVER, REPORTER,
LIBERATOR

BY ANITA LESLIE

BLOOMSBURY
LONDON · OXFORD · NEW YORK · NEW DELHI · SYDNEY

BLOOMSBURY CARAVEL
Bloomsbury Publishing Plc
50 Bedford Square, London, WC1B 3DP, UK

BLOOMSBURY, BLOOMSBURY CARAVEL and the Diana logo
are trademarks of Bloomsbury Publishing Plc

First published in Great Britain in 1948 by Hutchinson & Co
This edition published 2018 by Bloomsbury Caravel

A catalogue record for this book is available from the British Library

Library of Congress Cataloguing-in-Publication data has been applied for
ISBN: 978-1-4482-1668-0

ISBN: HB: 978-1-4482-1683-3; ePDF: 978-1-4482-1685-7; ePub: 978-1-4482-1667-3

10 9 8 7 6 5 4 3 2 1

Typeset by Deanta Global Publishing Services, Chennai, India
Printed and bound in Great Britain by CPI Group (UK) Ltd, Croydon CR0 4YY

MIX
Paper from
responsible sources
FSC® C020471

To find out more about our authors and books visit www.bloomsbury.com
and sign up for our newsletters

This book is dedicated to
Jeanne de l'Espée
and her *ambulancières* of the 1st Armoured Division

and to the memory of
Lucette and Odette Lecoq
who were killed near the Danube
24 April 1945

TRAIN TO NOWHERE

At the station near my Irish home the porter used to walk up and down the platform shouting: 'This train goes Nowhere'. He meant of course 'All change'. And that is the point we seem to have reached today. We are not really going Nowhere, we have just got to shoulder our luggage and continue the journey on a new line. Thus far I have held a first class ticket.

ANITA LESLIE
Glaslough,
Co. Monaghan, Ireland.

CONTENTS

Introduction by Penny Perrick   1

Part I: Middle East

1   Mechanized Transport Corps   7
2   Step Off   12
3   Cape to Cairo   17
4   Souls in Khaki   27
5   Desert's Edge   33
6   Eastern Times   39
7   Beirut Base   48
8   Syrian Kaleidoscope   56
9   Transjordania   61
10   Ladies of Lebanon   71
11   Good Works and Bad   77
12   Goodbye Middle East   82

Part II: Italy

13   Spring in Italy   87
14   'Air Evac'   94
15   *Simple Soldat*   104

Part III: France and Germany

16   My Kingdom for an Ambulance!   113
17   Debut in the Vosges   123
18   *Le Repos*   135

19 Alsace at Last   139
20 Beside the Rhine   151
21 Christmas 1944   160
22 Winter Wait   168
23 Hospital   173
24 Battle of Colmar – Snow   180
25 Battle of Colmar – Thaw   190
26 Aftermath   197
27 Home   206
28 Bullets in Our Bonnets   216
29 We Finish Pétain's Wine   229
30 The Murder of Lucette and Odette   235
31 'Der Krieg ist Beendet?'   241
32 Occupation   250
33 Extermination Camp   261
34 And so to Potsdam   269
35 White Wine on the Moselle   294
36 All Change   299

A Note on the Author   311
Index   313

Introduction
by Penny Perrick

Anita Leslie was not the sort of person usually found on a battlefield. During the first winter of the Second World War, when both her brothers and most of her friends were active in the fight against Hitler, Anita was cubbing in Northamptonshire. She wrote to her friend Rose Burgh: 'I feel I am "helping the war effort" by having as pleasant a time as possible which is just what he [Hitler] doesn't want.' Later, from London, she wrote to her mother, Marjorie, in Ireland: 'You can't imagine how bored people are with the war here. No one wants to listen to fancy speeches.' The fancy speeches were made by Anita's cousin, Winston Churchill, and inspired a nation.

What persuaded Anita to volunteer for active service was a need to escape from an exhaustingly tangled personal life, circumstances not referred to in her searing war memoir, *Train to Nowhere*. She enlisted as a driver in the mechanized transport corps (MTC), a voluntary organization much favoured by upper class young women such as Anita, who could afford to pay for their own chic uniform designed by the couturier Hardy Amies. As she sailed to Pretoria on the *Arundel Castle* through U-boat infested waters, she revelled in the novelty of freedom, writing to Rose: 'Never again am I going to live a dull domesticated existence – I'm just going to be naughtier and naughtier! He he.' She may sound shallow but she came from a class that required its young girls to be light-headed and giddy. 'Smile dear, it costs nothing,' Anita's grandmother, Lady Leonie Leslie, often admonished her. Marjorie's advice to her daughter, about to head off to the Desert War, was 'Don't get sunburned in Africa – men hate it.'

In Cairo, the MTC tended the wounded in intense heat, hot winds and 'maddening discomfort' before being incorporated into the auxiliary territorial service (ATS) when the unit reached Alexandria. Anita, sensing correctly that it would be stuck in Egypt when the war moved elsewhere, manoeuvred herself into more adventurous roles – editing a newspaper, the *Eastern Times*, joining the Transjordan Frontier Force, where she delivered supplies to isolated field hospitals in Lebanon and Syria with her friend Pamela Wavell, who made these hazardous trips wearing a white dress and picture hat.

In 1944, after three years in the Middle East, she asked the Red Cross for a transfer to Italy, wanting to be in 'the fight that lies ahead in Europe.' In Naples, feeding the casualties from Anzio and Cassino was 'like trying to run a canteen in Dante's *Inferno*.' She remarked of the British Tommies: 'Somehow it is their humour and courage that no one else seems to have when blown to bits.' It was dauntingly rewarding work but Anita wanted even more involvement. In *Train to Nowhere* she wrote: 'I had a faint selfish hope that the war would not end before I had time for some startling achievement.' For that hope to be achieved, she had to join the French Forces which, unlike the British Army, allowed women on the front line. And now what might be called Anita's real war, the one that gave her the reputation of *une Anglaise formidable* began. On 15 August, the day of the allied landings in southern France, the Red Cross handed Anita over to the French Forces. Dossiers were demanded, including 'a certificate stating that the British Government did not mind what was done to me … there were unpleasant clauses about deserters getting shot.' In October, Anita landed at Marseilles. She was now *un simple soldat de 2ème classe*.

They did things differently in France. *Train to Nowhere* is dedicated to Anita's commanding officer, Jeanne de l'Espée. Her first command to the new recruit was 'Whatever happens, remember to use lipstick because it cheers the wounded.' In England, the iconic blonde bombshell recruiting poster designed by Abram Games for the ATS was rejected as being too glamorous. Amid the sound of gunfire, kitted out in American soldiers' outfits, including 'comic underwear' – a far cry from Hardy Amies couture – eating tinned beans off tin plates, Anita was a front-line ambulance driver in the 1st French Armoured Division and played a vital part in the liberation of France. Driving in the pitch-dark through woods full of Germans, Anita wrote to Marjorie that she had never enjoyed life more. The fighting went on for months as the allies drove north-eastwards towards the Rhine, with heavy casualties on both sides. How sharply, and horrifyingly, Anita describes the battle-fields: 'In all directions, men advancing through the fields were suddenly blown up in a fountain of scarlet snow.'

The story told in *Train to Nowhere* is one of dancing among the skulls. The *ambulancières* splash about joyfully in Marshal Pétain's bathtub and drink his delicious wines just hours after he has been hastily evacuated. Then two of the girls, sisters Lucette and Odette Lecoq, are ambushed and murdered by retreating Germans. Lucette's body is 'still warm' when found; the Red Cross flag is still flying on their ambulance. Anita's final war work is as sombre. She is sent to bring back to France the survivors of the Nordhausen labour camp. These 'shivering, exhausted wretches' were scarcely alive. Anita wrote: 'Better if the whole earth remained desolate as the moon if this is all mankind can make of it.' On 15 August 1945, in Wittlich, the Rhineland city on the Moselle, Anita in a freshly ironed skirt cut out of a GI's trousers, polished boots, neatly-turned down white socks and white gloves had the *Croix de guerre* pinned on her shirt as the band played the Marseillaise. In September she was demobilized.

Train to Nowhere, subtitled 'An ambulance driver's adventures on four fronts' was first published in August 1948 and was widely considered to be the best book about the war to have been written by a woman – a dubious compliment. Reviewers recognized Anita's 'impersonal integrity' and her unique point of view, 'a terse, keen reticence and the summing up of deadly situations in a line or two' *The Times*. The book sold out quickly, was reprinted twice and then forgotten. In the early post-war years, women were under pressure to revert to their pre-war role of angel in the house. Nobody wanted to hear about their exploits in bombed out villages or rescuing the dying in fields of blood. Anita herself didn't write or talk about the war until 1983 when she wrote a lighter version of her wartime life. By that time, she had become well known for her gossipy biographies of her Churchill and Leslie relations.

How gratifying that *Train to Nowhere*, the most heartfelt and absorbing of her books, is being revived for a new readership.

Penny Perrick 2017
author of *Telling Tales: The Fabulous Lives of Anita Leslie*

PART I

MIDDLE EAST

1

Mechanized Transport Corps

Any girl in England could have applied for that job and so few did. It was a sultry evening in August, 1940, when picking up a London newspaper I read the advertisement for women drivers ready to go to Africa. A shiver of excitement went up my spine and as sometimes happens I knew by instinct that I would go. But the clipping did not summon an eager crowd. When I applied at the headquarters of the mechanized transport corps in Chelsea only a handful of fidgeting girls stood asking each other if such a plunge-off might be a 'good thing'. Good or bad? Fate would take her time in giving an answer to each. Speculations ended when a red-headed, red-nailed girl in khaki arrived with a notebook to brusquely ask, 'Special talents?'

A murmur went up. We all knew 'something' about engines. One by one we were led off to be interviewed by a matronly Major, whose tactful enquiries were presumably intended to plumb our morality. Then, before we could gather our scattered senses, we were given sheafs of forms to fill up and led to a trestle-table to face an intelligence test. Faces grew long at this prospect but the ordeal proved bearable. Only a few showed signs of jitters when given a handful of screws and bits of wire to convert into bicycle bells, clothes pegs, sparking plugs, and distributors while the clock counted ten minutes.

Then we were marshalled outside to have driving tests in the oldest car in the world.

Two days later I was among eighty selected for camp and my kit list arrived by post. Camp-training was to take ten days, the list of clothes and accessories needed covered two typewritten pages. I set about borrowing from friends.

Laden with canvas basins, rolls of bedding, and suitcases of new uniforms we travelled to a beautiful beech grove at Hertfordshire which had been lent to the MTC. Here we were sorted into platoons and harassed corporals hung coloured labels around our necks. A band of girl guides had been peeling potatoes and boiling cauldrons since dawn. All we had to do was pull luggage out of the lorries and put up the tents. A call went around for anyone who had put up a tent before. None answered. Dusk fell while the sergeants shouted inexpert advice to bands of struggling girls who were hammering fingers and pegs alternately, and tripping over guy ropes while poles crashed down on their heads. For two hours hubbub arose to the moonless sky. Happily the first aid tent had been the first to get hoisted; it was soon buzzing with clients who had to be bandaged and plastered by candlelight. A few girls, instead of helping the distraught brown owls and guide captains who had come to instruct in camp life, retired from the danger zone and had hysterics in the dark woods. These were classed, 'not the sort of girls we want'.

Every dawn we rose up from the coppery beech leaves to drill and make camp fires in the moss and construct twig furniture that might be useful when stranded in the jungle. We learnt about Corps Spirit and, better still, we learnt about the Magnetic North. Set free with compasses we floundered across ploughed fields trying to work out where we were on the map and each night we slept blissfully under the stars. We could stare up at the dark sky across which searchlights waved like white arms and aircraft hummed. We did not know that the Battle of Britain was beginning over our heads.

It was a strangely carefree time. One afternoon a group of German bombers, having plastered Luton, roared over the camp and whistles blew – which meant we had to run like rabbits and take cover in some low holly trees. Everything seemed funny in those days, even those humming, gilded bees that had shed death in a town eleven miles away.

On the last afternoon we were given a lecture about Virtue in Tropical Lands. Then a list was read of names passed for the Africa unit. Twenty gigglers were left out. These had 'blotted their copy books' but could redeem their faults later. Then the Bishop of St. Albans came in brocade robes to bless us, and we marched past swinging our arms like the guards brigade and gave him a bun for tea.

Press representatives from every big paper swarmed over the camp and we spread dummy wounded about the daisy fields, gathered them and bore them away triumphantly in our new ambulances while cameras clicked. They asked us to ditch a lorry and pull it out with a rope. 'Hold it! Hold it!' cried the press men. 'And now three girls waving spanners . . . big smiles . . . very nice.' Next day papers had headlines: 'Tough girls train for Africa' and 'Off to the Desert' and our photographs appeared on and under engines.

The camp broke up on 2 September and we all returned to London on the day the first blitz began. Bombing might be novel but it interfered with the next month's training.

A moustachioed sergeant major of the guards brigade drilled us in Chelsea Square.

'By the right . . .' he would yell.

'To the left *salute* . . .'

'Pick 'em up. Pick 'em up,' squeaked an obnoxious small boy marching beside the squad.

The 'as you weres' of the sergeant major silenced gigglers into sullen apathy, and we would sigh with relief when the drone of German bombers sounded and the shriek of guns and sirens gave us release.

God knows what we learnt in those sunny autumn, invasion-expecting days but the MTC certainly tried. An insect professor gave us a lecture on how to foil a fly on its frolic from the latrine (illustrated) to sugar basin (illustrated). While he talked and used chalk neatly on the blackboard we watched the window lit by a golden sunset from which bombs fell on Chelsea Barracks.

We were aware of the drama. Like children we ran to the windows to watch the ack-ack throwing orange stars into the sky, and my father stood entranced in the middle of Hyde Park composing a sonnet about the German plane being shot down over Victoria station. It was a good kind of war for a bit, interesting and gay.

It had not yet become a drab old story.

In October we were reviewed by Lord Lloyd, the colonial secretary, and the South African military attaché. As usual, press representatives appeared. We stood to attention in Chelsea Square while Vs of enemy bombers sailed like wild geese across the sky and the South African colonel started a charming speech of which we heard fragments through the crackle of guns . . . 'splendid gesture . . . brave girls . . . warm welcome awaits you in Africa.' . . . A piece of shrapnel landed on the bonnet of a car parked beside us and the parade broke up. But a reporter sheltering in a doorway got his story and more headlines blazed: 'Girls stand to attention under shell-fire.' We started to keep albums of clippings about ourselves.

My last day in London was rendered hideous because my tailor's 'button-holding-machine' had been destroyed by a bomb leaving my new uniforms incomplete. At 5 p.m. we had to report with kit, and two lorry-loads of girls drove off through the wet dusk to Euston station, where the lines had just been hit and trains were hours late. 'In two ranks get on parade' yelled our sergeants and we shuffled into line in the dark, deserted station. The dim blue lights shed an eerie glow on the row of girls standing to attention in tin hats, their backs humped by gasmasks and knapsacks. A thunderstorm added its voice to the gunfire as the charming lady major-general of the MTC appeared to make a farewell speech and give us a pep talk in public-school-leaving tradition. Against the roar of the raid outside we heard 'Cover yourselves with laurels . . . do your bit . . . bring credit to the corps . . . no longer raw recruits you are now the polished product . . .' She shook us each by the hand and then drove off in that dreary night where bomb after bomb was falling. At midnight, a single track having been cleared, our train rolled out.

2

Step Off

Embarkation on the troopship was slow and cold. We stood about the decks for hours staring at Glasgow dockland, unable to ask when we sailed or where to. Next day we felt the engines throb, and stamping our feet with cold we watched the last of Britain slip away as the *Stirling Castle* steamed down Clydeside . . . grey water and grey sea, grey buildings and grey funnels, and an icy wind and a sea-gull turned to gold for one moment in a brief ray of sunshine as the ship moved into a darkening Atlantic. We joined a convoy headed for America until, after three days, our ship swung southwards alone and passed through the floating wreckage of the *Empress of Britain*, whose SOS we had been too late to answer.

The captain of this ship that took us zigzagging through the South Atlantic was a character indeed. None of us ever met him face to face, he saw to that, but we knew him from remarks that drifted down to us. 'Soldiers must realize they are but soldiers' he said. 'No exceptions! Women cease to be women on a troopship!' Reading in orders, 'Other ranks will be confined to the lower deck' we pouted, for this meant we could not use the swimming pool or speak to officers in the first class. After all we had been newspaper headlines for a month! But what the captain of a ship says goes.

So we ceased circulating requests upwards through channels proper or improper, and enjoyed winds that grew balmier each day, and made friends with the squadrons of the Free French Air Force who were our fellow-travellers. Every morning we had our odd little parades on deck, and the Frenchmen watched us with solemn admiration, whispering :'*Qu' elles sont jolies!*' '*Qu' elles sont disciplinées!*' '*C'est formidable!*'

These Frenchmen were a bitter, broken-hearted little band who had either been in England when their country fell or had escaped there in diverse ways. '*Le cafard*' which had lain heavy on them at Glasgow, melted in the sunshine, but though they had personal courage they had lost belief in their country and wanted to be killed which, indeed, in the end they nearly all were. They brooded over their families in France with whom they now had no possibility of communicating for an indefinite period, but not so sorely that they could not fall in love, and engagements began to be announced. One dizzy-headed girl pulled a crumpled white satin wedding-dress out of her kitbag and said she wanted the cross captain to marry her to a small ardent navigator. The marriage was 'postponed' by fussed OCs. And what poems those Frenchmen wrote. All day they scribbled gallant rhymes to their lady loves or to the unit as a whole . . . One of these in fifteen stanzas began:

'*Amazones blondes et pures . . .*'

Meanwhile our three officers descended from the first class to inflict what parades and lectures they could devise. We recited Swahili verbs, the Latin names for every bone in the body and bound and unbound each other with bandages in the sweltering zones of the Equator.

When dismissed from these activities we lay about the deck or walked with Lord Dunsany, the Irish poet, who, giving himself a civilian's privilege of mixing with all ranks, would stroll the decks watching for that magic green light of sunset, or reading his short stories aloud, or even adding to our store of poetry. He was on his way to Greece to cheer and charm that brave people.

When darkness came the black-out made our cabins uncomfortably hot, and the entire unit would creep out with blankets and hide beside the funnels. Owing to the strict black-out our officers could search in vain and we silently laughed while our persecutors stumbled around calling 'Brown, Smith, where are you? Has anyone seen driver Wills?' all of which mystified the foreign legionnaires who had been at Narvik and were travelling out on this boat. They were a dour little party who kept to themselves, and the only one I got to know fairly well was a German, a short, stocky, unimaginative fellow who had fought through years of Moroccan tribal wars, in France, and at Narvik. He was pleasant enough in a dull way, typical of his race, very blond, and only interested in war.

He had no feeling about Nazi Germany although his mother and aunts lived there. The most professional of soldiers, he flared up at passing remarks of mine about the legionnaires being cut-throats, and gave a long lecture about his companions. 'I am afraid *Mademoiselle* has false ideas of the legion . . . You go too much to the American cinemas.' Despite this snub I invited him to the MTC concert which we gave one very hot night. The French airmen sat enrapt and appreciative throughout the charming little songs and sketches at which our girls had laboured. The legionnaires watched expressionless, then, not knowing I understood French, one of them turned and whispered, '*Dieu* how boring these *anglaises* are. Do you think we can slip out?'

Among the French Air Force officers were two brothers, the du Boisrouvreys, and their cousin Jean whom I had known in London. Owing to the captain's restrictions we could only speak after dark when their badges of rank did not show and they dared descend to the lower deck. These meetings gave us a thrill of doing wrong only experienced in the nursery and the army. The officers were less impressed than their men at the first sixty girls they had seen in uniform. 'What drives them to this folly?' they asked, 'Broken hearts or dull husbands?'

A fortnight after leaving Glasgow we woke to see the coast of West Africa lying gilded under the scarlet dawn sky and the French went ashore in little boats to make their way to Chad. Jean was posted missing almost immediately. The Boisrouvreys, who were both bomber-pilots, I was to meet again in Egypt.

In November we reached Cape Town and plunged into a new world, for it was spring. After the sombre, war-racked land we had left, the beauty of Cape Town with its weird mountain background and shimmering lights enchanted us.

Our unit was met by a Ladies' Committee for Entertaining Troops in Transit who seemed relieved at seeing only sixty girls. We drove off in fine cars to eat cream buns in old Boer farmhouses, and apparently we were a great success. The previous week several thousand Australian soldiers had been let loose for twenty-four hours in Cape Town and the committees had been ignored while Aussies swarmed the streets and found their own entertainment. Meeting a truck of beer they emptied every barrel within ten minutes singing that obnoxious song, 'Roll out the barrel . . .' They purchased ladies' underwear and dressed the policemen on point duty in scanties; then forced them by revolver pressure to continue directing the traffic.

Sixty well-mannered English girls were a great relief.

After a day at the races we were ordered to catch a train to Pretoria. 'Why?' asked the girls; but it was ours not to question why, ours but to do or die, and so after a long journey across a desert of weirdly-shaped rocks and hills we reached the capital of Transvaal and were informed that we must sign on as privates in the South African Army. This had not been in our London contracts, but we remonstrated in vain. Until we signed on the dotted line we could not be issued with shoes or socks or even a breakfast. Being hungry we gave in.

3

Cape to Cairo

From November, 1940, until February, 1941, we lived in barracks in Roberts Heights Camp near Pretoria, and the spring weather made life delightful. The troops lived in huts grouped around a swimming pool. Every weekend we drove into the veldt and slept out under the unclouded stars. The Transvaal is a high plateau with exhilaratingly dry air. Frequent thunder-storms, in which no rain falls but lightning flashes across the sky, give tense expectancy to the atmosphere. We took over the motor pool so the hard-worked South African women drivers could get leave, and this work enabled us to see the Rand country. We drove troops across the stony veldt on manoeuvres and rumbled in lorries to the gold mines of this strange, newly-rich strip of upland. At first we were thrilled by the wide spaces of Transvaal but after three months we pined to move to Kenya, where the East African campaign was in full swing.

General Smuts came to open the YMCA canteen beside our swimming pool. He had kind words for us all and some of our girls visited his home. We knew, however, that several thousand South African service women had sent him a petition that the 'sixty English girls' should not be sent to Kenya where their South African men were. This jealousy was understandable. The WAAS, as they were called who had enlisted, were treated differently from their men in every way and had not been allowed overseas. These

South African girls were splendid, healthy, outdoor creatures who beat us hollow at sports, but they seemed to be given little respect because they were women. Their superiors – whose minds were impenetrable Victorian jungles – insinuated that women, working near any fighting front, would hinder the war effort. Perhaps I misuse the word 'Victorian', for during the Boer War my English great-aunts ran front-line hospitals in areas that today would be stamped 'war zones unfit for women'.

When we arrived in Pretoria the jacaranda trees made a mauve canopy overhead and a mauve carpet on the pavements. But there was no stimulus in this old Dutch town; no theatre, no art, no intellectual life of any kind. And it was the same in Johannesburg, the mining millionaire city of sky-scrapers, thirty miles away.

Occasionally we were confined to barracks because pro-German Boers were constantly beating-up soldiers in British uniform. Many of these were Boers who could speak only Afrikaans and it was against them that the violence of the bearded anti-Britishers was chiefly directed. One hunter-farmer, called Willy, dared not return to his family at long leave for they were still bitter against the British. He tried to explain his family's bitterness. 'They live with thoughts that are forty years old. Understand? They hate Queen Victoria . . . understand? They think I am a traitor to Boer grandfathers who died fighting against British . . . understand?'

The English girls were puzzled. Their surprise turned to resentment when a Dutch Nazi threw a brick at one of them as she walked through Pretoria. She had twelve stitches and a lasting scar on her cheek. South Africa had declared war on Germany and her sons attacked each other with violence; my country had remained neutral and ten per cent of her populations served in the British Forces and were feted as heroes on their visits home. It was an oddly different atmosphere. The Irish are quick with their fists, but no one in Ireland would ever throw a stone at a girl and then run away fast to hide in a side street. The last I had heard of our local IRA leader was that he had been arrested after two days' violent intoxication, to celebrate his daughter winning a George Cross in the bombing of Coventry.

The South African women with whom we shared barracks were a charming, friendly lot. One of them said to me, laughing, 'We won't write any more petitions against you, but it would have been too much if you had gone north to drive our soldiers when we are all kept here.' Later on, when I saw South African wounded lying in forward casualty clearing-stations unwashed and untended I thought of their women, who would gladly have risked their lives to be there helping.

In February, orders came that our unit was to proceed to Crete or Egypt. We trained to Durban and set sail immediately. Our ship, the *Nieuw Holland*, loaded up with Cape Town Highlanders, stalwart South Africans surprisingly dressed in kilts. There were no poets, Irish or French, on this ship, and only the Dutch captain wrote a verse 'To the brave girls of the MTC.' With the Highland band playing we steamed out of Durban past a troopship packed with cheering Australians.

The heat increased as we passed between the windless shores of East Africa and Madagascar. I knew nothing about Madagascar except that before the war, on the Atlantic, the famous American financier, Bernard Baruch, had said to me, 'I'm going to chuck this turbulent world and settle in Madagascar. I've heard you get two fish for one cent there, and two women for one fish.'

We sailed due north through the flat, indigo-blue Indian ocean, till the Southern Cross disappeared in the night skies behind us. Two weeks of unbearable heat brought us to the Red Sea. We had lectures each day on the vile diseases we might catch. Swahili was now replaced by Arabic. We were fantastically clad in collars, ties, and hot, corduroy trousers. The only tropical kit that had been issued to us consisted of jungle outfits, mosquito veils and mittens, and anti-insect gaiters. None of this could be used except the topees, in which it was so difficult to salute.

The corporals made a sort of Gestapo with 'black books' in which to record bad marks every time they saw a driver 'slacking'. All this took place as we steamed up the Red Sea with the thermometer over 100 degrees.

On 3 March we woke to find the convoy steaming up the narrow Gulf of Suez. Before dusk we managed to anchor outside the harbour along with some two hundred other ships that were silhouetted in all directions with native sailing-boats travelling among them.

The canal had been blocked by a mine.

At last the port cleared enough for the *Nieuw Holland* to draw near and we stepped ashore. Our officers marched us, with swinging arms, down the docks. 'By the right' bawled our sergeant major. The native workers gabbled and pointed, while two officers of the 7th Hussars, sent to check troops arriving, doubled up with laughter and retreated behind a crate.

In a desert camp we found our famous ambulances; the gift of generous Americans, which had arrived straight from the USA and were waiting, lined up in the sand, guarded by Australian soldiers. One of these looked at us all frosted with sand and asked, 'British complexions underneath?' We climbed into our new vehicles and drove towards Cairo. Soon after midday we approached the Nile Valley and an escort of MPs on motor-bicycles came to meet us. They gasped 'Girls?' and wheeled.

Now the wide green ribbon of Egypt stretched below us. Beyond Cairo lay the great Pyramids, and beyond them the wilderness where General Wavell's Western desert force, consisting of little more than the 7th Armoured Division (later famous as the Desert Rats) and the 6th Australian Infantry Division had just destroyed Graziani's army of eight divisions in Cyrenaica.

Of the quarter-million Italian troops sent to Libya more than half had been wiped out in the two months' brilliant fighting. After the heartbreak of Dunkirk and the inquietude of the Battle of Britain it was a proud moment to arrive. Soon we shared the outlook of the men we met – 11th Hussars, 8th Hussars, 7th Hussars, riflemen, Aussies, New Zealanders, and some enthusiastic young fellows who were the beginning of the commandos.

No sooner had we arrived at Helmiah Camp – a horrible entanglement of barbed wire and petrol tins in the sand some miles from Cairo – than the air began to thicken with sand and the sky to darken.

Before we had time to clean the engines – which had stood so long at Suez awaiting us – we were needed to meet a hospital train from the Western Desert. For two nights, until we could organize quarters in the camp, we were billeted in a large hotel in Heliopolis. The male officers greeted us with amazement, followed by sour looks and complaints that our boots clattered in the corridors, but our ambulances were in great demand. We started work within four hours of reaching Helmiah Camp. March, 1941, was the month in which British Forces were pouring from Egypt into Greece, and on the day after our arrival we were called by our commandant to a meeting in which we were put on our honour not to say that our unit was going to Greece the following week. Until then we would continue to meet ambulance trains and serve the hospitals.

Any hour we expected to leave with the Australian and New Zealand infantry and British gunners who were sailing from

Alexandria and Port Said, but the days went on and we did not sail; indeed we wondered how we could, for who would there be to meet the trains of wounded that kept us busy day and night. We were less than sixty drivers, and we had replaced a hundred men who with their vehicles had gone to Greece. In the first week of April Benghazi fell. How much Benghazi and Tobruk, which we had hardly heard of before, meant now. A month of driving wounded men and listening to their talk made the desert battles live before our eyes; we shared the maddening discomfort with them, the heat, the sand, the flies, and from the very beginning we felt the pride of that little army of the Nile.

Through the soldiers we got an idea of General Wavell's personality. They liked him as a man and trusted him as a general. The Tommies said, 'The Wops have the planes and the guns, we just got the guts and the general, and it's us sees the blighters off.'

Nearly two years later – when Auchinleck had gone and Strafer Gott had been killed and for the first time British Forces knew they had the guns and the new army commander – Montgomery came from England amidst unprecedented publicity. I listened with amusement to a couple of soldiers disagreeing. One held the press campaign to be 'too much of a good thing'. The other argued staunchly that Montgomery, having obviously read General Wavell's lectures on the 'Relationship of the Army Commanders to the Politicians,' was the first general to act on them. 'Monty knows what he's up to . . . you'll see. He does it deliberately. He'll get himself built up until he can play the tune and it'll be him – not the politicians – that says how many troops does this and that and where the guns go. And if there is disagreement it won't be Monty that goes. You'll see.' In time we did.

Before we had been in Egypt two weeks we were meeting wounded who came back from Greece instead of from the desert, and then one day we got loads, not of soldiers, but of military nurses from the British hospital at Athens. They were unwounded but collapsing from exhaustion, after terrifying trips across the Mediterranean in cruisers which were bombed all the way. We lifted them into our ambulances and they fell asleep in heaps on the floor. We realized that our forces were evacuating and we would never get to Greece.

Nearly all the army vehicles which landed in Greece had to be abandoned. This made the strain on our forty odd ambulances heavy, we worked like troopers and used troopers' language too.

During hours off we fled anywhere to escape the sickening heat of our huts. A few miles from the camp lived Aziz al-Masri, who had travelled to Arabia with Lawrence on his first expedition. I had met Aziz in London and now he opened his luxuriant green garden near our camp to me and my friends. Whenever we got free evenings we drove there in some ramshackle Egyptian taxi and his Arab servants brought us meals and cool drinks. Aziz was born a noble of Arabia; he had been brought up in Turkey and had distinguished himself as a young officer in the Turkish–Italian war. He was a strange, smouldering, little man, strong of intellect and sincere of purpose, who felt that he had just missed greatness. 'When I finished the Turkish cadet school,' he told me, 'the commanding officer gave me a farewell talk. He said, "You will achieve great things, Aziz," and then as I left the room he added "if you have luck," and a cold chill went through my heart at those words. I knew then, by intuition, I would never succeed.'

He might have been a big man in Turkey but he quarrelled with Djemal Pasha and was imprisoned and fled. In 1915 he set sail with Lawrence and Ronald Storrs for Arabia, where he was to raise and lead the Arab officers for desert rebellion, but he learned of the secret treaty which promised Syria to the French and Palestine to the Jews, so forsook the venture. He talked a lot about honour, and later when I met many Arabs of all kinds the inevitable verdict on Aziz was, 'How could he achieve anything! He is the only straight man in the East,' and the more cynical said, 'He is mad.'

Aziz had later commanded the Egyptian Army and supervised the education of Farouk before he became king. In England he had tried to induce the fifteen-year-old prince to learn to ride and practise sports. 'At his age,' said Aziz, 'I loved the sound of bullets. I thought war the only profession for a man – perhaps I was in love even then with death.'

Now he was out of favour and he lived in seclusion within his beautiful walled garden. No one except the MTC visited him. He was tough and wiry but exceptionally short, and as I appeared with one tall slim English girl after another Aziz would exclaim in admiration, 'What stock – but it is giraffe-stock!'

When I remarked on the dirty face of a passing woman, he said, 'Her face may be dirty, but she washes her body, according to Muslim law, which the peasants of Europe do not. Once,' he continued, 'I met a beautiful German peasant girl when I was on a walking tour. She had a face like a goddess and when she came to my hotel that evening and said she was ready to abandon herself to me I sang with joy, but never again. . . . She was so dirty, only her face was clean . . . *C'était ignoble.*' We were sitting at tea in his garden during this recital and we tried hard to keep our faces straight.

Aziz had married a cultivated American. 'I could not stand the lack of brain among our own women. She is living in California with our young son.'

'How did you bring up your child?' I asked, 'as a Christian or a Mohammedan?'

Aziz answered: 'When he was five or six years old I tried to tell him about God. I said, "look around at the trees and flowers. God is the Creator, He made all that you see and He made you. You must try to copy Him. You must create not destroy." Later, I tried to teach him to love the earth. I told him, "We come of the earth, it feeds us and looks after us, we are made from the soil, and later we have to go back to soil." I did not want him to have any horror of the processes of decay, but to feel that, lovingly, one must give back one's body to the great Mother; so I took him out to the grass and said, "Look, when I die they will lie me there under-neath the green. Won't that be nice?"

'But the child's face fell. "No " he said, "it would make a bump on the lawn."'

Aziz spoke English, French, and German fluently but could not read much English. I occasionally translated bits of the *Seven Pillars of Wisdom* to him and he would say: 'No, no; it was not like that – but how well he writes, that Lawrence.' In return he attempted to translate a few bits of the Koran for me. 'The poetry is lost in trans-lation,' he would say; 'you cannot imagine how beautiful the imagery is.' He worked out for me the Muslim version of the story of Mary awaiting the Angel Gabriel, which he said contained the greatest poetry of the book. The Virgin Mary, waiting in the garden was described 'beautiful of body as a thoroughbred mare' – a curious simile to one accustomed to gentle Italian pictures of the Madonna.

'And what in the world,' said Aziz, 'is as perfect as a horse – Come, you must see the famous stud of the Egyptian Agricultural Society. They have the best Arab horses in the world – when you see their fire, their flowing manes and tails, then you will under-stand the poetry of the Koran which I cannot translate.'

Aziz regretted that break with the English when he fled from Lawrence at Jiddah. 'At the time I did not think them straight. Now I repent it. My luck has always failed me as I have always known it would. I have given up ventures which I did not feel compatible with my honour only to find in the end I was mistaken. Now my life is finished and I have nothing – not even an army to command – nothing, except the love of people who know me.' That he had indeed. The common people of Egypt trusted him.

One day he took me over the citadel, explaining its history with knowledge and intensity. We watched the sunset from the top of a minaret and when we left the great vulgar Mosque of Mohamed Ali the guide knelt down and kissed his hand and refused a tip – the most extraordinary thing for that scurrilous-looking knave to do. Outside in the streets a small crowd of poor people had assembled to cry out some pet name they had for him. They ran to open the door of his car, and when we drove off amidst this sudden spontaneous acclaim Aziz said, 'When I look into a face of those people I wish I could be their leader – But I am a failure, *ma chère* Anita, and so I can do nothing for anyone. Looking back over my life I can see all the wrong turnings, but it is too late. All I want now is to escape. The English will never trust me; the Egyptians make me sick – I want the desert that I came from.'

And then one evening he said, 'Anita, I am going away. I do not know where, but go I must – out of this cage—' and his hand designated the walled garden.

Next day the papers were full of the flight of Aziz al-Masri, for he sailed off in the middle of the night in an Egyptian Army plane with two young pilots who were his devotees. They crashed on the outskirts of Cairo, and Aziz hid for months in the city until he was recaptured and imprisoned. Through Fitzpatrick Pasha I sent him some English books and a dictionary to repay his hospitality, but I never saw him again. He was a strange, vibrant, little old man with some latent greatness in his soul. I only know that if Aziz gave his word he would have died rather than break it. And there are not so many men like that in the East.

4

Souls in Khaki

In May a heat-wave broke over us, the thermometer soared to 119 degrees and a *khamseen* blew. Our huts grew insupportable, as a large rush fence was erected which kept out not only the impertinent gaze of fellow troops but the rare evening breeze that occasionally sighed from the north.

Days and nights became one long jumbled series of convoys to meet wounded. At midnight we might go out to meet a hospital train that did not arrive. At dawn we returned to camp for buckets of black tea and baked beans, and after breakfast we called at hospitals. At midday the British Army would serve its tropical lunch – suet dumplings, sardines and more black tea. During the unspeakable sweltering afternoon the ambulance train that had not arrived at midnight was likely to approach. When we got back a meal of tea and beans would be repeated, only this time it was called supper, and then the night duty ambulances were sent out; but night duty or day duty made no difference, for as soon as one crawled under a mosquito net to sleep some harassed NCO was bellowing at one to crawl out again.

From the mists of Ireland my family wrote:

'Be sure to wear a hat, this modern craze for sunburn is so unbecoming – and we were rather shocked, dear, by your very

frivolous letter. Although we are all very glad you did get champagne do remember that after all there *is* a war on—'

The red trousers of the 11th Hussars – whose armoured cars had
been working for two years in the desert – the green forage-caps
of the 8th Hussars, and the wide hats of Australian and New
Zealand troops gave its special cachet to the Egypt of 1941. There
were plenty of rich traders who thought it smart to entertain
British officers, and every hotel bar had a cosmopolitan selection
of well-dressed houris; but a soldier fared less well, for as one
Tommy stringently put it: 'The tarts in Egypt is such snobs you
would think they was all Cleopatra.'

Through that burning month, the hottest in Egypt for fifty
years, our ambulances were loaded with British, Australian, and
New Zealand wounded, and with Indians whom we drove to
their own military hospital in the old citadel above Cairo. Egypt,
unchanged for five thousand years, made a strange backcloth for
the rumbling convoys, the tanks, and guns of modern war.

We learnt of the German invasion of Crete from casualties
who were in our ambulances within twenty-four hours of leaving
the island.

On 1 June I scribbled home:

'We love the starlit nights and hate the blazing day, hate even,
the pink dawn that is its herald. Last night I drove from five till
two a.m., kept awake by black tea and interest. Then, to my rage,
had to take three Cypriot mental deficients – unwashed and unwounded – to hospital! No sooner did I get back to sleep than
we were sent off to meet naval casualties from a cruiser.

'Some men were chuckling over the discomfiture of a thousand Italian prisoners on Crete who were well content with their

lot till German paratroops descended, recaptured them, distributed arms and sent them unwillingly off into battle. You should
see the black eyes gleaming of any Wop wounded we drive.
"*Bella, bella,*" they say when they actually realize the trousered,
black-goggled, and helmeted MTC are girls.

'Colonel John de Salis, the GHQ authority on things apper-
taining to the Vatican, was asked if Italian prisoners should be
allowed to say a prayer after Mass for the Duce. He signalled back
briefly: "Yes, he needs it."

'Yesterday a German officer, standing under guard, looked at
us and sneered in perfect English: "Out here to be photographed
for your society papers?" This, when we are exhausted by heat,
flies, and lack of sleep! One of my patients had had his arm
amputated by an MO in Crete and then walked eight miles to
be evacuated under fire – that was two days ago. His temper held
till asked his age, religion, unit, name and initials. He could not
remember them, only his Christian name, and as the conscious
are not carried out of the ambulance unless they have two initials
it held things up and the fellow nearly wept. There is a prevalent
view in HQ that our soldiers do not want frontline nurses and
that women-drivers would be a distraction. The fighting men
say they would give anything to know women would look after
them soon after being wounded.'

It was about this time that Father Blount, chief RC padre of the
Cairo Area began to look worn, and when we questioned him
about his file entitled: 'ladies – GHQ to Capt. the Reverend
Blount,' he told us that the Italians had abandoned a batch of prostitutes in Tobruk, whom the Australians marched to Alexandria
and dumped in a camp. GHQ, perturbed by an incident without
precedent, decided to hand them to the church for safe-keeping.

Father Blount was notified he had been made responsible for fifteen 'ladies' of easy virtue and enemy nationality, and that he was to proceed forthwith to meet them at Cairo station. 'It was somewhat embarrassing as they travelled with a train-load of nurses, who, having been evacuated from Greece, were clad in every sort of odd attire. Then suddenly I saw them – fourteen elderly peroxided brunettes who had trudged the desert attired in feather boas, black silk stockings, high-heeled green shoes and dangling earrings. A sheepish soldier handed them over to me with alacrity and disappeared.'

Ordered to find suitable internee accommodation Father Blount had appealed to an old friend, a Mother Superior, whom he cajoled into accepting the *signorinas* in her convent school.

Each time he visited the convent thereafter his charges, now dressed in checked gingham uniforms, clamoured that they were being badly treated. The light of friendship died out of the Mother Superior's eye.

Father Blount, in fact, was having a rough time so, when I got a week's leave with another MTC girl, we persuaded him to take a holiday and drive us three hundred miles to Jerusalem. We travelled the road which runs straight like a shiny black ribbon across the mud and sand, and crept slowly in the gold evening light from barren desert into the pale green hills of Palestine.

In the King David Hotel of Jerusalem, Betty and I procured a room which overlooked the old city's fifteenth century Turkish walls. HQ Palestine had been installed in the top floor of the hotel. Descending into the lounge we sat down and saw General Wavell, General Jumbo Wilson, the Australian General Blamey, General Spears, General de Gaulle, and General Catroux. At midnight we were told: 'At 2 a.m. we invade Syria;' and drove to a hill top to see what we could in the brilliant moonlight, but the northern skyline was dark and quiet.

The next few days we spent exploring Palestine. From Tiberius we looked down on the turquoise blue Sea of Galilee, while past us rolled trucks and armoured cars going north to the Palestine border and back rumbled lorries of captured Senegalese troops.

Twenty miles away in the serene Syrian hills and at the foot of snow-capped Mount Hermon, bitter fighting was taking place. Nearly all the French wounded came from the Vichy side, for the Free French brigade under the command of General le Gentilhomme, which had been rushed up by lorry from Egypt, showed a disinclination to fight other Frenchmen.

The Australians advancing up the coast road from Haifa had a sticky and expensive passage, but no reinforcements were available. The intense fighting which took place between Deraa and Damascus was done by an Indian brigade which suffered fifty per cent casualties, while the Free French followed bitterly in their wake and occasionally strafed by French planes picked up dying Frenchmen on the road.

It was indeed the oddest week of sight-seeing that two girls and a priest could have known. Every evening we got back to the King David Hotel where a tangle of intrigues flourished. Arab saboteurs and beautiful spies tiptoed in and out, and the British intelligence staff had installed the famous film star Asmahan al-Atrash, in a suite beside their offices. The first evening I saw her she was lying on a couch singing huskily in Russian; her deep throbbing voice and a trick of half swooning with passion, like the early film stars, would have brightened any office.

This exotic creature, with emerald green eyes and magnolia white skin, had been born in the black basalt Jabal al-Druze, south of Damascus. Her beauty was outstanding even amidst her good-looking tribe, and Hassan-el-Atrash, Emir of the Druzes, married her when she was sixteen. After a few years of marriage she got bored with her mountain stronghold and ran away to Egypt, where she won fame as a film star and as a singer. The British asked her to return to the Emir – who was still madly in love – and brought her to Jerusalem to dangle on the frontier thus tempting her former husband to bring the Druze tribe to the allied side. If the Vichy French should resist, a Druze rebellion could be staged.

Lovely Asmahan was waiting for the chance to ride back on a white horse to her mountain stronghold and rally the tribesmen. In the meantime she caused rather more British officers to lose their balance emotionally than the intelligence staff (who were paying for the champagne and flowers) had bargained for.

The invasion was supposed to depend on intrigue more than fighting. Never had one seen such flocks of spies and generals entangled together or heard so many rumours. Arab chiefs, Circassian-guarded French officers, and spruce British Navy whispered in the bar and vanished upstairs to the 'offices' to form fresh plots. The Aga Khan's son drove to and from the Syrian border on 'secret missions' in his peacock blue luxury sports car, and war correspondents languished around every corner. Meanwhile the Australians and Indians, fighting their bloody passage towards Beirut and Damascus, could have the consolation of knowing they were not supposed to be killed at all; it was meant to be a political walk-over, not a battle.

5

Desert's Edge

During that sweltering summer General Wavell, beloved of the fighting men (and stated by the German staff to be our greatest general since Marlborough), went to India and was replaced by General Auchinleck.

During the lull many Caireans opened their houses to the MTC amongst whom was Ahmed Sadikh Bey, the Egyptian minister to Tokyo, who wisely preferred to remain on his Nile houseboat.

The rich Pashas of Egypt were puzzled by the mechanized transport corps. One, on learning how we lived, shook his head sadly. 'But it is terrible . . . terrible . . . Girls out there in the desert and such pretty girls! Can you not find some general as a lover?'

Throughout the months of heat many of us got ill. Our unit commander, Mrs Newall retired to hospital in Cairo and I brought her special food in a bucket. In the next room lived a dejected Colonel Wingate suffering from a nervous breakdown. After making a great name for himself in Abyssinia he had returned to Cairo and been driven to despair by a disagreement with GHQ. He spent hours in Mrs Newall's room, talking and pouring out his difficulties.

This strange, harsh, magnetic personality would launch into unhappy tirades even on the most trivial subjects. He had an astounding intellect and memory, but I never knew what was going to upset him next.

On one occasion after a brilliant defence of the Roman Empire and Jewish emigration in Palestine he began to attack American development. He led me to the hospital bathroom and ranted over the lavatory plug which happened to be an American model pushed by a thumb. He maintained this was insanitary and enlarged germily in detail. Matron peered in at the door and I could not help smiling because I did not really care if a plug was sanitary or not but he snapped: 'It's not funny. It shows the idiocy of modern thought.' Later, when I heard he had returned to England and been posted to an ack-ack battery my heart sank for him. Then Churchill sent him on his famous mission to Burma.

Following a prevalent fashion I went into the military hospital at Abbassia with laryngitis and was promptly followed by my friend, Miranda Lampson, who had earache. Miranda was *l'enfant terrible* of the MTC and kept her uncle, the ambassador to Egypt, on tenterhooks for fear of what she would do next. He had sent her home to England just before the war on account of some prank viewed with disapproval in ambassadorial circles. She had been given what she called a 'classy education' in a series of schools in England and also worked as a groom, but until she entered the MTC, Miranda had not really followed any profession.

On the voyage out the captain, reading through the papers of troops aboard his ship, sent for Miranda's commanding officer and remarked, 'What very interesting personalities seem to exist among your drivers. I note that one has left a religious life to drive ambulances – her name is Lampson.' Dazed at this revelation the officer looked up Miranda's attestation paper and sure enough under 'Profession in Civilian Life' she read the word nun. Miranda was sent for and questioned until the truth dawned – it was not

Driver Lampson's holiness that should cause comment, only her spelling.

Miranda blithely refused to recognize discipline. She could not obey rules because she never knew about them; she took care not to. We all had our private methods of escape from camp, but only Miranda ever dug her way in the sand under the barbed wire fence in a silver lamé evening dress. Next morning the sentries gazed suspiciously at two tinsel rags that fluttered on the barbs, but they could not believe it was any of us, for the rulings about never wearing 'civvies' were stringent, and the penalty if caught included almost indefinite CB.

But as Miranda put it: 'I am always confined to barracks, anyhow, so I get a lot of practice slipping through barbed wire.' With her appearance it was not easy to slip past a sentry unobserved. She was six feet tall and very blonde, with huge, innocent, blue eyes that could open round as saucers with surprise when marched to the orderly room on a charge. She got away with a good deal more than they ever found out for she had trained outside friends, who, with knees knocking with fright, had to smuggle her out of camp on a forbidden night, but every now and again some outraged sergeant would shout for 'Lampson' all over the camp and discover Lampson just wasn't there.

On our last afternoon in hospital the ward was invaded with more patients. We already had an English quartermaster-sergeant's wife who talked without ceasing about her husband, always ending with; 'But he don't want to be an owfitzer for fear we might get all snobby-like.'

Then a little Greek woman came in who had recently married a British soldier but could only speak French. In the evening, amidst confusion and terse remarks from Matron, 'Madame' of the Italian Tobruk Brothel entered weeping volubly. She was placed in bed next to the Greek girl and I struggled to translate their Italian and French to the 'Bints' (servant girls), who gabbled in Arabic. The English nurse peered in and remarked that she was applying to be posted elsewhere.

Madame, whose copious tears continued while describing the horrors of being '*Prisonnière*', related their capture in Tobruk and how the Australians made them march for two days across the desert, and how their feet hurt. And now they had no sweets or cigarettes and were all very miserable.

At two in the morning Cairo had its first and only air raid. Awakened by the wail of sirens and deafening noise of an ack-ack battery, I found myself groping for slippers by the brilliant pink light of flares descending on parachutes right into our camp. The night-nurse arrived looking like some diminutive, prehistoric animal, with her tin hat perched on top of her veil. She roused the patients and ushered us downstairs to an empty ward. When a bomb fell near the hospital *Madame* of Tobruk began to weep again while the little Greek woman had a heart attack in the arms of the sergeant-in-charge who ordered us all 'under beds'. *Madame* could not make it, she was too fat; but Miranda and I made for the same bed and bumped our heads underneath it. We lay on the dusty floor giggling.

The bomb which fell beside our hospital killed a number of soldiers, and another outside the gates killed some thirty native taxi-drivers, with the result that taxi fares doubled. It had proved a dangerous profession.

In late October an air crash over the citadel cost the lives of Brigadier Russell, a famous leader in the desert, and Brigadier Pope, our new expert in armour out from England. Pope was replaced the following week by Major-General Norrie who invited Miranda and me to dine with him on the first evening he arrived at Cairo. We all 'talked horses merrily' and Norrie who weighed fifteen stone remarked blithely, 'No horse ever dares fall with me – I might roll on it.' He went off to bed. A curious chill settled on the party as they discussed the next 'push' which was going to be a big one. The next 'push', the next 'flap', 'caught with their pants down', that was the jargon of those days.

In October we held a party to celebrate the anniversary of our departure from England. The following morning we were lined up and drilled as usual by a kilted tank corps sergeant major who for some reason was instructed by GHQ to give us 'more discipline'. He shouted, 'Second man from the right hold your head up.' In my sulky trance I realized this was me. However, this phase of my military career was ending, for later in the day came an announcement that within two months the unit was to be disbanded. Individuals had to get new jobs or become ambulance drivers in the ATS. We had long known the ATS were short of recruits, and we insisted this was due to their grim senior officers and hideous hats. Now we were being pressed to sign on voluntarily into an organization, one of whose automatic rulings was that we would not be allowed in a fighting zone. That regulation alone made me decide to find another job.

Wanting to remain an ambulance driver in the British Army I was resentful that, apart from unequal pay, the ATS drivers were not given a man's treatment. I could have borne wearing a funny hat but not the ignominy of being a base ambulance driver, forever kept out of the fighting zone by regulations.

The British authorities made it such a handicap to be a woman that I decided when the time came I would seek a new job as far away as possible from headquarters.

In November the new 'push' started, and we were deluged with wounded who came in from the wet desert puzzled, weary, and depressed; but we heard their praises of Strafer Gott and Jock Campbell, who were the heroes of the day.

Meanwhile the MTC, reduced to thirty drivers, became ATS, and Sir Walter Monckton, head of the Ministry of Information, approved my application for a job with the British press liaison officer in Beirut who was starting the first English newspaper. Prince Peter of Greece, hearing Sir Walter tell me to take the 'first transport available,' kindly offered me a lift in his car.

In December my last day came with the MTC. We were driving wounded until after midnight, when I got back to camp. By moonlight I said goodbye to the girls who were signing on in the ATS under our charming, efficient second-in-command, Penelope Otto. Then it was goodbye to the old ambulance, and somehow I got to Cairo by 7 a.m. to leave for the new job in Syria – a land whose first enchantment would never quite be dispelled.

6

Eastern Times

Prince Peter and his Greek soldier drove me across the Sinai Desert. We lunched on caviar and chocolates – which caused the soldier to be sick – but Prince Peter proved good company and mended punctures with speed and skill. We reached Jerusalem by dark and next day I got a lift in the empty car of General Maitland Wilson.

Damascus was so beautiful that I felt a slice of my heart must be cut out and left there – the camel bells and the glinting minarets and the thousand years of history would draw me back – I little dreamt how many times.

Lieutenant-Colonel Kiltelly of the Transjordan Frontier Force drove me across a barren red mountain range until we looked down on Beirut jutting out into the flat blue Mediterranean. We found good food and good wine, a turquoise sea, and much laughter. Lebanon, a newly liberated baby, had recovered from its brief war and was having a naughty kick before the military administration could tie it up in red tape.

Beirut had no real beauty; the town resembled a soft, exotic woman. Little white villas with red roofs swamped in bougainvillea crept up from the too-blue sea to shimmering olive groves. Even the mountains seemed ridiculously pretty and one would in time tire of the brilliant mauves and pinks; but coming straight from a tangle of hideous barbed wire in the sand I fell in love with all Syria and the charm of Beirut caught me at first glance. When I reported to Major Rosselli, the British press liaison officer, he described my work which seemed complicated but I started in with the keenness of the innocent.

A month previously the best of forty Arab newspapers had applied to Major Rosselli to be allowed to produce the first English newspaper in Levant. Our press and propaganda departments were anxious that British troops, stuck in wild far-flung camps throughout Syria, should have news to read. The *Eastern Times*, launched by an all Arab staff, had in three weeks obtained a daily circulation of six thousand. My job was to see that it reached the farthest isolated camps quickly, and that as little news as possible should be printed upside down. Troops' papers were usually managed or edited by an officer who had been in the newspaper business, but I do not think any previous experience could have helped one tackle this partic-ular set-up. Major Rosselli thought I could at least spell, and cope with the paper's distribution across desert and up mountain passes. I proceeded through the narrow jostling street of Beirut to the big central square where the *Eastern Times* offices lay. Flabbergasted by the work I had taken on, I was shown up a staircase – heaped with garbage – to the enormous, icy, stone-floored office where a staff of eight Syrians argued, quarrelled, and ran about to the scream of an unanswered telephone. There were two big offices, one for the editor and one for the proprietor, who had a constant queue of visi-tors waiting to see him. On enquiring who this string of veiled women, weeping children, and men of every denomination might be, I learned that the proprietor, being also a lawyer, ran his business here and kept the paper going as a side-line.

The rest of the building consisted of smaller compartments in which the 'distribution manager', the 'financial manager' and several other 'managers' spent the day chasing each other round, shrieking like monkeys, fighting, pulling hair, arguing who was most to blame, and then making it up with tears and kisses. They simply hated me.

I was given a big, unheated, unfurnished room to myself where, wrapped in sheepskins, I could sit and ponder. The editor of the paper, Mr Racy, was a charming cultivated Lebanese, but he had not much more newspaper experience than I. Mr Malouf, the news editor, an excitable young man with eight children, spoke broad American and was trying to impose New York efficiency on the rest of the staff. I was installed amidst this throng in the capacity of 'military adviser'. I advised a lot but no one listened.

For a fortnight I hardly left the place. Every evening when we went to press I descended into the dark alley behind the office block and hurried past the thronging beggars and pick-pockets of Arab Cafés to the printing press. Here the pages were hand-set – by the hands, that is, of some fifteen Arab boys who could not read a word of English. If a line got dropped they reset it by guess work. Proofs were corrected by a dear eighty-two-year-old American missionary who for some reason had come down from the mountains and applied for war work. By midnight the paper had gone to press, and at three in the morning two taxis laden with queer passengers arrived to take copies off to Damascus and Tripoli. On the way, other passengers and parcels were gathered up and packets of the *Eastern Times* were dropped along the coast and in the Bekaa Valley for Arab boys to distribute to military camps. I would totter home and sleep until late morning, when I had to hurry back to the office and wait for Major Rosselli's daily blitz by phone.

Questioned why the headlines were back to front and photographs upside down, I never knew the answer. Everything had seemed all right the night before. The Greek king and his suite visited Beirut and were heralded in large type: 'King George has arrived with his suits'. One day an error was made about General Maitland Wilson's rank and the ADC rang up. The *Eastern Times* profusely apologized, and decided to publish a large photograph of the general next day with his correct titles. After midnight, when we had all left the press, an Arab boy upset and casually rearranged the line which held the letters representing the honours conferred on the general so that a lot of unheard of orders appeared after his name. The ADC rang up again and said to please not apologize any more.

The most disconcerting mistake occurred when a late Reuter reported 'Aust Mutiny, Troops run away and refuse to fight'. To the Arab staff 'Aust' had so far meant Australian, not Austrian, so they inserted a long story about Australian cowardice. As Syria was at that time packed with Aussies whose angry officers blamed me personally for the slip, I gave a gasp of relief when Major Rosselli ordered me off on a thousand-mile-tour to find out how the papers could be distributed.

Public relations sent me off in a staff car with a conducting officer to take me around the icy, sodden, far-flung camps of Syria, where we tried to co-ordinate ration lorries with small Arab boys on donkeys so that the troops in their godforsaken tents and huts could at least get one sheet of Reuter news a day. Also it was supposed to be good propaganda for the Arabs, who seemed wild with excitement over their own English newspaper.

I met enthusiastic Arab newsagents in every town and village who babbled that among the readers of the *Eastern Times* were the great men of Aleppo, Damascus, Homs and Hama, and even Druzes and Alouites (a tribe who were giving trouble on account of their self-appointed 'God'). Apparently even the unlettered but powerful Bedouin chiefs would gather their information from the *Eastern Times* and so might the Satan worshippers of the Jebel Sinjar.

My head swirled with accounts of probable customers, but we stuck to the policy of trying to cater for the soldiers by publishing plain news bulletins, countless articles on grouse-shooting and yacht regattas (issued by the Ministry of Information to cheer up the troops!) and, when we could get them, the *Daily Mirror* cartoons of 'Jane'.

My first trip led north to the Turkish border where the Australians were building a strategic railway through two hundred miles of banana groves. They had to construct nearly a hundred bridges and were frozen and cross, but they proudly carved their Rising Sun crest on the mountain rock at the Dog River like every conqueror before them, Assyrian, Greek and Roman.

It was the coldest, wettest December for twenty years. The Lebanon mountains grew white, and many roads were snow-blocked or impassable for mud. British troops enthused at the idea of getting a newspaper, but the Arab distributors had to be bribed and cajoled. One boy with whom I remonstrated for not taking the paper to Katena camp, lying in a mud waste beyond Damascus, excused himself on the grounds he never left bed in such weather.

We drove hundreds of miles through bleak, rainy desert and befogged mountains and found units living in intense cold and discomfort everywhere, and covered the great Bekaa Valley where defences were being built to meet the Germans – if they thrust down through the Caucasus – and visited far-flung Australian units in the wild forested hills of the Turkish border.

In Aleppo, the beautiful Arab city three hundred miles north of Beirut, we shivered snow-bound, and watched the strange mixture of spies and spy-catchers who hung around the hotel eyeing each other suspiciously – for all this Turkish border was alive with agents.

In Palmyra, the romantic capital of Queen Zenobia, we found the one hotel had been looted by the Arab Legion. Broken furniture and ripped mattresses lay around the open door together with an astounding catalogue of the hotel library which listed only those books known as 'curious'.

The French local commander, Commandant Moreau, invited me to stay in his square mud-house and took me out camel riding to see the ruins from afar. His camels were champion bred, small she-camels with fluffy brushed coats and scarlet saddles and perfect manners, but they would gallop all the time. In vain I tugged at my headstring, the camel turned her nose towards me but her great legs strode faster and faster. I thought I'd die if we did not stop jolting, die or faint or be sick, or fling myself on to the hard-looking desert that was ripping past.

Every evening there was a dinner-party in Palmyra. Moreau's Arab adjutant invited twenty guests to climb upstairs to his bedroom where a whole roast sheep awaited. Tent customs had simply been transplanted indoors. We crowded around the table, clambered on to the big brass bedstead and by lamplight crammed balls of rice and mutton into our mouths.

On my last evening an invitation came from Professor Amy, the French archaeologist who lived in a small house in a corner of the Temple of Bel. Amy blinked behind huge spectacles, had a pointed beard and great locks of untidy hair.

During dinner he talked piteously of the recent fighting when the temple got chipped. 'Come, I will show you a row of beautiful columns I have written a treatise on and now they are toppling.'

For ten years he had lived there, pestering the various military commanders for coal to run his little railway that carted away debris, or to lend him digging parties. War was merely a catastrophe that shook his ruins and passed on.

The professor's attitude had all my sympathy – what would we in turn leave to the wilderness we conquered? No marble columns, no fountains, no sculpture – a tangle of barbed wire perhaps – or a corrugated iron latrine forgotten in the sands?

Back in Beirut I decided to leave the hotel because it was so far from the *Eastern Times* office. My work finished late and I did not like walking home through black streets full of drunken soldiers and thieves, and I grew tired of snacks in Arab cafés, so the editor took me to search for a flat. He suggested going to an 'agent'. The 'letting firm' consisted of an old man in a tarboosh, sitting cross-legged on the pavement shouting the descriptions of rooms he had to let up and down the wet, empty street. I felt sorry for him and, when he folded up papers and umbrella and started off enthusiastically giving descriptions in Arabic I tagged along without much conviction. We visited several impassible premises and then, as if thunderstruck at the perfect idea, he led us to the apartment of a 'Lebanese widow of the very best family' who used to have millions but had lost it 'gambling'.

Turning into a narrow garbage-filled alley in the red light district we climbed an outside staircase to a bougainvillea-covered balcony. Here I could get a large bedroom with my own kitchen and bathroom, and the fat old widow assured me she would live next door and supervise her maid who would prepare my meals. So, as *monsieur l'agent* was howling for his commission, I paid him off and took the place, determined to ignore the red arrows pointing every way in my alley; for these, originally intended to lead to raid shelters were now used to lure the drunken soldiery to houses of ill-fame. I lived there just one week, Christmas week 1941.

In the morning when I sat up in bed and shouted for breakfast the 'maid' did indeed come in. She was nine years old, a pathetic waif, whose bare feet clattered in wooden sandals. She carried a thimbleful of strong black Turkish coffee and a glass of cold water to wash it down with. I sent her out to buy bread and a pot of jam. She took £1 and brought back stale bread and bright pink jam made of orange blossom. Then I asked for a hot bath, and understood this meant buying firewood, so out she went with more money and in time I heard groans; there came three little gnomes, plodding up the stairs laden with sacks of wood – half of which was sold to neighbours while I searched for more cash.

When I tried to cook my own dinner a terrifying hum started in the Primus stove, after which sheets of flame leapt up and blackened the kitchen ceiling. *Madame* rushed in from next door, turned on all the lights, and I found my little maid asleep on a plush sofa in the hall. It was her only bed and, having no nightdress, she slept in her cotton frock. Going to my own room I found she had been trying on all my clothes. The climax came Christmas morning. Awakened early by splashing in the bathroom, strictly reserved for myself, I hurried up and found everything covered with orange mud. I stamped angrily into the kitchen and found *Madame* dyeing her hair while all the saucepans were bubbling. She wept at my rage and, with henna running across her fat old face and dripping on the floor, explained 'Ah, but I want to remain young.'

So did I; so I moved.

After lunching alone in a small Arab café, I went to the *Eastern Times* offices to write a homesick letter to the girls in Egypt. Mme Khoury, wife of Sheikh El-Khoury who financed the paper, had suggested that she and her lady friends would get up a Christmas tea-party for three hundred British soldiers, as the boys seemed to have nowhere to go. There were as yet no NAAFI or YMCA clubs in Beirut and the streets were full of slouch-hatted Australians, blue with cold, buying poisonous ice-creams off Arab boys, or having fist-fights to keep themselves warm. I had sent out hundreds of invitations to the units around Beirut to send a few men to a party at the *Eastern Times* office at four on Christmas Day.

It was just two o'clock when hammering began on the back door and my heart sank. Opening I found the first hundred Australians had come straight from their beery Christmas dinner to ask unsteadily, 'Where is the fun?' Alone in the office I looked round in despair, gave them a piano to pound and hurried to the other premises where Mme Khoury, her daughters and ladies were arriving with baskets of cakes, tea-urns, etc. Then soldiers arrived in hordes. The Lebanese girls made gallant efforts to serve tea, offer cakes, and tip the more drunken ones downstairs.

Mme Khoury had thought up a lottery and tickets were distributed for the four dozen bottles of good whisky, which she had provided for the boys to take home. Amidst roars and cat-calls each winner would claim his bottle and then be promptly overpowered, and while one pal sat on his head the others finished the whisky. A couple of hooligans produced mistletoe and held it over the heads of the Lebanese girls who did not understand what mistletoe implied. It was definitely time to end the party, but the soldiers had now discovered 'the fun'. We began to cajole them downstairs. Some fell head over heels with ease. Others carried off the brass *Eastern Times* door plates as souvenirs. We watched timorously from the balcony while fifty men brawled in the Place des Canons. Then in the dusk we slipped off to our own Christmas dinners.

7

Beirut Base

All the snowy month of January I drove from the Turkish frontier to the Euphrates and back again to Damascus and Aleppo, Hama, and Homs, struggling to circulate news to the troops and learning unexpected things about newspaper distribution and travel in the Syrian desert, where winter tracks are of bottomless mud and it even rains mud. Sometimes I was in despair, but the paper slowly improved and distribution increased until most isolated places received a sheet of news daily.

When I drove to Transjordan, we crossed pale green desert with sand grouse and bustards and pigeons around the water-holes. Occasional Bedouin camped here, keeping the land barren by uprooting tiny trees for firewood and grazing their sheep on all that grows. Occasionally we saw troops of the Arab Legion (Bedouin commanded by Colonel Glubb). The legion had done well in the Syrian campaign but it could not be prevented from looting. The uniform consisted of khaki Bedouin-pattern clothes, a scarlet sheepskin-covered overcoat, and as many bandoliers of ammunition as the man could carry, spare holes being filled with daggers. Glubb achieved a greater influence over the Arabs than Lawrence, but he shuns publicity and his exploits will go unrecorded. He is, in fact, the biggest English character yet known in Arabic-speaking circles east of the Suez Canal. His word is law from Tigris to Nile and far into Arabia.

In the volcanic desert south of Damascus rose the black basalt mountain called Jabal al-Druze. The Druzes – a good-looking, white-skinned, blue-eyed tribe – had retired there from the Lebanon a century or so ago in order to carry out the rites of their secret religion. Asmahan, the beautiful Emira who had created such emotional havoc among His Majesty's officers during the invasion, had obeyed British orders by remarrying her divorced husband and retiring to this mountain strong-hold. Now she was living in her house at Soueida – the treeless, flowerless Druze capital. The ever-changing desert lights gave a desolate splendour to the rocky mountain, but Asmahan pined for the civilized world. Her sole joy at Soueida appeared to be the cocktail bar she installed under the stairs, from which she herself served the drinks. The fierce Druze tribe were still of interest to the British, and numerous officers were lured to Soueida on missions. They made their way up the grim moun-tain and shyly entered the exotic villa where their hostess lost no time in teaching them to address her as princess and treat her as if she were royalty. Dazed British officers were soon tamed, but the cynical French General Collet (who had crossed to our side with his Circassians and taken Damascus) arrived to see her and instead of addressing her as *princesse* asked: 'Pardon me, do I now call you *Madame* or *Mademoiselle*?' How she hated him!

Leaving the Druze Mountain we drove back to Damascus, and if the road over the Lebanon was not blocked with snow we might reach Beirut by midnight. No sooner had I got back from a trip like this than Major Rosselli would send for me to meet big-wigs up from Cairo for a Press and Propaganda Conference, and I had to gather my wits to try to explain the Syrian – Arab – Free French – Palestinian confusion in which this paper was produced.

During these conferences the proprietors of the *Eastern Times* were in a turmoil as to whether they would be allowed to continue running the paper or not. The Syrians and Lebanese were extremely anxious that any English newspaper sold in their territory should be produced by Arabs, not Jews. With amusement I heard ragged little newsboys shouting through the Beirut streets 'Eastern Timiss, Eastern Timiss Palestine Post no good!' At last a note arrived from Sir Walter Monckton that he had decided that the Arab-owned *Eastern Times* must continue. In eleven hours driving I tore down the four hundred miles from Aleppo, where I was wrestling with donkey boys, to Jerusalem; here we shipped a magnificent new printing press into three military lorries and returned triumphant to Beirut. Nejib, my decrepit ninety-year-old office boy who was supposed to run errands, and bring coffee when I got angry, congratulated me profusely and Sheikh El-Khoury, the proprietor, invited me to a celebration dinner in his immense unheated palace.

In late February the ten tons of paper which I'd been struggling to get from Cairo arrived in Jerusalem and proved the wrong size. The only British press officer who could give orders to change it had got snowed-up, on a skiing holiday at the Cedars. As we had only enough paper to go on printing for four days I phoned wildly till storm broke the wires. The proprietor kept begging me to go up to Cedars, '*Comme vous aimez le ski, Mademoiselle*' but happily I refused his offers to pay all my sporting expenses, for the officer in question eventually arrived, collapsing in Beirut after a fourteen-hour-walk through the snow.

Suddenly GHQ Cairo put a lieutenant who had been a journalist in charge of the *Eastern Times*. His job was not made easier by a little Fleet Street experience, for he arrived at a time when the chief problem consisted of dealing with a staff of thirty Arabs who demanded their pay not in money but in wheat. I retreated from the dispute and went off to cope with some other trouble in Damascus where Joy Goode, my old MTC friend, invited me to go out with her in search of 'the Street called Straight', where Ananias found Saul of Tarsus. But none of the seething market throng had heard of it, and when translated into French and Arabic it sounded odd.

'*Où est l'habitation de St. Paul?*' we shrieked at a local *gendarme*, but he baffled us by asking back, 'Who is St. Paul? Has he a shop?' The news spread quickly that two girls in uniform in a military car were looking for a Saint in a straight street, and staring crowds collected so that we could hardly drive over the cobbled alleys. After an hour of enquiry we were finally given to understand there were short streets and long streets but no straight streets in this part of the town. '*Not a straight street but the street called Straight*' screamed the indomitable Joy; but I had turned the car and was driving home fast.

In my Beirut flat I found Miranda Lampson on leave just back from Palmyra, where Moreau had treated her royally as he promised, producing 'camels, horses, wine, and petrol'. Miranda, brown from desert lorry-driving, lay on my bed and gave her version of the recent change of government in Egypt. Her uncle, the ambassador, went to King Farouk with a bevy of tanks in attendance and handed him an abdication form to sign, should he refuse to appoint Nahas as prime minister. The abdication form, being a confidential document, had been hastily typed by an ADC who did not excel at the typewriter when he was in a flap. It read something like this: 'I? King Farouk % ; do hereby resign ££ the throne etc. etc.' The king stared at it, raised his eyebrows and gave in. Meanwhile one of the tanks escorting Sir Miles leaned rather too heavily against the palace gate and broke it. The embarrassed crew scrambled out, mended it, and got back into their tank again before they were seen.

By April, the *Eastern Times* had improved enough for me to leave the editors alone and chase around continuously to the out-of-the-way corners of Syria. I explored Homs, a thousand-year-old city, whose silk looms were hard at work making parachutes. This time I stayed in the Arab Hotel Raghdan, where I had a spotless white room adorned with a large list of rules in Arabic and French. These read:

> *Monsieurs les voyageurs* will not smoke in bed.
>> Will not take in washing.
>> Will not obstruct the *canilsations* (drains?).
>> Will not cook in their bedrooms.
>> Reunions between the two sexes are forbidden except in the hotel lounge.

Next morning I found no food was served in the hotel. You were supposed to bring your own sandwiches and picnic Bedouin fashion. I bribed a small boy to go out in the rain and buy some breakfast at a café. He reappeared with local flat bread and a tiny lidless pot decorated with roses which contained a sip of tea. While I ate, the newsagent of Homs came in, and all the hotel staff gathered round to listen to our conversation and help my halting Arabic.

'We are anti-German,' they said. 'Good,' I replied; 'so is the *Eastern Times*.' 'Splendid,' they cried; 'we will buy it.' So joining in their laughter and agreeing with the thousand-year-old feud between Homs and Hama I shook hands with half the town, and went off leaving newspaper confusion in my wake; but by now I was carefree as the Arabs, and pious too, murmuring always when in difficulty 'if God wills'.

Not far from Homs lay Sulemya, the strong point of the Ismailis, fanatical Shias who worship the Aga Khan. In their houses I was startled to see framed *Tatler* photographs of a golden-haired English woman with two small boys: this was Princess Ali Khan (a daughter of Lord Churston) and her sons. When Ali Khan took General Wilson to visit Sulemya – mounted on horseback – the party galloped in escorted by a yelling crowd, many of whom deliberately threw themselves under Ali's horse in the hope of getting a limb bruised, for such a wound would earn money at perhaps £5 a touch. On arrival, the son of their holy one had a wash and there was a scrum for his dirty water. It seemed a singularly unattractive religion.

After the great Krak des Chevaliers – the most dramatic crusader castle in the world – ranks the Chateau Beaufort which towers above the Litani river. Richard *Coeur de Lion* enraged the local tribes by kidnapping a pretty Arab girl and keeping her here until she tried to escape and fell down the thousand-foot-drop to the river bed. No car could reach the castle, so we tramped up at dusk and to our amazement two camels stuck their heads out of the keep. We discovered a party of workmen engaged on restoring the walls which had been knocked about by artillery in the Druze rebellion. I insisted on making supper, and slept on the topmost turret. Never was there such method of news distribution, such an odd person to do it, or quite such a paper as the *Eastern Times!*

Not far from Sidon I found a zigzag track that led up to Juni, the hill village where Lady Hester Stanhope lived. There were pine woods and a stone-built village with a wonderful view of mountains to the east and blue Mediterranean to the west. Owing to shortage of building materials the last stones of her house were being carried away, but the villagers still spoke of the great 'Sitt'. I promptly wrote articles on Lady Hester and on Jezebel – who came from Sidon – in the hopes of interesting the troops around. But what cared they for kingly Richard or for the wicked, dauntless, Sidonian princess or for that embittered, brilliant Englishwoman who nursed her grievances and memories and dreams to death in the wild beauty of Lebanon!

Ordered by the British press liaison officer to scour the Euphrates and the Jazira plain which led to Persia for means of getting newspapers to isolated units, I had the wonderful idea of dropping bundles from the sky. French planes were supposed to cover the Palmyra-Euphrates area twice a week and so, to save motoring two thousand miles along desert tracks I now knew by heart, I went to the airport and asked a French officer if I might travel that day to Deir ez-Zor.

'*Oui, oui Mademoiselle* – As soon as we get the engine back in.' I did not know that aeroplane engines came out – very often! Mechanics twirled propellers and chattered, and finally a jockey called Wattat – who was well-known on the Beirut race track and who spent his spare time in the French air force – offered to pilot me to the Euphrates.

'I hope we get over the Lebanon,' he shouted. We skimmed the mountain tops and then hummed on over Damascus and Palmyra. It was cold, so the other passenger, an English brigadier, lent me his sweater without bothering to remove the badges of rank. At Deir ez-Zor the mail plane was met by Colonel Brosset, French commander of East Syria. He saluted smartly and bowed me into his car. Driving off, he gazed at my shoulder asking, 'Are you a brigadier?' I explained the sweater was borrowed from the senior officer he had left behind for the next car. 'Oh,' said Brosset blithely, 'I thought you were Princess Mary and that fellow your ADG. Perhaps we'd better go back and help him with the luggage?'

I spent two days travelling the flower-covered wilderness of the Jazira, trying to discover if and where the Taurus express ever stopped, if and where planes could drop anything and to whom. I waded knee-deep through a sea of wild larkspur and hollyhock and saw the snow-covered mountains of Persia, and explored great ruins that were the first cities of the world, but I never placed a single copy of the *Eastern Times!*

From Deir ez-Zor, Wattat flew me back to Beirut. Again he shouted, 'I hope we get over the mountains,' and again I smiled complacently. On the next flight his plane did not rise sufficiently and he crashed into the Lebanon and was killed.

In the following winter I motored back to Deir ez-Zor and stayed with Brosset, who had expended his unbounded energy for long enough in East Syria. He was champing at the bit to get off and fight. In 1943, he replaced General Koenig as commander of the French division that advanced in Tunis. In Italy, where his division landed in May 1944 and took heavy losses, he wrote me a piquant letter; but I never saw him again. In the fighting in France he became a legendary character, and one icy December night when I was dining by candle-light in a spahis mess near Belfort the news came in that General Brosset had been killed. He had been driving at his usual break-neck speed when a mine blew his jeep into a canal and he was caught and drowned.

8

Syrian Kaleidoscope

In May, 1942, the duke of Gloucester visited the Middle East and I was told to write up his tour for the Press Liaison Bureau to translate into Arabic. Incidentally, there were one hundred and forty-eight different Arabic papers published in Syria; Damascus alone produced fifty.

The duke spent a night at the staff college, Haifa, where officers were trained on the slopes on which Elijah held his competition with the priests that Jezebel brought from Sidon.

I was told to meet a public relations staff car at the Syrian border and join the royal procession with two war correspondents. The transport office in Haifa sent me, by error, in a hired taxi which also contained two unshaven French sailors in hats with red pom-poms and an Afrikaans-speaking South African, with a topee so large that it blinded him. We had not the speed or privileges of a military car and chased vainly along the ninety miles of coast road. Every time we approached a group of South African engineers or other soldiery, which the duke was inspecting, red-capped military police held us up, and by the time I'd produced credentials and got through we had dropped behind again. The Arab driver pressed his brown and white striped shoes on the accelerator till it would descend no more. Several times we nearly tipped into the sea, but the chase failed till reaching Beirut in the late afternoon when we caught up with the duke at Beirut airport, where he was reviewing the RAF.

The major who directed public relations peevishly asked where I'd been and signalled me to jump into the third car of the procession which was already moving off. My unshaven sailors threw my luggage in after me, together with two dozen grapefruit, which made the car look like a mobile fruit stall and we drove off to pay a state visit to the Lebanese president and then to General Catroux's Turkish palace by the racecourse. Here there was a *grand réception,* so I slipped upstairs to wash. No sooner had I bolted the door than pounding began and an ADC shouted to me to hurry because the duke was waiting. Flustered and dripping I opened the door and made way for HRH, who gave a broad grin but appeared to be in an even greater hurry than myself. So I scurried downstairs, where Mme Catroux mistook me for a French woman press photographer, and prepared groups for me before I had time to explain I possessed no camera.

At this point Prince Ali Khan – who was now Catroux's ADC – came up with an arm-load of my khaki summer shirts that he had kindly brought that day by plane from Cairo, and asked, 'What on earth has happened? You look sixty!' I seized a much-needed clean shirt and crept home to write a report. Next morning I had to set off in the same procession and same car, to drive north to Tripoli, where the defences had been built that were to hold up the expected German thrust from Turkey. On the sea-shore the 9th Australian Division, which had held Tobruk so long, was lined up; nearly a mile of lithe, tough, browned, not very polite, but extremely-amusing soldiers stood to attention with the wide blue sea as a backcloth.

HRH, with General Wilson and a bevy of ADC's, walked slowly along the ranks. I followed at a distance with the weary correspondents till a digger called out: 'Hey, there – look at the

Dook's girl-friend! We 'ad to leave ours at home.' An angry sergeant major strode forward but the offender was indistinguishable in the ranks. I thought it best to retreat to the car.

When the duke inspected the Naval Base, instead of accompanying the other correspondents I tried to keep out of the way by standing with a group of civilians. To my horror the royal party, having terminated the inspection, turned straight for my corner and I was for the fifth time in twenty-four hours introduced to the duke. Too late I realized that instead of hiding I had parked myself in front of a row of English women who were there to be presented, and I could hear their simmering rage as HRH asked if I was in charge of them.

Next day, in the Bekaa Valley, I kept well behind. The African native pioneers (Basothos, Zulus, etc.) lining the roads were fascinating. They were so proud of themselves, and so happy holding their spears, trying to keep a fixed military stare, but their wide black mouths just could not resist grinning with ecstasy at their importance as warriors on this day. These troops had no rifles, but they were so disappointed at the idea of parading with only spades that spears were allowed. The duke stood by the old Roman trade route while a division of New Zealand soldiers in their brimmed hats marched down the valley. In the background a camel, terrified by the tramping soldiers, bucked and retreated while a dazed Arab cajoled it along and peered over his shoulder at the king of England's brother addressing these men from a far-off land in this ancient setting.

In July I moved to a villa outside Beirut, where I had seven palatial unfurnished rooms and a bar. It had no address, but stood beside the French military prison and on several occasions friends, who enquired of the Senegalese sentry where I lived, were taken inside while records were looked up for an inmate of my name.

Rents had become exorbitant but my Muslim landlord gave me this place for a song because he said my friends were 'so gay'. He lived upstairs with a large family, and when his brother got married a hundred hired gilt chairs were put in my garden, where feasting went on for twenty-four hours. I had a dreadful little Arab maid but could not sack her because Moustafa, the gardener, liked her and he was indispensable. He mended the Primus and chopped wood to heat the bath water and arranged the flowers. When I arrived home late one night, after a hot twelve-hour drive from Palestine and found no dinner prepared, and no food in the house, Moustafa quelled my rage by placing a necklace of intoxicating jasmine blossom round my neck and saying his only English word 'Welcome'. Then he went off and picked me a bunch of bananas.

Beirut in the summer had a damp heat that provoked both Arab and European to brain-storm. All marriages broke up during July and August. The noise from the Place des Canons rose nauseatingly to my office window, the noise of taxis, trams, fighting boys, Arab street vendors, soldiers on leave; it rose above the motley surging mob like the roar of Piccadilly gone mad. From my desk I could watch the tribes of Lebanon doing their noisy shopping and driving herds of sheep and geese along the side-walks, while a minor riot was occasionally caused by Australian soldiers who, feeling warm, would strip and swim naked in the central fountain causing women to veil themselves and run screaming, while Lebanese *gendarmes* blew whistles for the military police and all the trams stopped so that crowds could climb up and use them as grandstands. Meanwhile above the chaos, beyond the old red-roofed Turkish Government House, rose the mountains of incredible loveliness tempting one always to play truant.

At sunset I would leave the office and walk the three miles home through side streets that smelt overpoweringly of drains and jasmine, to have an evening swim and feast on strawberries.

Meanwhile the desert flared up and I made tracks for Egypt. Cairo underwent that period called 'the Big Flap', and jokes were made about GHQ where they were burning all the secret papers and smoke literally poured from every window. Jerusalem was packed with refugees, the last of my Free French friends was killed at Bir Hakeim, Tobruk fell, Rommel reached Alexandria, and the few troops left in Syria were waiting for Stalingrad to fall. . . Then the Germans would sweep down through Turkey.

9

Transjordania

Unable to get the job I wanted in Egypt I went to Transjordan and worked in a motor repair depot at the oasis of Zerka, occasionally driving to Amman, to Madaba, or on across the desert to towns that flourished in Roman times, where the legions had left their arches and paved roads and nothing else. And at Petra . . . 'the rose-red city old as time' . . . there were charabancs of Australian nurses and lithe, soldierly sight-seers from New Zealand, as well as the occasional Cockney impressed with his own whimsy at making such a trip.

Studying Arabic, I found everything had thirty different names; that there were forty ways of forming the plural; that one had to use different verbs speaking to a man or woman; that there were three unpronounceable letters. Colonel Glubb, who occasionally descended on Zerka and, if no one objected would empty the larder and vanish with his Bedouin, said it had taken him fifteen years unremitting study to master the dialects.

In the workshop I learnt more about camels than cars. In the desert, they told me, an Arab can tell the footprint of each of his camels, he knows them miles off silhouetted against the sky, and in the dark he knows them by their smell. The Bedouin have up to two hundred names for the species, at different times of their lives. Arabic is probably the richest language in words in the world. We denote horses as foals, yearlings, etc., but the Bedouin breaks camels up again by the months and has a word for each.

There is no such thing as a wild camel in Asia — Bedouin say that a camel cannot live without the aid of man, that he cannot mate without human assistance, and would die out if left to himself. On the other hand the Arabs said that the desert gazelles, exquisite little creatures with delicate spun-glass legs mated as they galloped along without break of pace.

Emir Abdullah had the true Bedouin inability to understand money except as a thing to squander gaily. He never could see why, when he was short of cash, he could not send his son to the post office to ask for a hundred pounds' worth of stamps to pay his bills. 'After all, they are *my* stamps.'

He carefully kept his father's state robe of a Sharif of Mecca, embroidered with gold and small pearls, and one day he showed it to a British officer. 'It was too heavy to wear at the Coronation in London but perhaps some day I shall use it . . . I have served England well during these dark days and England will reward me when the war is over?'

He was thinking of a coronation in Damascus.

One evening I sat by a hillside village and watched some Bedouin chatter around the water-hole discussing the site for camp. These nomads constantly used a word *Howah* which meant the smell, or quality, of the air; and in the wide, unscented desert they would pick out special places where to them the *Howah* was good. Their talk about the different airs of the wilderness did not make sense to me, whose vulgar nose could only recognize drains or roses, but I soon realized that the Bedouin lived in a world that held far more to their glinting eyes than to mine.

The conceit of Arab women was very amusing. The ugliest believed that they must veil their temptation to men in the street.

As we motored by, peasant women hoeing in the garden would hastily hide their large, flat feet for fear of their irresistible lure to the men in the car. But in spite of a hundred strange conventions, they made no mystery of sex. The Bedouin are so practical that if a man finds himself sterile he has to pay another man (perhaps two goats or a donkey) to put his wife with child. No man will render this service free.

The modern Jews I knew in Palestine were unhappy. The Arab, like the Irishman, has a merry, irresponsible outlook on life. The Jews, originally of the same Semitic stock, bitter with brooding over their persecutions, seemed ill-adjusted to settle down to life on the land. When they first arrived as refugees they were ready to 'do anything'; but I never knew a Jew who took happily to the earth. Suicide is unknown in the Arab world but among the Jews in Palestine the rate was high. Their heritage through centuries in Europe had destroyed their peace of mind, their link with nature. When a man talks about 'my land' he means 'the land that owns me'. Palestine might belong to the Jews but they did not belong to it.

Professor Wasserman was living in Jerusalem at that time, and the only real Jewish friend I had was a scientist who was working on the separation of female and male spermatozoa, so that the sex of a child might be determined at will. He used to say laughingly, 'Once I am successful I will come to England with my method and there I will make my fortune, because it is the only country where, if there is no son to inherit, a man's properties and titles go, not to a daughter, but, to some distant cousin. In Spain and France and Italy women inherit in their own right. Nowhere is so much legal importance attached to a child's sex as in England. Yes, I shall go there and produce little peers and get made a peer myself . . . you wait and see.'

I suggested that Chinese peasants might receive him gladly, but he insisted it was less bother to pop a female infant in a bucket of water than to trouble with cellular research. Then I wondered if his purpose was in accordance with nature and suddenly he became serious and said, 'My child. Do you really imagine that the great laws of life cease to be natural; just because we study and understand them?'

One night I spent in a Jewish settlement above Haifa with a quartermaster of the Transjordan Frontier Force. He and his wife and children welcomed me to their home. They cooked a big, stodgy dinner, and let me sleep on their sofa in a trim European bedroom. In the morning they showed me over the settlement, the rows of clean white modern bungalows, the well-worked gardens and orchards. They were cheery, kindly Jews.

Far more discontented in atmosphere was Tel Aviv, the big noisy modern city of shops and night clubs, wide concrete streets, clean cafeterias, and a busy Jewish population with resentful faces. Whoever served you, whether it was unsmiling chemist or sad-eyed waiter, you sensed he disliked you, and disliked life.

It was a relief to get out of this atmosphere to the dirty old Arab town of Jaffa where the inhabitants had some capacity for enjoyment. I sat there one hot night when the *khamseen* blurred the yellow egg-shaped moon and watched a torch-light procession proceed through the dark streets with the wild music of bagpipes. The cook explained, 'One chap he gets married, he make lovely night, he rich Arab, much music, wife and many girls they dance.' And his face lit up with the fun of it.

Gaza, with its filthy-looking mud-houses, is a stronghold of Arab merchants, but the houses are clean and attractive inside. They don't bother about the exterior. The sand dunes outside the town are covered with half-finished villas, which the Arab tradesmen build slowly, adding a few stones each year, so that in the end they can retire into a house that will last. No modern jerry-building for them – a tent or a castle!

Ten Arab girls of the 'highest class' were recruited into the Transjordan Frontier Force as clerks. They were keen to join, but no Arab women would go to the Palestinian ATS, for they could not mix with the Jewesses. When these girls arrived I found them well educated but Victorian in outlook. They were 'anxious to help Great Britain', but so modest they could not undress in front of each other. They wept all night with home-sickness, but typed efficiently all day. The experiment failed, for Palestine HQ would not authorize them unless they joined the ATS which they refused to do for fear of their 'reputation', and they returned, once again weeping, to their homes.

Meanwhile Ramadan came on, cannons thundered until they broke from over-firing; singing, dancing and drumming lasted all night in the Arab villages. After forty days it ended with more banging of drums and cannon. The jabbering of the cook in the kitchen had made me ask who he might be talking to; 'To himself,' came the answer. For a people so poor and near starvation, so lacking in medical and scientific knowledge, the Arabs seem inordinately happy. They never do anything that bores them! The Bedouin, who have the hardest life of all, contain themselves in mental stateliness and grandeur unknown to harassed town-bred Europeans moving as they will, and when they will, across a vast world of sand and stone.

There was a great difference of character between Colonel Glubbs' Bedouin and the agricultural Arabs, but the Emir Abdullah lorded it over them all. His red-roofed 'palace' (Oriental Ruler's Residence 3rd class) lay on the hillside of Amman. The Emir, himself a jovial little man, and strict Mohammedan, clung to old conventions; he would not allow any woman to work in an office in Transjordan, and had husbands reprimanded if their wives wore transparent veils in the street.

When the officers of the district paid an official *Bairam* visit to the Emir, I went with Mrs Glubb and the English ladies of Amman to the celebration *levée* of his wives. It was terrifyingly formal and boring. The two official wives standing side by side in a doorway received us, the third wife (and gossip had it the favourite) was ebony black, not royal, and did not receive. Wife No. 1, the 'Royal Lady' of Sharifian blood, was a grand old dame in white head-dress, with plenty of character and queenly manners. Her humorous black eyes twinkled, and she showed great interest in the lives of women ambulance-drivers, which I tried with effort to depict. She had two sons, and the eldest had been sent unprepared to Woolwich, where he was ragged and given pack drill, and has never liked the British since. In fact he became so bitter that the Emir has appointed the second son as heir.

The daughter, who has since married, sat beside me. After much staring, I discovered she spoke French and we could chatter fluently about Jerusalem and Cairo where she 'liked the shops and cinemas'. The dreariness of these women's minds was horrifying. The Arab does not transplant from the desert. The boys are ruined when, instead of sharing the hard life of the men, they are brought up indoors and pampered by women, and these poor, pasty princesses were pathetic compared to the common women, who might slave but were full of fun and laughter and bawdy jokes. I looked at the fat little legs squeezed into cheap high-heeled shoes; at the hideous modern furniture and linographs of the Emir; we nibbled chocolates, sipped coffee, and after an hour of strained conversation and long silent pauses, when not even Mrs Glubb whose Arabic was fluent could think of anything to say, we filed out, over the most exquisite of Persian carpets, to visit wife No. 2 in her separate apartments.

The second wife, very fat and Tartar looking, was clad in a red plaid sports dress; she had straight black bobbed hair and large legs in wrinkled stockings and high-heeled shoes. She had nothing to say in any language and could only beam aimlessly. The modern villa-palace with its utter lack of taste or homeliness appalled; especially as the Arabs have a great history of art behind them, and the interior of a Bedouin tent is delightful with glorious rugs, and saddle-bags, and objects of fine workmanship strewn about.

Abdullah's second son had married a young Turkish Sultana who was now eighteen and the mother of one child. We gasped when she suddenly came in looking like a Vogue fashion advertisement, blonde hair dressed in most modern fashion, slim figure, smart grey dress, lovely shoes and stockings. She sat down with us and conversed in perfect French and English. I wondered she did not go mad, shut up in this fashion. Her handmaidens, a group of Arab girls with tattooed faces and the usual black robes flittered around the open door, while another servant girl in an ill-fitting European dress, thin black silk stockings, and orange leather high-heeled shoes on which she could hardly balance, handed sweets and coffee.

Next day we paid two more lengthy visits to the daughters-in-law of Abdullah, who lived in their own stone villas some way from the palace. We saw the little fair-haired Sultana in her own home, where she spent days sitting about in numerous Paris gowns and sighing for the smart world of Egypt. The 'sitting-room' had bare walls and was furnished with a plain 'set' of chairs, reminiscent of a dentist's waiting-room; two hideous modern French china vases; a gold piano; an exquisite sixteenth century carved wood table and the usual beautiful carpet. Her husband (the heir) was modern enough to shake hands with us at the front door.

In the other villa I met for the first time the wife of Tallal (who went to Woolwich and was to be disinherited). She was a Sharifian princess educated on modern lines in Alexandria. For the first time among these royal ladies I found one person charmingly easy to talk to. She had great tragic black eyes and vivacity. She might have been a smart Frenchwoman in her black satin gown and silk stockings, and there was pathos in her eager questioning. 'Seven years ago I married,' she said, 'and since then I have not returned to Egypt.' Asked how she liked Amman, she looked at me wistfully and said, 'I am in prison.'

In November, General Alexander came to the Middle East. He had been born and brought up at Caledon House, three miles from my home in Ireland. The walls of our estates meet, although his land lay in Ulster, ours in the Free State. His father, old Lord Caledon, a great character in the Ireland of the 'nineties had explored North America in the early cowboy days and had lived with the Blackfoot Indians. He brought home large, live, grizzly bears and stocked his park with different kinds of deer, and there was a summer-house which we children solemnly believed to be compiled of human bones from an imaginary dungeon. The old earl was extremely unsocial. On one occasion, when he met a London friend after a three-week-trek across the prairies, he just waved and rode on. Lord Caledon had four sons, the third of whom, named Harold, was my grandmother's pet. She often talked about his career in the Irish Guards, and what a good shot he was.

The first time I saw Harold Alexander was when he came over for a shoot. Aged about five, I sat and watched the 'promising soldier' banging away while Tay, the labrador who lived in the nursery, retrieved from the swamp. That evening, when the

Alexanders had gone home, old Tay committed murder in a premeditated manner, unique among dogs. He picked up our spoilt pet Sealyham, who was as usual teasing him by nipping at his tail, and carried him by the scruff of his neck far out into the flood water. There, deaf to our piercing screams, he drowned the small dog by deliberately holding him down, just out of the frantic reach of me and my three-year-old brother.

My grandmother had been in Paris in 1870, had lost a son in 1914 and thoroughly disliked the Germans. From her I learnt the word 'boche!' When I listened to her conversation, there were always stories about young Colonel Alexander and her nephew, Winston Churchill. Little did she dream that one day the sour-faced little girl, whom she used to beg to 'smile dear, it costs nothing', would stand in the centre of Berlin, watching British troops parade in front of those two men in whom she had been interested since they were boys.

Since that horrible duck shoot – which must have been in 1919 – the slim athletic figure of 'Alex' had occasionally reappeared in our home, walking over from Caledon for tea or to watch the plays we wrote about county families. He had visited Caledon just after Munich, and had discussed the possibilities of Czechoslovakia as a battlefield over a vast Irish tea-table with my grandmother 'feeding him up' with honey. I had not seen him since. Now he had come to the Middle East to replace Auchinleck and to plan and launch the battle of El Alamein.

Before that offensive broke he paid a formal visit to Transjordan and, after inspecting the Arab Legion and Transjordan Frontier Force depots, dined with the Emir Abdullah. The Emir, being a real little Bedouin with charming manners, loved big talk about war; he explained exactly how to drive the Germans out of Africa, and where to invade Europe. Alexander listened, and politely agreed with the Emir's ideas. Meanwhile, behind the doors of the reception room the prime minister of Iraq and Haidar Pasha from Syria, were hiding like naughty schoolboys to smoke their cigars and take nips from the prime minister's hip flasks. The Emir being a strict Muslim would not allow alcohol or tobacco to be enjoyed in his presence, but the two large men felt safe to puff and sip, as long as they could watch through the hinge of the door and see the Emir deep in military plans with the general.

When Abdulla produced his visitors' book, the general signed his name in well-written Arabic, and all were delighted; 'Iskander' had been the most famous of soldierly names ever since Alexander the Great swept through Egypt. The Emir, easily touched and excited, put his arms around the general's neck and kissed him saying, 'Mahaba' which means 'I love you', a sincere expression between Arab men.

10

Ladies of Lebanon

In the Autumn of 1942 I had to leave Transjordan and resume working with the *Eastern Times* in Beirut. Abandoning ideas of running a flat I lived in the St. George's Hotel, a diverting building jutting into the bay, which resembled a stranded aircraft-carrier. I had a room overlooking the sea and the music of a dance band drifted up with the sound of lapping waves. Black-out was vaguely enforced in Beirut, none knew why or paid much attention to it, but occasionally Lebanese *gendarmes* came and blew whistles around brightly-lit windows, and had to be bribed to go away. The St. George with the silvery Mediterranean lapping beneath its balconies looked so innocent without, while a hotbed of intrigues and excitements flourished within.

Staid British colonels, Indo-Chinese cocottes and Balkan revolutionaries lived side by side in rooms linked by balconies running round the building. A beautiful mannequin, who had lived there for several years, told me that in peace time *un mari enragé* had been known to give chase, leap-frogging the partitions right round the hotel. This balcony construction proved even more useful for the wartime dramas of spy-ridden Levant.

No day passed at the St. George without incident. Sometimes it would be the Greek prime minister who was warned of a plot to blow up his room (which was under mine), on other occasions mysterious arrests would be made on the hotel steps. I could sit on my balcony and watch people bathing and dancing and sipping their drinks and plotting. A few doors along lived a beautiful blonde French girl who had a number of admirers, among whom were certain young officers on the staff of General Maitland Wilson's HQ on the mountain top above Beirut. When she wished to travel to Cairo by air her swains received instructions they were to take her heavy baggage down by car. One morning her trunk was unfortunately placed on the back of General Wilson's own car, and while crossing the Sinai Desert, her large bottle of Chanel 5 broke and soaked through into his personal luggage. On arrival in Cairo the general wished to change hurriedly for a conference and sniffed suspiciously at his clothing which reeked of the perfume while his aides nervously blamed the over-scented Egyptian porters.

For those who had time to look there was no dearth of startling women in the Middle East. Among the most alluring were the Balkan 'countesses' who crept mysteriously across the Caucasus. They had guileless blue eyes, and they borrowed money and husbands and returned neither. The British authorities did not like glamorous women sitting in vital information centres – each with a pack of officers 'devoted to the poor little thing' – but whenever arrangements were made to remove them to some other clime they pleaded so prettily with the officers in charge of their removal that they never seemed to get very far.

Of all the women in the Middle East none caused such a stir as Asmahan, the Emira of the Druzes. As I grew to know and like her well, she told me her life-story; how she married the Emir when she was sixteen and found she could not love him.

'He cared so much for me, and I was just a tormenting spirit in his home. I was beautiful and ambitious. How could I sit on that bare black mountain listening for ever to a dull husband and to the tribesmen boasting of their exploits? I ran away to Egypt and there, as I could sing and act, I became the first Arab woman film star. I heard that my husband brought records of my songs and listened yearningly to them, but he divorced me and married a Druze woman who produced children. When the British contemplated invading Syria they brought me from Egypt to Jerusalem, and kept me there as a bait, knowing the Emir would do anything to get me back. What a time I had waiting . . . !'

I remembered that flower-filled room and the queue of officers anxious to discuss the military possibilities of the basalt mountain with its green-eyed princess.

'Do you know that the English paid me £50,000 sterling and I tried to get it in gold . . .' She laughed, and said, 'I wonder if I was worth it . . . but, oh la! how quickly it went! I can't seem to keep money; I like squandering it on clothes and champagne and presents . . .' She was a reckless, generous creature. Drinking nothing but champagne at £5 a bottle, she did not expect her guests to have lesser tastes. 'After the French Armistice I remarried my poor husband, who was censured by the Druzes because he put his other wife aside. The British expected me to settle in the Jabal al-Druze, but instead I went to Ain Sofar . . .'

There was a large luxurious hotel at this mountain resort, and Asmahan held court there during the days of the Armistice Commission; in the evenings she would descend the wide hotel staircase dressed in her magnificent tribal costume and more than one senior officer lost his head.

One winter night, long after all this occurred, she asked me to drive up into the mountains for a party in a house near Ain Sofar, and as the car crawled through a snowstorm she cuddled up to me and cried a little: 'You can't imagine how in love I was at Ain

Sofar. I've never found anyone else to care for since, and I'm miserable and lonely. Now my friends are the rich men of Alexandria whom I need to finance me and pay my debts. But I did care for just that one person, and we were such good friends too, *bon copains*. The British sent him back to England because of me. They said English generals should not fall in love. Why? Anita, why? The admiral and the air marshal did not get sent home, only him whom I really wanted. He had a ruby brooch made for me, it was the emblem of his division and I wore it all the time. Why shouldn't a soldier give me presents. Why? I never could understand, and now I love nobody and life seems stupid. The British made me marry my husband again and then they take away my beloved. Why? I wish they had really paid the £50,000 in gold,' she added, 'then, maybe, I wouldn't have spent it all.'

We arrived at last at the house of a Beirut millionaire, built on the very edge of a gorge with a sheer drop of a thousand feet into the valley below. The door opened and through the swirling snow we saw a luxurious room with a blazing log fire. There were several Levantine magnates waiting, with a lavish supper spread out with unprocurable wines. One of them had been made minister to the interior, on which his first act had been to pass a decree that none but himself would be permitted to build hotels in the best resort. We were welcomed to the party, praised for our courage in driving through the blizzard, and champagne appeared. Asmahan preened herself and lounged on a sofa, smoking and singing huskily. She gave her own fire to those queer fierce Arab songs that sounded so discordant in the villages. As the snowstorm did not abate, we accepted our host's invitation to remain the night. Asmahan and I were given a bed with sheets of finely embroidered pink satin. Sleep overcame me long before Asmahan ceased 'talking business' with the men in the next room. Towards dawn she came and woke me up.

'I have made a contract to go to Egypt,' she said, and her huge tigerish green eyes looked haunted. 'What does it matter where I go? I am destroyed. I have nothing to care about. I will make films again.' She pulled aside the curtain and we looked out at Ain Sofar, snow-covered in the dawn. Asmahan sighed and laid her head on the sill. 'It was summer when we were there together. I will never see him again, will I? If only I had had a child by him,' she said, 'I could have gone to the British Government with a child. . .'

I could imagine the humourless reception this effort would have achieved.

When the sun rose we drove hastily down the hairpin bends as I had an appointment in my office at nine, and I was getting rather tired of snow, champagne, and forlorn love. A few days later, Asmahan came to my hotel to say goodbye. She wore a veil so as not to be recognized, and when she stepped on my balcony and slipped it aside in the bright sunshine I thought again that no woman's face could be more beautiful, her features might have been carved from white marble, and I pitied indeed the men who had gazed too long into those emerald eyes.

She did not return to Syria and I never saw her again. Having played every card she possessed with the British Intelligence, she returned to films, then a jealous rival cut up her fur coat and expensive clothes in the King David Hotel in Jerusalem, and she had hysterics in the corridor which surprised officers going to work at HQ on the top floor. She was only allowed to return to Egypt because the British Oriental secretary guaranteed her demure behaviour and she swore to create no scandals.

She meant to be good, but within a fortnight of her arrival she went out to dine with an Egyptian cavalry officer, a jealous rival came in with a revolver, fired at his brother officer, shot the waiter dead by mistake, and caused an uproar that Asmahan in her role of demure temptress found hard to explain away. A few weeks later she herself met with sudden death. Tired and upset she went off alone for a quiet weekend at Ras El-Bar. Her car crashed into a water buffalo and overturned into a canal.

When they dragged her out it was to find her neck had been broken at the first impact. Her few enemies immediately said she had been strangled by a jilted lover, but it was not necessary to invent tales about Asmahan, and her funeral was attended by throngs of sincere friends. I was glad, having left the Middle East, when one of them wrote to me, 'I sent a big bunch of flowers from you.'

She was a lovable person. A wild flower, grown in the midst of a warlike tribe on a black stone mountainside, she was not made to grow old. Yes, Asmahan, being really fond of you I was glad you died when you did for you were two thousand years out of date. A Roman general could have given you a ruby brooch and kept his command.

11

Good Works and Bad

For a year the submarine flotilla based on Beirut was commanded by Captain Philip Ruck-Keene, who cured his exhausted submariners of every ill by making them ski from one end of the Lebanon to the other. Playing truant from the *Eastern Times* I joined most of these expeditions and we skied by moonlight across the whole range and when it grew warm camped in the beautiful high valleys. One of the most war-worn submarine commanders, Bill King, arrived from Malta in a state of collapse. Ruck-Keene said thirty mile tramps over the mountains would cure duodenal ulcers. They did. Bill went off to add to his DSOs in the Pacific, saying he had never before realized how restful life in a submarine could be.

I now lived with my cousin, Lilah Fortescue – an ATS officer in counter espionage – and Patsy O'Kane a slim, amusing girl who also struggled in a press job. We shared a villa owned by a delightful Russian couple, who behaved as if they were actors in a comic play. We loved them but how we groaned at their wonderful plans for making money. They thought up a new scheme every week and we usually got involved. When one lives with Russians one becomes just like them.

The servant problem in Beirut was acute. We had an old guards sergeant of the Tzarist Army who spoke no known language but loved us all dearly, and when I got bronchitis he left his gardening to mix brews and place jam-jars full of flaming cottonwool on my back. I screamed with terror, but the treatment worked. Alexandre, as he was called, never left, but a succession of housemaids came and went. At one time we had a Russian soldier recently demobilized from the Foreign Legion. Under Alexandre's eagle eye and deep bass directions he swept and dusted with enthusiasm, handling the broom as if he was in barracks again. But on Alexandre's day out he got at the vodka, broke every kitchen plate and disappeared into town.

Lilah, Patsy, and I were alone in the house and wanted to go out to dinner, but at the garden gate we found several very drunk and fierce foreign legionnaires shouting what sounded like, 'We want Lladiiiiiiinir,' so we quavered, retreated, and went supperless to bed. In the morning we felt that even with the servant shortage we could not have a housemaid with a black eye tottering about in an alcoholic stupor, so he was given notice.

At the end of November, 1943, the French, who still administered Syria and the Lebanon, arrested President Khoury, breaking into his house with Senegalese soldiers in the middle of the night to do so. Then came the 'Beirut riots'. During my years in Syria I had noticed how few top-class Frenchmen were spared for the responsible job of administration under the mandate. As a result there were perpetual incidents which made a feeling of seething bitterness that characters like Commandant Moreau and other French officers could not dispel.

When President Khoury was arrested in Gestapo manner the allies all protested. I knew the president and his family well, for he had financed the *Eastern Times*, and to him I had to apply for the money needed to buy new machinery. It was Mme Khoury who had given that vast, dreadful, but well-meaning tea-party for three hundred soldiers on my first Christmas day in Beirut, and since then she had often entertained British soldiers in her home.

A curfew was imposed in Beirut, during which Senegalese sentries took pot-shots in all directions while the rifle brigade patrolled the town. The negroes posted on our garden wall promised never to fire towards the house; but they were frightening, for so few of them understood French, and if stopped by a bayonet against the stomach it was impossible to explain' one's rank and business by gestures alone. The rifle brigade drove me daily to the *Eastern Times* in a command car bristling with guns. The office had been taken over by our military and the paper continued to appear under a new name, *Ninth Army News*. Fourteen soldiers of the rifle brigade were on guard in the offices; that is, they slept on the floor at night and chattered to the editors all day, while the same old squad of ancient office boys brought them coffee.

I visited Mme Khoury and found her in bed. The big hall where she had got up her jolly teas for our soldiers was packed with weeping relations. The method of the arrest had been unbelievable; Senegalese soldiers had broken open the door in the middle of the night and gone around stealing every trinket; they had even taken the old servant's savings. It was all stupid, and no one ever explained why that unfortunate order had been given nor who was responsible for the deplorable methods used in the actual arrest.

The tense atmosphere continued until one evening when explosions, crackers, and fireworks started to go off all over Beirut. As the result of British and American pressure President Khoury was to be freed . . . but without explanation. For the next few days Beirut was full of crowds marching in tribal costumes, sword-dancing, singing, and waving green branches. The Lebanon-Druze leader, Emir Majid Arslan, who had embarrassed Ninth Army HQ by camping nearby with five hundred men 'awaiting operational orders', rode into town on his horse amidst cheers, while French officers embarrassed and humiliated by the whole episode refused to appear in public. General Catroux – that wise and understanding character who had unfortunately left Syria – flew up from North Africa and General Sir Edward Spears gave a dinner for him to which I was invited. It was a strained and miserable function; although General Catroux had straightened out the mess, he looked so weary and we all felt a thunder cloud of depression because Anglo-French relations had received a real blow.

Escaping from Beirut was like disentangling the clutch of an octopus. When I finally abandoned the *Eastern Times* and asked Lady Spears to attach me to her hospital in Tunis she pinned me down instead in her Syrian branch of the Red Cross. Lady Spears had the maddening capacity of making you like her so much that you found yourself doing the things you hated most to please her.

She said that General Wavell's daughter, Pamela, who had been sent to organize the distribution of medical comforts in military hospitals throughout Syria needed someone strong and not particularly intelligent to help her drive and carry boxes – someone just like me in fact.

Pamela was lovely and frail and overwhelmed with work. Clad for some reason in a uniform consisting of a snowy starched dress and a large white picture hat, she had to motor hundreds of miles in a dilapidated staff car to the isolated field hospitals with loads of jug covers, pillowcases and anti-fly gadgets. When she travelled the three hundred miles of semi-desert to the north she had to change wheels and mend punctures alone in the wilderness, and because she had no helper she had to carry crates of stores that would have made a stevedore sulk. The vision of Pamela struggling alone with a breakdown on that eternal Aleppo road was more than anyone could endure so I sat down and sewed red crosses on to my uniform.

The new job entailed motoring the same old roads, but we got plenty of laughs. I remember one winter day when we drove three hundred miles north to Aleppo where a dismal CCS was in need of Red Cross equipment. There we had orders to pay special attention to the needs of two VADs in charge of the Greek refugee camp. These two Scotswomen were the only military VADs ever sent to the Middle East. Their virtue, efficiency, and strength became apparent at first sight. They were the type of woman who make the backbone of an Empire, red-haired and with shiny pink faces that had never known a powder puff. They worked alone, without encouragement or supervision, at a nightmare job in the vast, unheated Turkish barracks situated on a hilltop outside Aleppo.

They organized hundreds of starving, verminous, discipline-abhorring Greeks who arrived in unpredictable numbers every day. The idea of separating men and women in the icy stone-walled dormitories had to be abandoned, but in some unbelievable manner these valiant Scotswomen did manage to instil a certain amount of order into the most lawless of people. They supervised daily the de-lousing, and insisted on fresh air and a certain amount of washing, which was not easy with one tap of cold water per thousand bodies and no wish at all to be clean. At one time the Greeks sent a protest to military HQ against 'cruelty' in this camp, which was eventually traced to the VADs who briskly opened dormitory windows every day and made stringent rules about going out in the cold to the latrines.

12

Goodbye Middle East

The war had now completely left the Middle East. In the Spring, George Jellicoe, son of the famous admiral, came back from the unsuccessful Aegean campaign to take a hard-earned leave in Beirut. I remembered him as a small boy, the winner of races and source of rage to other children. Now at twenty-five he had won a DSO, MC, and *Croix de guerre* in three swift years of raiding by car in the desert, and by boat and parachute in the Greek islands. He said he did not know how to spend his leave, so Patsy O'Kane showed him. She took him to every crusader castle in the Lebanon mountains, to Palmyra, Byblos and Baalbek. Then she lamented that she had never seen Cyprus, where Richard *Coeur de Lion* spent his honeymoon. George, his pockets stuffed with guide books and his head whirling with the histories of Phoenician, Assyrian, Roman, Greek, Nabatean, and Saracen ruins said: 'All right, Cyprus; only couldn't we find time to get married too.'

So Patsy had ten hectic days in which to prepare her marriage festivities. The Russian villa, in which we three girls had spent a happy year together, became a scene of turmoil. Carpets, flowers, and champagne arrived in hand-barrows. Olga, Michel, and the dear old gardener worked like slaves to provide a splendid setting. Orange blossom provided itself, for the trees were in heavy, scented bloom. When the day arrived we were all over-tired and over-excited. At eleven Patsy and I realized we were alone in the house because everyone else had gone to the church. We were, as usual, busy trying on each other's clothes, and I am ashamed to say that instead of dressing the bride I made her dress me in her best Molyneux frock.

We arrived at the chapel and a military policeman came forward. 'You can't park here. We are waiting for the bride.'

'I know,' cried Patsy, as she finished dressing and ran out.

There was a wonderful party afterwards and, like Richard and Berengaria, they honeymooned in Cyprus.

A week later I left the Lebanon to follow the war in new countries. Snow was fading from the mountain tops and blossom from the shore as I motored wistfully down that coast road for the last time. My friends were scattered. Patsy had married. Lilah returned to England, where she received a pompous epistle from the War Office stating she might call herself Subaltern for life. Captain Ruck-Keene had left to command the aircraft-carrier *Formidable*, later to make her name in hard combat with Jap suicide planes. Bill King, who had plodded the heights with us, was commanding the submarine *Telemachus* in the Pacific. Randolph Churchill, who had been the *Eastern Times*' most determined critic, was in Yugoslavia. The guards brigade, who had trained near Damascus, were mostly killed at Salerno and Anzio. The household cavalry, that had chased about the Middle East during four years without getting into action, were now being used as infantry in Italy; and Charlie Lansdowne, my cousin in the Wilts Yeomanry, which had camped in Lebanon all the winter, wrote that he enjoyed driving back thirty miles from the front line for red wine and opera in Naples. My three years of peregrinations in Egypt, Palestine, Syria and Transjordan were ended.

I flew from Jerusalem to Cairo in a Flying Fortress with Paulette Goddard who wore American colonel's badges of rank and three rows of medals! I applied at Red Cross HQ to be sent to Italy, and within a week General Sir T. Sergison-Brooke had packed me off to Alexandria where I boarded a hospital ship in charge of bales of medical supplies. My own luggage was not heavy. After three years in the Middle East I had only my uniforms, some Damascus sandals, Aleppo sheep-skins and a horde of memories. By night we sailed out into the Mediterranean with decks lit and Red Crosses gleaming on the ship's side. Egypt disappeared in the dusk.

PART II

ITALY

13

Spring in Italy

In May, 1944, as our ship arrived at Taranto, the news of General Alexander's offensive broke. As I stepped ashore, streams of wounded were being carried up the gangways. The embarkation officer sent me to the 'transit camp', a large, stone palace where I slept alone on a straw palliasse in a suite of spooky, deserted rooms. Southern Italy looked green and cool to my eyes. There was no taste of sand in the air and the blue sky hummed with bombers.

The next night I was ordered to an ambulance train and we rolled northward. Before dawn the train stopped and an officer woke me, saying, 'You must be out within ten minutes. This train has new orders.' I slipped my great-coat over my old orange pyjamas and made a spectacular descent into a siding. It was not yet light, and there seemed nothing for it but to dress and sit – dumped on the railway lines – until I could get some message to the Red Cross in Naples; but there was no station in sight. A soldier came up and said we were at Caserta, and that a battle was raging at Cassino twenty-five miles further north. One could hear distant artillery but all seemed peaceful here.

With a medical officer who had also been flung off the train I went in search of breakfast. We walked up a wide avenue to a vast palace, and tentatively asked a sentry if there was any transit mess. We had had no supper, and were so hungry that we spent nearly an hour wandering through empty courtyards and up and down-stairs, for since this palace was army HQ I was sure there must be something to eat. At last we did reach a dining-room where a soldier gave us cups of tea. Then we hurried back to the railway and the medical officer found transport. I resumed my vigil on the Red Cross stores and wondered what king of Naples had built the huge palace and why. I had not heard it was considered the most magnificent of all baroque buildings, nor had I read the English traveller of 1818 who wrote angrily, after seeing the great stone façade, 'I hate kings more than ever.' And then 'the staircase is fine . . . the gardens and waterfall, of both of which they so much brag, are quite horrible.' Nor had I yet waded through Ruskin's tangle of words on the subject nor Sacheverell Sitwell's essay 'The Serenade at Caserta'. To me, the new sort of traveller in a khaki greatcoat, this vast building of fairy-tale magnificence that was revealing itself in the morning mists was just another lousy dump that hadn't got a transit mess.

Now, as the world began to wake a soldier strolled from the RTO's shack to chat. There was a caravan rail-coach just down the line which he informed me was General Alexander's sleeping-quarters. 'The general used to have a villa but too many people came to see him there, so he prefers the siding where they can't find him.' I watched with interest, for I had to sit beside those rails for nearly seven hours.

I nearly called on the general, but then it struck me it was just 'not done' to roll in for breakfast with the commander-in-chief in the middle of a battle. Suddenly he came out looking spruce in a grey shirt and corduroy trousers, climbed into an open command car and drove jauntily off to the front. I almost waved as he passed a few yards from me, but there was a bevy of ADC's and military police who would have thought it unseemly, and he might not have recognized me in beret and great-coat. Another soldier drifted along towards mid-day and told me Cassino had fallen and I felt all Italy was being taken while I sat on the line.

At length transport did arrive and I reached Naples to find the Red Cross billeted in a villa overlooking the bay. The workers were busy dealing with wounded at ambulance check-posts, and in spite of the distant thunder of guns a curious unreality hung over the town.

I was immediately given a mobile canteen to meet the wounded from Anzio who arrived by hospital ship. The much bombed, sordid, ruined docks were brightened by American Red Cross glamour girls with pink ribbons in their hair and dulcet voices. They lavished slabs of chocolate and cookies on the British wounded. On several occasions English soldiers begged me to remove 'something horrid, like dead baby birds' from their chests, and I would pull out doughnuts and restore the patients' morale with strong black tea. I never could understand how anyone, even in the pink of health, could swallow that loathsome lump of flour called a doughnut, but to the Americans they seemed a basic necessity of life. At the Anzio beach head, war correspondents were proudly invited to see the 'Doughnut Operation'. Under shell-fire huge machines turned out fifty thousand an hour while guns roared around. In fact the story was that on the days these machines broke down a whoop would go up from the American troops, 'No doughnuts, no battle.'

Day and night the wounded poured down to Naples in two streams, by sea from Anzio and by land from the army surging past Cassino. To help me brew the tea and climb about the ambulances I had a party of stretcher-bearers detailed to this job because they were 'bomb-happy'. As the hundreds of pitifully wounded men passed by, I felt it was like trying to run a canteen in Dante's *Inferno* with the Marx Brothers as assistants.

The docks of Naples had been startlingly decorated by the New Zealanders with enormous hoardings such as 'Is VD your souvenir?' 'If she is willing – she's got it.' 'What has she got your girl back home hasn't got? VD,' and 'Lice breed typhus. Have you searched?'

Most of my friends in Italy were in the Inniskilling Fusiliers at Anzio. When they got a 'day off' they came to Naples and we would go out to dine at one of the only two places which served food – the British officers' club or the allied officers' club – where one could see a medley of nationalities, American, British, French, Pole, Brazilian, Greeks and Japanese. Incidentally the two US Japanese infantry divisions in Italy won a very fine record proving themselves soldiers of almost inhuman discipline. They were never late on parade or absent without leave. The only case of disobedience recorded was that of two sick soldiers who left hospital without permission in order not to miss a battle. Nevertheless it was surprising to hear Japanese talking with a broad American accent.

When I got a rest I went south to the Inniskillings regimental base, where the wounded officers recuperated in a macaroni factory painted with pink cherubs. The proprietor – who had eight pretty eligible daughters enamoured of the *Inglesi* – kept inviting us to feasts and reporting his enemies in the village as being Fascists, while the latter tiptoed in at the back door and reported the same of him. 'Lili Marlene', the melody that had been stolen from the Africa corps and sung all over the desert, was now bellowed at the end of every evening to the accompaniment of smashed glasses. One evening six Russian officers came to a British club and the Italian orchestra, eager to please, struck up the 'favourite tune', 'Lili Marlene.' The Russians got up and indignantly walked out. Only the British soldier could humorously steal the enemy's marching song . . . in fact, no matter how successful the Germans were our Tommies thought them rather a joke.

Near our Red Cross villa lay the beautiful old red stone palace where Lady Hamilton had lived waving to Nelson from its windows when his ship returned to harbour. Admiral Cunningham had taken it over as his residence, and the sentries on duty used to warn off Italian boats that approached the shore. One day a dinghy rowed by a small man in a straw hat with a tall lady fishing in the stern came too near and the sentry roared at them to explain their presence in these hallowed waters, and to give their names. In perfect English they answered:

'We apologize for the intrusion. We were just out for a little fishing. We are the King and Queen.'

And they were. They rowed away leaving the sentry polite but perplexed.

Four French divisions were now in Italy, three North African divisions, and General Brosset's division of Fighting French. They slogged with heavy casualties through the mountains west of Cassino and General Sergison-Brooke sent me to look at their overflowing hospitals along the coast. They were very rough. The CO of the biggest hospital showed me with enthusiasm into the operating theatre, where a woman surgeon held up her work while he explained that *la Croix Rouge Britannique* had sent *une gentille demoiselle* to make lists of pressing requirements.

Then I was taken round the wards of the seriously wounded, and to dinner in the mess, a meal of red wine and garlic, scented soups, and salads. The tables were filthy, the food superb, and the conversation witty; it was the opposite of a British medical mess. Nursing seemed non-existent. I left them some 'cradles' to keep the weight of bedclothes off amputated stumps, and enough bed-pans to make a crazy paving to Rome. The French officer who drove me home said his sister had been killed the week before while giving cigarettes to the wounded. I also learnt that the Moroccan divisions used women ambulance-drivers at the regimental dressing-stations, and I pitied my old MTC unit, which, since it had been incorporated in the ATS, had never left Alexandria.

The Poles – who had lost two hundred officers taking the Monastery at Cassino and were fighting like tigers up the East coast – also used their women in the front lines for driving supplies, dressing-stations and canteens. Knowing the keenness of my own ambulance unit, and the spirit of the women in ack-ack batteries in England, I thought it a shame that one never saw ATS near the front. 'Where are your two hundred thousand service women?' asked the French, and I tried to explain. Some of the young ATS officers, women of ability and spirit, were putting up a fight against the unbending views of the War Council, but they had to struggle to obtain consent to do jobs which foreign women had been handed automatically by their army commanders. British women are public-spirited and hardworking, but they are also meek and unquestioning.

Whatever the achievements of the ATS the tendency of male authorities was always to scoff, and keep first-rate women subordinate to second-rate men.

The wounded soldiers suffered from lack of women nurses at the advanced dressing post, and our medical administration for dealing with wounded in the desert was archaic. A slight improvement occurred after the Americans arrived in North Africa and it was seen how efficiently their nurses worked at the front. But in Italy there were many CCS's where wounded British soldiers lay for three days without even being washed, because there were only a few male orderlies about who did not even trouble to sponge their patients' faces. General Sergison-Brooke, who had commanded a guards' brigade and himself been wounded, made a great effort to get his Red Cross workers as far forward as possible, because he knew from personal experience how much women meant in the dressing-stations.

14

'Air Evac'

Soon after the fall of Cassino and the link up with Anzio wounded began to be evacuated by Dakotas from air-strips which followed the rapidly advancing front. I was posted to work with 'Air Evac' at Capodichino airport on a plateau above Naples. Hundreds of fighters squatted on one side of the field and big American planes swooped down in another corner. There was a constant roar of engines overhead and everything inside our big tent was covered with oily dust, churned up by planes as they took off. Three hundred wounded arrived each day. The planes dropped down with their loads, ambulances rolled out and brought the stretchers back. They were carried into the big tent, where they lay in the dust and the noise for a hectic half-hour, while two MOs sorted them and other ambulances took them off to the big overflowing hospitals in Naples area.

Most of these men were seriously wounded and the flight jolted and frightened them, but it was the quickest method of getting them to base hospitals. Twenty odd stretchers could be suspended in each plane and a US nurse in fresh blue linen and a male orderly looked after them during the trip. Doctors at the loading and unloading could give morphia. During the sorting of patients I raced around with drinks which often had to be given through rubber tubes, or laid gauze over burnt faces to keep the flies off, and fought the vain hopeless battle against clouds of oily dust.

One's body had to be abandoned to sweat and dirt; one's hair became a stiff grey mass one hardly dared brush in the evening for fear of suffocating oneself; one's face wore an unlovely earthy mask all day; eyes smarted, and the stretcher-bearers got skin disease from the oil in their pores. But this meant nothing in the wild rush to help the wounded in their least-drugged, most weary, seasick moment when they were carried from the plane. And every time a plane took off with its tail towards us the white trays of fresh tea and cold lemonade would receive a thick layer of dirt. Everything had to be thrown away, frantically we would wash the mugs and trays and prepare more drinks; then, as the stretchers were carried in, I and a couple of soldiers would hurry around till a gust blew the covers off everything and it all happened again.

It was worse for the MOs and medical orderlies, who had to try to keep their gauze and dressings clean, than it was for us who merely went demented over lemonade. We got a sort of insane irritation with that dust for when the tent was carpeted with wounded figures, it would fill the air so that the thirsty men choked and buried their heads under the blankets.

Occasionally I flew up to the front-line air-strips to see what they wanted in the way of Red Cross stores. Every few days as the front advanced, the field would change. At first it was Frosinone, where the wounded lay amidst poppies and golden-meadow-flowers, sheltered from the sun by the wings of planes. Then on towards Rome. The flight lengthened from ten minutes to an hour. In the end it took two hours from Siena back to Naples.

Overhead against the blue sky, out of the noise and squalor of the airport, huge purposeful formations of our bombers flew northwards to blast the villages of Italy while our guns smashed on.

The Italians did not seem to care about anything. They said, 'We are a destroyed nation. Why should we bother any more. You have licked us and now you must look after us.' AMGOT strove to cope although there was only just enough food. Meanwhile, Greece starved. The Italian nation is soft on top and hard underneath. Upper class Italians buttered up the allies just as they had the Germans, but the more we knew of the peasants the more we liked them. Occasionally I saw Italians being cruel to their horses and I usually stopped my car, seized their whip, and drove off with it without a word.

For three weeks General Alexander's offensive swept forward and Italy was the centre of world action. On 5 June Rome fell, and my friends of the Inniskilling Fusiliers were surging through the streets cheering the Pope (yes, even the Protestant boys laid by their orange drum and were shouting *'Viva Papa!')*. The girls of Rome were in the streets throwing flowers to the troops, and in the hotel which General Mark Clark selected as his HQ a well-known duchess could be seen listening agog to two privates who after a little *vino* were relating how they personally had led the advance. General Brosset (far now from the Euphrates) and his French were dining in the restaurants, while on the outskirts of the city sniping continued. The first capital in Europe had fallen to Alexander's Army!

On the morning of 6 June the wounded poured in, burnt and ghastly. I was kneeling down trying to get a tube into some man's mouth when an American Red Cross girl ran in and cried: 'It's begun. Eisenhower has just spoken on the radio.' That was D-Day. Fresh news leaked in as we worked. The men in the ambulances forgot to drink their tea and we handed them instead the special army papers with the biggest headlines we had ever known 'Invasion'. In a way they thought it a shame that their own advance was so swiftly overshadowed by the new landing, but we all felt the war might end in a month. That night I got back to the villa and there was a big moon silvering Naples bay. I thought of Normandy, and of the wounded I had talked to that day; an Indian lying quietly with both hands off, and a twenty-two-year-old lieutenant blinded forever by one rifle bullet behind his eyes.

The very beauty of Italy in its spring turned one's heart. The nightingales at Cassino had made a mockery of war, and the scent of wild roses were, a French soldier told me, blended forever in his memory of that great artillery roar which opened the battle.

I spent one night in Rome, seeing the sights from a jeep, and slept in a lorry by an ack-ack battery near the airfield. The luxuriously dressed Romans seemed to think the allies should be grateful to them, 'for giving in'. A duchess, who had been an old friend of my grandmother's gave unbelievable tea parties at which the minor inconveniences of civilian life such as commandeered telephones and lack of taxis were discussed as catastrophes of magnitude. The feats of that endless stream of smashed bodies carried back from allied lines meant nothing. Only the peasants showed themselves sturdy of heart and ran risk of death and torture to help our prisoners of war. When wounded Italian partisans came down with our men, the MO took care to send them to a British hospital and not to a filthy ill-run Italian one.

An uncle of mine, Lionel Leslie, was in charge of a camp that followed the advance to deal with our POW who escaped. He told some odd stories. The allied and German lines in this part consisted of scattered posts facing each other, with only a few hundred yards in between. Having been a week in one small village he noticed an electric plant pumping away, and asked,

'Who is that engine working for?'

'To provide Pennapiedimonte with electric light,' answered the Italians.

'But the Germans still hold that village.'

'Oh yes, it's full of Germans. But no *Inglesi* said they were not to have light.'

The Poles who deserted from the Germans wanted to take off their jack-boots, put on battle-dress and start fighting on our side right away. They were always admitted, but sometimes they could not obtain British uniforms immediately and one beheld the puzzling sight of stalwarts in German uniform lining up in an ENSA queue.

Indian POW arrived, after terrible months of hiding in the mountains, with extraordinary requests. One Gurkha reached the British post in a dishevelled, starving condition to ask for a rifle so that he could return and do in some Germans he had noticed on the way. His companions, after two years as prisoners, only wanted to know if there was any football match they could play in that afternoon.

As many of the British arrived in the last stages of hunger, exhaustion, and nerves, my uncle applied to welfare for comforts. They sent back some medicine balls! Oh England! my England! ...

Perhaps the oddest little incident occurred when a German officer, speaking fluent English, came to my uncle's cottage to desert. He walked in with his hands up, collapsed weeping on a chair, and addressing the senior British officer present as 'My dear' asked if he could have lunch.

Unlike General Montgomery, who insisted on having only the best British troops at his disposal, General Alexander had twelve nations fighting under his command in Italy and he welded them into an efficient, harmonious force. We saw little of the Yugoslavs except in the hospitals along the East Coast where they drove the

British matrons demented as men and women wanted to share the same wards, and no partisan could understand why he should not bring his wife and children to hospital with him.

Of the Russians we knew nothing. One morning in July, I was at Capodichino airfield waiting for the first load of wounded, when a large machine swooped down on the strip reserved for ambulance planes and out got a Russian general in scarlet and silver and some twenty officers in ill-cut green tunics, unpolished belts, and baggy trousers with long boots. They were followed by two very fat women in garden party attire of brilliant design, veiled hats, high-heeled, patent shoes, and wrinkled stockings, who turned out to be the wives of the general and his staff officer. A little girl of four, somewhat plane-sick, completed the party. They had flown from Moscow and expected to be met by American transport which never appeared.

They stood about while our soldiers gathered in a crowd, as if a circus show had dropped from the skies. Thinking this a poor reception I wandered up to the general and saluted just for fun. He spoke fluent English, so I led them to the tent and offered cups of lemonade while the stretcher-bearers nipped to attention. The general made very precise polite conversation. He introduced his little daughter and said seriously she was going to be a fighter pilot in the next war. I made a slight joke which he did not understand so I tried to explain. He grew distressed and suspicious that I was laughing at him. 'Just a joke,' I tried to explain, 'a joke – a pun – you know.' But the word was not in his well-studied and extensive vocabulary so I turned the conversation to our organization for the wounded. This was a tactful subject. His face lit up. 'I myself have been wounded three times,' 'Oh where?' I asked meaning what battles. 'I'll show you.' And he proceeded to, stopping in the middle of the airfield, 'Here, and here and you see again here.'

Meanwhile, the wives in harlequin crêpe-de-chine waddled behind and the other officers strode off across the dusty airfield. Afterwards I reflected on the manner in which these young men had accepted drinks from me without a smile or a thank-you. I think they were embarrassed. They were unsure of my status and did not wish to damage their dignity by a polite word to what might be a mere servant.

Every week the Red Cross got up an afternoon boating trip for fifty convalescent soldiers, and once I went with them. We chugged around Capri and served tea and cakes to the patients who loved it, save three little wounded Gurkhas, who looked dumbly around as if wondering if there was no end to the horrible things war might do to a man. During the entire trip they lay face down-wards on benches, refusing offers of food. We could not understand if this was due to sea-sickness or because female shadows had contaminated the sugar buns. Brave as the Indians were in combat, they turned into weeping, moaning, incomprehensible idiots as patients. If one offered them a plate of biscuits or sweets they would empty it into their blankets and pillows, and lemonade they would rinse their mouth with, spitting it out in sprays.

In July I flew up to work at the air-strip where the planes loaded with wounded. From the Dakota one got a perfect view of Cassino, and the hill range we had smashed through, and of the flooded Pontine Marshes and Anzio. How strange it was to see that little bare piece of coast which the troops called 'hell in a hat-box', over which a veil of grass had already grown. The German lines of retreat were marked by water-filled bomb craters which from the air looked like trails of silver pennies.

Our advanced air-strip had moved to Lake Trasimeno. A South African fighter squadron shared the field and invited us to dine. As they drove us home along the dark road we ran into a row of soldiers standing with hands raised. Our escorts leapt out of the car with revolvers drawn, thinking they were about to take a bunch of prisoners but they proved to be a work party of unamused English soldiers holding up a broken telegraph wire.

General Alexander's camp was now at Lake Bolsena, some fifty miles to the west. He wrote me a charming invitation to dine, which he probably never thought it would be possible to accept. But within a week I appeared at his advanced headquarters having been dropped by an observer plane on to his private air-strip. The faces of the ADCs when I walked up to their tent and said I was delighted to accept the commander-in-chief's invitation were very funny. They just could not think where I had come from. They sent me swimming in the lake while the general had a conference with General Juin who commanded the French corps which was reaching its halt . . . Siena.

We had a magnificent dinner of beautifully cooked rations in a tent overlooking the moonlit lake. General Harding, the chief of staff, was there and the American General Lemnitzer who had landed in the submarine with General Mark Clark in North Africa prior to the North African invasion, and Brigadier Sandy Galloway who said 'that officers before going into battle should read *No Orchids for Miss Blandish* to make them callous.' The general himself was in grand form, and thought I was rather clever to reach this little group of tents well hidden by trees which was his secret head-quarters. Air Marshal d'Albiac promised to fly me back to work in the morning in his own plane, so I spent a comfortable night in the 'guest tent' which was furnished with fancy Italian tables and a real bed. Next morning at dawn I left in the Marshal's plane for Trasimeno. It was the best 'day off' I had in the whole war.

Back in Naples, George Jellicoe rang up the airfield and asked if when work finished I would drive to Rome for dinner. We got as far as Cassino and gave up. Only white ghostly walls were standing above the rubble, surrounded by barbed wire with notices 'Beware Boobies'. Nevertheless two small boys were searching in the ruins. It did not look like a bombed town, but some unhuman, weird city of the dead. George and I were so moved we ate ten peaches each in complete silence. An occasional exploding mine still rent the air, so we proceeded carefully. We stared at the little cemeteries where German and New Zealand and Polish dead lay side by side, and at the graves of some war correspondents killed on the road. In the British cemetery was the grave of Lieutenant-Colonel Goff, whom we had all known in Beirut, where his wife June, worked in Spears Mission. On the wooden cross his battalion of London Irish had written in pencil 'a hundred per cent'.

General Maitland Wilson's secretary, Hermione Ranfurly (whose husband, Lord Ranfurly, having been captured with General O'Connor in the desert, had just escaped through the Italian lines) now worked at Caserta Palace. I first met Hermione in Jerusalem when she was secretary to the High Commissioner. She had gone to General Wilson when he was in Baghdad, then to Cairo and Algiers.

Whenever I could get away from the airfield, where there was usually a long midday pause while the Dakotas flew back 400 miles to pick up a second load, I would hitch-hike on some ambulance in the direction of Caserta Palace and arrive white with dust in the supreme commander's office to lunch with Hermione. After she had tidied her files we would drive off in a jeep along the stately two-mile-wide avenue which ran straight up behind the palace beside enormous basins of water, fountains, and formal statuary to the Kennels, a building in the woods which she had arranged attractively to lodge Marshal Tito and other VIP's when they visited General Wilson.

Here, where the hunting dogs had once been kept, we lunched with the ADCs and then walked for an hour over the stony hills, panting in the shadeless heat; Hermione's quick wit turned the most scorching exercise into an excursion of amusement. Foreigners thought that the 'beautiful English countess' must be a modern version of Princess Lieven, and tried to win her confidence in seventeenth century style, hoping for a favour here, a quiet hint there – but, as Hermione remarked with annoyance, the Congress of Vienna is long past, the modern 'woman behind the scenes' just pounds a typewriter or is an army cook.

Apart from her ability as a shorthand typist Hermione possessed tact unusual in a person of such vitality. When a forty-page confidential report had to be typed overnight, when two fiery Greeks came to reveal each other's subversive activities to the supreme commander, when a Tito Yugoslav and a bitter, fuming, anti-Tito Yugoslav sought audience on the same day, when the ADCs felt the situation just too tricky to be fun, then the job was Hermione's.

Through faultless efficiency she managed to keep a job which administrative circles openly spoke of as 'too good for a woman'. We were both of us sore on that point, and as we panted back to that colossal slave-built palace, which had become a nightmare maze of Anglo-Saxon offices, the summer woods, where the kings of Naples used to hunt, rang with our indignation. Eve Curie had been given officer's rank in the French Army and afforded every facility to swoop around the front with a notebook. They were proud of her because she did well. The English would never have allowed any woman to travel as an ordinary intelligent war correspondent.

15

'Simple Soldat'

In August, after the French landings around Marseilles, I realized the air evacuation from the northern front could not continue much longer. There were no driving or press jobs with the British so I went to Lieutenant-General Sir F. McLeod, who now commanded the Red Cross, and asked if he would allow me to join the French Army as an ambulance-driver. I was frightened of the general and thought my request would annoy him, but he knew the French divisions had fought well in Italy and were in need of drivers. My heart leapt when he said, 'You might do that job well. Go to the French.'

Our forward air evacuation post was now outside Siena and General Alexander had his HQ camp in a wood nearby. He approved my new job, and I paid a farewell visit. Winston Churchill and Sir Alan Brooke were there at the time, so I was given an open touring-car to whirl about mediaeval Siena and see what I could of that beautiful town. Florence, that I had known and loved well, was still under bombardment. When I dined in the camp with the chiefs of staff we discussed, oddly enough, the unforgettable Emira of the Druzes who had aroused the curiosity of every man she met. General Alexander dined with the prime minister in the villa commandeered for his benefit, and late in the evening the ADCs returned with much of the talk from the great table.

In the morning I breakfasted alone in the mess with General Alexander before he set off with Winston to tour the front. All along the sunlit roads of seeming victory they were cheered by troops and enthusiastic Italians. The end seemed so near. Returning to Naples, I heard that all French units were embarking and I must immediately leave the Red Cross, so, at the airport, I said goodbye with affection to the soldiers who had worked with me in the dust during four hot months, and went off to sign on as an ordinary soldier in the French Army. Happily, I found an old friend, *Comtesse* Elizabeth de Breteuil in charge of all feminine personnel in Italy. The French demanded a huge dossier; as well as the letters I carried from General Alexander and General McLeod they wanted X-rays of my lungs, a certificate of good morals (given by my dazed uncle in the Cameron Highlanders), a certificate that I had not just left prison (given by Rear Admiral Morse, who commanded the Naval Base), a certificate to say I could clean a carburretor (which I wrote myself) and a certificate stating the British Government did not mind what was done to me! This was difficult to get until Elizabeth de Breteuil and Hermione Ranfurly together approached officialdom and obtained a grand document hung with his Britannic Majesty's seals which handed me over to the discipline of the French Army. There were unpleasant clauses about deserters getting shot; but Elizabeth laughed. 'Don't worry. You would always manage to *te débrouiller*' (untranslatable verb meaning to disentangle yourself successfully when in the soup). Then she took me to sign on at the French HQ. It was very simple. We found a colonel, packed to sail for France the following day. He grumbled, unpacked a form, said I was a funny sort of recruit and, 'Here is your first ration of French cigarettes. You will no longer receive them from the British.'

And so I found myself *un simple soldat de 2ème classe* and we walked out into the hot, bustling streets. I was attached to an ambulance company due to sail shortly from Naples. Until then I could live with the Lieutenant de Breteuil. We went out to celebrate at the allied officers' club, driving our own five-ton lorry, which was all the transport we could raise. As military vehicles were constantly stolen we had to remove the rota-arm. After dinner we could not reinsert it without a torch. Two drunken Tommies helped us with matches, then clambered aboard for lifts. We tried in vain to drop them in town, as Elizabeth wished to introduce me to the British commissioner to Italy who lived in a villa overlooking the sea. With some difficulty we swung the lorry in past a sentry at the sharp gate turn, dropped our load, who were profuse with drunken instructions, and continued down hairpin bends to the sea. We had to reverse at each bend and arrived at the villa door with a crash. After wiping the engine oil from our faces, we went in to a civilized drawing-room where Lady Dorothy Macmillan and Lady Diana Cooper, in satin evening gowns received us gracefully.

'But why don't the English use their ATS anywhere near the front?' asked a French officer who was there. I didn't know, so I answered, 'It's all a question of male jealousy.'

The Frenchman laughed: 'So you have come to us body and soul?'

I replied, 'The soul like my British passport remains my own.'

When we left, I, who had been introduced as the ace of ambulance-drivers, was mortified at the explosive sounds that issued from the engine. We readied the gate with horrible gear grindings to find our soldier cavaliers still waiting. Scraping the post away but missing the sentry, we swerved out, and as the old lorry bucked and hopped down the road we heard shouts from our drunks, and then a disappointed Cockney voice:

'Give it up, Bert. They're too – proud.' So ended my first day in the French Army.

Apartments were difficult to find in Naples so Elizabeth had installed her office in a flat in one of those numerous little streets labelled 'out of bounds' and allowed me to stay there with her for three days. I cut the Red Cross badges off my uniform, sewed French ones on and sat on the sunny balcony from which I could watch the admirals and generals, whom Elizabeth had invited to lunch, nipping up the alley sheepishly, hoping no military police saw them sprint the twenty yards of forbidden zone. Underneath the balcony in the odoriferous, shady street bloomed a gay little black market restaurant which delighted us with wine and music and deliciously cooked fish straight from the beautiful, sewer-laden harbour of Naples. This restaurant, from which sounds of concertina and angry cooks issued day and night, was even more 'out of bounds' than the alley for being 'feelthy'; but a back stairway linked it to Elizabeth's apartment so we could shout down and order meals to be carried up.

After two days of Elizabeth's glamorous social activities, I was ordered to a great barracks at Pozzuoli, outside Naples, which I found packed with hideous Senegalese soldiers and devoid of running water or any sanitary arrangements. I was about to post myself back to Elizabeth with a wail, when the other girls put their arms around me: '*Allons,*' they said, '*C'est infecté.* Come out for a walk by the sea.' So we strolled down to the small romantic harbour of Pozzuoli where a regiment of goums and their ladies were embarking on a spruce American ship. The goums were a wild mountain tribe who had fought long years against the French in Morocco. Their first excursion out of Africa took place when they were formed into brigades to accompany the French infantry divisions in Italy. Warriors by tradition and inclination they found European warfare full of fun.

It was they who first broke through in the harrowing mountain country that lay alongside Cassino – no other infantry could have made it said a British officer who watched them crawl off across the crags and heights, each with a knife in his teeth and joy in his heart as if on some splendid *chamoix* hunt. Enfolded in their blanket robes with only the steel helmets giving a modern Yankee touch to their traditional dress they moved into the night, fierce and happy. No one who fought near the goums will query their achievements. They were without fear. They liked killing. Unfortunately there were other things they liked as well and when they broke forward they never stopped. Some who had vanished in the Cassino break-through travelled on ahead of the allied armies all the way to Siena. And they claimed the privileges of warriors according to their own lights all the way . . . they had killed plenty of Germans, necklaces of human ears attested to that fact; but their French officers found it difficult to explain away the complaints that rolled in from the Italian villages which had lain in the path of their advance. Courts-martial took place, and at one of these a young French lieutenant translated for, and staunchly defended, his soldiers who were accused of raping two Italian women of eighty. 'They were tantalized,' he protested. 'What form did this encouragement take?' The lieutenant answered stoutly, 'The old women peeped through the shutters as my goums went by.'

Another officer told of the only time he heard of goums running away. This occurred when an ancient farmer came in recounting a tale about his wife's false teeth. The crone had been working in a field when two, swarthy, black-moustached, blanketed goums came up to her. Their intentions were obvious, even to an octogenarian, so she bit one fellow in the arm, until her false teeth came out and fell to the ground. Whereupon the amazed warriors fled across the hayfield shrieking '*Djin! Djin!*' and never reappeared.

The French being logical in these matters attached a unit of tribal women to each goum regiment, and as long as their lorries managed to keep up with the advancing troops trouble in the countryside was averted. Now, as we strolled by Pozzuoli harbour, we saw an American ship on which a party of these goumesses were merrily embarking. Classed as army personnel, they were attired in American soldier's trousers, which gave a very remarkable effect to the wide haunches which were evidently a tribal characteristic. Of self-consciousness they had none. Their faces blue with tattoo marks were wreathed in smiles and their black eyes sparkled. Above the khaki shirts veils and spangled scarfs, which their boyfriends had managed to loot in Italy, were twisted tantalizingly around their heads. Instead of kit-bags they carried kittens, doves, rabbits and bunches of roses. The American captain of the vessel stood incredulous as this horde filed aboard his naval craft.

Each night at Pozzuoli I arranged my own blue blankets and my own small satin pillow and slept happily enough on a carpet of insect powder on the barrack floor. In the morning a Senegalese burst in with a bucket of blue-black ink, which proved to be coffee and chocolate mixed, shouted '*La Soupe*' and thirty odd girls scrambled up. Those who had mugs dipped them in, swallowed the vile mess, and lent them to those who had none. That was breakfast.

Everyone was kind, and good-natured. Only *I* seemed to think it Hell. Then one morning a sergeant shouted in at the door that the company was to embark that day, and we carried our kit down into lorries and drove off to the docks, where after K rations had been distributed, we sat for hours in a grey drizzle. I nibbled vitamin sweets and tried to keep my spirits up by remembering I had moved heaven and earth to get into the French Army and now I had just got to take it. I'll like it, no matter what happens, I swore to myself. I'll like it if it kills me.

PART III

France and Germany

16

My Kingdom for an Ambulance!

The sea was calm and blue for our three-day voyage. As we passed the island of Corsica the spirits of my French companions rose. There was dancing and singing on deck all day and all night. I thought of that other voyage from Britain four years before with the wistful Free French Air Force and wished the few of them who were left could be sailing high-hearted with me now.

When at last we saw the coast of France shining in the light of a cloudless dawn the French grew quiet. They were wondering what they would find in their land and many had homes in territory which the Germans still held. There was a touch of fear in their happiness; but I, as a foreigner, found it very moving to return to France with her own exiles, sharing their excitement and hearing their hunger for French soil echoed in the voices that were singing the Marseillaise.

Owing to the destruction at Marseilles we had to climb into small craft and scramble ashore in the tiny old harbour. Then we were solemnly marched through the streets while the inhabitants cheered and clapped. Women put down their baskets in the roadway to blow kisses, *'Ah les braves coeurs . . . Elles ont du courage celles-là!'*

Soon we began to smile and wave back. The girl in front of me carried a satchel from which the indignant face of a kitten protruded. Inwardly I began to laugh and wish friends left in Italy could see me. I had only been in this army for a week and already we were having a triumphal march.

Our company reached a large white chateau on the Toulon road in which we were to be billeted in large rooms devoid of furniture, but already occupied by black Senegalese soldiers who insisted the chateau was a reserve hospital and they were the medical staff. I made Anglo-Saxon remarks about sharing the bathroom with Senegalese. And by *share* I mean they came to shave and wash in the same basin in which one was brushing one's teeth. I was horrified, but the other girls lay down in their blankets and went to sleep on the floor happily enough. Next morning several of us went for a walk through the rocky, shadeless countryside. The sight of girls in French uniform aroused a pathetic welcome everywhere. Old women ran out to seize us by the hand and gaze into our faces while tears filled their eyes.

It was the real *Midi de la France*. Passing a garden with vast grapevines overhanging the gate we stopped to ask a timid little man if he could sell us grapes. He signalled us inside the garden and there we met an oldish man in a beret who spoke perfect English. He questioned me about my war career and then, as the others could not understand a word, he looked at me wearily and said:

'I will tell you my story, and perhaps some day in London you will ask a question for me because I shall never go back there.' He paused, and then went on: 'It is curious that what has been so secret all these years I can now talk about openly for it is over, over and forgotten, and only a few of us with the bitter knowledge remain.'

He told me about the Resistance Movement of the Marseilles area in which he had been a leader for two years, since the night he had been dropped by an RAF plane on a secret airfield near his own village in southern France. There were thousands of young men in this district who were trained, armed, and ready for a signal from London which was to be given by a certain word in a BBC broadcast. Their attacks on munition dumps and sabotage of military transport and communications were to synchronize with allied landings along the coast.

On D-Day, as the invasion of Normandy started, the BBC gave the *phrase d'alerte* meaning landings could be expected in the south of France. Next day the alert was cancelled and then, a few hours later was given again with the sentences which meant all sections of the Plan must start. On 6 June fighting began, and for five days the whole Marseilles region was held; then ammunition ran out and no communication came from London. The Maquis had launched their carefully prepared plans to aid an army which never arrived. When the BBC spoke again it was to give orders to disperse without any reason. Astounded and heartbroken, the Maquis withdrew into the hills. The whole scheme had been revealed to the Germans, which meant that it could not be repeated at the proper time in August, and the Gestapo sent out a drag-net which resulted in hundreds of the bravest and best trained men being arrested, killed and tortured.

'And under torture, *Mademoiselle* – wholesale torture applied to dozens of people – secrets leak out. My own men who had for two years risked their lives to train for this moment came to me in anger, crying, "We have done our part. Why is there no invasion from the sea? There is treachery.""No, you have not been betrayed – someone in London has made a mistake – they sent the wrong signal. You must hide your arms and disperse." So that was that. Our effort was for nothing. When the French Army landed two months later hardly any of our trained men were left. When I identified the mutilated bodies of my friends who had borne their pain without revealing our secrets – men who had died under torture for nothing – I did not feel like telling them "it was only a mistake"...'

All this time the man was staring at the unlit kitchen fire and now he looked me straight in the face.

'I got away because it was easier for old men to allay suspicion, but the young ones were nearly all arrested. You cannot imagine the moral courage it takes to fight when you are not in soldier's uniform; the haunting endless fear; the loneliness of dying alone without all that talk of an army's glory to keep you going. Because of that mistake I saw the finest young men of my region go to the carnage pits. My work is over now, but they will be missed in the France of the future. You'll see...'

Before I had been in France a week a chill descended on my spirit. The boisterous gaiety of military life in the Middle East and Italy seemed to belong to another life.

My companions were also getting depressed, for they wanted to visit families they had not seen for years and the authorities refused all leave. 'If we granted compassionate leave the entire army would be travelling over France in search of lost relatives,' said the angry colonel, who had been badgered for a week by tearful women. Two or three girls whose homes were within fifty miles of Marseilles were allowed to hitch-hike off for the day, and they returned with long faces having found their families in a state of starvation.

I decided to take my rations each morning and see what I could of the surrounding countryside. Friendly American jeeps stopped to my signal and ran me to the region of Barcelonnette, where the Maquis, under a Captain Lecuyer, had held out from 10 June to 15 August while the RAF dropped supplies. The people told me that a Scotsman, Captain Haye, had been dropped by parachute to instruct the Maquis in the loading of PIAT guns and he had been killed here – *'Un brave écossais'* they called him. When he was hit, Mme Charon, a Maquis worker, had carried him to her house and tried to staunch his wound; but clothes pegs will not clip an artery.

At another village called Signes I sat about nibbling grapes and wondering at the apathy of the south until I learnt that on 19 July, just two months before, the Germans had lined up and shot thirty-eight of the leading civilians. 'Why? Oh, they were annoyed at the Maquis rising; they threw the bodies into a pit over there—'

The words of the old man came back to me 'the flower of France has gone to the carnage pits – they will be missed in the future.'

Everywhere the same tales damped one's spirit. In the dreamy old town of Aix-en-Provence I tried to appreciate the seventeenth-century houses, the cobbled streets, the silent *Musée*, but here the half-starved caretaker told me less about the tapestries than the street fight on 17 July when the Maquis killed Totora, a professional boxer of Italian origin who worked for the Gestapo and was responsible for its efficiency because he personally devised the tortures which got at the truth.

How sick I grew of these tales – how could one want to live in such a world? It was a great relief when American officers invited me into Marseilles to 'have a bath' and tour the crowded night clubs – where there was no food and no drink but an astonishing assortment of peroxided blondes.

When the company's ambulances arrived by sea we moved northwards, hoping to catch up with the French Army which was chasing the Germans up the Rhône, but to our disappointment the convoy turned down a country road and drove into a small deserted race-course beside Aix-en-Provence. Here the men of the company had set up a field-kitchen. The girls parked their ambulances in a row in the open stalls and when evening came went to sleep in them. It was icy at night and we had no candles, so as soon as the sun set we went to bed. The first morning I opened my eyes and stared straight up at a blackboard with the names of horses and their weights still chalked up – and the date of that last race was 1940!

After a few days in that cold south wind – the *mistral* – which penetrated body and soul I decided that I had not joined the French Army to shiver in a field and peer down carnage pits. It was time to *me débrouiller,* so I applied to be posted on as promised.

The harassed colonel in Marseilles told me to report at seven next morning and find what transport I could going north; I was delighted for French camp life had palled. I longed for bully beef and good black tea instead of the bucket of sickly, artificial coffee we had for breakfast and the cauldron of sweet-flavoured 'meat and beans' served twice a day on tin plates which we then washed in a dirty stream.

The French transport office sent me to the Americans and I was squeezed into a charabanc of US officers going to Lyon. After a ten-hour journey up the Rhône through the debris of abandoned German equipment we reached the transit hotel in Lyon and I learnt the French HQ had moved on north to Besançon.

Bitter weather had suddenly come and my bare legs were so cold that I tried to buy a pair of angora woollen stockings from a rabbit shop. I had no coupons but the woman behind the counter said she could not refuse *une brave fille* in French uniform and I could have them without. The price was £3 a pair, and I had only a few francs so I went back to the transit hotel to borrow. The French manager took me into his office and said he was proud and glad to lend whatever money I wanted and *Madame la directrice* shook both my hands and stuffed my pockets with notes. This sort of treatment heartened one.

In pouring rain I drove on to Besançon, where the 1st French Army had installed its HQ. I reported to the Major in charge of Ambulance units and he said:

'Why were you so long getting here? I have just the job. You are to be posted as an *ambulancière* to the 1st Armoured Division which is now fighting in the Vosges ... It is very chic. You must be pleased.'

For two days I had to stay in a large mixed mess with Totote de Chambrey, a charming woman I had met in Italy where she commanded an ambulance company of two hundred girls. I was issued with a complete American soldier's outfit including gaiters and big boots and comic underwear. With feelings of respect and despair I realized how casual French women are about comfort. We slept on sacks of straw which was warm enough but, for a base unit, the arrangements seemed appallingly primitive. I had nothing to do but try to make a fire out of furniture that had been smashed in the fighting and block up the broken windows with sacks. Up to this point I had been very hazy about the military set-up in France. Now, as we huddled around the crackling flame, I learnt that for the first time since 1940 a real French Army had been formed. Under the command of General de Lattre de Tassigny seven divisions had landed in the south of France and chased the Germans north as far as the Vosges mountains where a hard battle was now being fought.

The 1st French Army which landed in the south of France consisted of:

1st Armoured Division,
5th Armoured Division,
9th Colonial Infantry Division,
4th Moroccan Mountain Division,
3rd Algerian Division,
2nd Moroccan Infantry Division,

1st Free French Infantry Division (the original French division which had fought in Middle East under General Koenig and in Italy under General Brosset).

Another French Armoured division under General Leclerc had landed in Normandy under British command and was not yet incorporated in the French Army. All except the Free French division had been trained in North Africa.

De Lattre, who I had scarcely heard of to date, was the hero of the day. General de Gaulle, head of the government, was outside the orbit of military discussion. I never heard de Gaulle harshly criticized by Frenchmen (and they love to demolish their leaders with wicked wit) but they said he was 'not supple enough to be a statesman' and they called him 'as stupid as a saint' . . . *'que voulez-vous'* they said 'what can a saint do in politics?' . . . And then, talking about his past brilliance as a divisional commander and expert on armoured warfare, they would analyze him: 'What you love and understand you will in time resemble; de Gaulle's mind is steel-plated. His brain is as un-agile as a tank . . . but he is straight.'

How often I was to hear Frenchmen using that word 'straight' as if it were a virtue so rare among politicians that it made up for any other faults.

The 1st Armoured Division to which I had been posted was fighting in the mountains forty miles north of Besançon. All equipment was American and for simplification each armoured division was divided American fashion, into combat commands instead of brigades. Totote said that Combat Command 1 to which I was going consisted of a tank regiment the 2nd Cuirassiers, the 3rd Bn of Zouaves (infantry), one armoured car squadron of the 3rd Chasseurs, and a medical company which had twelve ambulances with women drivers. Everyone congratulated me on being *une ambulancière divisionnaire*. I had as yet no idea what these words signified nor could I imagine that from henceforth Combat Command 1 with its cuirassiers in their Sherman tanks and its zouaves in their muddy boots was to be my entire world . . . a small, intimate world of lovable human beings and good friends.

The twelve ambulances were supposed to have two drivers each; but they were short-handed and Jeanne de l'Espée, who commanded the unit, had applied for spares. My future commanding officer seemed to have made a great name for herself in the army. Everyone spoke of her with admiration. She was the daughter of the famous General de l'Espée. They said she was a real soldier's daughter who had been decorated in the last war when she was only sixteen for bravery while nursing in the front lines and who astounded the Americans in the brief fighting in North Africa by driving through the lines in the middle of a bombardment to look after and translate for the French wounded. 'She is an enchanting personality and very chic. She ran Patou before this war and speaks perfect English, and lots of Englishmen *très bien connus* have been in love with her.'

So, in spite of the wet autumn weather, I was purring with pleasure and pride when Totote de Chambrey set off with me in search of Combat Command 1. As we drove the mountains grew wilder, their steep slopes were covered with dense pine forests, while the valleys gleamed with the red and gold of wet leaves. There was a gloomy beauty in these heights. I had no idea the French were fighting one of the hardest battles in their history. I had no idea of anything except that I felt conceited at having been attached to Jeanne de l'Espée's unit and I had a faint selfish hope the war would not end before I had time for some startling achievement.

In the afternoon we heard artillery booming in the valleys. A sign read, 'Front line. Complete black-out'. Reaching a small village called Rupt, where two batteries were firing each side of the brigade casualty station, Totote de Chambrey stopped. Jeanne de l'Espée's ambulance relay had moved forward two kilometres that day. I was told to wait and get a lift on the next vehicle going forward. Totote turned her jeep and said goodbye.

'Well, *mon vieux*. You wanted to work in the front line, so here you are. Good luck . . .'

I wandered into the school-house, which had been transformed into the brigade operating theatre. The wounded lay on stretchers waiting for transport back to an evacuation hospital. There were no nurses, but hideous, native Algerian and Moroccan orderlies carried the stretchers. I stood in the road waiting, while our artillery began to roar up the valley shattering the damp evening air.

17

Debut in the Vosges

Dusk had fallen when a radio liaison truck came along and I was handed over to a young officer who introduced himself as Lieutenant Pêche. 'The advanced post is at Thiéfosse the next village along. When we go into action it works between the regimental posts and the brigade station,' he said, slapping on his ear phones. We drove up the mountain valley. I could see nothing from the back of the truck, but the crash of guns seemed to increase. After a time we stopped and I heard voices, *'Oui, mon général . . . Non, mon général.'* Pêche lifted up the canvas flap: 'Crawl forward. The general wishes you to be presented.' I leaned out and shook hands with General Soudre, who remarked:

'You have arrived at the right moment. We are in full attack and there's plenty of work for the ambulances . . . Nice to have *une irlandaise* in the division . . . how have you got here, anyway? Well – hurry off there's plenty for everyone to do . . .'

The sound of cannon roared in all directions and the flash of guns lit the forested slopes. Again the truck stopped and I tumbled out into the dark. I could see a few soldiers hurrying about and in a large barn, originally used for making tombstones for local villagers, I found two resuscitation trucks, where blood transfusions were being given to wounded, who were carried in from ambulances which had churned the mud outside into a quagmire.

The barn was lit by firelight and a party of Moroccans were heating their supper. There seemed to be feverish activity. A stout little woman called Mme Kleber and a doctor were working swiftly in their clean, white, electric-lit trucks pouring blood into the wounded and examining dressings. I learnt the ambulances called in here on their way from the regimental aid posts to see if patients were suffering from haemorrhage or shock, in which case they would be given treatment and several hours' rest before going another four miles to the mobile operating theatre at brigade HQ. It was a strange, crude scene with the firelight flickering over the wounded, who were carried in on stretchers to be laid on rough wooden trestles while the native orderlies cooked merrily away a few feet from the dying. The medical treatment looked modern and efficient, while the swarthy faces of the gabbling Arab stretcher-bearers might have been Neolithic. Then Jeanne de l'Espée came in; she had merry blue eyes and a quiet voice and looked very small in her lumber jacket and American helmet. Reading my papers she said, 'So you are the new driver. Good. I need spares badly.' She lent me a tin plate so that I could snatch some of the Moroccans' supper and a mug for the sour red wine that was issued to French troops in petrol cans.

Squeezed in between a heap of blood-sodden blankets and the sizzling pan of beans we stood and ate by firelight while she described the ambulance system. When the division went into action the girls were posted to the regimental doctors and worked under their direct command driving the wounded back from the regimental aid posts. 'Now we are in full attack, and the girls are driving day and night and getting short of sleep, so you must begin work tomorrow.'

Jeanne de l'Espée led me out into an orchard where there was a stationary ambulance, saying, 'Squeeze in here for tonight.' So squeeze in I did, trying not to disturb the two girls who were already asleep on the floor. 'Who on earth are you?' they asked, as I slung a stretcher above them. 'A new driver.' 'Thank God for that,' they said, and went back to sleep.

Jeanne went off to stand in a foot of mud all night waiting for her girls who were driving wounded back from the front, creeping along the dark roads with only the tiny blue headlights known as cats' eyes. I curled up and slept happily despite a big gun in the next field that went off at intervals all night making the ambulance quiver.

In the morning a flicker of early sunshine lit the orchard and gilded the mist-covered mountains. A party of Moroccans were digging deep trenches which I smugly thought were latrines, but I was disillusioned when two jeeps came down the road laden with dead bodies. I should have learnt by now that the French Army does not bother about latrines. These were graves. The padre of the 2nd Cuirassiers, our tank regiment came down in one of the jeeps and said the funeral service. So it was that I met Father Condeau for the first time and we became great friends. He was a twenty-nine-year-old priest possessing wit, charm and intelligence, who had escaped from occupied France through Spain to join the French Army. Someone asked him how he liked work in the thundering valley ahead where he was kept busy dressing wounds and giving morphia as well as administering the last sacraments. He laughed: 'It's not as bad as having to listen to old ladies' confessions.'

No one in the barn had slept that night. Stretcher after stretcher was carried in for blood transfusions, and the dead were laid in a row by the roadside. A general sigh of distress went up when the body of Commandant de la Forcade, second in command of our tank regiment came down. A mutual friend, Edmond de Pourtales, had given me an introduction to him. I pulled the letter out of my pocket and tore it up. It was the only outside contact I had with anyone in the division.

When more girls arrived to park their ambulances and snatch a few hours' sleep, Jeanne, looking fresh as a daisy after her night in the mud, joined us for a cup of coffee. 'You see the girls have been taught to spend every possible moment sleeping and you must learn to do the same. We eat well whenever we can and, whatever happens, remember to use lipstick because it cheers the wounded.' I soon learnt that behind Jeanne de l'Espée's whimsical humour lay a character of steel. The first soldiers I talked to told me that 'last Sunday' she had driven out at nightfall and managed to rescue wounded parachutists from a mountain top where they had lain for three days surrounded by Germans. They saw her driving up the rough track and opened heavy shell fire as she came down but no one was injured. '*Enfin elle a du style cette femme*,' said the soldiers.

The tiny village of Thiéfosse had been captured by us on Thursday. I went to Thanksgiving Mass in the little church on Sunday. The cottages were hung with tricolours and bells rang out although a battle was in progress only four miles further on. The small white-washed church with its smashed windows had been decorated with satin banners hung over the Altar and the plaster Saints had on their best dresses. All the children were dressed in oddments of red, white, and blue with ribbons in their hair, and the old women wore their best bonnets; *Monsieur le curé*, big-eyed with excitement, gave a slightly tremulous sermon amidst the crash of gunfire in the hills around. He was a frail old man and seemed to falter for words of thanks but when an enemy plane roared over and dropped a stick of bombs nearby, neither he nor the congregation flinched an eyelid. These were the first newly liberated French people I had seen. Their pathos and gratitude was very real, but they were terrified the advance was going badly and the Germans might return to wreak indiscriminate vengeance.

After Mass I went out with an ambulance to drive three wounded soldiers and a small boy back to the brigade station. Everything went wrong. A Bailey bridge had sunk below water and we had to do an eight-mile detour over appalling tracks. By the time we arrived the child was begging for air, which meant internal haemorrhage, and he died as we carried him into the operating room. The soldiers lying on their stretchers looked up disconsolate. 'They could not save *le petit*?'

It was the first time I had ever seen a child die. It was more poignant and terrible than the death of any grown-up; and, by curious coincidence, when we moved the advanced post forward to the next village called Saulxures a distracted woman named Mme Amet called at the cottage where I was trying to dry my clothes to ask if I knew anything about her little son who had been wounded in the thigh. I steeled myself and asked her into the kitchen. She came in out of the rain, a young peasant woman with a black shawl over her head and asked me quietly, 'Is Ramon dead?' Flinching I answered, 'Yes.' She had a very pink skin and very bright blue eyes that somehow did not fill with tears as she stood there listening while I assured her he had died without pain. The child had chattered bravely enough, and when I mentioned his twin sister a look of relief came to her face. She knew I was not inventing comfort.

The wet October days dragged on. Hundreds of grey-faced German prisoners began to slump back along the road from the narrow mountain passes ahead and the peasants looked at them with loathing. But every soldier who marched back past my waiting ambulance, whether German or French, was devoid of expression.

They had all been wet, cold, hungry, and without cover for a month. There were parties of drenched Germans, lost in the mountains for days, trying to surrender and too exhausted to move.

The weary French did not feel like carrying them or sharing rations so they would be disarmed and left in the rain, perhaps for several more days, until our front could move forward and organize a POW counting post. A zouave officer, with his hand off, looked at me stonily and said: 'It is the limit of what a human frame can endure out there. Is it true the American infantry have waterproof boots?' The Americans had every comfort gadget – anti-wet, anti-cold devices with zips that made our men writhe with envy, but the ordinary, rubber-soled American Army boot which had been supplied to the French was quick to leak. And what virtue can a pair of boots have except to keep out the wet?

The village of Saulxures had been bombarded for two weeks and shells still whistled overhead, but as our troops advanced through the narrow defiles beyond, the gaunt-faced inhabitants began to creep out of their cellars. A young woman who allowed me to heat coffee on her stove told me casually that her father had been shot four days previously by the Germans. Six French POW had escaped while passing through Saulxures; so the retreating *boches* seized six old men who were working in the fields and shot them in front of their houses. She said: '*Mademoiselle*, you will soon learn *la vraie haine du boche* that all we French people have.'

Trying to analyse reasonless German cruelty I remembered the philosophy of Keyserling, whose books had stood in autographed rows in my grandmother's library. Deliberate cruelty he said has its source in fear.

The peasants of the Vosges whose relations had been indiscriminately shot kept asking our soldiers to bring them back German prisoners. A soldier told me how he had marched a couple of

Germans to a frantic woman who had seen her sick boy dragged out to be shot a few days before. She asked for a revolver and he gave it to her. The Germans were too tired even to lift their hands. Whatever they saw in her face they were beyond caring and she also was expressionless as she shot them.

'The curious thing,' said this solemn little man, 'is the way women shoot. She looked away when she pulled the trigger. Then she gave me back the revolver and went back to her house without saying a word and closed the door.'

Thus it became a tooth for a tooth and a son for a son.

One morning the body of a woman in German uniform was brought down from the mountains. The parachute troops had found several women snipers tied in trees. Their bodies were bound so firmly they did not fall, even after they were dead, and the soldiers said they had cropped hair and were indistinguishable from men. *Blitz Mädchen*, they were called.

The pouring rain hindered the French attacks, yet there was drama in that setting of mist-swathed mountains, and sometimes the forests were lit to gold with a moment's brief sunshine. When not working we would sit for hours in the ambulances watching the road where all the traffic of war rushed to and fro, where files of fresh infantry trudged up to attack along the right-hand side while the wounded came down on the left. Many of the Moroccans marched down from the front lines with bare or bandaged frost-bitten feet, carrying their wet boots as if the pain were more endurable that way. Their faces were too stiff to smile; but when our armoured cars advanced into Cornimont they related its capture with typical French-soldier wit.

'*Mademoiselle, imaginez vous* . . . we drove in carefully at that end and as we looked, a shell fell plumb on a small house. We waited for the dust to subside and out of the debris ran a man shouting angrily, "Where the hell is that plumber?" So we advanced cautiously and asked what the plumber had to do with it. "Blast the fellow," cried the good man, "he has been working here for a week . . . I've paid him the Lord knows what to put my drains in order and this morning I go to the lavatory, pull the plug and the whole blooming house falls down . . .'"

I had reached the unit with the reputation of being *une anglaise formidable* panting for work in the front line, who could drive anything on wheels. I was, therefore, given a captured German ambulance to drive, whose worn-out battery and unpredictable petrol pump were far beyond my technical capacity. Jeanne de l'Espée had installed her office in it, so she could crouch out of the rain, and check the whereabouts of her twelve ambulances, and at night we shared it as sleeping quarters. We would lay out two stretchers in the tiny space and struggle out of muddy boots and wet clothes, pull off our fantastic men's underwear and wriggle into flea-bags.

'What on earth made us go in for this?' Jeanne would say. 'At least I have no one to blame for this discomfort but myself, and you, too, I suppose? But if we had not brought it on ourselves how indignant we should be.'

At nightfall those ambulances which were not out with the regiments crept into various backyards of Saulxures village, and six ambulances of the American Field Service joined us squeezing their vehicles between the houses as best they could.

For the first few days I was tone-deaf as regarded shells. In the perpetual noise I could not tell the difference between ours and the Germans, but the villagers were always jabbering about *les arrivés* and *les départs* and before we had been a week in Saulxures I learnt the lesson myself. One night at the end of October, when we were still stuck in this gloomy village, brigade HQ moved up to us and with it came the operating theatre which installed itself in the Schoolhouse.

Several girl drivers were back from the regiments and we had a noisy dinner by candle-light. The arguments grew deafening, for the subject was clothes, and French women discuss clothes with that fire which the Irish reserve for politics. The girls sat about on the floor, heatedly discussing the merits of a black tailored suit as the basis to any wardrobe. All through the meal (tinned beans on tin plates) they asserted their views and Jeanne (who ran Patou before the war) dominated the conversation. 'Only shoes, stockings and gloves really matter,' I learnt. 'For the rest, *mes petites*, you cannot dress too plainly, and black is better than navy blue – a well-cut black *tailleur* will take you from breakfast to midnight, and the hat is of great importance.'

Jeanne – who was the real Patou expert – continued the argument till we were snuggled into our blankets and dozing off to the patter of rain on the ambulance roof. We had just got warm when something like a railway train rushed by and exploded in our yard. Actually it was a large shell that landed plumb on the radiator of an American boy's ambulance a few feet away and it was the first of many. In a second I was out in the rain and ready to run – but where? The next shell hit the house beside us and its blast knocked me flat. Jeanne said: 'Make for the house of the baker. It has a real cellar, and put this on your head, it's better than nothing.' She gave me the outer steel casing of a helmet and wallowed off through the mud to round up the other four girls who were back for a 'rest'. Saulxures was a bottle-neck and crammed with military stuff but the few civilians left slept underground. As I struggled through the dark, trying to find the house Jeanne had told me to make for, shells kept crashing down covering me with plaster and bits of roof.

Soon I found my legs were running very fast although they felt as if made of cotton wool. Nothing interested me except getting out of this hideous noise, but I could not find the *belle cave* of *monsieur le boulanger*. Never had my addled brain worked quicker. Each time I heard a shell scream over my head I flung myself down behind a wall and in the split second between the whistle and the crash I found that somehow I was selecting quite sensible protection, and my timing got quite good. I was covering twenty feet between each shell. At last I stumbled into a backyard and found steps leading to a cellar. While I hesitated a shell landed on the house next door and with an incredible movement of self-preservation I held the helmet casing over my head like an umbrella to protect me from the tiles that rained down.

Then I realized that in flight I had snatched up Jeanne's tin washbasin by mistake. I leaned against the wall to giggle before diving for the cellar, where a flickering candle revealed some twenty terrified old men and women with a huddle of children who had not left this place for weeks. There were brass beds and feather eiderdowns with whole families peeping out. It was bitterly cold, so I perched on the corner of a coverlet and listened amused to a little girl who, woken by the repeated crashes, kept pounding her pillow and saying furiously, '*What* a night!'

Then the field service boys came tumbling in. One of them in a very American accent kept shouting *mong dough*. Suddenly we saw he was trying to call attention to his back, where a piece of shrapnel was embedded. Another American, called Dean Fuller, arrived wrapped Roman fashion in a khaki blanket with his helmet over one eye. He had been asleep when the first shell landed on his ambulance radiator, the engine was blown to pieces but although the blast hurled his stretcher out of the door he was unscathed.

'Anyway, I found myself stark naked crouching under the ambulance, but somehow I had my helmet on . . . you see I have only one pair of pyjamas and was getting them washed.'

The Americans had been with the New Zealanders through Africa and Italy and were full of complaints about the one thing that I missed in the French Army . . . the lack of cups of tea! They also said no medical staff could survive this sort of treatment long. My face must have fallen, for I was at that stage of bewilderment when one believes anything and they all laughed. Then one of our doctors arrived, running so fast that he fell headlong and took all the skin off his shins. He attended to the American, and we learnt with distress that shells were landing around the schoolhouse where the wounded we had brought in that day were lying on stretchers. Two of the company doctors had been hit already, and men whose limbs had just been amputated were suffering from shock. The brigade operating theatre was always supposed to be out of range.

Jeanne then arrived with the girls who were not frightened but angry. They blamed brigade HQ which had moved up during the afternoon. 'It's all the fault of that colonel . . . who is attracting all this with his radio,' they said. 'Evidently there is some battery up there that no one has found. They ought to send out some more goums . . .' I brightened a little at this. goums were the obvious answer.

As dawn came the village filled with troops rattling forward to attack. Jeanne doled out what rations she had for breakfast. I got a packet labelled Funny Folks Fudge, which made me feel a lot better. The brigade workshops had moved up, and scores of Arab mechanics were milling around, ducking and darting to cover each time a shell burst. I walked down the road carrying my half-helmet, to ask a question of the chief mechanic. If I put it on it covered my eyes, and if I walked bare-headed officers shouted, *'Votre casque Mademoiselle!'* The French have a curious courtesy, even when being cursed in the middle of an attack it was *Mademoiselle*.

Orders came for us to retreat. While the road was under fire vehicles set off separately at intervals of ten minutes. With six men pushing, my captured ambulance started and chugged slowly along, stalling in each boggy patch, at which I would lean out of the window and shout, *'Poussez, Poussez,'* and Moroccan infantry would crawl out of the ditch and heave while shells made mud fountains around them.

Soon after we had left the baker's cellar received a direct hit, and an exhausted medical officer who had come down from the mountains for a rest was killed, while the poor civilians in their brass bedsteads were blown sky high. After twenty-four hours I tried to improve my morale with lipstick but my fingers still trembled, and I dreaded the idea of going forward again. I began to wish I had never heard of the French Army.

18

Le Repos

'Greveuse est la guerre, et dure a l'endurer; Quand ailleurs est l'été, en Galle est hiver,' wrote a mediaeval poet, and I understood full well what he meant.

The fighting in the Vosges lasted for two months. The French suffered heavy casualties and took only 4,500 prisoners and 60 cannon as against 58,000 prisoners and several thousand big guns they had captured during that spectacular summer sweep up the Rhône. The German dead lay uncounted in the mountains, and the French dead were too numerous to be revealed.

The American Seventh Army, commanded by General Patch, worked just to the North of our division. His son was killed leading his squadron into action quite near us in the forest. Everyone liked fighting with the Americans although envious of their superior equipment. They had mobile baths, cinemas, libraries, doughnut-machines, hot-coffee stalls, glamour girls, and relief troops. Behind the perpetually-employed seven divisions of the French Army lay nothing but hungry, disorganized France.

In early November the 1st Armoured Division pulled out of the Vosges to refit. The regiments were spread far and wide in small villages through the wooded flooded countryside and the *ambulancières* enjoyed what was mockingly called *un repos* in a vile village called Port-sur-Saône.

The ramshackle attics in which we were billeted were hideously uncomfortable, but we learnt to wash cunningly in small bowls of water heated in a kitchen that was permanently packed with soldiers, and which we carried into the ambulance for privacy. Stunned at the squalor in which we were supposed to recover from battle-strain I watched my companions, happy as larks in the smoky old loft where our stretchers were spread on the rotting wood floor. They preened and prinked and manicured their nails and spent hours devising new hair styles. I myself, frozen and frightened by the Vosges battles, did not care what I looked like any more; and any vulgar craving for danger I had ever entertained had vanished.

One of the most attractive girls was Jeanine André, a blonde Alsatian of twenty-three, whose father had been killed commanding a battalion of Chasseurs in 1940 and whose two brothers were officers in this division. No sooner did she get out of a battle than Jeanine would pin up a pocket mirror and begin arranging the long golden hair, which she wore twisted in complicated coils on top of her head. It caused her such pain to ruin it by pulling on a helmet. Her large blue eyes were fringed by lashes that looked artificial, they were so black and thick, and she just hated to be dressed in khaki. In fact she spoke with open annoyance of the destiny which had forced her to the wheel of an ambulance.

It was her mother, a lady of the military caste, who wished Jeanine to go into the 1st Armoured Division as well as her two sons and in France what *Maman* says goes. So Jeanine André did her duty but she was always a little cross about it, and she could not understand why I had forced my way to this unit. She was completely devoid of fear; even her nerveless companions remarked on her calmness, and in the end she was decorated for extricating wounded under heavy fire and mending her ambulance in full view of the Germans. No one who watched her working in the front lines could have guessed that her real desire in life was for what she had never possessed, 'a long evening dress that sweeps the ground'.

During our ten days we grew to know the inhabitants of Port-sur-Saône intimately. In spite of the rich agricultural land around, the village houses were poorly built and most uncomfortable. There was no running water or sanitation, but there was a smart *coiffeuse* and we all made friends with her, for she lived opposite our loft.

Mme Paillot was twenty-three years old, extraordinarily lovely to look at, and quite contented in a nightmare struggle to run a house, a garden, and a hairdressing shop single-handed. Her blond, two-year-old baby was well tended although, like all the other children, his countenance was marred by spots. Every evening, when her husband came home from work, she cooked their meagre rations into a dinner which excelled anything a Paris restaurant could produce. For every vegetable she knew a dozen sauces, and she would cook a hoary old chicken with white wine and mushrooms, and a piece of the cow which had stepped on a mine was served in four different ways, each more delicious than the last. With amazement I watched her preparing these dishes on a dirty little stove and at the same time washing the infant's clothes and running at intervals into the front room to curl the hair of her clients. 'My mother taught me to cook,' she said. 'Grandmother was famous. I never look anything up in a book. I know it all; and, besides, one must invent not merely copy.'

All the water for her kitchen, laundering, and shampooing, she had to carry herself in pails from the village pump down the road. Yet she found time to make herself an assortment of elaborately veiled hats which she wore when going to the market. Sometimes I helped with the chores or bought the bread for her.

The bakery was run by two fat, garrulous old sisters, in their sixties. They wore carpet slippers, wrinkled black stockings, a variety of woollies and shawls and their large, shining faces were permanently crowned by halos of curl-papers. Both of them talked and gossiped until they made your head ring, but in opposite tones. *Mademoiselle* Marie was jolly and optimistic – the war would be over by Christmas, things were improving already, *la belle vie* was coming back, the French soldiers that she met when pushing her bread barrow to the surrounding hamlets were all *braves garçons* of *splendide politesse*. *Mademoiselle* Margot had a very different tale to shout over the counter. She would launch into rhetoric about the degeneration of France. 'I shiver with shame when I see what the new generation has grown into, and as for our government . . . ! The bread is getting worse and worse – look at the children – patriotism is dead, *le belle vie* is dead, and morality is dead. I tell you, *Mademoiselle*, I am ashamed to be French. Let me shake your hand. You can tell that in England when you get back. I predict that France is finished.'

Tolerant as her compatriots were about political argument, I wondered that no customers took offence. But the expressions of those within ear-shot showed only sly amusement and Mme Paillot remarked, 'Poor thing . . . she was in love, what do you expect?' 'In love? That fat old monster?' Then came the story. *Mademoiselle* Marie and *Mademoiselle* Margot having never found husbands lived together happily enough running the bakery and gossiping until the disaster came . . . *Mademoiselle* Margot fell in love! 'She had no pride,' said Mme Paillot. 'Every day she would waddle here to have her hair dyed or frizzed "You must make me beautiful" she pleaded . . . Can you imagine?'

The cause of this trouble was said to be a young man of sixteen who worked in a garage. He urged her to run away with him – which she did. The elopement was not a success, for the young man left her after two days! And so the villagers excused her sour temper. '*Que voulez-vous . . .*' they said.

19

Alsace at Last

When we were put *en alerte* for a move from Port-sur-Saône the villagers baked us cakes, and little Mme Paillot asked me to come and stay after the war. The farewells were touching and, because I was the first British person these villagers had ever met, they gave me all they could of delicacies. 'Come again,' they cried. 'Finish the war quickly and come back in better times.'

At two in the morning orders arrived to depart. We rolled up our blankets, tied our kitbags on the ambulance wings and folded the stretchers. The village was alive with headlights and roaring motor engines. Our friends offered us bowls of hot milk while we floundered in the mud. At dawn, we moved off towards the Vosges again and, by mid-day, all knew we were going to join the French attack in Alsace.

A passing convoy shouted, 'Montbéliard has fallen. All goes well!' The famous Belfort Gap, where the army had been hung up since September, would soon be breached. Our company spent the night in a dilapidated old chateau. The Stars and Stripes fluttered in the garden where month-old crosses marked a thousand American graves.

By this time I had collected a Moroccan 'fag'. He was an Oran taxi-driver, who spent his spare time cleaning my boots and accepting tips (perhaps bribes would be a more exact term). We billeted ourselves as best we could in the old farmhouses grouped around the chateau. My fag reported he had found a splendid place for me – 'the best kitchen in the village.' I found a low-beamed barn with an old woman, and the refugees she had taken in, cooking and sleeping at one end.

Not until I had curled up in my blankets did I realize that an all-night party was beginning. Three Moroccan orderlies had caught a rabbit and brought it in to be cooked by the girls. An Arabic sing-song by firelight ensued. I put my head under the blankets, but sleep was impossible and before morning, in spite of sprinklings of DDT, I had been lavishly bitten by bugs.

As always we were roused for *le depart* at 2 a.m. We floundered round in the dark filling up the tanks of our vehicles which were parked in a bog.

Dawn came with dramatic beauty, a herald of clear weather for our attack; but the whole day passed and still we waited. At 9 p.m., just as we decided to sleep in our ambulances, the word came. We moved off and drove through the night, in slow convoy, always making way for tanks to rattle past. '*Attention, aux chars!*' came the cry, and we drew into the hedge. Later on, when the attack was launched, it would be '*Attention ambulances*', and at our shout of *blessés graves* all would make way for us. There was a fantastic quality in that long drive, with the boom of guns flashing ahead as the artillery barrage lit up coppery clouds against a momentary pale blue, like a great flash of lightning.

As a second dawn without sleep came, I beheld a country different to any I had yet seen in Europe. The purple Vosges mountains loomed in the background and we were swooping along the Swiss frontier into the great plain of Alsace. The black-and-white timbered cottages looked Elizabethan, with high sloping roofs. They were hung with tricolours and peasants ran out waving, smiling, and weeping, to hand us apples, and the people who had no flags set their children in windows to wave branches. But most houses had kept a flag hidden away in some cushion. Women ran out imploring our busy soldiers to 'Come inside, just one minute and watch'. Then they would snip open the hiding-place and triumphantly pull out the long-forbidden Tricolour.

As our convoy stopped I leaned out and asked a woman, 'When did the Germans leave?' 'Two hours ago. I heard them march out and did not dare open the shutters till dawn. Then I saw French tanks.'

I realized that we were liberating Alsace. Most of the country-side had been silently evacuated during the night.

The sun shone bright and we passed some villages where there had been resistance; shelled farmhouses, over-turned vehicles, abandoned ammunition, and in one ploughed field a big smashed crucifix with a wrecked German 88 gun beside it.

Yvonne Moreau, our second-in-command, came up during a stop and said: 'My husband's squadron has just gone forward into the attack.' She had married a young officer of our 5ème Chasseurs tank-destroyer regiment two days before the division sailed from Algiers. Their honeymoon had consisted of the invasion and the route up the Rhône and the Vosges.

An hour later she drove a load of wounded to the brigade station and heard a surgeon casually remark that Captain Moreau had been sent off with a piece of shrapnel in the brain. They said he had continued to direct his squadron for an hour, and then became dumb. Yvonne never flickered an eyelid, even when she learnt he might die or become mad. She asked as a favour to be allowed to drive a load of wounded out of turn, in the hope of seeing him at the evacuation station; but he had already been sent to a brain specialist at the rear. She carried on, though the strain showed through her calm, until Moreau's doctor asked for her presence, to see if he could recognize her.

Jeanne sent her off saying, 'Your duty here is finished – go and help your husband.' We heard from her occasionally afterwards, he did not die but he did not recover either. They had been such a brave, handsome, young couple.

That evening we reached Waldighoffen on the Swiss border and while the cuirassiers waited to attack Altkirch I was sent back with a load of German wounded. It was late at night when I turned back to the advanced post and hurried the ambulance ahead of a roaring line of tanks. By now I was very tired, and feeling my strained eyes could not be trusted in the dark, I switched on the headlights – which was of course forbidden when in sight of German artillery.

The villages were black and silent, for the inhabitants had either fled or were hiding, trembling, in the cellars. Only the sky crashed with the theatrical light of guns. The Germans had not had time to destroy the sign posts that stood at every cross-road, but the names of Alsatian villages were impossible to memorize. I drove on until I spotted three burning tanks that had not been there on the journey down, and knew we were lost. I turned off the head- lights, stopped, and got out. It was a moonless night, full of the roar of cannon.

Two soldiers loomed out of the hedge with bayonets and asked who the devil I was. They said I was driving smack into the enemy lines, the next wood was full of Germans. 'Where is the tank column we are waiting for?' This I could tell them was rattling along behind. 'You'd better turn and go back,' said the soldiers. I swung the ambulance round in the dark narrow lane, terrified lest the roaring engine and grating gears would attract the enemy's attention. Driving back past the advancing 2nd

Cuirassiers, I realized that I had been sailing into Altkirch ahead of the tank attack!

When I found the turning and reached the advanced post at Waldighoffen it was late, and with relief I realized no one was about to ask me embarrassing questions. Pulling out a stretcher I went to sleep in the ambulance, shoving aside in the dark those blankets wet with German blood.

Next morning we heard the attack on Altkirch was going successfully and the division hoped to reach Mulhouse and the Rhine that day, but the Delle road, our supply line, had been cut a few hours after I had travelled it the previous night. Waldighoffen clattered with armoured vehicles and weary civilians with packs on their backs were plodding against the stream. They spoke an extraordinary dialect of Germanized French, hard to understand.

The 9th Colonial Division and the two Moroccan divisions were attacking to the north. Belfort had fallen and the German line through the Vosges mountains was breaking up. Our division held the southerly sector. We could see Switzerland only five miles away, and I think the soldiers looked wistfully at those mountains of peace. The French Army had advanced swiftly for two days but now the Germans began launching counter-attacks behind us. The first ambulance to leave next morning narrowly escaped capture and had to make a detour along the Swiss frontier which took twelve hours. No one seemed to mind our supply line being cut, but I thought it could not be a very good thing. 'De Lattre is a fox for cunning – don't worry – he has thought out this campaign,' said the soldiers when we heard gunfire behind as well as in front. Then Altkirch fell, and advanced tanks of our division traversed Mulhouse and reached the Rhine. This was on November 21st. Smugly I wrote in a pocket diary, 'My twenty-ninth birthday! Reached the Rhine.'

In action the combat command divided into three *Groupements*. The ambulances waited under the orders of regimental doctors. When a message came in that there were wounded, either the doctor or his intern would go out in a jeep or half-track to find them while our ambulances got as near as the terrain would allow. After morphia and brief dressings we drove the casualties back to the advanced dressing post and sometimes back to the operating theatre. During a swift advance everything would become madly mobile, the advanced post and brigade station might be together in one village or suddenly separated by several miles. All units changed position every few hours, and owing to mines and broken bridges maps became almost useless, so one had to memorize the routes.

I was now attached to the *Groupement* of Commandant Vallin who commanded the 3rd Zouaves. This meant I worked under the orders of Lieutenant Husser, the zouave MO.

In spite of their withdrawal, the Germans had left groups of men fighting in every wood. The *Groupement* Vallin advanced to Illfurth, a village on the main Mulhouse road, which was under mortar fire from a nearby wood. The tanks rattling along with us got a hot reception, and we left two smoking Shermans by the roadside. Their crews were killed. Wrecks of war lined all this route; broken Panthers and guns that had shivered and flamed and roared for the last time, and among them were multitudes of women either crying hysterically or offering flowers, or trying to kiss us and talk. A very fat man who had come out on a bicycle laid it down on the grass and just stood beside the road wildly blowing kisses with both hands while tears poured down his cheeks.

At Illfurth – a village about eight miles from Mulhouse – the zouave doctor, Lieutenant Husser, set up his regimental dressing

post while the infantry attacked a nearby wood. This was the first
time that I saw with my own eyes the importance of infantry, for
our tanks could not be risked amongst the trees; they were like
kings in chess, so precious they could hardly move while the poor
old zouaves creeping through the bushes on their flat feet were
the pawns.

As the sun went down violent fighting started around us, and
Lieutenant Husser ordered us into a cottage. The two ambulances,
his jeep with its stretchers, and a much-shouted-for vehicle,
Lafftraak (which I learnt was merely a half-track used to pick up
wounded on rough terrain), stood outside the door. As the rattle of
machine-guns increased and mortars began to fall, I asked the MO
where he would like us to sit – meaning which was the safest place.

He replied, 'Where you like.' I thought him a detestable little
man and sulkily chose my own corner away from the window.

Towards the Rhine our planes were sailing low over the
retreating enemy and swooping up again like hawks after attack.
Troops passing through Illfurth brought us news. St. Dié and
Gérardmer, that we had been pounding towards in the Vosges, had
fallen and so had the fort of Le Thillot, where more French soldiers
had died than in the whole sweep up the Rhône.

Our supply line, the Delle Road, was still cut and the Germans
counter-attacked six times behind us, while isolated bands of men
were fighting hard all over Alsace.

I had been allotted as co-driver a young girl who never let an
hour pass without setting her hair with lotion from a bottle. As her
fashion was to have it waved on top in a sort of pompadour, the
steel helmet made life very difficult. She turned the interior of the
ambulance into an untidy beauty parlour. Pots of cream and rouge
fell out of the tool-box and rolled about the floor. She stuffed
make-up and hair brushes in the map-case and showed a constant

desire to take off her trousers and don a skirt. Having a plump figure, she knew that trousers were unbecoming, especially the rear view, so campaigning was agony for her.

'No one cares what your *derrière* looks like,' I said, 'especially not the wounded.' I wondered why an eighteen-year-old girl should have plunged into an ambulance unit. Now, as mortars began to fall in the village, she sat there, phlegmatically polishing her nails while the native orderlies scurried from one corner to another, and I could not resist asking, 'Why did you volunteer for this work?'

'I wanted to feel proud,' she answered, waving her finger-nails in the air to dry.

Before nightfall Lieut. Husser went out with his jeep to collect wounded from Heidwiller wood, while the intern took the half-track ambulance to the next bridge, which had been blown up. Here an Alsatian farmer had worked all day rowing soldiers across the Canal under heavy fire. During his last trip a German had tossed a hand grenade into the boat and he was badly wounded. The two soldiers with him had bits of grenade in their buttocks. They called this '*rien du tout*' and lay on their faces talking about the farmer. 'Drive quickly,' they said 'for he is a grand chap and his poor wife was watching from the bank, *affolée*.' But we had to creep back along the shell-pitted roads to Altkirch. '*Route Minée*' shouted an officer as we approached the direct road; so we had to cross and recross streams. The advanced post took the soldiers and sent us off with the farmer, to the big civilian hospital at Altkirch. We stopped in the dark, silent town which our cuirassiers had taken just before dawn. The civilians were bolted behind their doors and there was not a light or sound.

By the time we reached the hospital, our charge was bleeding to death. No one answered the door, so we carried the stretcher

inside. A nun appeared with a candle. She said, '*Mes pauvres enfants.*
The electricity was cut in the fighting so there are no lights and
the lifts do not work. The operating theatre is on the third floor.
Can you carry him all that way?' I and my young mate panted up
three flights carrying the stretcher. We chased up and down dark
corridors looking for a surgeon and at last we opened a door and
found four doctors dining by candlelight. They left their food and
wine and helped us lift the patient from stretcher to operating
table and cut off his bandages and clothes. Two more white-clad
nuns appeared with a flickering oil lamp, chloroform, and a
crucifix. It was too late. He had died as we gasped our way upstairs.
'Is he Catholic?' asked one of the nuns; and I answered, 'Yes,'
though I knew nothing except that he had worked courageously
with the zouaves who had been his comrades for a day.
Despondently we drove back to Illfurth.

Next morning a great din woke us. 'They attack again,' said
Husser; then, 'Aha, they reply!' as mortars landed outside.

'What is the difference between a shell and a mortar?' I asked.

A soldier sheltering from the drizzle explained for twenty minutes.

When silence came we went out to meet the wounded, who
were carried, dripping, from the wood. Machine-gun rattle kept
bursting through the soft patter of rain. 'They have plenty of
ammunition although they are surrounded,' said the wounded.
'They are tough, those Germans. . .'

At dusk we got the first wounded enemy. He was slightly hit in
the leg and, after a dressing, Husser sat him in the ambulance to
await fresh cases. He was a big bearded man and he never spoke,
but just sat there, with wide apprehensive eyes as if wondering
what in the world would happen next. Then a mortar fell in the
village street making a crater outside a prosperous-looking, mauve
villa. The windows were smashed, but one could not have guessed

that two children had been hit inside the house until a little man, covered with plaster, rushed out waving his hands.

Husser sent orderlies to fetch whoever was hurt. They brought back a boy of seven with his skull broken open, and behind came *Monsieur le dentiste*, owner of the house, carrying a little girl of four or five. Husser bandaged her head and told me not to wait for the boy. 'I'll send him by the next ambulance,' he said; but I saw the child was dead. The dentist climbed into the ambulance with his little daughter unconscious in his arms. Now the village began to creep out from shelter and a commotion started. Nothing arouses anger like the sight of wounded children. They wanted to drag our POW out and lynch him. 'Are you SS?' they asked in German. '*Ja ja,*' said the man. He answered '*ja ja*' to everything. I slammed the door, shoved up the step and drove off hurriedly, to cries of '*Sale boche*' and 'Let us get at him.'

The dentist sat behind me with the child in his arms. He kept very calm and quiet, from shock – I think. I noticed the little girl's head bandage growing scarlet.

The endless detours needed to get to Altkirch drove the dentist demented. He insisted he knew a short cut and foolishly I listened. We found ourselves on a road strewn for half a mile with dead bodies and blown-up carts. I realized this was the *Route Minée* we had been warned about and turned the ambulance.

We reached Altkirch Hospital and evidently the dentist was well known here, for he carried the little girl straight off to a surgeon of his acquaintance. While they operated he came back to me and asked again: 'Your doctor said he would send my boy by the next ambulance. Is he alive do you think?'

And in cowardice I flinched. 'Yes; another ambulance will bring him.'

The wounded prisoner still huddled in a corner like a terrified animal . . . All the journey he had kept as far as possible from the dentist, fearing that revenge for the wounded child might be taken on him. Now as I rearranged the blankets, to drive him off to the brigade post, he shrank away murmuring *'Ja, ja'* as he had when the villagers asked if he was SS. At our dressing station he suddenly burst into Russian. One of the doctors understood and questioned him. Yes, all the men fighting in that wood were Russian. Did they know they were surrounded? Yes, but they had ammunition still. Why did they fight in German uniform? They were told to. Did they like their German masters? Blank.

He was a simple peasant, a frightened, captured bear who did not know what it was all about and he would have been ready to take off his German uniform, put on a French one and fight on our side the next day without explanation.

'I was told to,' or 'I don't know,' were his only answers.

But the others carried on till shells and mortars were exhausted and few of them remained alive. It puzzled the French, who were emotional fighters, to know that a band of sodden peasants could fight so well without a country, without a master and without a reason.

Back at Illfurth, Lieutenant Husser told me to put on my helmet and walk down to the village to give the dentist's wife what news I could. *'Monsieur le dentiste,'* said our Alsatian neighbour, 'has *la plus belle maison du village – la maison violette.'* There was a shining brass plate on the door and so I learnt the name of that little man whom I felt I knew so intimately. I went round to the back of the mauve villa and shouted down into the cellar where most civilians spent their time. A wild, tousled-headed woman came up.

'Madame' I began, 'your husband spent the night at the hospital and returns today by bicycle. All possible is being done for your

daughter.' I saw she was demented as, seizing my arm, she dragged me into a room on the ground floor. Beside the dentist's chair lay one of our stretchers with her little dead son.

Later, I learnt the little girl also died after three head operations in the Altkirch Hospital. The young nun who told me this had hyacinth-blue eyes and they clouded with tears as she said, 'The father was here all the time and we prayed so hard.' It is not often that you see a nun cry.

That evening Heidwiller wood fell and, arriving with a load back at the advanced post, I ran in shouting:

'We have taken Heidwiller.'

The surgeon laughed.

'We?' he queried, 'so you are really one of us!'

They handed me some letters from home and I read: 'No one here knows anything about the French Army. Do they fight well? Let us know.'

I did.

20

Beside the Rhine

By chance I heard a BBC broadcast announcing: 'Strasbourg has fallen. French Forces have cut off the enemy salient between Belfort and Mulhouse'. That's us, I thought! And now we heard of the successes outside the section of Combat Command 1. All Alsace had been cleared of Germans except a strong pocket around Colmar.

Lieutenant Husser had been born and brought up in Mulhouse so he was excited when we got orders to advance across the canal, where a Bailey bridge had been constructed. He drove up to the house where his mother lived and knocked with trepidation for no news had got through for a year. But she herself opened the door and gave a cry of delight.

Unlike mediaeval Strasbourg, Mulhouse is an industrial town without charm. It had been smashed by British bombers and now the Germans were fighting in the northern suburbs.

We drove in and, as in the villages, tricolours hung from every house but there were no people about, owing to the constant shelling. Commandant Vallin's group installed itself around a large schoolhouse. We put the two ambulances in the courtyard and Husser found the concierge, picked a piece of shrapnel out of her daughter's large rump, and asked if there were any rooms where four girls could be billeted.

'The apartment of the SS lieutenant!' she cried with enthusiasm, and led us up to a smart flat where a recently fled SS and his wife had lived. There was an enormous feather-bed to bounce in, and a kitchen where we cooked our rations into a delicious dinner, and a series of hideous uniforms hung in the wardrobe, in which we speedily dressed up. '*Mon Dieu*,' said Jeanine, with a crested helmet down over her eyes 'it takes a *boche* to think out uniforms in such taste.' They were sky-blue, trimmed with vivid green, chocolate brown and silver. There were buttons everywhere, up and down the sleeves and on the jacket's behind. His Frau had left perfume bottles on the dressing-table and photographs that showed her as a pleasant blonde woman with two children. Some of their toys were still there, and Mimi, being very small managed to sleep in a cot. The downstairs tenants came up to gossip and with them were two youths just back from the interior of Germany. They were all terrified the Germans might return. 'You have heard how they shot the inhabitants of every house that had hung out French flags when they retook Metz.'

Late that night Husser sent my ambulance back to the advanced post with two wounded soldiers. It was eerie driving through the deserted streets, unlit save by the lightning flicker of landing shells. We crept through the devastated station area, where a square mile of buildings had been flattened and the bridges had large shell-holes through them. We were allowed no lights, so sometimes we had to stop and do a short reconnoitre on foot. There were no troops about and the silence was only broken by the boom of our guns followed by the whistle of the shells they sent sailing into the moonlight to crash in the German infested suburbs. The weird laughter of our shells was strangely exciting.

We reached the advanced post and Jeanne de l'Espée came out to scold us for not wearing our hateful steel helmets. 'Come on in, *mes petites*, you must not sit within enemy range for pleasure.' We got back before dawn and learnt that the Combat Command 2 was fighting through the Harth Forest, which lay between Mulhouse and the Rhine and their new girl drivers had already met with disaster.

One of their ambulances had got lost in the forest, driven into the German Lines just outside Mulhouse and been captured. Another had taken a wrong turning in full view of a French battery and been hit by machine-gun fire. One of the girls got out and was seen running wildly down the road. Then a bunch of Germans stepped out from cover, caught her by the arm and dragged her away. The French could not fire for fear of hitting her. They watched the ambulance smouldering but the other girl (aged seventeen) never got out, so she must have died in it.

Taking Mulhouse was like taking a ghost town, grim, silent streets, invisible inhabitants. Fear reigned everywhere – fear of the Germans, fear of shelling, and fear of hunger.

The spahis regiment, with which I had left Italy, arrived on the outskirts of the town, and Charles de Breteuil asked Jeanne de l'Espée to bring me to dinner in the mess. We ate by candlelight, and the proprietor of the village restaurant produced the famous white wine of Alsace and a bottle of rare raspberry liqueur. 'How long I have had to keep this bottle hidden!' he said. His friends came to form an orchestra. They did not play very well, but their faces shone with excitement. 'They play from the heart,' said the spahis officers. This was the only gay evening we had, and it was tempered by the news that General Brosset, who commanded the *division France Libre*, had been killed near Belfort. I had not seen him since the Euphrates.

By 8 December, the French Army had liberated Alsace except for the pocket around Colmar – and there they stuck, for the

Germans were strongly fortified and well supplied from their bridges across the Rhine. Dreams of getting into the Black Forest by Christmas vanished as the hard cold descended, but the French soldiers always spoke with confidence of General de Lattre de Tassigny. We lived now in squalor and discomfort, warming our hearts at cottage hearths with brave strategic talk. Our division had daringly whirled along the Swiss frontier while the Belfort Gap was breached, and Germans were encircled everywhere. There had been a hundred small fights like Heidwiller wood. We had lost many tanks, and the Germans had left the great plain, so suitable to armoured warfare, strewn with the blackened carcasses of Tigers, Panthers and Jagdpanthers.

The last tank we lost in this advance was hit by a bazooka at Lutterbach. We were a little way behind the village, 'listening'. That was the worst part of the medical service; sitting about, listening to a fight, and knowing there would be nothing to do until someone got hit. On this occasion the cannon-loader, a young fellow called Peters, got out and borrowed a tommy-gun from the supporting tank and went alone on foot through the mortar fire. He killed two Germans who had the bazooka, and brought back four prisoners. Then he collapsed from wounds and we evacuated him, grinning and triumphant. 'It's my twentieth birthday,' he said.

There were ten to twenty soldiers in every room in that village – which made it impossible to wash, to warm up, to cook or to think. I asked permission to go for a walk every afternoon to get out of the bedlam.

'What?' said the officer, 'walk alone in the drizzle? Very, very, English.' Hiking in winter over ploughland has never been the Continental idea of *un joli sport*; but I was allowed to wander as long as I did not 'imprudently walk into the enemy lines'. They thought the British capable of any eccentricity.

It was a cold and dreary landscape. On the Rhine ice crackled and in the air sounded the whistle of German shells and the fluttering, feathery laughter of our own, laughter that died away eastward. In the cold air you could hear the rattle of machine-guns and the neat short crack of a rifle as soldiers sniped at each other across the swift grey water. Even the rifle bullets had their baby whistle.

The Rhine-maidens must have been sulking downstream, and their melodies were lost in the sounds of war, I reflected, plodding along in big boots that were always heavy with mud, for we slept in mud, ate in mud, and drove in mud, and, if it had been possible to get near the seething village pump, one might have washed in mud.

During the evenings, when we had cooked dinner for the MOs and the padres, and washed it down with wine, we would sit for hours in discussion. The French alleviate unpleasant situations by talk. They were full of spiteful witticism which made the dirt and din more endurable. In an advance, hardship passes unnoticed, it is static discomfort that makes an army groan.

The English have a curiously erroneous concept of the typical Frenchman, whom they associate with lively amorous adventures. In reality they are extremely unsentimental. They treat women unemotionally and with respect, which makes comradeship easy. No Frenchman I met would have dreamt of making up to any girl working in the army. They would have considered it bad taste, and whatever else may be lacking, the French keep their taste.

The Moroccans, of lurid reputation, evinced no interest in anything, save stealing poultry and having secret feasts in barns. Latin standards of morality, as a whole, seemed to me more logical and kindly than the Anglo-Saxon. For instance – if a man leaves a girl with a child, opprobrium falls on him, and pity on her.

Occasionally new *ambulancières* attached to another unit visited us. One of these, Anna, was a pretty creature of twenty with sad brown eyes and delicate features. Understanding little English she brought me letters from an American officer to translate. They were very warm and loving, so I would scribble them out on a bit of foolscap and give them to her to read.

As there were constant references to presents of clothing, sent to her baby son in North Africa, I asked one day about her husband.

She answered, 'I have no husband.'

'Oh! Are you a widow?'

'No, I am not a widow.' There was not a tremor in her voice, only wistfulness, and I felt hot with shame at my own bluntness and at the expression that must have passed over my face. She told me, quite simply, of her life as an *ambulancière* in North Africa where an American officer had fallen in love with her. 'You see he was a foreigner and did not understand our ways. We think it sensible to see if you can have a child and then, one goes to Confession and gets married. My American did not tell me until it was too late that he was a married man.

'It was a terrible shock and my unit were very angry with him. He loves me still and sends me presents, but he should have realized that one does not take *une fille serieuse* unless one intends marriage. My unit, of course, stood by me and the girls clubbed together to buy baby clothes and now my little boy lives with friends. The unit sailed for France without me, but I rejoined as soon as I was strong enough, and so I have just arrived. On the way I saw my mother and, of course, she understood.'

A few days later the girls were discussing Anna and what a good wife she would make. They passed on to another *ambulancière,* whom they said no one would ever want to marry.

'Why?' I asked.

'Because she is frivolous.'

'But what has she done?'

'Nothing; but her character is not serious.'

'How do you know?'

'By instinct. No; Anna will make a good wife and is the one that all the nice men want to marry. What a tragedy she had to suffer, poor thing; but the husband who gets her in the end, will be lucky. You'll see.'

But no man got her, for in the spring Anna was killed.

In spite of the discomforts of regimental life, when orders arrived that our ambulance was to be relieved my heart sank. But 'rest' was compulsory, and in the dusk we drove back to Landser, eight miles from the Rhine. All around the village our artillery was banging away and each battery had built a huge bonfire where the men warmed themselves and roasted anything they could lay hands on. It was a fine sight, the roaring guns and gay looking fires made one feel cozy and safe.

Jeanne de l'Espée and some half dozen girls were billeted in an empty, unfurnished house and all the medical company vehicles were parked in a sea of mud in the garden. Having backed my ambulance into its allotted place in this bog, I climbed upstairs and found preparations for some kind of reception. As fast as I arranged a place to sleep, it was swept away. 'Les Invités will want to sit there,' said the girls. They built a table and arranged boxes for chairs. Tins of beans sizzled on the stove, and heavy petrol containers of red wine and kirsh were being carried upstairs. Everyone was giving directions and tasting the wine, and burning fingers in the beans while the windows shook from our guns outside.

For some reason Jeanne de l'Espée, chief figure of the dinner-party, sat amidst this din reading a story book aloud, by candlelight, to a huddle of quarrelling cooks. Having learnt that the causes of all this commotion were Colonel Durosoy, who commanded the 2nd Cuirassiers, Charlie de Breteuil of the spahis and an officer from brigade HQ I retired downstairs and poked my head out into the noisy night. Something sounded wrong. Certain explosions had not the right tone. The Moroccan medical staff who inhabited the ground floor had already vanished and I shouted upstairs, 'There are *arrivés* falling in the village.'

Amidst the booming, a new kind of crash sounded. The Germans across the Rhine were not just taking it! They were answering back! The cooks and wine tasters hurried downstairs, and the next shell landed amidst our ambulances in the garden.

I might have expected it. *Le repos* was always like this. All cozy feelings had vanished. I ran into the cellar and worked out a problem . . . if we could fire into the German lines from here they could reach us back! Somehow I had never thought of this before.

In the cellar a lot of queer soldiery fussed around trying to make sandbags for the windows out of straw. There were angry orders to don helmets. Obediently I put mine on but it was full of apples which, falling on my head, frightened the life out of me.

The company doctors joined us from a house across the street and we stood in the murky dark, some thirty people, helmeted but helpless, listening to shell after shell falling in the garden outside. A wail went up each time glass tinkled, for only ambulances had enough panes to make that sound, as of a Japanese wind bell struck by a gale.

Then with satisfaction we heard our own guns replying. When a pause came, we slithered out into the darkness to find a shell had landed in the middle of our rations truck, while the four ambulances had smashed windows and burst tyres, pierced radiators and shrapnel embedded in the engines. Screams of rage went up as the girls pulled their precious uniforms out, riddled with shrapnel. Into this chaos a jeep rolled up with our three forgotten guests. We sat down amidst the wreckage to a burnt dinner and a couple of hours lively conversation. The men teased us, insisting that war was a fascinating sport women could not appreciate, but when a few more *pruneaus* landed, they announced this was the last time they would ever accept dinner in a feminine mess and drove off hurriedly without lights.

We were ordered to sleep in the cellar, and struggled down the narrow dark stairs carrying blankets and trying to avoid getting electric shocks from a broken cable that dangled in the dark. After midnight there was silence from all the guns so I wandered out in the bright moonlight. Peace seemed to lie on the world, silvery peace and beauty.

Next morning brigade HQ looked at the shell holes around their doorway and moved smartly elsewhere, but they informed the *ambulancières* they might continue to 'rest' where they were while the vehicles were mended!

21

Christmas 1944

The division returned to Mulhouse and for three weeks we were confined to one dismal barrack-room. Here we slept and ate and talked, above all – talked! We spread out stretchers on the floor and woke as late as possible to make the day seem less interminable. Then having folded blankets and dressed and made a cup of coffee we went into the courtyard to fight our way to the only tap of that squalid building. Here one could elbow aside the tattooed Moroccans who were shaving, the company cook and his satellites who were cleaning saucepans and emptying garbage on your feet and make a firm effort to wash. The tap was an excellent one in that it did not, like all the other taps I met, run dry after two days of such treatment.

At midday an Arab kitchen boy yelling *'la soupe'* brought us a bucket of hot stew, and then having eaten and washed our mess-tins at the same tap we spent the afternoon trying to find something to do to our ambulances in the yard. When the cold afternoon terminated there was nothing for it but to return to our room and wait for the evening cry of *'la soupe'*. From across the Mediterranean I had imagined the excitement of capturing cities in Europe, but in Mulhouse there was no laughter, no lights, no fun, and no music save the howl of Arab songs in the room beneath. Mme Kleber, the plump little woman I had first seen working at the resuscitation truck in the Vosges, joined us and her reminiscences were a change from the others: *'Eh bien ma belle'* she would address one. 'I am working-class and proud of it. All my life I've worked and it hasn't been a pretty story, that I can tell you. Look at my hands – I've had something better to do than paint my nails—' and finding an audience who sat on the floor absorbed by this or any other story she poured out her life which had been a series of disasters. We shared her early disappointments, and boiled with indignation at the ne'er-do-well husband who gambled and drank and squandered the earnings of her grocery shop. We lived through the hard struggles to maintain and educate two sons, through the bad moments when husband reappeared to make scenes, and in the end we praised and consoled her. The boys were now leaving school and wrote affectionate letters to their *Chère maman courageuse* which we read and approved of, and their photos we admired. 'I can tell you about men, *mes belles!'* she would say. And, meanwhile, a new fat jolly girl, who had just joined us from the Red Cross, having related the history of her seven brothers, two of whom were priests, would kneel down and unselfconsciously say her lengthy prayers, holding out her arms in the shape of a cross.

It was during this wait in Mulhouse that the fascinating drama of Paulette's rabbit reached its climax. Paulette had got married at Port-sur-Saône. It was not considered quite the thing to occupy your mind with marital thoughts at this stage of the war but Paulette met her fiancé who she had not seen for five years and it was too much for her. Marry she must. So she went off on the day we left the Vosges and as she could not obtain more than three days' leave, the honeymoon had to be spent at Port-sur-Saône. I felt a sneaking pity for the bridegroom when Paulette led him daily to our mess for food and he sat nibbling nervously beneath the gaze of twenty girls who did not approve of husbands. When the call came at 2 a.m. to move off and capture Alsace, Paulette had to leave her better-half waving pathetically in the roadway.

A few weeks later, when we were shelled at Landser, everyone remarked that Paulette turned a peculiar shade of green, and soon after this she extracted a promise from a company doctor. Then she offered a large reward to the Moroccans – who were constantly scouring the countryside for fat geese, poultry and such like, to add illicitly to their rations – if they could produce *une lapine vierge*. Owing to the German artillery which kept us constantly on the move and the unvirginal habits of rabbits in general it was some time before a splendid young doe made her appearance, with the farmer's written guarantee. Paulette carried her around in a large cardboard box, feeding her cabbage leaves at frequent intervals. Now, during our incarceration in Mulhouse, we guarded her day and night for although the native troops understood her to be reserved for magical rites pertaining to fertility, we still feared their ability to steal Paulette's precious proof and make rabbit pie.

It was all very complicated and colossally interesting . . . it was in fact our only interest and when the tests had been made and the rabbit slain Paulette could triumphantly demand a release from the army. A long correspondence followed between HQ, who seemed reluctant to accept proof of a Wasserman test conducted in the front line, and after two months during which Paulette was cherished and kept as far out of enemy range as was possible the release order came through and she left the division to await her baby in Paris. 'How nice for Paulette,' said the girls; 'but no one else must marry until the war ends.' And no one else dared.

It was an exhilarating moment when we were given a move-ment order to 'proceed in helmet' to the public baths. Gleefully carrying towels and soap we walked through the deserted streets and found the water was boiling. This was my first hot bath since Marseilles three months before. I can still remember the tiled cubicle, the old wizened woman scrubbing the tub, and the little window that let a ray of sunlight sparkle the water.

Jeanine André and I were sent for a few days to the suburb where Jeanine's brother commanded his armoured car squadron. We had meals in the 3rd Chasseur Mess and, as legend decreed that one of my nationality should be constantly preparing tea, the officers of the squadron always turned up in our room for *le five o'clock*. One evening I had just come in when a zing rushed past my head and a bullet embedded itself in the wall. Its blast blew out our lamp, and all was indignant commotion while we shouted to the soldiers outside to arrest all the Moroccans who wandered around shooting at pigeons. I did not mind much until I found the bullet had singed my beret. They never caught the culprit, and after a chase for *les types qui se promènent avec des carabines* the soldiers came in, ate all our biscuits, and admired the hole in the window pane.

Then, just before Christmas, the division moved back thirty miles to wait *en réserve* while the battle for Strasbourg began, and we were awakened at midnight to drive under cover of darkness to a new village.

We reached it at 3 a.m. and although it was arctic we slept in the ambulances till the first glimmer of dawn. Then, stiff with cold, we climbed out and stared at the village shimmering in hoar frost. Smoke crept up from a timbered cottage and a few lights showed. We tapped on a door and found a bevy of soldiers making hot coffee and ingratiating themselves with the farmer's wife. She told us she could not give us billets, for there were three or four native soldiers curled up in every feather bed for

miles around. Only one dilapidated three-room cottage in
Tagsdorf could be secured by the billeting officer for the eight
ambulancières au repos. There were no beds, no stove, no water-tap,
no sanitation of any description.

For Christmas week, Jeanine went to her brother's squadron
and I was sent on duty with a Corsican girl of nineteen to
Commandant Vallin's zouaves in Franken where we were billeted
in the apple-loft of a farmhouse. We spent most of our time downstairs sitting on the stove with the farmer, his buxom wife, and
their four little daughters. The man, like all Alsatians who grew up
between 1870 and 1914, spoke only German. His wife belonged
to the slightly younger group who knew French also, but with a
gutteral accent; and, as it had been strictly forbidden to speak a
word of French in Alsace for five years, the children only German,
though they soon learnt to ask our soldiers for things that were
good to eat.

There was nothing to do but to keep the ambulances warm,
running their engines every three hours day and night and wrap-
ping them well in blankets. The rest of the time we sat indoors
with the clamorous children and their noisy good-natured mother,
Frau Schmidt, deafened by German voices and raucous laughter.
A great feast was prepared for Christmas Eve. We sat on the tiled
stove, watching, until we had to join the noisy party. The Alsatians
had big Teuton appetites and, unlike the rest of France, they had
never suffered a food shortage for they had been incorporated in
Germany. The farmer and his yokels ate hugely and greedily.

Our hostess plied us with more and more food. 'What! it's no
good?' she would cry, if one refused a third wedge of greasy
pudding and, if we did not constantly talk, her big hand would
smack one between the shoulder-blades, *'Mademoiselle fâché?'*
During the cooking of the last dish – which necessitated a long

wait – the four little girls were ordered to stand in a row and for the twelfth time sing us the Marseillaise shrilly and off key, but with good heart. My small, fat, Corsican companion was overwhelmed by home sickness. I begged her to keep the tears back for fear of offending the farm people, and she tried to beam and join in the conversation.

A Moroccan batman, billeted with his officer nearby, had far more success. He stuffed pudding in his mouth, made tea, roared with laughter at incomprehensible jokes with the farm hands, swung the children round his head in a happy gabble of German-Arabic.

Frau Schmidt, a garrulous extravert, determined that we should know the villagers intimately, recited her neighbours' immoralities until our heads were spinning. Friends came in and kept up the recital in dialect French.

At nine we escaped to a troops' concert in the village. Three hours of songs and jokes about the company cook dragged on while a barrel of hot red wine was served out. Then suddenly our Brigadier Gruss appeared with General Béthouart (our corps commander). The last puerile jokes petered out and silence reigned in the stuffy barn until Béthouart spoke. He said that one of the hardest and most concentrated battles of the entire war was raging in the Ardennes and that the Germans were thrusting around Strasbourg. According to captured enemy papers an attack on the plain of Alsace might be expected any hour. The whole French Army was *en alerte*.

As General Béthouart's brother-in-law was killed with the zouaves in the last war he had decided to spend tonight with the men of this battalion. 'I want to tell you all that, no matter what American troops are evacuated, the French will not leave Alsace. No matter what is thrown against us we will not retreat.'

Meanwhile, Christmas bells mingling with a far-off roar of guns, echoed over the white, frozen land. As we walked to midnight Mass, the little village looked like a picture from some fairy tale with gleaming windows and sloping roofs. The church had a square tower from which gargoyles put out their tongues at the centuries.

Within it was freezingly cold, but there were candles and white chrysanthemums, a whiff of chilly incense and a feeble organ. The cracked voices of an ancient choir struggled with the hymns, old women in black bonnets knelt with bowed heads, praying for daughters deported to work in Germany and sons in danger.

General Béthouart and Brigadier Gruss, in their fur-collared military lumber-jackets, shivered in front of us, and a cold crept up from the stone floor that seemed to paralyze us. I thought of other midnight masses, in Beirut and Egypt, and in the South African summer and of the far-off, hot-house atmosphere of Farm Street, and then I thought of the twenty-eight American divisions recoiling in the Ardennes, and of the seven under-strength, French divisions waiting in the Alsace plain, and – at intervals of such thoughts – perhaps said a few prayers—

When the generals had gone off to visit other units we walked back with Frau Schmidt to the farmhouse. The children, waiting for us on the tiled stove, were as usual eating. We sat around the spangled tree and drank coffee. Several women came in and talk turned to their sons in the German Army. 'There are no young men in Alsace, *Mademoiselle*. They are all fighting in Poland or in Budapest. They are never used now on the Western Front, for they would escape back to us;' and the same old question would be asked by some wide-eyed peasant-woman: 'When will the war end, *Mademoiselle*? When will my son get back?'

A kindly soul – who had allowed us to wash our shirts in her kitchen – told us she had only one child, an eighteen-year-old boy who had just left school and been conscripted a week before we arrived … 'You see it is better to have only girls,' bellowed Frau Schmidt to her husband, and the four ugly brats grinned.

So we spent Christmas night 1944 comforting the mothers of enemy soldiers and running the ambulance engine to keep it warm. The evening ended with excitement as a farmhouse in the next village caught fire from the exhaust of a military car, and burned to the ground. Water had to be passed in buckets by hand and it froze between the pump and the flames.

At last we went garrulously to bed in the attic, which was cold but smelt sweetly of apples.

22

Winter Wait

The *Alerte* only lasted forty-eight hours and although German divisions were gathered as if to attack Strasbourg they only made thrusts. During the weeks that followed we had few occasions to drive out. Several soldiers had frozen feet and one native, too stupid to blink, got frozen eyeballs! Never had the war seemed to me so unhappy, yet we lived in boisterous gaiety and there were days of unbroken sunshine. Even the dreary village pump now had a loveliness as a fantastic lacework of ice glinted around it.

We moved a few miles to another village, Zassingen, where the two *ambulancières* were offered the mayor's house. This sounded very grand, but it was just a big simple farmhouse like the others. We had an icy attic to ourselves and could share the kitchen with a tank crew. Instead of Frau Schmidt and her clacking children we had as hostesses the mayor's wife and her three marriageable daughters. It did not take us long to realize that we two *ambulancières* were distinctly *de trop*. In the morning we would wait till the moment of least chaos to carry a pitcher of water into the kitchen, then make our breakfast and wash our teeth, while the men shaved and the daughters made cakes and flirted. When we tumbled round the stove, spilling our bowls of milk the household scowled and sighed. But whatever the men dropped or broke, they were beamed on, for they represented potential husbands for three handsome daughters, grown up in a world scraped bare of men.

Perched on the hot tiled stove munching vitaminized barley sugar, malted milk tablets and 'energy crackers', I tried to keep out of the fray and yet listen to the gabble in German as neighbours dropped in.

In Zassingen, as in the other villages, most of the women were anguished at being unable to obtain news of sons or brothers in the German Army. A lonely old creature brought us a cake saying she had made it out of the ingredients saved for her boy expected on leave. 'He'll not be home now till war ends. I'll pretend you are my daughters, so please come to dinner tonight.' We went across the road and found she had one officer billeted in her sitting-room whose Moroccan batman, a good-looking innocent who had been wounded, spent most of his time in the kitchen trying to tune in to Arab wails from Tangiers on the radio and preparing huge non-pork meals for himself. I firmly switched the radio from North Africa to the BBC at news time for the Ardennes thrust had frightened this people, who knew the possibility of the Germans sweeping back and reoccupying the plain of Alsace.

We sat down to supper with the woman and her old husband. The Moroccan making a great show of polishing the table with spit, and bringing his own collection of sweets, joined us. Conversation in German-Arabic made little sense but was studded by smiles and polite gestures.

The Moroccan told with childish simplicity, about the wife who was waiting back home for him to buy her. Wide smiles showed his pleasure at being listened to. I was fascinated by the beauty of his teeth and, as the conversational subjects at this sort of meal could leap smoothly from wives to dentifrice, asked if he ever brushed them. '*Non, non*, only this,' he took a splinter of fire-wood and scraped.

Then the woman started talking, and as her mind revolved always around the missing son, she showed his photo. I wondered inwardly if some day we would see him lying dead in his grey uniform and to us he would be just another *boche*. She went on about the German soldier-friends he used to bring home on leave, nice young men, very clean, very correct.

'There was one,' she said 'who used to come and see me alone, and he would sit up late at night brooding, weeping, and talking of things he had done in Poland, been forced to do, of course. He poured out descriptions of the lines of Poles brought out to dig trench graves and then he and the other soldiers would be ordered to shoot them. "We had to," he would say, "but it's the children I cannot forget," that's what he used to say, and yet he was clean and honest this boy, and his pride was easily injured. If there was any suggestion that Germany might lose the war he would turn white with offence. But night after night he used to come back here into the kitchen and weep saying, "they were human beings like us and the children – and I can't get over it."'

We were invited to celebrate the New Year in a zouave officers' mess, which had been established in the smoky, stuffy, scruffy, gay little village pub. French infantry regiments are less smart and cosmopolitan than the cavalry. These eight zouave officers had no contact with the world outside France. They were more isolationist than any middle-class English, and I was the only intimate British friend they were ever likely to have. I liked them enormously and they liked me. If they hadn't, they would have shown it because they were touchy and petulant about the 1940 defeat, so easily wounded at any mention of their country's fall that a foreigner in their mess might easily jar. But because I found that hurt pride natural (just the feeling I would have myself if my country failed), they would discuss their own faults. They were the real conventional Frenchmen of France of whom the outside world knows nothing.

No one ever gets tight in a French mess. Even on New Year's night when we had champagne no one was inebriated except with his own chatter. As midnight rang we drank to the first offensive of 1945, and the wireless bells died away into a voice announcing that the Ardennes salient was held. Late in the evening a liaison officer came in and told us how Patton's 3rd Army on the southern front of the salient had driven the Germans back *swimming* across the river Sauer! We could not have wished a worse fate to any enemy.

Rumours were pouring from the North, and the people around besieged us with questions. Why couldn't we take the great German pocket around Colmar? Was it true that American soldiers were retreating? Might Strasbourg be given back to Nazi revenge? We reassured them, for none of us knew that General Eisenhower had decided to pull all American troops out of Alsace to wait behind that old defence line the Vosges Mountains, and if necessary be rushed to the Bastogne salient. We did not know the High Command was ready to abandon Alsace to save the Ardennes and that the civilians had reason for their panic. General de Lattre and General de Gaulle were protesting that at all costs the French Army must be allowed to hang on because of the German habit of reprisals.

Later, it was revealed that on January 3rd, de Gaulle telephoned Churchill, who flew to France to support the French appeal that in this case human considerations made the military gamble worthwhile. After all night discussions Eisenhower agreed not to abandon Alsace but on condition that the French Army took over all responsibility for the defence of Strasbourg. Every available French unit was arriving in Alsace and all commanders were giving 'no retreat' pep talks on the lines of General Béthouart's Christmas chat.

As soon as the snow went, as soon as it was spring we *must* attack. . .

That was in the first week in January, but I was entirely obsessed with my own difficulties. Our ambulances stood in the open, and in spite of anti-freeze we had to run the engines every two hours at night. One morning before dawn I went out to run the engine. Sitting there admiring the starry winter morning with dark sky and blue snow, I caught what I soon thought was pneumonia. As concertina wheezes issued from my chest I was sent back to *le repos* where the girls could but offer me the choice of asphyxiation beside the smoky stove or lying on a paillasse of tickly straw without heat. Then Michele, another girl, came in with a hacking cough and we were both packed off to the evacuation hospital at Belfort swearing we'd get back before the next attack 'somehow'.

23

Hospital

Being ill in the French Army is a special experience. After the diagnosis of the *une belle bronchite* you are laid on straw by large-booted Moroccans and left to cough and seethe with self-pity. If you have a thermometer, you take your own temperature at intervals and make petulant remarks. No one pays the slightest attention, nor will lung-splitting whoops induce a native orderly to be sorry for you. Those accustomed to the ways of a nanny with hot gargles and a camphor rub will find Arab sympathy sadly lacking.

On arrival at the empty evacuation hospital (which was waiting for the coming attack) they did not want 'women with sniffles', but a nice doctor forbidding us to travel on in such a state put us together in a room, where we lay quietly and tried not to turn over, as any movement caused the rustling straw of our mattresses to fall out. After a few warm hours in bed, an orderly made us get up and wade vainly protesting through three feet of snow to another building to be X-rayed.

There were no nurses. A Moroccan in an overcoat, with his sidecap pulled down over his eyes and swathed in mufflers, brought a bowl of blue tepid coffee in the morning, green tepid soup for lunch, and red tepid soup for supper. His large dark thumb was always deeply immersed in the liquid. The invariable announcement of each meal '*la soupe*' seemed singularly apt.

The doctor, when he did appear, was charming and full of amusing anecdotes. Intended complaints died in one's throat before the flood of his affability. 'The first two *ambulancières* in my hospital! What a lot I have heard about you all. Admirable girls, splendid, brave devoted to their work – the whole army resounds with compliments – Tomorrow, *Mademoiselle*, I will listen to your chest.' One afternoon the door opened and in walked General Soudre, our divisional commander, whom I had not seen since that first evening in the Vosges. The doctor seeing the three stars (major-general rank) was most impressed. Everyone talked volubly for fifteen minutes, when General Soudre left to visit one of his sick officers and we fell into the jolly sleep of fever and conceit. Next day the doctor said he was *désolé* but we must be moved as, if there was an attack, even the corridors would be packed with wounded. After five days in bed we had recovered sufficiently to stand a sixty-mile drive to Besançon, where there was a large base hospital which had a women's section where we could convalesce.

The frozen canal and old citadel of Belfort looked grim as we floundered out and climbed into an ambulance already crowded with sick soldiers. We drove back along the road they had captured in November. They chattered and reminisced as we raced at 60 mph past charred ruins and dead trees, silhouetted against the snow. At the wheel sat a typical Paris taxi-driver who had been in the army about a week. Cap over one eye, cigarette hanging from mouth, he practised invectives as we swirled, dodged, and skidded past long convoys of army lorries.

In Besançon we were taken to a large building overlooking the river Doubs, and dragged our knapsacks along big stone halls to the 'reception office,' which looked like a Heath Robinson version of a railway-station waiting-room in Tartary. Some twenty

Frenchmen in various fantasy-uniforms bickered and fought in the smoky room whose dingy walls were lined by wooden benches on which slumped the figures of patients, hospital personnel, or perhaps just tramps who had wandered in for a snooze. Those who did not sleep ate. The floor was covered with nutshells, peelings, and old paper. In one corner was a sink piled high with unwashed plates; in another a big gas jet, meant for sterilizing, shot out a perpetual flare at which members of the mob could light cigarettes. Some kind of nurse, Mae West in type, and distinctly technicolour with orange hair, purple lipstick and scarlet dress, flirted with a harassed doctor who was apparently trying to sort the dying from the merely scrofulous among the tramps.

I peered around for some queue leading to a registration table, but there was no distinguishable exit from the general whirlpool, so Michele and I pushed our way to a bench and sat among the eaters of nuts and spitters of tobacco, hoping a method of formal entry into this hospital might presently reveal itself. Meanwhile, I stared around. In the middle of the floor sat a woman of the goums in full native dress. Bangles glinted, gold coins hung around her head-dress and she was veiled to the eyes with a blue cotton yashmak. They were black, bewildered eyes, like those of frightened cattle on a fair day. She had probably been sold, at the age of twelve, to the military *Bordel* of her tribe where she would lead a moderately orderly existence. (The word *Bordel* is a sordid one to attach to those bands of native women who trailed in the wake of their fighting men, but the official French designation was BMC – *Bordel Militaire de Campagne*.)

Heaped around the goumess were her bundles and belongings wrapped Arab fashion in red carpets. She sat cross-legged amidst this litter, as if waiting for some camel to trot up and take her off across the desert. A moustachioed escort fussed around, patting her on the shoulder and translating her particulars to two small hysterical Frenchmen in berets who sat at a desk in another corner writing like fury in huge registration books. No sooner had they got it all down in pages of spidery writing than it was discovered she was not entering hospital at all but being returned to Morocco and should have been taken to a different office, so all her information had to be scratched out. This was too much for the scribes; ears were boxed, and amidst furious screams and kickings she and her red bundles were carried away to some other place.

Meanwhile a fist fight started over 'three lost stretchers', and those who had slept on the benches all night awoke to gape. When the writers in the big books ceased scolding I pushed up to their table and found our rank had magical effect. There was no toad in the French Army who would not be nice to *mesdemoiselles les ambulancières.*

Michele and I were led to the top of the building where the feminine military had a ward all to themselves, with a stove where one could heat water and warm up the bully beef and macaroni which appeared twice a day, every day, all other food supplies being cut off owing to the cold. Everyone said that the farther you got from the front the worse the hospitals became because the Germans had blown up or taken every bit of medical equipment they could lay their hands on. The Americans were re-equipping the French hospitals slowly and they had begun with X-ray machines, so that no matter what the affliction we had to go *à la radio* every other day.

Apart from a pneumonia case the thirty inmates proved lively conversationalists. There was a hardy *ambulancière* of the 2nd Moroccan division, and a very excitable little creature who had worked four years with the Maquis near Calais. She was petite and elfin, bitter and dramatic. All she wanted to do was kill a few more

Germans. She had been dragged out by the Germans one night to watch the punishing of four Maquis youths. The Germans poured petrol over them and, as they burnt alive, the villagers were forced to look on. Her face while telling this story sealed its truth.

The conversation for a sick ward was truly astounding. I wished I could catch the various accents, for these women came from different provinces, and the *patois* of the Pas de Calais was as strange to my ear as that of the Midi. One troublesome topic arose every evening. They kept it bottled till then, so that hoarse participants could fall out and recover during the night's sleep. The theme of this argument was exploits of the French Regular Army versus exploits of the Maquis. The *ambulancière* protested that no one here knew how the French divisions had fought in Italy or cared about the 60,000 casualties they had sustained. The Maquis girls cried out for the unnamed Frenchmen who had been shot during the four long years of occupation, when the army enjoyed itself in the sun of Africa.

Crouching beneath a flaming barrage of words I formed my own silent opinion. The true Maquis had disappeared. The best men, who escaped being killed by the Germans, had volunteered for the regular army, slipping into units as it moved up the Rhine. Only the fellows who had done little, but could talk much, still called themselves Maquis. They could boast of great deeds without being checked, and now, in truth, they were bringing ridicule on an heroic name. The real Maquis who might have squashed them were dead or training in the new army units.

This parrot house of passionate invalids was presided over by a matron in crackling apron, whose ribald humour reminded me of the nurse in *Romeo and Juliet*. Standing, hands on hips to scold us all, she would get in her say about the *boche* and then launch a tirade on young women of today. We were cocky; we were no-goods; instead of producing children and being good cooks we spent our time in political argument, *ça alors* she had never seen when she was young!

Rubbing the ice off our window-panes we could look down on the little snow-covered roofs of Besançon, the high twisting chimneys and house fronts, a picturesque setting for an army HQ with the river and the old citadel and cobbled streets now hidden beneath the snow. It was the town of Victor Hugo, and it gave him the atmosphere for his gloomy mediaeval novels.

Beneath our window, in the hospital yard, lay a twenty-foot deep pile of tin cans which a group of lazy Indo-Chinese soldiers were trying to burn. They spent all of one afternoon throwing petrol on them and setting it alight, oblivious to the fact that tin cans do not burn especially when snow is falling.

We had no fresh food and owing to the cold no fresh air, so after a week of convalescence I was ready to go back to Alsace. Michele's X-ray had shown weak lungs so she was sorrowfully sent off to a Riviera Recuperation centre, and I had to return to the front alone.

After a long tramp to the other hospitals of Besançon I found an ambulance returning eastwards. We drove slowly, for two feet of snow covered the countryside and the roads were solid ice! The ambulance dropped me at divisional HQ, where I found Jeanne de l'Espée, who had now left our Section to command all the new women who came to the division. The other combat commands were changing from men to *ambulancières*, so there would be eighty women drivers, apart from those who worked in the clerical, radio and supply lines. Now that a comfort fund had been opened in Paris, and a certain amount of welfare could be provided for the soldiers, each battalion had two *assistantes sociales* or welfare officers. They lived in the officers' mess and were permitted to wear the regimental side caps, insignia and buttons, and had officer status. They attended to the personal affairs and troubles of the men, investigated appeals for compassionate leave and distributed comforts. They did exactly the same work as the British Red Cross welfare officers in hospitals but they had a more personal touch because they remained with one unit and had to know the men individually. When a battalion went into action the *assistantes* worked at the brigade clearing stations, and as the wounded came in they could speak to each man, write letters, fulfil any possible request, and notify the next of kin if they died. This system gave maximum attention to the men in a simple and prompt manner.

Jeanne de l'Espée, who now had over a hundred girls under her command, was frenziedly sorting and packing cases of army shoes and socks. 'Gone are the carefree days at the front,' she said, 'how I miss you all, *mes petits choux*.'

I spent one night at Dannemarie. Taking a mug of water up to bed to drink in the morning I found, on peering out of my flea-bag, that it had frozen solid. It was 20 degrees below zero. 'How does one make war in this?'

'You'll soon see,' said Jeanne. 'You leave for Mulhouse this afternoon. A terrible attack has just started.'

24

Battle of Colmar – Snow

I found the whole medical company installed in a college in Mulhouse. The ambulances were parked in the courtyard, with a foot of snow on their roofs. The onerous task of running the engines every two hours at night had been taken over by a soldier, so the girls obtained a good night's sleep on the stretchers which they had spread on the classroom floors. I had a new co-driver, Lucette Lecoq, who had come to us in January. She was twenty-three and very lovely, with eyes of a curious light brown flecked with gold and green. I was fascinated by her. I have never known anyone more watchful of other people's happiness, more attractively unselfish.

On 20 January, with the temperature at 19 degrees below zero, the 1st French Army launched a heavy attack in three feet of snow. This date was relentlessly set, because captured German plans revealed the enemy's intention of attacking on January 30th. We had to forestall their long-deferred offensive to regain the Alsace plain, which we had expected ever since the Ardennes thrust. For over a month our division had waited in the snow, fidgety at the idea of what any moment might bring. And I think we all had a rather weak feeling in the stomach at the thought of six or seven Panzer divisions launching thunderously into a plain which gave every advantage to armour.

The soldiers now knew that General Eisenhower had considered Alsace was untenable on account of the big German pocket dug in around Colmar. But he had been confronted by the cry of the French generals: 'We cannot give back Strasbourg or Mulhouse or one foot of French soil. No civilians can again be abandoned. We know what happens to our people when the Germans retake a town.'

So they made terms. General de Lattre had accepted the responsibility and we had hung on, shivering and waiting, in the icy discomfort of snow-covered Alsatian villages. De Lattre had given an assurance to his nation that the Germans would not get through unless the entire French Army were annihilated, and there was not a soldier who did not approve the general's courage.

But personally, I could not enthuse at the prospect of annihilation. The blossoms of cowardice, whose seeds had been sown by the freezing rain of the Vosges, now flowered. Just as the sun calls plants to life, so the hidden seeds of fear, lurking deep in human nature, can be brought forth by sheer physical discomfort. Fear has little relationship to danger; it is the product of winter, grey skies, and cold winds. It takes a month of brooding in wet boots to teach you the real thing. The French were blue with cold but seemed to mind it less than I did. But frost gave us all a secret desire not to be wounded, because everything *hurt* so. It even hurt to pick up a spanner and investigate the petrol-filter.

For over two months not a day had passed without the sound of artillery plastering each other across the Rhine. Waking in the night to that constant boom I used to hope the roar would not suddenly increase to the thunder which would mean a German offensive had begun.

It was a relief when the waiting ended and the French themselves attacked, with violence and brilliance. The enemy, believing it impossible to launch forth in such weather, were unprepared, but fought back like tigers and sent for reinforcements. Our division, and three North African Infantry divisions, forming the 1st Army Corps under General Béthouart, attacked from the south while General Monsabert's 2nd Army Corps joined the attack from the north. The 1st French Army had now swollen to 10 divisions, of which seven were concentrated on the Colmar pocket, together with two American divisions which General Devers had incorporated in the command of de Lattre. On 29 January, after ten days of desperate fighting, General Revers put the whole 21st American Army Corps (consisting of 28th, 75th and 3rd infantry divisions) of General Milburn under the command of General de Lattre. This placing of an American corps under the French commander not only showed the confidence felt by Eisenhower in General de Lattre, it also turned the tide when the French troops were nearing exhaustion.

Those are the facts of the Colmar campaign as recorded, perhaps, in some military text book. The historian may call it a hard campaign, and mention that it was well planned against an enemy dug-in to a fine position ... just a few dull words ... But to us who lived through it, how different!

The 1st Armoured Division attacked from the city of Mulhouse with the 9th Colonial Division and the 4th Moroccan Division. After seven days of terrific fighting in blinding snowstorms the Germans still held those northern suburbs of Mulhouse. Casualties came pouring in. The stretcher-bearers waded knee-deep in snow, gasping with the weight of their loads, lifting stretchers over fallen trees, losing their own feet on mines. The 9th Division fought beside us and shared aid posts. They immediately lost two regimental doctors, and one of their *ambulancières*, a girl called Denise Ferrier, was killed by a shell-burst on the first morning of the attack. Three days later Isabelle Boraud was wounded beside her ambulance and had to have her leg amputated above the knee before she could be evacuated.

There was something fantastic and ghostly about this winter battle. Our tanks, painted white, crunched across the snow, rolling like phantoms past the dark woods or disappearing against white fields. White jeeps, ludicrously resembling ice-cream carts, skidded to and fro with shouting, blue-faced liaison officers, and the infantry, wearing white cotton gowns over greatcoats and tin hats that resembled large white puff balls, crept through the snow, lay in it, froze in it, died in it.

Our ambulances ran to and from the brigade operating station established in the Mulhouse schoolhouse and the battle raging in what had been neat industrial suburbs. We could see the far-off Vosges cloaked in mist and storm, while around us the landscape remained white and black and scarlet – for wherever men had been there was blood, frozen tracks of rubies that glinted in the snow and wide red paths leading into the roofless villas that were our aid posts.

'*Cité*' is the French name for a small garden city. We fought through *Cité* Anna, *Cité* St. Barbe, *Cité* Therese ... innocent names for a desolation of little smashed homes, in whose ruins our doctors kept small fires going so that their fingers should not grow too numb to dress wounds. We melted cans of snow – there being no water – and helped as best we could the stretcher parties, who were having heavy casualties themselves as they dragged the wounded through the snow.

There was something ludicrous about having a tank battle in a garden suburb. As our Shermans crept along the avenues, playing their horrible hide-and-seek with the greater, stronger German tanks, zouave infantry took house after house in desperate fighting.

One January dawn I watched an attack on the village of Wittenheim. All night long our tank crews had warmed their engines every two hours, but nevertheless when morning came three Shermans had been put out of action by the cold and their commanders were hopping mad. One of them, a Sergeant Major Olivares, asked to accompany the attack on foot and ran along shouting: 'Those . . . saw me running at Bir Hakeim but I'll see them run yet. . .' He gave directions to the creeping tanks until one of them skidded and as a bank of snow gave way, slipped into the ditch pinning Olivares by the ankle. Seeing a tank had stuck the enemy opened up with machine-gun and mortar fire. Olivares continued to give what directions he could while a message was sent back for medical aid.

Wounded were calling for help in all directions and the only doctor available was a young intern called Pariante of the Colonial Infantry. He reached Olivares as the enemy, who had the trapped tank well sighted, launched a hail of mortars. The two wretched stretcher-bearers commandeered on the way prostrated themselves in the ditch but by lying head downwards in the snow Pariante found he could just reach the trapped foot. He gave a morphine injection, put on a tourniquet and proceeded to amputate. It took twenty minutes. During all this time Olivares continued to give directions to the tank that held him, and it was not until he arrived at the post that he realized that his foot had been taken off. Then he asked for his captain and said sadly: 'I am afraid it's goodbye to the squadron.' Pariante himself seemed slightly shaken saying: 'I do hope I made a good job? It is difficult to do one's first amputation while hanging upside down.'

Now the sandbags on our ambulance floors which had always seemed such a nuisance, were carefully arranged to guard our legs for every day the wheels of vehicles were letting off mines by the

'Now Girls!' cartoon by Anita.

Members of the Free French Forces who accompanied the Mechanized Transport Corps (MTC) on the *Stirling Castle* leave 'in little boats.'

Betty ♡ me seeing Africa

Betty and Anita see Africa.

Sudie   Betty   Self.

March 1941.

Christmas day 1940.

Christmas day 1944 (Anita front centre).

The women of the MTC get issued with tropical kit.

Betty under — self on top

Anita and Betty servicing an engine.

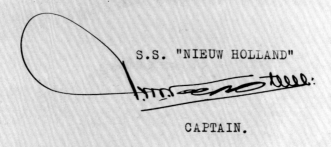

```
           OUR VERY BEST WISHES TO THE
        BRAVE GIRLS OF THE M.T.C. ON
        ARRIVAL AT SUEZ ON MARCH 3RD 1941.

        MAY THEIR LUCK AND JOYS BE
                    AS DEEP AS THE OCEAN,
        THEIR WORK AND TROUBLES
                    AS LIGHT AS ITS FOAM.


                        S.S. "NIEUW HOLLAND"


                        CAPTAIN.
```

'To the brave girls of the MTC' the captain of the *Nieuw Holland* offers a warm welcome.

Anita riding a camel in Palmyra.

'And what in the world … is as perfect as a horse' – Anita takes a break from camel riding.

charles Johnson Serge Muanda Olya George Patsy

Patsy O'Kane and George Jellicoe get married.

Convoy of our ambulances

Convoy of MTC ambulances.

General Alex at his H. Q.
Lake Bolsano
July 21 1944

General 'Alex' in a moment of contemplation.

Naples

Anita's cousin, Winston
Churchill, in Naples.

US

Anita and friends in a rare moment of calm.

Anita with her ambulance.

Jeanne de l'Espée and Solange.

Women of the 1st Armoured Division.

Cernay (note wall sprayed with bullet holes).

Anita and soldiers posing with a tank.

The first tank to enter Mulhouse and reach the Rhine, 21 November 1944.

Group photo with locals (unknown location).

The Leqoc's ambulance when recovered.

Lucette Leqoc, who was killed with her sister Odette whilst driving the ambulance, 24 April 1945.

Anita in Germany – 'Now the endless miles of ruins were impressive, strange and horrible.'

Posing with a tank in front of rubble – Anita was skilled at finding levity in the most difficult surroundings.

How she hated this hat.

Anita had the reputation of being '*une anglaise formidable* … who could drive anything on wheels.'

Anita at Germersheim with paintings of allied tanks showing their weaknesses.

Anita and Colonel Peter Wilson at Potsdam.

Genny and Anita wearing their *Croix de guerre*.

July 23 1945

BERLIN W 8, DEN
REICHSKANZLEI

DER FÜHRER UND KANZLER DES DEUTSCHEN REICHES
ADJUTANTUR

Darling Ma & Jack —— On the 19th I arrived in Berlin & stayed four nights with the 11th Hussars — saw their parade up Unter den Linden on Sat & yesterday Winston had me to lunch with him at Potsdam —— Mary was there - charming - & I sat between himself & Anthony Eden —— they talked Conference shop —— hordes of Germans being turned out of Czechoslovakia without notice —— chaos sizzling in fact —— food or nat out in the sun & dined then staff men —— had a talk with F.M. Alex —— he was so nice & made kind remarks about my decorations —— Now I am with my French armoured car with 3ieme Chasseurs —— all rather irregular as only elements of our Div. are here yet —— they are around Treves —— Berlin is grim & unbelievable —— Russians duty beyond words — riding about in convoys of hay carts —— Don't you like my note paper scrounged from Chancellerie? —— Love Nitu

Letter home on Hitler's notepaper, given to Anita by a Russian officer at the Reich Chancellery as a trophy after the fall of Berlin.

roadside; and occasionally the Germans, themselves in frantic retreat, ran through a field and were blown up by their own contraptions. Legless German soldiers, abandoned by their comrades, lay calling for help while our own sappers advancing cautiously with detonators had terrifying casualties. There was an inhuman horror about the explosive cobweb which had been woven into the countryside. In all directions, men advancing through the fields were suddenly blown up in a fountain of scarlet snow and their comrades would drag them back, themselves sinking above the knees at every step.

Lieutenant Husser, our glum zouave doctor, shed his bad temper after he had spent five or six nights without sleep, without taking his clothes off and, if possible, without shaving. Now that water shortage made an inch-long beard inevitable he seemed really happy. He bullied his exhausted frightened native stretcher-bearers till they were ready to weep, and imposed a tyrannical discipline in the dingy cellars where, by the light of an oil lamp, he dressed wound after wound. One afternoon, during a pause in the fighting, Husser wandered out to look at a field from which the enemy had been driven. A German had stepped on a mine in the middle of the field and since morning had lain with one foot off calling for help. The stretcher parties looked and turned away, for no one dared take a heavy risk to his own legs to help a German. When Husser decided to go, and called for volunteers to follow him with a stretcher no one answered. So he chose two Arabs and showed them how to walk in his tracks across the snow. They followed at a distance, with much trepidation, carefully fitting their large feet into the doctor's track; after Husser had given morphia they brought the German back.

'Why did you do it?' I asked, for we all feared losing a doctor. Hands in pockets and swathed with mufflers, he looked out from under that steel helmet, even less becoming to him than to others, and answered: 'The reason was pity.'

Outside *Cité* Anna stood a queer, pretentious chateau with the name Hohrenderhubel, which became the object of a bloody battle. Perhaps it had been the home of some local industrial magnate who put his fortune into this oriental fantasy of minarets. Hideous stone lions guarding its entrance were blown off their pedestals as shell after shell landed around the front door. After several days of fighting, the chateau was captured and Husser established his post in the ruined drawing-room.

It was a bad moment for the stretcher parties. Owing to the terrain the half-track ambulance could not be used. Wounded had to be carried three kilometres, lifted through a tangle of smashed trees, and the bearers could scarcely drag their loads through some of the snow drifts. Thirty or forty zouaves a day lost their legs in the blackened woods around this chateau. It seemed that every wood, hedge, and field resounded with the mixed cries of French and German wounded. No ambulances could approach the Chateau Hohrenderhubel, but from a distance we could see that the enemy were concentrating their fire on the building. A shell exploded in the centre of Husser's tapestried drawing-room. By a miracle no one was wounded, but the blast knocked out several already stupefied medicos and bearers, and the wounded quietly fainted on their stretchers, Husser himself, in his dirty little red zouave cap was, like the others, whitened with fallen plaster. He counted his crew, counted the wounded, counted the scattered surgical instruments, and when the zouave commanding officer walked into the debris, Husser greeted him with a wide grin:

'Come to inspect the post, sir?' It took a lot to amuse that doctor.

On 1 February, when we were still outside *Cité* Anna, the thaw began. Our zouaves had seventy men wounded that day, fifty of whom had their left legs amputated. As the Germans retreated the nightmare of mines increased.

Our company surgeons cried out as the stretchers were carried in, 'What! not another left leg! Is it possible?' The eyes of our chief surgeon, Captain Benishu, had become mere slits from the strain. *'Jambe gauche amputée – Jambe gauche amputée,'* scribbled Mme Kleber on the docket tied to each stretcher.

While Husser worked inside the shaking walls of his chateau, we waited with the ambulances at a post which had been established in the least damaged of a group of small houses. The top floor had been blown off but the ground storey had two rooms intact, except for windows. We stuffed the frames with mattresses and sacks to keep the wind out. It was better to tend the wounded by a lamp than have them freeze while the clothes were cut from them.

Occasionally faces would peep like frightened mice from the cellar door, and one realized that civilians still existed in these shattered homes.

The regimental padres worked with our doctors, cutting away clothing from around wounds and administering morphia. It was good to have priests there, men with kindly bearded faces and gentle hands. The courage of a priest has a certain quality; he leaves no wife or child; death is almost the aim of his life – in battle the priest comes into his own.

While the stretcher parties carried their loads up the little path of trampled crimson ice that led to every post, we waited ready with hot tea and the merciful needle, and then drove off our loaded ambulances, before shock had worn off and pain begun.

Jeanne de l'Espée insisted that the *ambulancières* should not neglect their make-up even in battle and men did give a sort of gasp of relief when they saw us. We would go up to the waiting stretchers, kneel on the floor and try to get a hot drink between their chattering teeth, and reassure them. I felt, at the time, that no words of mine would ever matter more to a human being and although we were there as workers, not as comforters, I am sure we fulfilled a psychological need. It gave one a kind of conceit to know one mattered so much and to so many.

Although our nights were bound to be disturbed by calls, we nevertheless observed the formality of saying good-night. Doctor, soldiers, ambulance girls, and priest all snuggled in the straw, then ... *'Bonsoir, mon père'*; *'Bonsoir, mes enfants'* and someone blew out the lamp. It was peaceful lying there, watching the frosty stars through the sacking that flapped in the window-frame, while the far-off thump of shells indicated the German retreat.

Our last casualty was a sapper whose leg was blown off as he walked back with eight German prisoners in front of him. They had long sticks and prodded prudently as they went while their captor followed last of all keeping to their tracks. Suddenly his weight let off a Schu-mine. The Germans turned and picked him up. We saw them walking up the road with the bleeding Frenchman in their arms, just as we had seen so many weary French bearers gaspingly carry the German wounded. This sapper kept saying, 'I can't understand it. I didn't think this would happen to *me* somehow – not to *me*,' Everyone felt that – such things could happen to others but never to the person called Me.

In February, the softening ground allowed graves to be dug, and the dead were gathered on carts. At one turning we met three shire-horses dragging one of those wide platform waggons used for transporting tree trunks. And its load looked strangely like trees, for the hundred or more dead Germans were frozen stiff in every attitude, their arms, held out like branches, showed how they had been killed in movement; but their faces, crystallized by the cold, had the peace of all dead faces.

The little old farmer, trying to control the plunging horses, waved to us merrily. His apple face was wreathed in smiles. 'Haven't I a funny load!' he shouted.

At the schoolhouse, buzzing with rumours, we heard that Colmar had been taken from the north. The American 109th Infantry Regiment were ahead of the French 5th Armoured Division and, as the town surrendered, their commanding officer courteously sent a message:

'*Messieurs les Français*. To you the honour. We wish to follow French soldiers into Colmar.'

Most of the wounded had been evacuated to the big base hospitals outside Mulhouse and our worn-out doctors were sleeping in the classroom next us. We supped gaily and agreed to go to a singing rehearsal for a Mass for our dead. With undying energy the *ambulancières* practised till ten that night. Then we went to bed, arranging our stretchers in rows on the floor. Not only were we tired after ten days of action, but our shoulders ached from all the stretcher lifting. We took it for granted that the division was pulling out for a short rest but the rest only lasted four hours.

25

Battle of Colmar – Thaw

At two in the morning orders arrived saying we must leave in an hour. Lucette, who had the capacity of rising up from sleep at any hour in nursery spirits, ran along the corridors shouting:

'*Allons! Allons – à l'attaque!*'

At four a.m. the advanced post, consisting of eight ambulances, two doctors and a dozen stretcher-bearers moved off into the black drizzle. A grey dawn found us in Kingersheim, a village which our combat command had fought over during the last week. German tanks were burning by the roadside and every house was a blackened shell; dead dogs and dead Germans made a foul stench.

For ten days the Germans had held fast in hard frost. Now for another ten days they were to dribble away with the melting snow.

Our division moved out of Mulhouse to follow the retreating enemy towards Colmar and join up with the two northern corps.

We established our advanced post in Kingersheim's wrecked *Mairie*, amidst scattered papers and records. Underneath the house in a large dank cellar there were mattresses. Evidently the villagers had carried their bedding to the safest place and slept there when the fighting began. Not liking the look or smell of what the orderlies called *une très jolie cave*, I preferred to make coffee on the ambulance step with a flickering spirit lamp under my tin mug of water. This activity was interrupted by the whistle of nearby shells which caused me to hurry cellarwards leaving the alcohol lamp alight and untended. Presently, overcome with desire for coffee, I returned and, while I mixed the brew, a little man who must have been the last civilian left in the village emerged from some wreckage and asked:

'Have you come to fetch the dead?' Cold, sleepy, and breakfastless I answered curtly, 'No; we are *en pleine attaque.*' He said timidly, 'My wife and two daughters were killed eight days ago in the kitchen — I cannot bury them in the hard ground — A soldier said someone would come and fetch the bodies. I thought perhaps, *Mademoiselle*, it was you.' Not until the battle was over did I realize how callous I had been.

At ten our attack began with a thunderous artillery barrage that lasted perhaps an hour. How comforting it was to the soldiers, that boom of guns filling the sky overhead with the lovely fluttering laughter of our shells. We stood gaping at the low grey clouds until it was our turn to drive forward some four miles into another industrial suburb of neat villas with little gardens and white fences. The fences had been ironed out by passing tanks and dead Germans lay stretched on the fancy flower-beds which melting snow revealed. The inhabitants had either fled or been cowering in cellars for weeks.

One old woman climbed up from the cellar of the house and seemed delighted to find French troops. She laid out our tinned food on plates and we started a meal with a sapper officer who told us we were closing in nicely on the German pocket and ordered us down to the cellar where he lectured us on taking needless chances when a village was being *arrosé* (descriptive French term meaning 'sprinkled' as from a watering can).

Just then an orderly panted up, with a call from Husser. We drove forward to the end of the village where, for the first time, I had the chance to see a tank battle at close quarters. While we waited for the wounded to be carried into some ruins, I watched the tanks nosing, like angry dinosaurs, around the wood. Our beautiful white Shermans had lost their paint in a fortnight's fighting, but as the earth returned to brown, their mud-caked armour did not need new camouflage. Now they battled on in disreputable array like old harpies in some street brawl, tousled and smudged!

In the field between us and the wood jeeps hurried about, while zouaves and sappers poked about for mines, and shells sent up fountains of mud. It was tremendously exciting to watch the deliberation of heavy armour in action, and I felt a curious elation at not being afraid; I wondered if my nerves were getting stronger or if explosives were losing their force.

As we lifted the first stretcher into the ambulance, the shells fell nearer, bursting in the road a few feet from us with an acrid smell. The Algerians disappeared like rabbits into the ditch. One moment they were helping, the next we could not even see the tops of their helmets. Young Guillot, the intern, came out with the fourth stretcher and told us to drive the long flat mile to Wittenheim as fast as we could for the Germans were watching from the wood beside the road.

As dusk fell we returned to Husser's post. The fighting was still so hard we had to wait well back from the dressing-post. When there were wounded some soldier would be sent back with a slip of paper describing where they lay, and Guillot would go out with the half-track to pick them up. Hours passed and it was whispered 'Guillot is lost in the German lines'. But at midnight he reappeared with a full load of blood-soaked bodies whom Husser dressed in the dark half-track. We could not even use an electric torch in vehicles which were in view of the Germans. Fumbling in the dark we transferred the stretchers into our ambulance. At the front we did the actual lifting of stretchers ourselves for the bearers always seemed so rough.

Driving back to Mulhouse with our load took us two hours to cover eight miles as it was pitch black, with heavy fog, no moon, no lights. The burning church of Wittenheim alone guided us. On the long stretch of road where we were supposed to drive fast the fog forced us to a walking pace. Many times we had to stop and search the road for the big shell holes we had noticed by daylight and we called loudly at each house hoping to make certain of the way, but our only answer was the crash of burning beams. And nothing could have been weirder than the vision of Wittenheim church with its roof a skeleton of golden timbers; while on the altar flames danced like living devils. At last we reached the three burnt tanks that marked the advanced post at Kingersheim and awoke the doctors who checked our silent wounded in their wet, reddening blankets, and reckoned they could stand another four miles back to the company. The fog was now so thick that twice we took a wrong road. No one who has not driven wounded, without lights on a pitch-black night, and got lost near the enemy can imagine the agonizing responsibility.

Husser's post advanced to the outskirts of Ensisheim, a town of factories where the Germans were fighting like wild cats, and painting up on the factory walls, 'We will never surrender.'

Now we could hear the rumble of our own artillery in the north, as we closed in, slowly cutting the pocket in two. We found Husser and Guillot working in a cellar by candle-light, where we sat listening to the shells, fearing our ambulances would be hit and that we should not be able to evacuate the wounded. This happened to Jeanine André who was working with her brother's armoured car squadron down the road. A direct hit landed on the house roof and Jeanine ran out, covered with plaster, to find one of her wheels smashed. She and her companion Maxime (the daughter of Agnes Borea, the Paris dressmaker) changed the wheel hectically while the German snipers courteously withheld their fire!

I was busy making coffee by the light of the single candle when our Arab stretcher-party, for some reason, carried in the body of a young zouave officer who we all knew. Husser, who was sitting bolt upright, fast asleep against the wall woke with distress to see his friend lying at his feet – for this man's wife had just lost her baby in North Africa. The zouave must have been killed instantly for the back of his head had been blown off, but the face remained intact – a stiff white mask with the expression of peace peculiar to the dead.

Lucette's lovely face shone white and madonna-like in the candlelight. The helmet made her look ridiculously childish as she stared down and said gently:

'I also knew his wife. Death always comes at just the wrong moment, doesn't it?' We sat silent in the half-dark thinking of that woman in Algiers already mourning her child.

Suddenly the shelling increased and the orderlies began to fidget.

Husser woke up: 'Listen *mon vieux*,' he said to the nearest stretcher-bearer. 'Don't be scared. If one of those prunes comes down directly over you it has got a roof to penetrate, then a floor, then your steel helmet and then your skull, and I'm wondering if that wouldn't be hardest of all.'

Then a burst of machine-gun fire sounded in the street outside; compared to the cannon it was like a canary twittering in a parrot house. I was still tone-deaf to different kinds of firearms but Husser exclaimed: 'That sounds German?' We heard French voices shouting for a tank and then a cannon roared once only. Husser went out and brought back two highly excited zouave soldiers, slightly wounded but voluble as only Frenchmen can be, and this was their tale.

They were searching house after house and as they approached the door of a villa next door several Germans opened fire from a window and hit them both in the legs. They had flung themselves down behind the low garden wall and shouted to their comrades to fetch a tank. They were in great spirits at refusing to be rescued, and giving successful directions. When their comrades returned with the tank they shouted to the Germans to surrender, but they refused. The tank rolled forward, machine-gun bullets pattering uselessly against its hide, the cannon lowered and blew the house to pieces from the garden gate and *that* was the noise! It was *épatant* they said, the three *boches* were blown out through the roof. We drove these two back to Mulhouse, just as Ensisheim was being taken. There were long processions of German prisoners slogging into the city and, over-stimulated by morphia, our wounded addressed some pretty language out of the windows. Then: '*Pardon! Mademoiselle*, that was a bit strong but we are just a little pleased with ourselves – you know.' We knew!

That night Ensisheim fell and our 3rd Chasseurs armoured cars met the Americans between Colmar and Cernay. We learnt this in the cellar at Kingersheim when an officer stumbled in to ask who we were, where he was, and the way to the front. No one knew, because the front had surged forward into the arms of the 5th Armoured Division. Only a small surrounded group of fanatical Germans fought on to the last in what was left of that thorn in the side of the French Army – the Colmar pocket.

On the next night the Americans astounded General de Lattre by attacking at night by *artificial moonlight*! They brought up some amusing great gadgets that threw light up on the low clouds reflecting down on the enemy and leaving themselves in darkness. The Germans moved back and blew their last bridge at Chalompey, leaving about half a division strewn through the Harth Forest to be captured in bits and pieces. Little parties stood in the road with their hands up, and others stepped on their own mines.

In a few days the Forest had been cleared, and long weary trails of German prisoners marched expressionless through Mulhouse streets. '*L'Alsace c'est fini,*' said the soldiers excitedly. 'Can you believe it! No more *boches* in France! Next time we fight will be on German soil?'

On 9 February, just three weeks after the first attack in the snow, the Colmar campaign was over. The ambulances were now ordered to reassemble at HQ in Mulhouse. We drove back through the Harth Forest and suddenly realized birds were singing in the wet woods and a faint feeling of budding filled the air. There was blue sky and sunshine, the snow had gone, and the face of the earth had changed. It was quiet. The sound of guns, that had not ceased for three months, died away with the first breath of Spring.

26

Aftermath

Of the fifty gleaming white tanks of the 2nd Cuirassiers who had sailed proud as brides into battle three weeks before, only fourteen dishevelled, mud-plastered, dented old monsters rattled back to the repair depot.

This meant a break. Whatever happened on the rest of the front we could not move for a month or more. So we settled down in Mulhouse and watched the town coming slowly back to life. Throngs of civilians returned from the country and we could walk about freely in the sunshine.

We still lived in the schoolhouse, where there were no washing facilities and, owing to war damage and accommodation shortage, we were unlikely to get better billets. It was irritating to get back, weary, dirty and tired, and not have a decent place in which to relax. We had two rooms in which thirty stretchers were spread on the floor and there we slept and ate, and waited.

Apart from having to be on call our life was easy. We slept with blankets over our heads till nine, when '*la brave* Mme Kleber' would crawl angrily off her stretcher and go clumping downstairs to fetch a petrol-can of hot water, which was all the cook-house contributed to our breakfast. This was not as brutal as it sounds, for we had packets of Nescafé. We got up, dressed, and arranged our blankets into the semblance of armchairs. When the room was brushed and tidied we could go out and stand in a queue on the stairs for the one water-tap in the building, but we only had to share it with the doctors.

Now that we had, as Captain Dautany who commanded the company put it, 'returned to civilization,' the floor lavatories were to be reserved for *ambulancières* and medical officers. 'Out of bounds' notices were put up and a native orderly appeared with pail and mop to clean up. The doctors, supervising this procedure, applauded, '*Bravo, mon garçon* – go to it.' The orderly grinned conceitedly and wielded his mop with such zeal that, within five minutes, he had somehow smashed the whole lavatorial system and floods of water deluged the building.

Owing to every road being studded with mines along the verge, occasional lorries loaded with horribly wounded soldiers and civilians still came in, and we were all lectured daily on the importance of driving in the middle of the road, for no corner of the Harth Forest would be safe for months. One morning a lorry, driving evacuees back to their homes, swerved a few inches off the edge of the road just outside the city and touched a mine. The soldier driving was killed and the passengers riddled with shrapnel. A passing truck stopped and the driver filled his vehicle with straw which made a rough mattress for the dying evacuees. He drove on into the town until he saw the Red Cross placard outside our yard.

I happened to be hanging out of the window admiring the green plane tree buds bursting open in the new spring warmth, when the truck drove in and backed to the doorway as if to deposit a load of coal. We all ran out, stretchers were fetched and the doctors tried to sort that heap of bodies in the red straw where men, women and children lay in revolting confusion. It is curious how the tidy shelving of wounded bodies on stretchers takes away from the horror of such a sight.

The spahis who took Geubwiller found one of our girls who had been captured in the Harth Forest, lying in hospital there. She had been burnt when the ambulance was hit. The Germans who caught her running down the road had treated her moderately well according to present day standards, that is they put her in hospital, interrogated her almost daily, and slapped her face when she gave stupid answers. Apart from bruises she seemed fairly fit, and at this period of the war merely hitting a sick girl could be reckoned as decent treatment. As she was nineteen years old and had only joined the combat command ten days before getting captured, she knew nothing about numbers of tanks or guns, but she took pleasure in spinning tales which she hoped were not accurate. As the French troops closed in around Geubwiller, the nuns in the hospital secretly gave her injections which produced a high fever so that she could not be evacuated to Germany with the other patients. When the spahis entered the town she ran out barefoot to hug them.

The Germans were usually decent to the people they caught in uniform, that is they merely slapped them. It was a very different story with civilians. At the Concentration camp near Strasbourg I heard that four English WAAF officers had been drugged and cremated because they were dropped by parachute on a special mission and caught in civilian clothes. It seemed unbelievable that, knowing what we did about the Germans, they had not carried poison. Although it sounds strange to say it, they were lucky to have been spared worse torture. Such are the charming truths of twentieth-century Europe.

As they regrouped, our friends of the regiments wandered in to see us. One afternoon, Jean, a twenty-two-year-old lieutenant of the 2nd Cuirassiers, came in ashen-faced to tell us that morning his tank had run onto a mine in the forest which blew its track off.

He went back to the repair company leaving the rest of the crew sitting about waiting. Seeing friends down a side road, they ran forgetfully on to the grass verge and touched off another mine. The cannon loader, aged eighteen, had both legs blown off and the others were severely injured. Jean had just brought them in to be operated on downstairs and in the meantime he came to unload his distress to us. 'Stupid, so stupid,' he kept saying; 'they were well trained in the tank – how could they have been so thoughtless.'

It was Jean who drove us out in his jeep to see Colmar, the little town whose name had been a legend with us ever since that November afternoon when we heard that Colmar had been taken and then 'not quite'. Now it seemed strangely exciting to drive there in an hour and a half, making detours at the blown bridges and speeding along the flat plain. Happily the exquisite mediaeval core of Colmar had escaped destruction. We drove through the outer ring of ruined modern suburbs and spent a happy hour *faisant du tourism* around the central square with its cathedral and tiled fifteenth-century *Mairie* and tiny streets of old-timbered houses that were miraculously intact. In Mulhouse there was nothing of beauty or interest. Our only outings were to the public baths, where we could get a much-needed scrub for a shilling. There was nothing to see but mile-long processions of German prisoners; nowhere to sit or get a cup of tea; nothing in the shops to buy (except paper flags!), and as there was no electricity or hot water, the hairdressers would not shampoo unless bribed with bully beef.

We found the public baths full of Americans. As we sat on benches waiting our turn, thinking I was French, they began whispering 'Look! dames!—' (really the American soldier is dame-crazy!) 'Dames in our boots, our socks . . .' After twenty minutes of this I asked them in English what *they* were, and why

they wore *our* sort of trousers. They gaped and said, 'We're the
artillery lent to the French Army for that attack.' Remembering
the good steady thunder, our hearts warmed, but we teased
them: 'How nice it was to hear the noise you made back there.
While we work a hundred yards from the Germans, it is
delightful to know the chaps in the rear are busy too.' Puzzled
they shook their heads. 'Dames' it couldn't seem to register –
'dames in pants . . .'

Soon after this we were allowed skirts *'pour se promener en ville,'*
and as the spahis as well as our own division were re-forming
around Mulhouse, a vague social life began. The French were so
civilized. They cared for the graceful forms of life. No meal began
without a formal recital of the menu by the *Popotier* (messing
officer) – followed by *'Bon appétit! Nobles Invités! Bon appétit! Mon
lieutenant, etc, etc.'* Then the traditional shout, *'Et par St. George, Vive
la Cavalerie!'* or in our case, *'Par St. Christophe Vive les Ambulancières!'*

The discipline imposed upon us was that of soldiers, not school-
girls. As for being 'improperly dressed', no girl wearing the
divisional emblem (a tank with the cross of St. Louis) would have
dreamt of appearing in public unless in her smartest, correct turn-
out. Once in Mulhouse we saw a girl in uniform, capless and
tieless, wearing our company badge. My nineteen-year companion,
swollen like a dowager duchess with righteous indignation,
requested her to remove emblems to which she had no right,
ending up with a tirade about *l'honneur de l'armée française,* which
would have done credit to Fénelon. No one thought it 'not nice'
for men friends to roll in and sit on our bedding at all hours. I
don't think they knew what 'not quite nice' meant. They only
knew what was good or bad taste.

The rigid morality of these French girls was astounding after
the Middle East. The only people I ever saw intoxicated in the

French Army were occasional non-Mohamedan Arabs, who had no capacity whatever for wine, and they would be led off quickly before knives came out. The girls told me, wide-eyed, that in Oran they had seen open lorries of American soldiers embracing women in uniform. They took it for granted that the women were military prostitutes.

The *Bains Publics* closed for lack of coal, and as far as I could make out there was no such thing as a hot bath in all France. I teased the girls because they did not care about comfort so long as they could make up in front of a mirror. Mimi, who had been cited for a *Croix de guerre* for standing out, like a little elf in her big helmet, directing military traffic at a cross road under heavy shell fire, answered heatedly: 'But it's perfectly logical; if you want to be happy you must catch a loving husband by dressing up and looking nice.'

'Or else you must be able to cook well,' said the prosaic Mme Kleber.

Soon after the Colmar campaign the French held a big parade in Mulhouse. Mme Kleber dragged me with her to see 'dozens of generals strutting like peacocks with the mayor'. In fact, we saw de Gaulle and Béthouart and our divisional commander, Soudre, reviewing what was left of our armoured vehicles, which were dripping with new green paint. The zouaves and spahis infantry made a fine showing but they were less stared at than staring, for the route was all lined by pretty girls in traditional peasant costume who had come out to smile and wave at the conquering heroes. The full skirt with ribboned bodice and wide black taffeta ribbon head-dress of Alsace made the plainest girl look a beauty, and there were some fine rosy-cheeked specimens to cheer the soldiers' hearts that day.

Far from having become cynical at military display, Mme Kleber grew enthusiastic *'Les petits soldats'* she cried; *'ah, les braves gosses* it is good for them to be applauded. See their eyes roll!'

A few days later we were ordered to turn out 'in full dress'. That meant we ironed our skirts carefully and curled our hair the night before. Then, in white gloves and white socks, we marched through Mulhouse to form a line behind Jeanne de l'Espée while she was decorated by General Soudre with the *Croix de guerre avec palme*. Her citations of 1918, 1942, and the last for rescuing wounded parachutists in the Vosges, were read out loud, trumpets blew, the good folk of Mulhouse who had collected to watch, clapped enthusiastically. General Soudre had to pin the cross on her and kiss her on both cheeks, to her delight and his embarrassment.

We marched away with great pride in our leader and the general sent his ADC with a kind message to say he liked the way we kept in step and also the manner in which we had managed to tan our legs to the same shade. We laughed. Evidently the general had been puzzled, he did not know we all painted our legs from the same bottle of artificial *sunburn*.

Conscription brought fresh French recruits. The army that had sailed from North Africa could gradually reduce its native element, but the infiltration was slow because there were neither barracks, uniforms, or training equipment for the young men who were called up. The armoured divisions naturally contained a higher percentage of Frenchmen than the colonial infantry divisions. In the mechanized regiments all personnel was French except for a few 'pourers of petrol'. The zouaves had French officers and NCOs but the men were thirty per cent Arab. The farther you got from the fighting zone the worse impression you received of the French Army. Base troops were ghastly Senegalese while the flower of the nation was at the front.

Our doctors were too busy to deal firmly with the native orderlies allotted to this company. If there was a disagreeable mission, the regimental doctors usually tried to inspire the

rudiments of heroic action into their stretcher-parties by asking
for volunteers. The natives usually stood like a row of unhappy
children and no hands went up. Then the intern would select two
or three with words of encouragement and they would follow
him out to find some wounded man and carry him back gently
and submissively. They never disobeyed, they just could not help
showing how they hated it. After all it was not their war. They
might have been happily washing bottles back in Oran.

When I complained that the dreariness of our life was entirely
caused by the dirty, thieving, undisciplined Arab element of the
medical company, the doctors said, 'Yes; but it is inevitable. Our
nation had six million casualties in the last war. Fifty per cent of
the Frenchmen between eighteen and forty were killed. One does
not skim milk three times and then expect to find much cream
left. We are the remains of the old French Army and have its spirit,
but we have to use any manpower we can get.' The Maquis had all
been swept into the army, as with their fighting experience they
could be taken on half-trained. The new recruits who were now
drilling beneath our windows seemed heartbreakingly young. I
felt a chill at seeing these youths of eighteen and nineteen go off
in tanks, they looked such babies.

Living, as I did, a foreigner in the heart of the French Army,
seeing so many Frenchmen die, I realized that they had the soul of
a great nation. One of the officer's wives, discussing the women
who had been killed working in the French Army, said with
typical logic:

'It seems dramatic and creates a momentary stir when a woman
gets killed because it is less usual for a girl to risk her life at the
front than in child-birth, but the loss of these young boys and the
men who leave families matters far more. None of us *ambulancières*
leave children; we do this work precisely because we are not the

centre of a home. It is much less of a tragedy to lose a childless woman like me than a *père de famille.*'

French women are so sentimental about the family, so practical about death.

27

Home

On 1 March I received news that my mother, whom I had not seen for nearly five years, was seriously ill in Ireland. Brigadier Gruss gave me compassionate leave as far as Paris, where the French Military Bureau presented me with two free metro tickets. They could not do more, for leave to *Grande Bretagne* had not yet become official. At SHAEF HQ in Versailles I found Lieutenant-Colonel Rothwell, the British camp commandant, who with great kindness procured me a seat in an RAF plane, and I landed at Croydon with the last of the doodle bugs.

Within three days of leaving Alsace I was with my mother in a Dublin nursing home. As I walked across St. Stephen's Green that evening the notice board at the gate made me pause:

RULES GOVERNING THE PARK OF ST. STEPHENS GREEN

No idle or disorderly person, or rogue, or vagabond or person in an intoxicated, unclean, or verminous condition shall enter, loiter, or remain in the park, or lie upon or occupy the ground, or any of the benches thereof.

Persons carrying ladders, planks, boards, fish baskets or other articles of a size, shape, or character likely to inconvenience other persons are not allowed to enter the park.

No person may bring into the park any carriage, cart, barrow, truck, bicycle, motor-bicycle, motor-car or other vehicle except a bath chair or perambulator.

Horses, cattle, sheep, pigs, goats or other live stock are not allowed to enter, nor any dog in a rabid state.

The swimming and bathing of dogs is strictly prohibited.

No unauthorized person shall drill or practise military evolutions or use arms or play any musical instrument.

Brawling, fighting, quarrelling, gambling, playing with cards or dice, begging and telling fortunes are prohibited.

No person shall FISH, WASH or BATHE in the ornamental-waters therein.

I was back in my own country at last!

After sleeping on stretchers for six months it seemed exciting to climb into a real bed with white sheets, but on my first night in a Dublin hotel I had strange dreams that an animal was digging into my hair with his claws and jumping on and off the bed. I woke and switched on the light several times but saw nothing until morning when, by broad daylight, I lifted up the eiderdown and found a large rat was curled up in bed with me. At my yell he jumped off the bed, scuttled under the wardrobe, and there the hall porter found and killed him. Rats had been my one real terror when sleeping on the floor in France. I did not realize what luxurious tastes they had.

The welcome which the Irish people gave to their returned warriors was an amazing contrast to that meted out in Transvaal. I use the word 'amazing' because South Africa had declared war and

Eire remained a neutral country, so that one might have expected applause in Pretoria, and stones in the bogs.

I would have given anything for the 1st Armoured Division to have seen that fleeting visit to my home in Monaghan! Cheering school children presented me with a bouquet at the station while, that evening, the local boys' brass-bugle band came and played outside the house. My father was just back from the west of Ireland where he tried to describe to an old fisherman the different nations now fighting Germany. The fisherman could not read newspapers or hear a wireless, he only knew that every young man had gone from the villages around and he listened with interest: 'I'm glad to hear it,' he said; 'I'm glad to know that other nations are helping Ireland in her battle.'

How could I describe to my French friends this neutral country in which half the men were off at the wars? Or explain the candour of a local woman who answered an enquiry as to why her large stout son had *not* volunteered: '. . . He's afraid of getting his feet waat!' Or cite the charming solemnity of one of our kitchen maids who, after an unfortunate romance with a departed American soldier, was left unmarried 'pushing a pram', the chubby occupant of which she had proudly christened 'Alexander Montgomery'?

On the day before the air battle of Arnhem I returned to England and, sitting by the Romney marshes that Saturday morning listening to the flights of planes overhead, I fumed for fear the French Army would attack again before I got back.

On Good Friday, the prime minister invited me to lunch at Chequers. Winston Churchill had all his life entertained a tender spot in his heart for the French, for their great history and culture, and for all that French thought has given to the world. I think he grieved most bitterly when France failed and now he longed to see her rise again.

Winston Churchill's mother had been my Great Aunt Jennie. When I was a year old she had given me all 'dear Winston's little baby clothes'. I was strong and plump, as he had been and, alas, I wore them all out except two white dresses and some little knickers. He was first lord of the admiralty at the time, but my nurse evidently had no respect for that title for I was allowed to romp in and destroy an infant *trousseau* which would someday have made museum pieces!

'Himself', as the Irish would say, received me in bed; he was not ill, but found it the best place to work. I had not seen him for years, not since a lunch at his house in Westerham at which I was in disgrace because, having gone out riding on a horse I could not control, I arrived dishevelled and in breeches half an hour late. Now he sat, regal among the pillows, with heaps of papers over the bed. Phone calls to Eden and 'Ike' and Roosevelt were put through while his secretaries scurried about with sheafs of secret documents. It was fascinating to listen to our greatest war leader after spending such a long time in the lower stratas of the fighting machine where all one had to think about was the keeping of one's vehicle – and oneself – intact.

Winston seemed in rollicking form. He knew the war was reaching its end at last, and that his great task was reaching a triumphal close. He gave me a cousinly kiss and said:'Well! tell me about the French. . .' I tried to. I could only tell him about the army; of France itself, the hungry broken country that lay behind us, I knew little, only the unhappy stories of comrades who returned from leave.

Six days before, Winston had flown to the Rhine to watch the Airborne Army descend at Arnhem. He sat up in his dressing-gown and, puffing at his cigar (yes, he even smokes in bed), described the battle with that strong emotional vitality with which he writes his books. He let himself go in a flow of words until I also felt the drama of that spectacle, the sky full of white parachutes opening in the sun, and the wounded planes turning back or falling in black smoke. He faltered for some moments to convey his personal reaction to the splendour and the tragedy, and I sat spellbound for I had only seen battle from close at hand and with eyes of terror, not of a historian. In fact, I had heard from other sources that the prime minister of England behaved like a naughty schoolboy when he got to the Rhine, and drove the officers in charge of his person nearly frantic. He had shed the bevy of generals who were out to explain things and insisted on standing on the most shelled bit of the river bank 'to see better'. Then he went up in a spotter plane and made the sweating pilot 'just drive a bit further' till they were almost amidst the descending parachutes. I told him his staff had been through torments for fear something would happen to him. He just grinned and said: 'Well, I am an old man and I've worked hard. Why shouldn't I have a little fun?'

I wished that Hitler and Mussolini could have seen their great antagonist that day at Chequers looking a mixture of a cherub and a bulldog. How little they ever understood the mettle of England.

When I left, the prime minister gave me a pat on the head and said:

'Give my love to the French . . . I think they are rather fond of me . . .'

Next morning I flew back to France. Paris looked delicious from the air with all her gardens full of blossoms and the Seine curling round the old familiar landmarks. I went to Easter Mass at Notre Dame, and then to lunch at a naval HQ at St Germain. After a lunch with smart, well-groomed wrens and naval officers amidst a delirium of Gothic carvings, we drove around Paris, which was hung with flags and garlands in preparation for an Easter Monday Parade...heralded as the 'biggest triumphal march since Napoleon'. But there was no armoured display. I guessed why, and hoped my own division had not crossed the Rhine without me.

After a farewell dinner in a resplendent officers' club (NAAFI gone wild in a Rothschild mansion), I took the night train back to Mulhouse. The division, which had spent the last month refitting, had not moved. The girls greeted me with hugs and kisses, and the men recited the charms of their new tanks fitted with a 90 mm cannon that ought to knock sparks out of any Tiger.

Each *ambulancière* was *marraine* (godmother) to a tank. Mine, the Peronne had been smashed near Colmar, but only one member of the crew was hurt. I had to inspect the new Peronne II and rave over its strangely long-barrelled cannon. There was a real thrill in having at long last better guns than the Germans, although our armour plating still remained inferior to Tigers and Panthers.

Nearly all the 2nd Cuirassiers tanks now had II or III after their names, a kingly reminder of others lost in the fray, and the Peronne II crew were painting with pride the white letters on their vehicle's steel side. *'C'est du snobisme!'* they said, laughing; 'but, all the same, it's *chic.'*

When I mentioned that I had lunched with Churchill – there was a scream, *'Mais comment? Allons – raconte!'* What did he think of the French Army? He likes it. What did he think of the Colmar fight? He thought it splendid. What does he know about the *ambulancières*? Everything!

The whole division soon heard, and I gained a fresh interest in its eyes. Soldiers came up to me in the street. *'Pardon, Mademoiselle.* Is it true you saw Veenston Churchill in England? To speak to? What did he say?' I repeated in English, for it was untranslatable, '"Give my love to the French", that's what he said.'

Brigadier Gruss invited me to dine at brigade HQ and asked, 'Is it true, *Mademoiselle* Anita, that you met Churchill and that he said: "Geeve my loov to ze French?"' Yes. I answered other questions and saw that every officer was dying to ask how much interest Winston Churchill took in the French Army? They were so human, far from wanting to hear his views about the war, they just longed to know what he thought of them as soldiers. Having been a nosy-parker in London I could answer truthfully that our prime minister had a map room which he visited every day to see what the different armies were doing, that he knew exactly what the 1st French Army had accomplished, and knew that the Vosges and Colmar had been *très dur*. He was always pleased at French achievements and (this I invented) when our last campaign ended he said '*Bravo*'. Eyes gleamed. They wanted to hear more and more, these regular army officers. They did not care a hang what anyone else thought about them but *Monsieur* Churchill – *celui la, quand même!* – It was all '*très intéressant – très très gentil* – You must give our LUV back—'

Several new girls had joined the section. Lucette Lecoq was no longer my *co-équipière,* for her young sister Odette had arrived, and they naturally wished to share an ambulance. My new co-driver was a Lorrainian of twenty-four who had been working all the winter with General Patton's 3rd American Army. A number of girls in the French Army were used to do reconnaissance in the parts of the country they knew. Genny had been born in Nancy and brought up in the border country of Lorraine. The French attached her to the American 3rd Army who used her in the land she knew so well. She and several others were sent out separately, during attacks, to find out where the German guns lay, and to identify German units on the battlefield by their dead. Having lived four years under the German military they knew most of the insignia. Genny's partner had been shot dead by a wounded German officer whom she had approached to search. I thought ambulance driving must seem rather tame after crossing the enemy lines eleven times bringing information about gun-sites. She was a very quiet girl, good-looking in a boyish way, unmade-up compared to the others who preened and prinked. She was not pretty, just handsome and fit. '*Très sportive*' the girls classed her; and Solange, who commanded the unit, put us together immediately.

During the first days we were on duty together Genny spoke very little. I dragged from her the story of her *mission spéciale* with the Americans.

'Why have you come to us?'

'They moved into Germany – into country where I would be useless; so, having heard of Mlle de l'Espée's unit, I applied for posting.'

'Won't you miss the old job?'

'It was exciting,' she said. 'I could do that work well. They usually sent me out at night when bombardment was in progress, for then no one was about and I had more chance of getting back. If the Germans caught me, of course, it would not have been pleasant – but I liked the work. I knew I did it well and I liked being alone.'

I had been long enough in Europe to understand that fear is comparative. The courage of those who risked being caught and tortured by the Germans made the soldier's bravery seem a joke. I had been brought up soft, and so I quailed at the idea of being wounded; but Genny could not see what there was to be fright-ened of in mere shelling. After all, if you did get hit your own people tended you – to die with morphia was nothing.

As always, the order to move came suddenly. I was dining with Edmond de Pourtales and Charles de Breteuil of the 4th Spahis

Regiment, who were *'en garde'* along the Rhine. Solange de la Brosse, who now commanded the section sent a message: 'We leave at six in the morning.'

So it was goodbye to Mulhouse. We moved out in the dawn driving slowly in convoy through those shattered northern suburbs where we had fought in January. Already life was creeping back, the blackened shelled houses were half hidden by masses of lilac and blossoming fruit trees and with the tenacity of ants the owners were living in the ruins, digging their gardens, mending as best they could the smashed roofs. In the village of Ostheim where only one chimney remained standing, a pair of storks were nesting, they had come back to their own traditional chimney and while mother-bird sat on her big twig nest father-bird peered at the desolation around with a long face. Storks like people, and by his expression it was obvious that he disapproved of what human beings had been up to during the winter.

We drove through the lovely orchard that is the Plain of Alsace to a mediaeval village outside Strasbourg, and there we waited several days drinking white wine beneath the flowering chestnut trees and listening dreamily to the German planes that fussed about the starry sky each night.

Just when we expected to be off, General de Lattre visited Strasbourg for a review. None of us realized this was a ruse to mislead German reconnaissance planes which were taking a great interest in the large troop concentrations in North Alsace. Four of our ambulances drove through the apple blossom and lilac and dust to line up along with the brigade in an avenue of flowering chestnuts. As we had merely come as passengers, I went off with the Lecoq sisters to explore the mediaeval part of Strasbourg and drink grenadine with our 'pals' during the four-hour wait for de Lattre, who had a five-kilometre walk along the line of armoured vehicles while the crowd cheered and waved bunches of lilac. Just in front of us a hideous old woman ran out and plastered the general with kisses.

It was a merry afternoon, full of good humour, while across the Rhine the cannon thundered as the French Army fought down through the Black Forest. A frightened woman ran up to me in the street and asked in German if she should hide. I indicated with my hands shells going away, not arriving, and she smiled. How smart I had grown since the Vosges!

On the following day Genny and I drove two hundred miles through the Vosges mountains depositing convalescents at rest camps. We should have realized our units were getting rid of softies with sore throats in order to move far and fast. The scenery was so glorious in the wooded mountains that we made the drive last as long as possible. It was eight at night when we drove back into the shimmering plain of orchards, and at Obernai the Lecoq sisters rushed out to say: 'You must fill with oil and petrol at once. Orders have arrived – We are just having the Mass for quitting French soil.' The romantic moment had arrived. We were going into Germany. It was eleven at night by the time we had put finishing touches to our ambulances and attended the brief lecture on how to behave *chez les boches.* Promising Solanges we would remember the military regulations about looting we snuggled down on our stretchers for a few hours' sleep.

28

Bullets in Our Bonnets

At three in the morning we drove off under a clear, star-lit sky. As always when in convoy there were numerous stops. Once, while we waited, a nightingale sang just by my ambulance, thrillingly beautiful in the warm night. Then came a cloudless pink dawn, and light showed we were rolling through the woods of northern Alsace. Jeanine André saw her own town, Haguenau, half in ruins but, like the mediaeval villages around, it was hung with tricolours. We crossed a great line of fortifications without realizing it was the Siegfried Line – the very one where we had, unfortunately, not hung our washing five years before, then we passed an American signboard: 'You enter Germany by the courtesy of the 19th Engineering Company', from hence the flags ceased and the villages grew deserted. A few peasants stared without waving. We knew then we were really in Germany.

Before midday, in brilliant sunshine, we crossed the Rhine, and drove on through enemy fields and orchards, hazy in the summer heat. The civilians we saw were bent over their work in the fields; gaunt, unsmiling women pushed barrows of their possessions along the roadside, while healthy-looking, barefooted children gaped. It was a curious sensation, the emptiness of the countryside under a bright blue sky, the long roads bordered by flowering fruit trees, the expressionless faces watching from cottage windows, and the lines of German prisoners tramping past in clouds of white dust. For the first time I saw a German prisoner weeping. He was marching towards France in a long column and the tears poured down his face. Surely he wept not for himself, but for his splendid, stupid, cruel, loathed, broken country.

We whirled through desolate Baden and burning Rastatt, where the convoy halted in a big square whose name-board 'Adolf Hitler *Platz*' hung by one nail on a charred ruin. A middle-aged German came up to speak with us in French. He was ingratiating, almost welcoming. We could hardly believe it, but in the afternoon we stopped for rations of bread and cheese in an orchard and the old proprietor shambled up mumbling: '*Enchanté, Mademoiselles.*' We thought at the time he was mad.

The 3rd Chasseurs squadron of armoured cars that accompanied us shared their wine when we halted by the roadside, and one of the officers, Lieutenant de Bellefond and Susanne Coignard chose this of all moments to announce their engagement. We drove on south through the Black Forest with the 4th Moroccan Division, leaving open country of sunlit orchards for the beauty of forested mountains and mossy green valleys. We wanted to eat and sleep and, for once, we had not been issued with rations. At ten that night – having driven since three in the morning – we halted at Freudenstadt, which had been our destination in orders, but the town was in flames and as soon as our convoy drove in, enemy planes roared overhead dropping bombs and machine-gunning, and then the artillery opened up. From miles away they must have been able to see anything that moved in the brilliant light of the burning houses. So we crept away slowly and without lights into a dark, slumbering village and got the order to sleep in our ambulances.

'Wake up,' squealed Genny the next morning, 'we're miles inside Germany and look.' An extraordinary sight met my eyes.

Our doctors were busy installing the advanced post in the school-house, and, all up the prim line of German cottages, super picnic breakfasts were being served. The terrified Fraus of this village had heard vehicles stop in the night and did not dare put their noses out. Then, after sunrise, our orderlies had tapped on front doors to ask for hot water and milk. When the inhabitants realized that a medical company had arrived their fears abated. We knocked at the nearest door and affable handmaids brought bowls of hot water and towels. Then we sat down in the sunshine and quietly absorbed the fresh boiled eggs, buttered bread and milk that was smilingly carried to us. 'We are conquerors at last,' grinned Genny with her mouth full.

At nine o'clock Solange began to send ambulances to the regiments. Our ambulances, and that of Susanne Coignard and Mimi, were the two attached to Commandant Vallin's group. That meant we would serve with Husser for this campaign.

No sooner had we left for the post than we were stopped by two excited Moroccans. They had been running around a farmyard trying to shoot a chicken and had plugged a pal by mistake. We found the man lying in the ditch with a rifle bullet through his stomach and transported him hastily back to the post. Before we could cover the mile, however, another native appeared waving his hands and howling. He, also coveting a chicken, had shot himself through the foot! We squeezed past our squadron of tanks in a narrow hill lane and the men shouted: 'What! wounded already?' 'No,' I yelled back, 'just a couple of idiots chasing hens . . .'

Having dumped these nitwits with our indignant doctors, we made our way back to Husser who was establishing his regimental post in Horb, a town on the Neckar. We still had the holiday spirit, so Husser gave us permission to lunch in the inn where a company of Foreign Legion invited us to share a fine repast.

They were cooking in the large kitchen using copper saucepans, and saying: 'At least we won't have to wash up.'

They were due to attack with our zouave infantry at three o'clock. 'Our reception is finished now,' they said at half-past two. 'You had better find cover before the scrap begins.' 'We don't find cover,' we answered grandly; 'we go to our post.'

We walked down the deserted street which we now saw ran parallel with the river. There was only one bridge which had been partly demolished, but it could still carry a jeep or infantry with light guns. On the other side of the river the mountain side rose up steeply. We could just see a road of hairpin bends twisting up the forested slope. It was a natural line of defence. Our troops would have to cross that one bridge under heavy fire and then struggle up through the pine trees which gave perfect cover to the Germans waiting with machine-guns, while their artillery could shell the town of Horb as much as they desired. We wondered if they would really destroy a German town as we had been forced to destroy the towns of Alsace.

From the corner house a road led straight to the bridge. 'I must take a photograph,' said Genny, as our zouaves began to creep up from a gully and ran across the bridge. Machine-gun fire came from the watching Germans, then a shell landed smashing every window in the street. 'Go to your post,' yelled the foreign legionnaires, 'can't you realize the Germans are watching you from across the river?'

We pelted down the street to the boot-shop where Husser was installed. He was particularly proud of the Red Cross sign which he always stood outside the door of his post. It had a red glass cross that glimmered at night in the faintest light. The next shell landed right beside it and shrapnel came through the wooden shutters into our boot-shop. 'Oh, my beautiful sign; it's gone for good,' said Husser, peering into the desolate street.

Mimi and Susanne came running in from their ambulance. Mimi thought she had been wounded. She had actually seen a shell land on one of our Shermans, that is she saw the tank give a sort of bounce and the blast knocked her against the ambulance driving wheel and bruised her. The tank had been hit on its thickest armour and the turret was closed, so the crew suffered no ill effect, but one of them peered out and yelled at her, 'Was that an 88?' 'I don't know,' answered Mimi faintly, 'How does one tell when it lands a metre away?'

A platoon of zouaves came into the shop and tried to find an exit through the cellar which might lead out under the bridge, but they did not succeed and the men filed back with long faces. They had to wait with us until further orders, and suddenly I realized how much they hated seeing the medical equipment being laid out – the table arranged for a stretcher, the bandages and instruments, all the cold-blooded preparation for operations on their flesh. To hang about doing nothing before attack is the worst a soldier can go through. Jokes sound false and silence is irritating. When a film got stuck in Genny's camera four men struggled to help. They were grateful to spend this hour in our company, but, as we heard burst after burst of machine-gun fire from across the bridge, their faces set a little; Mimi, rummaging in the back of the shop, found some silk stockings, squealed excitedly and gave each man a pair for his girl. They went off to the attack laughing: 'What would we do without our *ambulancières* . . . !'

Ten minutes later the wounded began to be carried back. Two of the Foreign Legion we had lunched with were killed before they got to the bridge. Their corporal came in with a piece of shrapnel in his thigh, angrily took his trousers down and asked Husser to pick it out quickly so he could return. He was an enormous blond man and extremely cross when little Husser suggested he should be evacuated. I gathered he thought zouaves were sissies!

Every house along the river bank had been deserted but two German policemen were found and ordered to commandeer forty men to come and reconstruct the half-demolished bridge. Marching along in fours, with picks and shovels over their shoulders, they had a frightful resemblance to the Seven Dwarfs but, although in step, they did not sing. We thought the Germans would withhold their fire when they saw their own countrymen at work, but they intensified it and soon two old men were wounded and carried back to us. After the usual attention we drove them to their homes, dumped them in bed and comforted their hysterical wives.

Meanwhile wounded zouaves were pouring back. Guillot, working the other side of the bridge, had to get the stretcher-parties across under steady fire. Captain Gillet, who commanded the zouaves here, and Lieutenant Aries were brought in dead, and several officers were hit. Their commanding officer came back from his post to question them while Husser gave morphia and sulphur drugs.

Dusk came; the fighting still continued fiercely and our tanks, unable to blunder into combat on a mountain slope, still huddled amongst the protecting houses. We had dinner in the house next door – where plates and food had been left on the table as the owners fled in panic. Mimi was in raptures. We would have *un joli petit diner* with a tablecloth! She was looking for wine glasses of the right shape when Husser shouted outside: 'Come out of that house. Can't you see it's in a direct line from the bridge?' It had, in truth several shell holes through the walls, so we decamped, dragging the table-cloth as a symbol of civilization with us.

Hearing a growl in one room I found a poor little dachshund crouching under the bed, his owners gone, his world turned into a thunderous nightmare. He ran out and hid in the hen-house, where I caught and calmed him, and also picked up several eggs. I thought he would like human company for a bit so started down the street. But *Whezeeze* sounded a shell and, as I started to run, he struggled violently in my arms. The eggs broke all over us both and I arrived breathless in the post covered with raw egg and clinging to a demented dog. Husser said: 'Really I think my *ambulancières* are going mad. Kindly realize that we are in the middle of a battle.'

Mimi and Susanne left with a load of wounded after nine at night and Husser told Genny and me to get some sleep, as he would need us later. Genny was too excited to keep still an instant; she was comparing American and French infantry in action: 'The Americans are courageous, but oh la! the war bores them so,' she said. 'The French advance with *élan*.'

I curled up on a pile of kit-bags, pulled two greatcoats over my head and tried to get an hour's sleep, but the native orderlies were having a row. They were short of rations and someone had stolen and eaten *une demi botte de pâté*. They screeched and quarrelled in high-pitched Arabic, while half-a-dozen wounded Germans who had just been brought in watched them with popping eyes.

Abandoning sleep, I sat up and watched too. Enemy wounded always have a look of fear. These weary men, who had been dragged in from the forest, sat in terror, evidently thinking the natives were quarrelling over the pleasure of cutting their throats. Genny and I gave them water, until Husser came to dress their wounds and procure them beds in the town hospital. But at this point a young zouave NCO who had been lying in a morphine-stupor awoke in a state of hysterical nerve-excitement, saw the

Germans sitting there and thinking he was still fighting across the river, got up and tried to attack them. Genny and I sat on his chest and explained soothingly that he must not move his broken leg, but he struggled on until we knocked him out with morphia.

At last, when it was nearly midnight, Husser had our ambulance loaded with French wounded and again we started back along the twenty-mile road to the advanced post.

It was the first time we had driven alone at night in Germany and the dark forests made it unpleasant, for we were forbidden any lights but the cats' eyes, and we knew these woods must be full of German soldiers. Army lorries had to travel in convoy of at least twenty accompanied by two tanks. Only the ambulances rolled alone through enemy country.

It was three in the morning by the time we had delivered our wounded and got back to Horb where our sappers said: 'The zouaves are scaling the hillside. We'll have the bridge ready for tanks by dawn.' So the attack had succeeded! Around us the town smouldered and the street was an inch deep in broken glass on which our boots crunched loudly.

At six next morning, Husser woke us and, breakfastless, we drove off. In triumph we crossed the battered bridge and crept up the hairpin bend roads through the pine woods. The elation of advance quelled hunger. The 2nd Cuirassiers tanks who now ground their way up the hillside went roaring into action.

We saw the monstrous splendour of a line of Shermans sitting outside a dark forest, spitting fire into the trees, and we drove on until halted by enemy shells which sailed over our heads and fell beside the road. Husser signalled the convoy to stop and got out his maps. We *all* got out our maps in fact and started to argue. The village ahead was the place where we were supposed to have breakfast but it seemed to be full of enemy. After half an hour in

the ditch Husser said: *'Demi-tour!* We will withdraw, I am puzzled.'
We all reversed.

It was a sweet little convoy, the two doctors in a jeep, the half-
track ambulance, two padres in a bright yellow two-seater they
had commandeered at Horb, and our two ambulances. As we
drove back our mobile artillery lined up their lorries in a green
flower-carpeted valley and opened fire. For a moment it looked as
if we were driving into a row of dragons roaring flame; it was a
fantastic sight, savagely beautiful, and we cheered the crews who
were running to and fro feeding shells to their guns.

Husser remarked that, in future, he would try to keep his convoy
behind the tanks, discretion being the better part of valour where
the medical services were concerned.

We did eventually halt for *le café* in a quiet village – hung with
white surrender flags – which had been captured that morning.
We had now learnt the form. One just walked into any kitchen
and said, *'Milch, butter, brot'*. It delighted us to have all our
requirements appear as if by magic, but how *could* these women
smile at us?

All that day we drove on slowly through villages whose inhabitants had hung their sheets and pillow-cases out of every window
as a sign of surrender. Sometimes whole families stood on the
doorsteps in open-mouthed terror and even the little children
were holding their hands up. Coming across a flock of sheep we
halted while our Arab orderlies gave chase across the field. They
loaded three or four into the Red Cross half-track, which
resounded with bleats. That evening they roasted mutton to their
hearts' content. This was *their* idea of war.

Later on I found a description in *The Times* of this day:

'The French made a spectacular dash of thirty miles to reach
Rottweil, capturing a number of villages as they swept forward.'

Towards dusk we drove into a village called Rosenveldt where there had been a hard fight. Several buildings were burning while blackened guns and tanks smouldered on the torn grass amidst numbers of German dead. Husser installed us in an excellent little hotel and drove on further with the advancing zouaves. On the way back he and Guillot, alone in their jeep, suddenly came on eighteen German soldiers with a lorry. Guillot collected their arms and then the whole procession came back to Rosenveldt. Husser was tickled to death at his capture, especially as he had long coveted another lorry for his medical stores: 'That's the way to get things, instead of applying for months and filling in forms.'

The excellent meal we ordered for ourselves was interrupted by requests to our doctors to visit German civilians who had been shot that morning by retreating SS as they hung out white flags. A hysterical Danish woman begged me to get Husser to see her husband, who had received two revolver bullets in the face as he pinned a sheet out of his bedroom window. Our doctors attended to the civilians and left them in their beds. It was impossible to operate or evacuate them.

One woman doctor lived in Rosenveldt and she sent a message asking us to help with the wounded who had been picked up outside the village. I walked over to her clinic in the moonlight and found she spoke fluent English. Seizing my arm, she half-dragged me upstairs into the small clean surgery. On the table lay a German soldier who had been dragged from the mass of burning tanks outside the village. With a terrible obstinacy life still clung to this travesty of a human body. His legs were both half-off, and from a shattered arm held up by a weeping girl spurted a stream of blood. The doctor implored me: 'Please, please let me drive him to Rottweil. He must have both legs and the arm amputated immediately. I want to save his life.'

I wondered why, for every bit of flesh had been blackened by powder burns. In spite of morphia his glazed eyes remained wide and his gasping breath might have been cries of pain.

'Give him another injection,' I said.

'His heart won't stand it,' wept the doctor; but she gave him another shot.

'I am trained to assist at births, not deaths,' she went on, and her fresh good-looking face, framed by golden hair was drenched with tears. Still she pleaded to save her soldier, saying: 'I have never done an amputation. I am not a surgeon. Let me drive him off.'

I said: 'It is impossible. Listen!' Gunfire sounded in every direction.

When the young girl collapsed I stood by the German holding a lighted candle in one hand, keeping his torn arm up with the other. He was finding it very hard to die. I could not help noticing that if his arm was allowed to hang down he would bleed to death in a few minutes. Yet I stood there foolishly, holding him, and the hot candle grease burnt my fingers while the doctor-midwife sobbed and stared wide-eyed at that burnt, shrapnel-riddled form which breathed on and on.

'Do you know this man?' I asked.

'No, no,' she shook her head; 'but he, too, has somewhere a mother.' Sentimental she obviously was, and rather ridiculous, and yet there was something pleasing about the tenderness of her woman's heart. As my own hand began to ache I lowered his arm slightly and then with a gasp and a tremor he was dead. I handed her the candle and walked back to the inn hoping no one would take a pot-shot at me in the dark alleys. Husser was sorting prisoners and he decided to off-load all German wounded into the local hospitals so as not to overburden our own medical lines. On hearing about the Clinic he sent me off with a jeep-load of lightly wounded Germans. Frau *Doktor* received them gratefully and we left them sitting about the floor where she could busy herself with maternal, gentle care. She was glad to look after them.

'Thank you, thank you;' she took my hand. Queer thanks for queer presents!

Back at the inn the other three girls were enjoying hot baths and the proprietor had prepared a table of roast chickens, all lit by a single oil lamp. The doctors dined with us, and our merry laughter must have sounded through the shutters into the dark streets which had been patrolled by angry SS the night before.

Next morning we drove on proudly with the new lorry. We would lunch in one village, take another in time for tea, and capture a fourth to order dinner. All the people looked healthy and pink-cheeked; they had masses of food, and it was evident no German had been short of anything during all this war. I thought of the thin children of France covered with spots from the filthy bread, compared with these strong, fresh-skinned little tow-headed brats who were running round enjoying themselves, waving small white flags. And already the Moroccans were giving them sweeties!

Some of the 'typically German' women, with blonde pigtails, turned out to be deported Russians. They looked bovine and fat and happy. Each time the convoy stopped villagers came out with jam sandwiches and if we refused their offers they would nibble it themselves to show it was not poisoned.

All day we drove through the sunlit country, with our convoys raising dust along the blossom-lined roads, and in the fields of golden flowers lay heaps of stiff bodies, German soldiers in their grey uniform lying beside a burnt-out lorry or broken gun. No one picked them up or buried the German dead. They just lay as they had died, and meanwhile their wives and mothers and sisters were waving welcome to the invaders!

That evening one of our artillery soldiers was stricken with acute appendicitis. Much as he disliked having to send an ambulance back thirty miles in the dark, Husser ordered us back to Horb. It was a rainy evening when we set off. Darkness was falling when out of the woods crept a sodden little German who stood by the roadside with his hands up.

'On s'arrête?' asked Genny. We had gleaned three revolvers and a carbine so we fancied the idea of taking a prisoner ourselves. The appendix case also cocked a revolver! Genny got out in the rain and searched the German while I could not resist snapping a photograph. Our captive was soaked and shivering and had been in hiding in the forest for two days, so he stumbled gratefully into the ambulance and collapsed on the floor. We felt gleeful and decided *not* to say how easy it had been and that he was green with terror and his knees shook while we searched him.

It was pitch dark when we reached the steep descent down to the Neckar. Finding it impossible to see the hairpin bends I asked Genny to climb on the ambulance bonnet and yell instructions. 'À droite – à gauche,' she cried, and, as even from her perch she could not see, we switched on the headlights. Then someone began shooting at us and it was no fun at all. From the bonnet my poor mascot was shouting 'File vite! On tire!' but I could not do more than crawl or we might have ended over a cliff. A dozen bullets zinged before we reached the bridge and found our advanced post. Genny had a bullet-hole right through her jacket, and its passing heat had made her think she was wounded. Our prisoner was blubbing and looked about the most miserable, terrified, little specimen in the whole German Army.

We lay down to sleep in the ambulance, and while we arranged blankets the Lecoq sisters came to talk. They were full of their own exciting tales saying: 'We wouldn't have missed this for anything.'

29

We Finish Pétain's Wine

At dawn we drove off hoping to catch our zouaves and cross the Danube with them. We reached a small grey stream on which were a number of ducks and, as we waited our turn over the small bridge one of the armoured cars stopped beside us, a nineteen-year-old member of the crew, elated by the taking of the Neckar, leant forward and shouted scornfully: 'Can you believe it . . . that trickle is the famous Danube!' Meanwhile the rest of the division was taking the Tuttlingen district around the Danube's source, and released prisoners of war were now streaming back along the roads. Seeing the tricolour painted on our ambulances the Frenchmen would run up shouting: '*Français? Nous aussi! Nous aussi!*' We gave them what cigarettes we had and helped them strap up their belongings and set out on foot for France.

Before he sent us off the previous evening Husser had spoken of Stockach, on Lake Constance, as the next likely stop, so we drove on there alone. Outside the town we heard sounds of battle and stopped to look at our map. Our heads were bent over it in concentration when a face appeared at the ambulance window. There stood a German soldier with a bicycle and a rifle slung over his shoulder. As he took it off I hoped he was not the sort who would shoot us. He took out the cartridges, threw them away, and handed us his gun through the window, '*Nicht gut*' he said, jerking his head towards Stockach. Evidently he was running away from the fight. We wondered if we ought to take him prisoner but it seemed rather difficult when we were driving towards the front, and then he pulled a photograph out of his pocket and said it was his mother who lived in the next village and he was going to her. Before we could make further comment he cycled off, waving and leaving us to add the rifle to our increasing accumulation of fire-arms.

At Stockach we found heavy fighting in progress. A harassed staff officer said the *Groupement* Vallin had switched eastwards along the Danube. The division was in fact fanning out all over the great plain south of the river.

After two weeks' sunshine it had suddenly begun to snow. We followed the Danube downstream until an excited soldier stopped us saying there were a hundred German soldiers on the road ahead. We thought they probably wanted to be taken prisoners but had no intention of capturing any more. Not wishing to take risks, we drew up by the side of the road. A jibbering farmer's wife came out and thrust bowls of milk through the window. This section had only been taken over an hour before and, as German propaganda had been broadcasting that the entire French Army consisted of negro troops who would rape and lay waste the countryside, these honest bovine Fraus thought they had better appease the invader quickly with food. They seemed reassured on seeing women's faces under the steel helmets.

A command car drew up and in it we saw Brigadier Gruss. He said: 'Well! I'll go ahead and see what all this is about, and you two had better follow with the tanks.' I don't know why we were always just ahead of the tanks instead of just behind!

We travelled on jauntily with twenty roaring clattering Shermans – fair company it seemed in that snowstorm – and we saw batches of Germans running, hands up, in every field. They were, in fact, begging to be taken prisoner and no one would stop. Brigadier Gruss himself was accosted by some forty whom he waved aside.

We reached Sigmaringen, where the Hohenzollern Castle towers over the Danube. The bridge was blown up so we deployed with the tanks, bumping over ploughed fields until it was too rough for an ambulance to follow. We then followed a track and, when we were alone, a band of Germans appeared, hands over heads, and began to run after us begging to be taken prisoner. To be captured by two nice girls in a comfortable ambulance is, of course, the dream of any surrendering soldier! But we were sick of them by this time, the novelty had worn off; also someone began shooting, so we did *demi-tour* and drove back while the Germans, who had thrown their guns away, ran after us, shouting 'Stop!'

We drove into the town of Sigmaringen at two o'clock. It had been taken without resistance at midday. A few dead German soldiers lay in the streets, and an old wounded policeman was being led home by a weeping girl. On the balcony of a large military hospital, bandaged Germans and nurses were standing with their hands up. Groups of frightened civilians were hurrying along the streets with shot-guns and knives which they had been ordered to hand in to the mayor, while their police in green-blue uniforms chevied them and scolded hysterical women who kept asking what to do with their penknives. Commandant Vallin and his zouaves were billeted in the great Hohenzollern Castle.

When we reported to Husser he just said: 'At last!' and took us around the *Schloss*. Laval and Pétain had been kept there in regal semi-imprisonment, and the old Marshal had fled that morning at three o'clock. His confidential reports and newspapers were still lying on his desk with *'Monsieur le Maréchal'* written on them in pencil.

Two nice bedrooms had been allotted to the *ambulancières*. Mimi and Susanne were already splashing in Pétain's bath tub!

Then we strolled to the big kitchen, where our Moroccan comrades were busy plucking chickens. Each cooked his little mess under the gloomy gaze of the Austrian chef who had lorded it in this kitchen for a decade. We organized our own dinner and were waited on by the kitchen-maid, a deported Yugoslav woman, who kept begging us to cut the throat of every German. I think she had a grudge against the chef. We found the wine cellar excellent, and began to approve of war. The date was 22 April, 1945.

The next day we awoke late, wandered out to breakfast through halls hung with antlers and stuffed heads, and peered at the magnificent views. Appeals were now coming in from neighbouring villages to help German wounded. Husser sent both ambulances off to scour the country and collect serious cases. Genny and I enlisted a tubby local policeman to direct us. He looked pretty miserable when we ordered him inside the ambulance. Then I discovered he spoke fluent English and once he grasped the routine for gathering up wounded he became quite agile and even dictatorial to the civilians who kept running up with more and more tales of dying men. He liked to be given orders and we gave them! Before long he was our devoted servant. I thought to myself, *anyone* could lead this nation, anyone who took the trouble to study them for five minutes. They are like plasticine!

The first batch of German soldiers we found were in a barn, where they had been lying on the blood-soaked straw with terrible wounds for twenty-four hours. They were shivering and their only covering was a huge cotton Nazi flag.

Looking for the next batch we were directed to a manor house eight miles away. It resembled a derelict English country house, with remains of lawns and untended flower-borders. There emerged from this house an old lady in black who, to my amazement, announced that she was English. She appeared to be a governess or companion. Two blonde girls and two young men followed her, also speaking perfect English. When I asked how they had acquired such good accents, one of the girls explained she had been educated at Roehampton Convent . . . We had, in fact, been there for one term together. The old lady addressed them as 'Your Royal Highness', and introduced them to us formally as the prince and princess something or other of Bavaria, of Hanover, etc. I could not follow the flow of names but I gathered the older woman with her distinguished-looking husband of about fifty were the heads of the Hohenzollern family.

On the previous afternoon the fighting had swept through their garden, and in the evening they had crept out to carry badly-wounded soldiers out of the rhododendrons and cabbage-beds into their house, where they lay on the drawing-room floor. Several had died; the rest were in a bad state, and we had to lift them carefully on to our stretchers. While this was being done the Princess Hohenzollern told me that Sigmaringen Castle had been her home until they were ordered to make way for Pétain and Laval. 'I have two sons fighting in the German Army,' she said; 'when on earth will I hear from them now?'

It was the same question I had heard from Alsatian peasant women all the winter, but this woman in her tweeds and cardigan looked exactly like an English country lady. When we drove off with the ghastly load we had fetched from her house she came out and graciously bowed goodbye and wished us 'Good luck' in the old-fashioned way of an Edwardian hostess seeing her guests start off on a pheasant shoot.

We drove carefully down the rutted drive with our moaning load and left the remains of German royalty living like some actors in a Chekhov play, completely out of every world, in an unreal, tumbledown chateau.

Back in Sigmaringen we deposited the wounded, and a French *déporté* ran up panting to ask if we were Scouts. I felt dazed, as my Brownie days were long forgotten, but Genny was ardently *un scout*, on learning which he requested us to accompany him to a villa where a German man had just been shot. Here a weeping Frau told us that a Moroccan soldier had chased their daughter in the garden and, when the father remonstrated, had shot him in the stomach and run off into the woods. This was the only case of attempted rape I had heard of, and I did not see how native soldiers could be expected to understand the friendly overtures of German women. We carried the father off to the German hospital and asked that he should be taken directly to the operating room, but organization seemed to have broken down.

A number of hospital staff and nurses stood idly about while the German wounded we had brought in from all over the countryside still lay unattended. I lost my temper when a nurse began to laugh. Perhaps it was nerves, for there was certainly nothing to laugh at. The faces of the wounded were grey; they had not been given any morphia. For all we knew they might be dying of haemorrhage. So I shook the sniggering girl by the shoulders until she pulled herself together. Our German being inadequate we made the fat policeman our interpreter and induced some kind of activity. Then we drove back to town and dropped our little policeman at his home, where his Frau was wringing her hands at the window. In six hours' hard work we had become friends and, when we drove off, he waved his green and silver, eagle-encrusted helmet at us in fond farewell.

Returning to Sigmaringen we dined again in the great courtyard where some English war correspondents joined us with the news that Berlin had been taken. We emptied Pétain's last bottle of white wine.

We drove slowly back in the dark to the post and found Husser anxiously awaiting us. Guillot ran up and said: 'Thank God you are back for the Lecoq sisters were killed today.' My heart froze while Guillot went on: 'The girls left the advanced post this morning with some wounded, and while we were waiting by the Danube they must have been caught by the retreating Germans in the next village which the cuirassier tanks have just recaptured. I went forward to see if there were any wounded and found the sisters lying dead in a barn.'

That morning at about ten o'clock a cuirassier soldier, slightly wounded in the hand, and two seriously wounded Germans had been brought to the advanced post, and after treatment they were sent off in the Lecoq ambulance to the brigade station which was some twelve miles back near Sigmaringen. Lucette and Odette drove off in bright sunshine at about eleven o'clock; at midday the advanced post heard sounds of heavy shell fire all around, and learnt they were cut off from the rear by several thousand retreating Germans. In the village of Sauggart the Lecoq's ambulance drove into a crowd of enemy soldiers, and realized too late that these were not surrendering troops. They stopped, and Odette – the younger sister who was not driving – stepped out, pointing at the large Red Cross flag that waved on the bonnet. She was not wearing her helmet so there could not have been any possibility of mistaking her for a combatant soldier. A group of Germans approached to within a few yards and shot her dead with a tommy gun. Lucette jumped out of the other door and put her hands up. They shot her through the chest. Then, treading on the girls' bodies, they hurled themselves forward on to the driving-seat to shoot the wounded with revolvers, but the two terrified Germans lying on their stretchers yelled out and stopped them just in time to save their own lives and that of the third patient the French cuirassier, who was sitting holding his bandaged arm in stupefaction.

There was a pause while the Germans argued together; then they carried the girls into a barn, commandeered the ambulance and drove it on southwards for two days until they reached Ravensburg. The cuirassier knew enough German to understand his captors and his wounded companions spent a lot of time discussing the incident. 'The war is nearly over,' said the German wounded, 'the French treated us well when we were in their hands. Why did you have to shoot the *fräuleins*?' At the end of two days' remonstration the men who had done the shooting seemed to grow rather ashamed.

At Ravensburg the ambulance was driven into a yard and the patients were put into hospital. Two days later, when the cuirassier heard sounds of fighting and saw tanks of his own squadron rolling into the town and ran out waving to them. That was how we eventually learnt what had occurred. The ambulance was returned to our unit. Its windows were smashed by bullets and the girl's personal kit had disappeared. The two wounded Germans had vanished from the hospital, as they were probably frightened they might be associated with the killers. The cuirassier's hand had healed sufficiently for him to remain with his squadron and continue in the advance towards the Tyrol. He was desperately hoping to find the men who had done the shooting, as he swore that he could recognize them, but among the thousands of retreating *boches* they were never caught.

On the evening that Guillot found the Lecoq sisters lying in the barn, we knew nothing of this story. Guillot could only tell that both girls had been shot through the chest at close range. Odette was stone cold, but Lucette was still warm, so she must have died in the late afternoon. We hoped that she had been unconscious. The 2nd Cuirassiers who recaptured Sauggart that evening, found their bodies and swore that every house would be burnt to the ground to avenge the *ambulancières*. All Frenchmen hated the Germans, and this incident inflamed a real anger. The men leapt from their tanks and ordered the people to leave their houses and drive out the cattle, while they prepared to set light to each building. The officer commanding the squadron had known the girls well and, white with anger, he stood watching and approving his men. After all, it was the sort of reprisal that the Germans had inflicted hundreds of times in every country they occupied. But when the houses had been cleared, and one old woman knelt down before them in the road and held up a Crucifix, the men hesitated. They were Frenchmen not Germans, and suddenly they knew such vengeance was not in them.

This was not because they were pious, or had self-control or because they considered themselves civilized, it was simply an innate inability to kill helpless people or destroy their homes. Many Frenchmen went into Germany with bitter memories, bent on revenge, but when the time came they found they could not do it. That was the difference between the races.

As dusk fell over Sauggart village the cuirassiers carried out the two young bodies and set fire to the barn in which they had laid, but they did not touch any other house.

Guillot brought the sisters back to Hailtengen in his jeep and laid them on stretchers in the parlour of our little house. They looked frail and lovely and so very young, like two sad little madonnas laid side by side in the white sheets. The padre found candles and brought his Crucifix, and we four girls who were on duty at this post, Mimi, Susanne, Genny and I, kept vigil in turn all night. As the soldiers around the village heard the story they came in to cross themselves and kneel a moment by their *ambulancières*. Even the Moroccan stretcher-parties, silent for once and wide-eyed, came to pay their respects, and one of the most cowardly orderlies volunteered to be sent off on a lone commando raid '*pour venger ces demoiselles*'.

When dawn came the two padres said Mass for the sisters in the village church. Only Guillot and we four drivers were able to be present, but the local German curate, having heard what had occurred, asked if he might serve our priests. After Mass we walked back in the light of the just risen sun and we thought of the sisters waking excited, eager, and full of life in yesterday's dawn.

Lucette had been the beloved of Lieutenant Pêche, who hoped to marry her when the war ended. When he came along in his radio liaison truck — just as I had seen him on that first evening in the Vosges — he stopped cheerily to ask for news. The girls told him and his face turned white but it was not only of himself he thought:

'They were only children,' he said. 'Their poor mother will be left without anything.' Of course we realized now that sisters should not have been risked in the same ambulance — but they had been so happy together.

From the parlour we carried the two stretchers into Mimi's ambulance ... how light they seemed compared with the men!

Dark red pools of blood lay on the parlour floor which the woman of the house weepingly washed away. She was a sentimental soul, who had to cry at the sight of dead girls. Then we blew out the candles, the priest took his crucifix, and Mimi and Susanne drove sadly back to the brigade station.

They were buried that afternoon with full military honours.

31

'Der Krieg ist Beendet?'

For the next two days we remained at Hailtengen while zouaves and tanks cleared the surrounding countryside. We watched thousands of German prisoners marching down the village street, and from the window we could chat with liberated Poles who were grabbing bicycles and setting off home. One of them journeyed six yards only to fall off and break his leg, so we drove him back to the brigade station, and on the way a band of hysterical French civilians rushed out from a village waving revolvers saying there were sixty SS in the railway station who might mow them down any minute. They were wild with fear, and begged for more troops immediately, because our squadrons had gone right through this village and they thought they had been abandoned to the SS. We asked them not to point the revolvers at our faces and swore that more soldiers would arrive.

When the road seemed safe we transported German wounded to their own civilian hospital across the Danube. They were always gushing and full of thanks; but their sentimentality, together with their capacity for indiscriminate shooting, had become distinctly boring. We had one young German officer who spoke English and I told him what had happened to the Lecoqs. He seemed genuinely horrified. 'It can't be true. No normal German soldiers would shoot ambulance drivers. Perhaps they were SS?'

As there were four SS divisions retreating from the Black Forest this was very possible. A large percentage of the German Army and Police was SS.

Hailtengen stood on a rise and we could watch the 2nd Cuirassiers deploying across a wide valley. The tanks would roll along, like huge cunning slugs in the golden meadows, then stop and their guns would slowly point towards the foe, much as an accusing finger might; then, as they boomed, fountains of smoke rose up in the pine trees and sometimes a black column of smoke rose up from some flaming house in an unseen village. When we drove back from the front we saw occasional shelled houses where weeping women were trying to pull oddments out of the smoking ruins, but our advance had been too swift for much destruction. It was not like Alsace, for I never saw wounded civilians or children. No German mother ever ran to us with a dying blood-soaked child in her arms, as had happened time and again in France.

The zouaves asked us to come out and watch the attempt to set fire to the forest around the OP tower with incendiaries, but the trees were too damp. I made an attempt to follow the fighting intelligently. Nearly all our armoured casualties had been due, not to Panzers, but to some fearless German who remained behind with a bazooka. In fact, so telling were these one-man attacks, I wondered if the bazooka might not mean the end of armoured warfare.

One morning, for some reason I never could fathom, our two padres drove off in their yellow car to say Mass in the next village near the enemy OP and were taken prisoners. Three hours later the zouaves advanced, recaptured the village, and found the priests sitting dismally in the church. They were unmolested, but the canary-coloured roadster which the zouaves had commandeered especially for them, had vanished with the retreating Germans, and it contained all their personal kit which they never recovered. Once again the padres, who had never had any transport of their own until we entered Germany, had to cadge lifts and two crest-fallen priests, without a sponge or tooth-brush to their name, climbed in our ambulance when the order came to drive on southward.

Bernard de Bellefond came by, driving a band of young German soldiers before his armoured car. These boys were aged between twelve and fifteen. We evacuated a little fellow, severely wounded, who looked about twelve years old, with his pink cheeks and golden curls. As he was prepared for a foot amputation the kindly, maternal, overworked Mme Kleber stroked his brow. He opened cherubic blue eyes and gasped: 'Don't you dare give me a transfu-sion of Jewish blood. You've beaten us this time, but just wait till the next war – we'll smash you—'

When the convoy halted for an hour or so we could hurry into the nearest cottage and say: 'Dinner for four in ten minutes,' and it always appeared. I remember one meal when the Frau introduced us to her *Mann* as if she were a happy hostess, and six red-faced children stood around gaping. I watched a German woman in the next garden feeding her ducklings. She picked one up and held it tenderly against her cheek. The gesture struck oddly against the background of crashing tanks and black smoke.

At dusk we reached Waldsee, a picturesque mountain town. The town crier, a meek little old man, was going through the deserted streets ringing a bell and proclaiming the death penalty for hiding arms. Meanwhile two eager women ran after Husser begging the *Herr Doktor* to stay in their house.

The next day we drove south without opposition until a line of snow-covered mountains appeared ahead and we caught our breath at their beauty. We were heading into the Tyrol!

Two whole German armies were now flying before us into the mountains of Austria and we were deluged with prisoners. Every wood was full of Germans and the French could not be sure if they wanted to fight or not.

When we reached Ratzenveldt, a mountain village of charming chalets, wet snow began to fall. There were over sixty lugubrious German soldiers in this place, all with Red Cross brassards on their arms, all claiming Red Cross protection, and talking about Geneva conventions. Husser scurried around and remarked ironically: 'Sixty Red Cross armbands and never were the wounded so badly looked after!'

Commandant Vallin had commandeered the inn as a mess and he invited us to dinner with a dozen zouave officers. From the radio in the inn we learnt that Himmler offered unconditional surrender; that Pétain was in France; and that Mussolini had been executed. One of the younger officers came in, halfway through dinner, elated at having just captured a German general and his staff. It happened thus:

We had just moved into the village when one of the locals came up and asked to speak to this officer privately. Then, eyes gleaming, he revealed that a general was hiding with his staff in a friend's hunting-box in the hills. There was no earthly reason for him to impart this information except sheer desire to ingratiate himself. They went with a squad, and found the general, two colonels and several other officers having tea. When the zouaves arrested them they seemed puzzled by the French refusal to shake hands and share their tea. Then the general explained that his sweetheart was in the house, it would therefore be a favour if he were allowed to stay until the morrow. He was dismayed when ordered into the awaiting truck.

I shall always remember our gay dinner in the just-captured chalet; the snow falling outside, the German girls serving us, the atmosphere of fantastic dream. Most of the officers present had spent some time in France under the occupation; Vailin himself had escaped through Spain. It did them good to see the lack of pride of the German people, for all the best Frenchmen had been hurt and humiliated by their country's defeat. They said, with burning satisfaction: 'Well! at least one never saw in France, during the whole four years of German rule, the *boche* being cheered in any village, and though Frenchmen did betray each other it was through fear and not without some strong compulsion.' *'Plat comme des punaises'* was the troops expression for the *Herrenvolk* – 'flat as bed bugs'...

By 29 April, when we reached Ratzenveldt, the cold was so intense we could not sleep in the ambulances. Husser commandeered a room with one large bed between the four of us. Mimi, Susanne, Genny and I had a hideous night, for there were no blankets, and only one huge cushiony feather eiderdown. We froze and boiled in turn, like a basket of miserable kittens all pushing and begging the others to lie still. I never knew anything as hellish as those German feather-beds. One's feet stuck out numb with cold while the rest of one poured with sweat. Our cannon were booming all night and a machine-gun rattled in the garden.

The climax came when a squad of soldiers clumped upstairs to search the house because they had seen a light signalling. They pounded on our door, and Genny pulled out the revolver she always kept under her pillow. *'Entrez,'* we yelled, and the soldiers came in with fixed bayonets. 'Who is here?' they demanded, flashing a torch around. 'We arrest you for signalling from a window.' 'But we are your *ambulancières*! Surely you recognize us?' The corporal flashed his torch on us suspiciously: 'In God's name how many are there in the bed anyway?' 'Four!' we answered in one furious shout, and he retreated quickly.

In the morning we drove on into the snow-covered mountains and now we only heard our own guns. The fleeing remnants of the German 19th Army no longer responded. Obviously our armour could not proceed much further through the wild forested mountains and snow-blocked roads. On May 1st we reached Oberstaufen on the Austrian frontier, and in the afternoon we passed through a dark, ominous forest where a tank-trap of solid trees lay across the road. The local villagers were ordered to hack it down. 'It took us two weeks to build,' they complained. 'Well, it must come down in two hours,' said Lieutenant Laporte who had taken Captain Fougère's place as squadron-leader.

In the cold twilight we drove into Oberstaufen along with the cuirassiers. Snow was falling gently and the usual white surrender sheets hung from every window. One chalet was decorated with four enormous Swiss flags and its jittering inhabitants ran out to announce their nationality in voluble French, English, and German. Lieutenant Laporte, who travelled ahead of his squadron, in the same half-track in which Fougère had been killed, stepped out to speak to the *Burgomaster*. A shot rang out and he fell. We hardly realized what had happened until his soldiers picked him up and shouted for Husser. By the time he had been carried indoors he was dead, with a rifle bullet through the head. It took five minutes to work out which house the shot must have been fired from. Troops surrounded it and broke in. They searched every floor but found it empty. Whoever fired the bullet had got away. All civilians were ordered to their homes; but a thorough search revealed nothing. The Germans, in like circumstances, would have taken fifty hostages and shot them. The French, being unable to find the man who did it, took no indiscriminate revenge though they felt sourer than ever.

We sorrowed for Laporte who like Captain Fougère and Captain Gelis had been among the division's most experienced and brilliant young officers. It was a tragic way to die, when the war was nearly over, especially as he had been wounded in the Vosges fighting, and had only just got back to the 2nd Cuirassiers in time for the invasion of Germany. This squadron had indeed been unlucky with its commanding officers, having four killed in eight months.

The next morning snow was falling heavily and we heard that armour could advance no further. We had hoped to reach the Brenner Pass. Husser was sent for by the villagers to go to the local doctor's house and we followed him. The German village doctor, a tall fine-looking man in the thirties, lay dead with his beautiful golden-haired wife and his two-year-old son beside him. The child looked like an angel asleep. They had all died painlessly from an intravenous injection which the doctor had known how to prepare and administer. He had been a sincere Nazi, and perhaps he believed the tales of French atrocities on the radio. Perhaps he had shot Lieutenant Laporte. We would never know. But what bitterness of soul, what anguished fear he must have felt to be able to kill his own small son.

The strange, morbid atmosphere of this mountain village was depressing so we were glad when ordered back from the snow-blocked roads to the warm golden-green Danube Valley.

We realized that in the last two days all sounds of war had died away. In four weeks the French Army had wiped out or captured nine Gorman divisions. Dazed by the incessant variation of directions of attack and by de Lattre's bold tactics the 19th German Army had been totally destroyed. Our Combat Command 1 had advanced 530 kilometres in their first six days in Germany, fighting most of the way. Our 3,500 soldiers had 25,000 prisoners on their hands and no one was popular who brought in anymore!

I did not know that in London the reports of this French Advance recorded: 'Hard resistance to the last. The Germans will not give in to French Forces.' I only knew that Genny and I had had the run of our lives!

Now came anti-climax. For three days we sat doing nothing, in a village where there was no water, no electricity, and no wireless-news, wondering if the war had ended or not. As the regiments were no longer in action the ambulances all came back to the medical company and we were reunited beside brigade HQ. The girls began to grumble. Some wanted the advance to last forever; others wanted to go back to the Tyrol and ski! I spent hours going over my Dodge engine, which had done 1,000 miles without a cough, and getting a nice old German woman to wash my clothes. Now the foreign workers had gone there were hardly any men left in the cottages. They had all been killed or made prisoner, but not before leaving a legacy of well-set-up blond children.

On 7 May, Bertrand de Bellefond arrived in his armoured car and told us that peace had been signed! A few hours later two of our zouaves in Ulm were hit by joyous Americans who were firing revolvers in the air to celebrate. The zouaves were hanging from a balcony and they fell like partridges, but proved to be only winged.

Eager for more news I went out to our mechanics who had indeed got a wireless working, but it was impossible to hear anything as they all had their heads inside the amplifier and were shouting each other down.

Genny and I wandered out into a field of yellow flowers and we sat looking at the sweeping Danube Valley trying to realize it was all over; that now, on this calm spring evening, peace was being signed.

The girls were quiet at dinner, too dazed and tired to celebrate. We had been the proud possessors of a dozen bottles of champagne but, as there was no clean water in this village, we had drunk it all up and now on the night of nights we had only chlorine tablets to flavour our victory toast.

I went out to collect my washing from the cottage woman next door, who was a dear old soul. The pictures of her two sons, one killed in the Western Desert and one at Stalingrad, hung on the kitchen wall. 'Is the war really ended?' she asked. *'Der Krieg ist beendet'* I answered, and she took both my hands in hers: *'Das ist gut,'* she said; *'Das ist gut,'* and her eyes were full of tears.

32

Occupation

Next morning we knew that peace had indeed begun for a series of scathing remarks about discipline appeared in Orders. General de Lattre, well known as a martinet, descended on his army like a fury, said that the rainbow assortment of commandeered civilian cars were making his convoys look like circus processions, and that if scarlet Mercedes-Benz were absolutely necessary for transporting supplies, they must travel in separate convoys and at night. He swooped unexpectedly on one of our zouave platoons where an unfortunate lieutenant, who thought himself still in combat zone and miles from army commanders, wandered out tieless and unshaved at midday. The earth did not open and swallow him as in kindness it should have. De Lattre ordered him ten days in *une forteresse* and swept on. Even we, the darlings of the division, were strafed about our *tenue*. The girls remarked airily they would just like to see *anyone* send them to a fortress; but, nevertheless, we pulled our socks up, or rather we turned them neatly down around our boots in the prescribed manner and we hastily painted Solange's splendid pea-green open roadster a correct khaki and procured her a military number plate.

At midday on 8 May, the whole division started to move back to a zone of occupation on the Rhine. We had hoped to move forward with the 4th Moroccan Division into the Tyrol, and were peeved when we heard Leclerc's 2nd Armoured Division was to hoist the French flag at Berchtesgaden. It was the hottest sort of day that Europe can produce. We drove for twelve hours in a meandering convoy with hundreds of waits and stops through a new fantastic Germany, a beaten Germany, where the women smiled and hordes of little Teutons did the V for Victory as we went by. Some of the tiniest did not understand and toddled out doing the Nazi salute until Mother saw it; then they would be smacked and whisked indoors. We had thought so often of this day of Victory, but no one dreamed we would spend it driving past cheering waving *boches*.

At dusk we passed Pforzheim, a fair-sized town which had manufactured precision instruments, bomb sights, and other intricate apparatus used in war. It had been raided once by the Americans and, in twenty minutes, 40,000 people were killed. Not one house was inhabited now, and even the villas on the hills around were gutted by blast. Every street was blocked by debris, but a single thoroughfare had been cleared through the centre for army traffic. In the middle of the town we had an hour's halt and we all climbed on top of our ambulances and looked around. It was macabre, like finding a city in the midst of the jungle that had been dead five thousand years. Not a soul moved in the ruins. There was no sound at all in the twilight. Occasional houses had the names of whole families, dead beneath the rubble, chalked up. It was weirder than Cassino, for that was a battle-ground, but this was a far bigger town in which life had ceased in one afternoon.

Late at night the convoy halted in a battered railway siding. As we arranged ourselves for sleep in the ambulances, one of the more tireless girls got her new radio fitted to work off her battery and we heard that VE day had been celebrated and that Churchill had spoken that afternoon. 'Blast,' said Genny, 'I don't understand a word of English but I would have liked to hear Peace announced by *Monsieur* Churchill's voice.'

Next morning we drove back through blackened Karlsruhe and recrossed the Rhine, leaving many good friends in German earth.

Our division was to occupy the Palatinate and the regiments were spread on both sides of the river.

We arrived in a big German barracks at Germersheim which had been shelled to pieces. The yard walls were decorated with life-size paintings of our various tanks, with the vulnerable places marked in red. In the evening we moved into the local casino, a large edifice standing solid amidst several blocks of ruins. It had no window panes and no lights, but we lit candles and lay down in rooms that were knee-deep in rubble, too tired even to think about supper. 'Don't let's forget we are conquerors, however,' sighed Genny, as she curled up on three dirty old cushions laid on a heap of rubbish.

Next morning we applied to the *Burgomaster* and hordes of German workers came in to clean and repair. They emptied loads of rubble out of the windows for other Germans to cart away and by nightfall we had installed ourselves fairly well. The girls were clever at making the rooms pretty with a few silk handkerchiefs and some paint. Three German women were permanently hired in the big kitchen to cook and wash up. Then, in the intense heat, we all indulged in a 'reaction'. We were too tired to move and very cross at not getting to the Brenner Pass. When our truck came up with kit from the rear I found my kit-bag had been stolen from it. To cap this, my down sleeping bag was taken off by one of the fifty German workers and several watches disappeared. We felt, irritably, it should be us, not the defeated, who indulged in any looting.

Swallows flew in and out of the house picking plaster off the ceilings with which to build new nests. All their favourite eaves had been knocked down and I had to discourage them building in my room. There was not a pane of glass for forty miles – but it was so hot we did not need windows.

We evacuated the town hospital which was taken over by our medical company. I drove the patients back to their various villages, through woods of glimmering leaves and dark pines which were a mass of tank traps, overturned vehicles, burnt-out tanks, barbed wire, pill-boxes, trenches and lines of defence, all the hideous junk of war. The smell of decomposing bodies turned one's stomach and did not suit the flowering gorse and tender greens of May.

Dozens of odd little happenings, such as the lack of any black-out, reminded us that the war was over and the whole tempo of life changed. We now drove with an Arab guard in the ambulance, and with him we dared to loiter and stop for cider at farmhouses. There was a very old man in the hospital who had to be returned to a far-off village; the first road we tried had a broken bridge and the second a river running over it, so, as we did not fancy submerging the ambulance, Genny and I got out and paddled to cool ourselves. Presently a tank came along, we waved and asked if they would take the patient. The crew was very affable and paddled too. We carried the old German across the river and lifted him on to the Sherman turret, complete with suitcase and crutches, and off the tank rumbled to drop him at his cottage door. He looked pleased and evidently thought it a fine way to come from hospital at the age of eighty.

On the first Sunday of peace – which was the feast of Jeanne d'Arc – we had High Mass sung in the undestroyed local church. We reserved half the Church, but the folk of Germersheim packed every corner and seemed to enjoy our hymns to Jeanne d'Arc and France. It was strange to see these same priests, who had worked beside us in action, helmeted and in khaki, now dressed in white and gold vestments.

General Gruss drove me to Div. HQ at Landau in his new open Mercedes-Benz, which had been presented to him by two SS officers who gave themselves up as prisoners in the Tyrol. The countryside was flat, full of barley and corn, women and children working in the hot sun with the Palatinate Mountains in the distance. There were numerous stone benches by the roadside with a sort of stone shelf over them and the general told me their history. This land used to be part of France and when Marie Antoinette left Austria and drove here, the people gave such a welcome to their new Dauphine that she decided to put up memorials which would be really useful. As the women in those days carried their produce to market in large baskets on their heads; Marie Antoinette devised these stone seats with the shelf above to put the basket on while resting. 'The benches of the Queen' remain, though the French tongue is long forgotten.

However, the people often asked us if they were to become part of France again. 'Do you want to?' 'We don't care, as long as we can live in peace,' they answered. I asked the French if they would like to have German peasants become French citizens. They looked rather irritable and said: 'Well, we do not want any *boche*; but see how nice and healthy their children are, and France needs children,' and they admitted frankly that the pathetic, scruffy children one sees in French villages are not entirely due to enemy occupation. The Germans take better care of their animals and homes; their kitchens are spotless, their gardens pretty, their children washed and brushed and gaily attired; even the bullocks, who pull their carts, are well cared for and led to some stream to be scrubbed with a long-handled brush each evening. What contradictory feelings one had about this nation! The more one saw their good points the more maddening it was to reflect on the misery they had caused. Life in the backwater of Germersheim was pleasant. Genny and I found it rather dull, but the other girls spent their days preparing for the numerous *soirées* that now started. They were in fact busy as bees choosing husbands.

Every fortnight each ambulance was posted to Div. HQ in Landau, and here within forty-eight hours we had five Arabs to transport to hospital who all had bullets through their legs due to silly accidents with guns. Then a Frenchman, who should have known better, got into bed with his pistol on and shot himself through the knee. We became less sympathetic at each call. The climax came when we were hurried off to collect *un noyé*. This proved to be another Moroccan who had gone for a swim immediately after lunch in the half-filled bathing-pool. Evidently he had a heart attack, for otherwise he could hardly have drowned in three feet of water. His pals, with their usual brightness, sat and watched him for thirty minutes before pulling him out and starting artificial respiration – to show the doctor what good-hearted chaps they were.

The little Saar towns had no charm and were half in ruins. Lorries of returning French slave-workers rolled along in the hot sunshine, waving and cheering, while overhead formations of planes roared all day. I watched them for weeks, wondering if one of them was bringing my brother home after five long years as a prisoner of war.

Genny and I spent one morning waiting for a sick parade to finish in the Palatinate mountains. We wandered into a huge garden attached to a lunatic asylum and bargained for the fresh-looking lettuces. I got a dozen for a few cigarettes, and a small boy helped me carry them. 'The war is finished,' he smiled grimly;

'Hitler *kaputt'* and he drew a finger across his throat in a revolting, gloating way, and laughed. It was a hideous gesture for a child.

Lieutenant Husser had set up a hospital for the Russians who were camped all along the Rhine. They had no medical organization of their own and lived merrily enough, in filth and chaos, sending for one of our ambulances when someone had a haemorrhage, broken skull, or was in the last stages of TB. There were five hundred Russians in the big barracks at Germisheim and we often drove them. I should not think any of them had ever had a bath in their lives, for the smell in the ambulance, even with the windows open, was almost beyond endurance.

Of this mixture of five hundred soldiers, deported workers, women and children, none seemed to have any desire to return to Russia or to their homes. All the other liberated peoples, French, Czechs, Poles, and Dutch whom I had seen, were weeping with emotion at the idea of returning 'home'. These Russians seemed content to live on in the barracks for the rest of their lives, saying, it was as good as anywhere else! Several men claimed to be officers in charge, but they did not seem to have any control, and they would not arrest miscreants. This made it difficult for French troops, who were supposed to maintain order in the country, for instances of theft and assault constantly took place. Some of our zouave soldiers patrolling a village at night heard piercing screams in a farmhouse and broke in. They found two Russians making off with loot while the woman they had just murdered lay with her head bashed in on the kitchen floor in front of her small terrified children. The zouaves arrested them by force and brought them back to the local Russian group who said: 'Well, what does it matter – the woman was German!'

One morning Genny and I were summoned to drive a Russian woman, stated to be dying of haemorrhage after a miscarriage in the Germersheim barracks. We unfolded a stretcher and were preparing to fetch the patient ourselves when she appeared half-pushed, half-dragged along by a couple of laughing men who hoisted her into our ambulance in a way that would have made our native oafs seem gentle. They thought it funny to see her in pain.

At the hospital Lieutenant Husser said, 'See how I have fixed them up.' We went in trying not to breathe, for every window was shut and even here they never washed. Tubercular cases and children with measles all dossed down together. 'I cannot induce the infectious and TB patients to keep in separate rooms, but this is fine compared to their own arrangements. Perhaps you find it hard to believe?' Having so often objected to the dirty habits of native soldiers I watched with amusement while a Moroccan orderly remonstrated against the prevalent Russian habit of using their bedroom floors as latrines. *'Nix, Nix'* the Moroccan was imploring, as he pointed to the filthy corners.

When Husser examined the new patients one old man pulled off his shirt and tried to hide a cross that hung around his neck on a chain. The woman interpreter laughed, and said in French, 'See! He is frightened of being reported for wearing his cross.' 'Do many of your people follow the Christian faith?' asked Husser. 'No,' she replied; 'a few of the older ones but those of my age know better.'

Physically these Russians were very much of a type, short, snub-nosed and with broad rather Mongolian features and a tendency to be fair-haired. I never saw one man as tall as myself (five feet nine) and the women were very stocky. Every evening several columns of men would go out from the barracks for a march along the Rhine. It seemed to be the only thing they ever organized. The first evening I met them by the river, I could hardly believe my ears as they approached singing *'Stenka Razin'* and other part songs the Russian choirs have made famous. Each group seemed to have one magnificent voice, whose fierce solos rose above the tramp of feet until the chorus burst in. No other people in the world can sing like Slav peasants.

'They are odd people, those Russians; they have funny heads,' said our Arabs, and the Moroccans, whom I had deplored for so long, were indeed trim and dainty and bright mentally in comparison. They at least washed and kept themselves free from vermin and disease. The Russian women were boisterous and simple and would play tag with our natives. Never in their lives had these Arabs met such females. I sat one afternoon and watched a band of Russian girls stroll along the Rhine embankment, strumming guitars and singing softly. They were squat and muscular, with flesh burnt red by the sun, and they were dressed in small black cotton shorts and *brassières*, with very dilapidated high-heeled shoes. In peasant dresses they might have looked pleasant. They met four of our Moroccans, also out for a stroll. I had learnt long ago in Syria, that it shocks a Mohamedan far less to see a woman naked than in a bathing suit, for to them arms and legs are indecent, whereas the trunk of the body is for utility not charm. I just wondered what would happen. The Arabs stopped, grinned broadly and made comments in Arabic. The Russian women looked at these moustached heroes and grinned back. There was no coyness. The men came up and felt their bare, bulging thighs and laughed again, while the girls giggled and wriggled and gave back walloping smacks. The Arabs gaped at women so coarse, so brazen, so utterly unafraid. Neither could understand the other's speech, of course, but a game of tag swiftly began. There were Arab shouts and Russian squeals and when the girls were caught and held teasingly over the river there were piercing screams while fat legs kicked. Everybody enjoyed it hugely for Russian males are sombre and Arab women do not indulge in horse-play. I left them scampering and hoped it would not end in tears.

Moroccan love-life along the Rhine developed oddly. Any member of the French Army caught 'fraternizing' with a German woman had his head shaved as a punishment. The first of these Moroccan cases in Germersheim were very shamefaced, but soon they all had shaven crowns, and it became *a la mode*, so had to be dropped as a mode of disciplining. But the extraordinary thing was, not that these simple-minded natives should be on the look-out for illicit love but that the clear-eyed German women, with all those years of race consciousness instilled into them, should be willing to accept men of dark blood.

At first the Frenchmen were all determined not to sleep with German women. They would let them wash their socks and that was all. But after a month of idling the feeling began to change. There were no French women to associate with and the occupation seemed exceedingly dull. One wondered how the socks of the French Army survived so much attention and the washerwomen were so amiable, so young and blonde and husbandless – poor things! It's no good trying to stop it, sighed the officers, as long as it is *avec discrétion*.

We lived in surprising intimacy with the Germans, for the units to which we were posted for a week at a time billeted us in the house of some pleasant German housewife, and every morning we would descend to the kitchen and heat our coffee and listen to her tale of woe. Heidelberg was our first glimpse of American territory. German girls in black satin dresses and fox furs were ogling negroes for cigarettes, while German soldiers with great packs on their backs trudged wearily along, heads hanging, unnoticed in the crowded streets, each making for his home town. It had always struck me that French women were finer on the whole than the men; but German women seemed devoid of pride whereas their soldiers kept a weary dignity. Perhaps if women are systematically treated as inferiors they in time become so.

Genny suffered from the inactivity to which we were now doomed. After her work with Patton's Army, and the exhilarating advance, she could find nothing better to do than clean the ambulance, with four tiny German boys helping. Being an ardent leader of Wolf Cubs in Lorraine she taught them the code of one good deed a day, and while she polished the engine a little tow-headed chap, aged about four years, would be at each wheel dusting it diligently.

At the end of May a Mass for the dead of the division was held in Speyer Cathedral. Three of our padres in black and gold robes chanted the service and the others officiated in their khaki surplices. General Soudre and the brigade generals wore full uniform, and the zouave band stood behind the altar and beat out on drums and trumpets a far sounding 'Last Post.' Bringing military music into church was most impressive and as the drums throbbed everyone thought of friends who lay still and quiet on battlefields. There were good voices in the division and they gave a rendering of 'Auld Lang Syne' which is the French soldiers' hymn for dead comrades. They use the words:

'Ce n'est qu'un au revoir mon frère . . .'

Later on our combat command organized a *Te Deum* to be sung at night by the Rhine at Germersheim. An altar was built beside the river and lit with candles. Most of the German townsfolk attended the service. As the voices died away the racing Rhine waters carried on the chant, and when a full moon rose up behind the altar all the river turned to brilliant silver and its beauty seemed to give thanks to the wide sky.

33

Extermination Camp

At dawn, on 4 June, three of our ambulances were detached to travel across Germany to collect sick French prisoners. Our instructions were simply to drive three hundred miles to Nordhausen, in the Harz Mountains, and report to the camp there. We passed Mannheim and Frankfurt and ate our K rations happily by the roadside. To travel through a new part of Germany in this Spring weather was delightful. At ten at night we halted far in the American zone. Genny, who prided herself on knowing American types, peered into the dark village street and said:

'There is a smart looking soldier with an intelligent expression.'

I could just distinguish a vague form and shouted: 'Hey! Can you put us up for the night?'

The soldier came up and peered in. 'Gosh,' he said in a fine Texas accent, 'Gosh, I guess so – but gosh.' He stepped on the running board and directed us to a commandeered college. Here we found a guarded park for our ambulances, hot showers and a kitchen that could be miraculously opened up to 'feed six famished French girls'. We supped and bathed and revelled in the luxury of beds with clean white sheets.

After a delicious night we left early for Nordhausen, which we reached about nine in the morning. Genny was driving and I was asleep beside her when we reached the entrance of a large camp

and an American soldier halted us at the barbed wire barrier.
Never having heard of Nordhausen we stared out at what looked
like a factory yard of small aeroplanes. It suddenly dawned on me
that these stacks of finished parts, the large balls of compressed air
and finned tails standing in rows, belonged to V1s and V2s. We
passed rows of huts that had been SS training barracks and were
halted by a second gate tangled with barbed wire. Here was a row
of huts where the camp commandant and French liaison officer
had offices, and an American snack bar was dealing out hot drinks
and sandwiches.

Having driven since five without breakfast we all tumbled out
when a friendly GI invited us to have coffee. We still had not realized that Nordhausen was an extermination camp, and that our
patients were to come from here and Buchenwald, so the next
invitation was rather dazzling. 'Say, girls,' said the jolly soldier, 'come
and see the swimming pool and the gibbet.' We followed him into
the camp proper where 15,000 wretches had lived in a square of
huts surrounded by electrified barbed wire. The wooded hill that
rose steeply behind the camp contained vast underground factories
for V weapons. There were over thirty miles of tunnels. The prisoners worked twelve-hour shifts in these subterranean workshops.
One thousand men died a month from exhaustion and starvation.

I had grown bored with the outcry about concentration camp
horrors, but neither film nor pen could describe the sinister
atmosphere. A French doctor, who had been an inmate and was
now tending the sick, showed us the rows of huts and the smart
modern swimming-pool used *only to conduct experiments*. This
doctor had seen men given hot soup and then thrown into the icy
pool, so that statistics could be formed on the number who died
of heart attack and pneumonia. Beside this pool – like a gigantic
football goal – stood the gibbet. Iron rungs made steps up it, and

as many as forty corpses at once had often dangled from it. Visible from all the huts, it was never without bodies.

In the centre of the camp a cement square was labelled '*Appell Platz*' where the two-hour roll-call took place daily. After their twelve-hour shift of work in the terrible airless subterranean factories men, standing in the snow, died at every roll. The doctors said their bodies would be held up and dragged off by comrades so that they could claim their soup. It was deliberately planned that a thousand humans should die each month; this toll was economic, as plenty more who needed 'political instruction' were always available to take their places. No one ever escaped from Nordhausen and no one was intended to survive. A few of the young men lived two years but most died within twelve months. If there was any shortage of prisoners the Germans, ever efficient, could slightly increase the rations and therefore add a few months to the average life. The system worked to perfection. It gave them free slave labour for the manufacture of their famous 'secret weapons' and the constant grinding out of the slaves' lives in the slowest torture so that none could divulge information.

'The crematorium was always smoking,' said the doctor, as he led us up the hillside heaped with human ashes. The books, recording that a thousand were burned here each month, were neatly kept. We stared at the brick building with its date 1942 proudly engraved on the smoke stack. We stared at the ovens, at the smart white porcelain dissection tables, still stained with blood, at the corpses of three Poles who had died that day lying on stretchers with skeleton legs and hands, and then at the big trenches half filled with burnt bones. The heaps of human ashes were the least of the horrors; it was the hideous craziness, the organized cruelty that had gone on before, that haunted the place.

It was a beautiful sunlit day and the camp, built in a hollow surrounded by wooded slopes, looked innocent enough. Yet warm and gay as the earth seemed in June we pictured this Hades in winter with rows of shivering exhausted wretches standing to attention in the bitter wind. A Pole came up to us and said:

'Fear keeps even a dying man on his feet. The noise and airlessness of the underground factories drove many prisoners insane. Others fainted as they worked, and the SS would kick and cudgel them until they staggered to their feet. If they did not get up it meant they were dead.'

Most of the huts were occupied by Dutch, Italian, and Polish prisoners and a number of DPs had been brought in. Under American supervision it made an adequate transit camp. The Poles, who still wore their convict uniform, were ill and lifeless and just sat about in the sunshine, beyond caring. A number had been wounded by shells when the Americans captured this camp, and many hundreds were shot by SS before they fled. We went to the hut which was now used as the French hospital and talked to women whose legs had been broken and purposely deformed.

The barracks in the first enclosure had housed some four thousand SS to look after fifteen thousand prisoners. Apparently it was a school for both men and women SS. No aeroplane could have discovered the large tunnels which led into the hillside where the underground factories were. The finished V weapons could roll out the other side of the hill straight into a railway yard and hence to the firing sites.

Seeing the camp was nothing in comparison to handling the men who were to come out of it and spend two days in our ambulances.

The French liaison officer asked us to pick up some of the inmates whom he had moved to a TB sanatorium a few miles away. This we did, though it seemed futile as they had only a few weeks to live, but they were desperately anxious to get back to France. Then we returned and loaded up with less sick patients from Nordhausen, and Buchenwald (about 40 miles away, which we did not have time to see, nor did we want to). It was five in the afternoon when we had loaded up completely. The American CO of Nordhausen who saw us off, was choking with rage about new horrors he had just discovered. It was strange to see an American colonel shake his fist in the air. As a parting gift, one of the Italian prisoners gave each of us a brightly-coloured belt he had woven from insulating tubes of the V weapons. Just outside the gate a German woman lifted her little blond baby up and smilingly waved its hand at us. The gesture was curiously irritating.

At ten at night we reached Mulhouse, where we knocked on the door marked 'Military Government'. Nice American officers came out and with great efficiency darted round the town and found a German military hospital where we could lodge our sixteen patients for the night. It was pandemonium, and the German officer in charge maddened me by coming into the ward, where we were all frantically making beds, and standing there smoking. I snapped at him: *'Nicht rauchen'* (learnt in trains) and he stood to attention, apologized, and threw away his cigarette. He spoke perfect English, and looked bewildered when I said: 'Look at these people. They come out of your prisons and are dying.' He was quite a young doctor, and as soon as he realized anyone spoke English he began a diatribe about the behaviour of the Russians in their zone. The American officers with us said: 'We'll discuss that later. For the moment we are only interested in the behaviour of Germans. Understand! You are responsible for these people.'

Early the next morning we collected our patients and drove fast along the *autobahn*, stopping at one village to commandeer milk and eggs. Here the American officer in charge helped and gazed with pity at our emaciated charges. He said: 'I've been all through North Africa and France, burying American soldiers. I've thought sometimes it was a terrible job, but I'd rather see men dead than looking like that. We try to make the German prisoners here go and see the film of those camps, but they won't look.'

After fifteen hours on the road with the poor devils I felt as if I had known them all their lives, although they could only talk in whispers. There was Jacques Wauters of Bruxelles, aged twenty-three, whose X-ray showed less than a quarter of one lung left, and an Italian, with deformed broken arms. The rest were Frenchmen, whose crime had been refusing to work in Germany because the BBC told them not to. 'Tell me why did the BBC say that? We thought there was something on, something going to happen soon, and that was two years ago.' A ghastly feeling of guilt stole over me, but I could not answer. How can one know that, because of some talk on the wireless, men, who have risked their lives to listen, will stake their all on a misunderstood phrase and suffer so terribly?

We stopped fairly often to give them drinks and got to care for each individual with an aching pity. They had a look I had never seen in human eyes before and the feel of their bodies was so light, like a bird's body, when one held them up to cough.

What a journey. Atrocities bored and revolted us, for we had heard of so many in France, but these sick men wanted to tell their stories before they died. One wanted to gasp out the tale of his friend whom he saw thrown into a lorry with a dozen others and driven to a trench where, as the back of the lorry opened and they fell out, a machine-gun opened fire. Dead and wounded fell together and were buried as they were, while the vehicle rumbled off for another load. It was the casual cruelty of Nazi-Germans that numbed one; they could kick a dying body as we kick a tree stump to see if the wood is rotten.

This journey never seemed to end. They were all spitting blood and two of them had TB of the intestines which gave them constant, appalling diarrhoea, and the smell in the ambulance became intolerable. We had no bed-pans so the only thing to do was to stop on the main highway, lift the stretchers down, roll them off into the grass, and hold them gasping with weakness. Their faces were pathetic enough, but their bodies even worse.

American soldiers came to gape and stayed to help, silent and gentle, but green in the face with horror when they saw the hip bones protruding so you would think they'd pierce the skin, their thighs as thin as a girl's wrist. The little Italian with big eyes was better than the rest, and he told me how he saw the Americans who took the camp lining up the thirty odd SS they could capture of those thousands, and mowing them down with a machine-gun. 'They were frightened, after all they had done – and died like cowards.' Genny, usually talkative, had collapsed with the inward despair we all felt and was now sleeping beside me, waking up occasionally to pass a drink or some gauze to spit in. These lung-less men helped each other touchingly. We gave up trying to disinfect the cups.

As the sun set with unusual beauty and the rich fields glowed in golden light, such a nausea came over me I could hardly drive, and looking at God's lovely earth I felt it would have been better if life had never crept out of the sea, better if the whole earth remained desolate as the moon if this is all mankind can make of it.

We crossed the Rhine by night and we were happy to tell them: 'Now we are crossing! You are nearly in France.' It was midnight when we got them to hospital, carried them upstairs, and tucked up their poor husks of bodies in bed. They were fainting with fatigue and soaked with sweat but I suppose the journey was worth it from the psychological point of view, for they died 'going home'.

During the days that followed a curious apathy crept over us. We did not want even to read. I preferred my nest of khaki blankets to the sunshine out of doors. I just lay there wishing one could vomit mentally. Genny slept, but another of the girls practised her new concertina, making appalling sounds, until she stopped and I saw she was crying. Thinking it might have been because I was so rude about her music I went over to her bed, but she said:

'Leave me alone! I can bear it because I am not *croyante* – at least I do not believe that any God watches these things. If I did, and knew that he had done nothing, then I could not stand it! But I just believe it is stupid, horrible chance that mankind is like this, and the world is burning out anyway so it is all right,' and Genny said: 'Nothing could ever matter again after this, could it?'

34

And so to Potsdam

French Army Orders granted leave to those who had a brother returned from imprisonment in Germany and as I now came in this category I applied. Kind Americans flew me to England, where a jolly customs man went through my belongings and passed the fur knapsack taken from the back of an artillery prisoner, my SS dagger, Iron Cross, brilliant Nordhausen belt and alarm clock and stockings looted at Horb.

The alarm clock was for our nanny who had sat imperturbably in England all these five years making prophecies about Hitler's downfall, which had, in the end, been completely accurate. All who have been brought up in an English nursery know that 'bad men cannot thrive!' The stockings were for my brave old charlady who had worked in London throughout the war and whose letter – when her son and his wife and children were killed by a V1 – is kept by my family as a reminder of what courage can be.

An RAF plane flew me over the Irish Sea and I met my brother on 'the Border' – the frontier of Ulster and the Free State, where the demesne walls of my home end and those of General Alexander's home begin.

When my leave ended an American Dakota returned me to Frankfurt, where I heard that my 1st Armoured Division was en route for Berlin. I proceeded to HQ for directions, only to find that SHAEF (housed in one of the biggest buildings in the world which had previously held the German Chemical Industry), was on that day being dissolved. I walked from one vast block to another, but every office sent me on saying they had got to transport their own staff to Washington or Tokyo and could not cope. On enquiring at a transport office, an American officer said triumphantly: 'We no longer exist,' and closed the door. No one had ever heard of the French Army, and no one cared how I reached Berlin as long as I cleared out and let them proceed with the dispersal of their own personnel. I climbed wearily into a bus and sat next an ATS girl who told me to go to the British camp commandant. To my delight I found there the same Lieutenant-Colonel Rothwell who had got me flown home in March. He was in the throes of moving to Berlin himself but he arranged for me to travel by the next British convoy.

For a few days I lived in an English officer's mess, and every evening we drove to the wooded mountains thirty miles north of Frankfurt where there was a spectacular allied officers' club called Frederick Schloss which had been the hunting-box of the Emperor Frederick and his wife – who was born Princess Victoria of England. The interior was untouched since 1914. In the library American officers perused leather volumes with 'Vicky's' bookplate. Her initials were on the plates and glasses in the dining-room, and on the walls were great combined coats-of-arms of England and Germany. Prints and photographs of Queen Victoria and the English cousins lined the corridors, and although the rooms were in 19th century taste they retained a nostalgic charm. Young men from all the States of America laughed along the corridors and asked if I would like a swig from the bottle of Bourbon whisky they had hidden in a vast gold clock.

In each of those bedrooms with the curtained four-posters and the knobs of brass we remarked the modest requirements of the modern officer on leave: a light aero-travel suitcase with zips, a gadget razor, and a bottle of liquor – different luggage indeed to the trunks of original visitors with their outfits for shooting and riding and dining. Even the bathrooms had retained their own ludicrous dignity with big, mahogany-encased tubs and platformed lavatories that were as ceremonial in appearance as thrones.

How much nearer we were to the Germans in those days! They had obviously liked and copied every aspect of sporting England; Vicky had brought the ways of Windsor with her. And if the Kaiser had not disliked his English mother, and been jealous of her country, perhaps he might not have provided the pebble which started the landslide in which we are slipping still?

When Colonel Rothwell sent off his staff in a convoy of lorries he gave me a seat with the officer in charge. We stuck to the big *autobahns*, reached Brunswick at dusk and were billeted in the best hotel. Military travellers were expected to provide rations, but if one ran short there would always be a friendly American with spare tins of meat and jam in his jacket pockets. We spent an hour looking at the ruins of this lovely mediaeval town. In spite of the warm sun, civilians, who camped in the streets like gypsies, looked frail and shivering. From this small state came Caroline to marry George IV. Never again will a German princess be able to write on her tomb the epitaph of even an 'Injured Queen of England'.

On the second day we kept solidly to the great Berlin *autobahn*. We passed Magdeburg, where the Russians and Americans had joined up in April, and in that great deserted plain it was easy to imagine the thrill as the tanks sighted each other in the sunlight and the dust.

We stopped to eat our lunch before entering the Russian zone, as instructions were that no British vehicles must halt hereafter. The sides of the *autobahn* now held a constant stream of German refugees wearily trekking in the hot sun. British soldiers hated the sight of old women trudging, with hanging heads, and expressionless young mothers pushing prams and barrows of belongings. I was glad, after my mixed war, to reach Berlin in company with London Tommies, for their remarks were full of kindness and wit.

As we sat by the roadside eating, the stream of refugees continued in silent single file, and of course before we had finished, the soldiers were giving tea to an old woman who was pushing her still older husband all the hundreds of miles to Bremen in a kind of bath chair, while behind them came a daughter carrying two heavy suitcases and her three small children dragging their little feet. We had to refuse lifts to those who were hiking towards Berlin, but there was something pitiful about the children that no soldier could resist. A little blond boy of about four got our last sweets, and the Cockneys sang out: "E'll probably be starting another war in ten years' time.' 'Ow, well, give 'im a bob and make 'im promise to be good.' Such were the English soldiers reaching the enemy capital. On the approaches to the city, when the vast Brandenburg plain gave way to fir plantations, burnt out in recent fighting, we stopped, and a couple of Russian soldiers trotted up on horseback. We had seen hardly anyone since entering their zone except a few horse-drawn convoys with men and women of the Red Army sleeping happily on top of carts of hay. Several times we passed villages where whole gardens were filled with red cones of painted wood, each about four foot high. These were soviet military cemeteries. Under each pyramid lay a hero of the Union. The effect was gaudy and Eastern, very unlike the neat crosses and crescents we were accustomed to see on soldiers' graves.

These Russians spoke no English but were amicable and managed to explain their rank – corporal and private. They looked pasty and ill, almost tubercular, their uniforms were of thin and very dirty cotton, their horses ungroomed, the saddlery never cleaned. One imagined them sleeping always in these clothes, indifferent to hardship, eating what they could get, very simple, easily pleased and demanding nothing of life. They were delighted with English cigarettes, slung their rifles over their backs and beamed while pointing out the painted hoarding which announced in Russian and German, that the Soviet held no animosity to the German people, only to their leaders. They were interested in the badges of rank of our soldiers and surprised that an officer should consort in so friendly a fashion with other ranks. A woman in uniform did not evoke the slightest interest, as the Russian Army is full of untidy women with bushy hair and cotton belted tunics.

It was late when we reached the big, bridged road-junction that led to the American and British zones of Berlin and we became thoroughly lost, for the signs were many and confusing, and huge placards announcing: 'Now you are leaving the American zone'; 'Now you are entering the Russian zone,' seemed to follow each other in quick succession until at last we came on the famous divisional sign of the Desert Rats. The 11th and 8th Hussars, those same regiments who had been fighting in Egypt under General Wavell's command when I had arrived as an MTC ambulance driver in March 1941, were now in Berlin! While billets were found for the convoy, I telephoned the 11th Hussars and was invited to their barracks. The second in command, Major Stuart French, came to fetch me in a jeep, and for a private soldier of a foreign army, I was royally treated and given officers' billets.

The 11th Hussars were lodged in a large barracks and had got it into good condition, burying dead cows and shovelling away the filth always left where Slavs have lodged. They had visited the Reich Chancellery and found smart Americans prying open, with bank-breaking gadgets a safe that had baffled the Russians, and removing diamond studded decorations that should startle the folks back home. They left the empty boxes however to be gathered up pathetically by the 11th Hussar. A band of Russian soldiers was busy smashing up furniture and cutting the carpets to bits. Having fought all the way from Alamein, the 'Cherry Pickers' thought they might at least have a bit of carpet too, and they cut themselves a slice to lay on the floor of their mess.

They were quite pleased with this mat from Hitler's private sitting-room and all the medals that the Americans did not want, but they soon got a reprimand from haughty British authorities who did not approve of 'looting'!

On the morning of 21 July the official Desert Rat Victory Parade was held along the Unter den Linden in front of Winston Churchill. Lieutenant-Colonel Wainman – who had been a squadron leader in Egypt and now commanded the 11th Hussars – sent me, with his batman, to balance on a box in front of the Grand Stand, which was decorated with mammoth posters of Churchill, Truman and Stalin.

In the Stand were Winston, Eden and Attlee, Field-Marshals Alexander, Montgomery, Alanbrooke and Wilson, and Mary Churchill who, in ATS uniform, got a big cheer from the soldiers. American and French generals drove up and a Russian car, whose driver must have been either dreaming or dazzled, drove smack into the back of the proceeding car just in front of the Grand Stand. It took a dozen military police ten minutes to lift and disengage the two vehicles, whose bumpers had become locked. We wondered if anyone got shot later.

I had seen armour in action, mud-covered, and flaming, and white in the snow, but never did I dream I would applaud an armoured parade with the tanks gleaming with paint and polished brass and German civilians cheering.

The troops' News Sheet of L. of C. Sub Area, dated 21 July 1945, is preserved among my papers, it reads:—

THE BERLIN VICTORY PARADE

Two hours before the start of the parade, British troops from the Berlin area and troops concerned with the Three Power Conference at Potsdam, began to arrive. A stretch of the Charlottenburger Chaussée on both sides of the saluting base had been reserved for spectators in uniform. A few American and Russian soldiers mingled with the British troops. German civilians were allowed to line the route. German policemen kept them on the pavement.

Just after ten o'clock the prime minister arrived. His sole military escort was some dozen military policemen in a jeep and on motor cycles. At the saluting base a salute was fired by the 3rd Royal Horse Artillery and the march past began. First came the tanks and guns gleaming in the sun. At the head of the marching troops came the band of the Royal Marines and behind them officers and ratings of *HMS Pembroke*. At this parade most of the army's representatives were drawn from the famous 7th Armoured Division, battalions of the grenadier guards, the Queen's Own Royal Regiment, and the Devonshire regiment. Almost all the men were wearing medal ribbons indicating they had fought in Africa, Italy, and Western Europe. The Canadian Berlin battalion followed the Desert Rats.

Before returning to Potsdam Mr Churchill opened a NAAFI club for OR's in the heart of Berlin's West End. Outside the club he made an impromptu speech to an audience of men from the 7th Armoured Division. 'Dear Desert Rats,' he said, 'May your glory ever shine, may the memory of the great pilgrimage you have made from El Alamein to the Baltic and Berlin never die.' Mr. Churchill was cheered by a German crowd which pushed its way through the police cordon.

The troops I was standing with had fought in the desert for nearly two years before Alamein and one of them said: 'There are three men I wish we could see standing by Winston's side ... the leaders of the Desert Rats when we fought the Germans with our bare fists ... General Wavell, General Strafer Gott and Brigadier Jock Campbell.'

Wavell of Cyrenaica had become Viceroy, Gott and Campbell were dead. But their soldiers remembered them in Berlin.

The Russians had not wished to grant any zone to the French; so the British, understanding the hurt pride of de Lattre's Army, gave them a suburb on the northern outskirts of Berlin. The zouaves of my division had already held a parade and enjoyed the pleasure of marching past the 1871 Sedan Victory Column, built to commemorate France's defeat and the incorporation of Alsace into Germany. When General Lyne gave them permission to fly the Tricolour above the giant figure of Germania which topped this memorial they had difficulty getting the flag up. At last, when all the steeple-jacks had failed, the zouaves found a Chinese acrobat in an internment camp, who skimmed up Germania's stone skirts and tied the Tricolor triumphantly above her head. As a reward the Chinaman was allowed to enter the ranks of the French Army (not as an acrobat but as a cook).

On 22 July, I received a note from Mary Churchill, asking me to lunch at Potsdam with her father. The Chasseurs with whom I messed had never forgotten that message I had brought from Chequers in April, 'Give the French my love' and were as excited as I was. The new badge of de Lattre's Army, showing the arms of Colmar with *Rhin et Danube* in big letters had just arrived. One was hurriedly sewn on my shirt, and I was implored to give Monsieur Churchill all their greetings and to bring Mary back so that the zouave band could play to her. 'After all' they said, 'if it were not for Monsieur Churchill we would none of us be here.'

A British car fetched me from Reinickendorf and we drove to Potsdam, where barriers of barbed wire, rows of Russian soldiers with gleaming bayonets and officers with tommy guns, together with the most serious of British and American military police, held one up. Pink and white passes decorated like Xmas cards had to be produced and one truly felt the eyes of the OGPU were fixed on one's name. The town of Potsdam had been well bombed, so the site chosen for the conference was a large area of luxurious suburban villas which must have belonged to the richest people of Berlin. The car drew up at a square white house set in a garden and Mary, whom I had last seen as a little girl at Westerham, now a captain of an Ack-ack battery assigned to 'special duties' for the conference, acted as hostess. It would have given anyone a kick to lunch with Winston in the heart of conquered Germany.

At lunch I sat between him and Anthony Eden. The sunshine lit up the modern white rooms which some rich Berliner had built without dreaming of the guests his villa would entertain.

The 11th Hussars had asked me to present Winston with a fine Nazi decoration hung on a red ribbon, and this pleased him greatly. He admired the flash on my sleeve of the First French Army which bore the arms of Colmar and the words *Rhin et*

Danube and he said to Eden: 'Why don't we call our own occupation troops Army of the Rhine? It sounds well.' I told him the French liked to think that he knew how hard Colmar and the Vosges had been for I do not think he realized to what extent they cared for him.

When I described the German people as we had seen them in the sweep forward, and how the women smiled and waved while their own men were being killed in the next wood, Winston said: 'That is the peculiar effect of Fear,' and he turned to his doctor, Lord Moran, who wrote the *Anatomy of Fear*, adding: 'He is the expert on that subject.' When men were afraid of battle they had a strained look and were over-gay but those emotions had little relation to the hysterical oiling-up which we had met with.

Another guest at this lunch was Professor (now Lord) Cherwell. I wondered what he was professor of, but that is a rude question to put to famous savants. In any case he could hardly have answered that he was adviser to the prime minister on an atom bomb that within three weeks would shake the world and end the war. After coffee Winston and Anthony Eden hurried off for an allied discussion on (according to my diary) 'the handling of Balkan problems, and the treatment of Germany.' A subject which seems to have lasted a singularly long time!

On the following day I myself explored Berlin, which I had not seen since 1935. Now the endless miles of ruins were impressive, strange and horrible. The devastation was revolting and so was the smell. The most interesting sector was that around the Chancellory where the great buildings of Nazi Germany, with their shell-pocked marble walls and smashed eagles retained a weird grandeur. A Tartar sentry held us up at the Chancellory door but we smiled and, trusting to luck, showed identity cards which he scrutinized upside down and let us through. We stared at the dramatic setting of Hitler's end, the smashed marble halls deep in rubble, the chipped eagles carrying their swastikas, the blackened desolate grandeur. We picked up fragments of black marble, knocked from the walls by shell splinters, to make table decorations for the 11th Hussar's mess, and a Russian officer gave me a piece of brocade which he said came from Hitler's chair, a German Motherhood Cross, and, most precious of all, some of the Führer's own note-paper headed with Eagle and Swastika on which my next letters home could be inscribed!

Near the grand Nazi building the foreign embassies stood in ruins. The Hotel Adlon, which I had last visited when Field-Marshal Mannerheim asked me to breakfast, had not one room left unsmashed. From the gaudy Japanese Embassy we gathered more brocade. A German came up and offered a beautiful camera for 200 cigarettes, but I had none, and the French contingent had not been supplied for three weeks.

The 11th Hussars were giving a grand dinner in their mess for Field-Marshal Alexander, Field-Marshal Maitland Wilson and Anthony Eden. A posse of officers had been sent off to the Hartz Mountains with orders to catch sixty trout, and I sweated around in a jeep with the 'flower officer' trying to find enough blooms to decorate the long tables. In the desolate suburbs of Berlin, this was not so easy. We found one small garden and cleared it. A woman asked us to come in and discuss payment with the proprietor, who spoke English. She led us to a very old man in bed with a banjo, who did not want to discuss the price of his flowers half as much as to sing us an English song.

This all took hours and as we had not got nearly enough we then drove to a dreary row of small gardens with huts, in which the owner of each plot could live. All the huts seemed deserted so we got out and cut what we could until a woman appeared and asked us not to touch the sunflowers, as the seeds had medicinal value. Sulky and exhausted, we stared at her and said: '*Wir wollen Blumen.*' She replied with a woeful tale. Her child was sick and had nothing to eat, but if only we could bring a bit of cake it could swallow that. Waving to neighbours' gardens we told her to gather all the '*blumen*' in sight and in four hours we would return with a loaf of white bread. This was most successful! The child arose from its sick-bed to don a party frock, and present an extra bouquet with a curtsy, and we got a whole jeep-load of dahlias which we arranged in flat tins. By twisting them over and around hunks of Hitler's marble we decorated all the tables in an attractive way. Then a new worry arose, the 'fishing officers' came back with their load of trout (caught, to their shame, not with flies, but by small boys with nets) and the army cooks announced they only knew how to make a white flour sauce!

The messing officer lent me the colonel's car to race twelve miles across Berlin and find immediately a Frenchman who knew how to make a real sauce. Nizola, the cook of the 3rd Chasseurs, wild with excitement at the prospect of cooking *truite au bleu* for *deux Maréchals,* tore upstairs to put on his '*plus beau pantalons,*' and with parsley in one hand and lemons in the other drove off in the staff car. He returned despondent, in the late evening to explain that by the time he got there the barbarian English cooks had cut off all the heads of the trout.

I recalled Voltaire's remark about the English having twenty religious sects but only one fish sauce.

Next day, Colonel Guibert, who commanded the 3rd Chasseurs, asked me to do what was possible for the welfare of his detachment of 750 Frenchmen. They had reached Berlin three weeks previously and were waiting the arrival of the brigade, but without wine or cigarettes. To the French soldier a pint of red wine a day means what the dozen-odd cups of black tea means to the British Tommy. The *poilu* only gets coffee and biscuits for breakfast, a meal at midday and dinner at seven. There are no elevenses or five o'clocks, but he does miss his wine ration and he hankers for cigarettes. Up to this time American cigarettes had been included in French Army rations, but in June this ceased, and the diverse units of the 1st Armoured Division were becoming depressed. They had no soap to wash their clothes but, as the soldiers said, one can wash without soap, it is worse to eat without wine, but to sit in Berlin without smoking is insupportable! They asked me to explain to some allied general that they were fighting troops anxious to enjoy the enemy's capital. I promised, and made quavering plans to find and vamp some NAAFI official.

The French had temporary billets until they could prepare the German Ack-ack Barracks, which were to be the winter quarters. I was allotted the absent padre's room in a villa next to the squadron mess and the German occupants of the house never ceased badgering me to help trace their missing son. The American WAACS at Mannheim had given me two cakes of soap and the German women of the house were grateful at being allowed to wash my clothes because they could do some of their own laundering at the same time. I soon became aware of their eyes watching my coming and going through the garden gate and occasionally some member would pluck up courage and ask if it were possible to procure tobacco or sugar. I told them frankly it was best to forget about smoking for several years, for our own troops were going short.

The English-speaking officers of the 3rd Chasseurs were invited to dine by one of Churchill's staff officers in the mess at Potsdam and we set off in Colonel Guibert's car for the mysterious, much-guarded conference area on its wooden hill. We had been supplied with identity cards by the British security and a huge pink card for the car and driver. I thought the Russian, American and British MPs looked at us sharply, for General de Gaulle not having been invited to the conference, these were the first Frenchmen to enter the compound. The staff mess was situated almost next to Churchill's house. It had terraces overlooking the lake where field-marshals and their attendant officers stood about in the evening sunlight, drinking aperitifs.

The 3rd Chasseurs, who had spent a month uninvited to British functions, found this invitation was most exciting. Major-General Laycock, whom I had not seen since Cairo when he led those first commando units against Rommel joined us and said: 'But I have never seen people enjoy themselves so much in any mess before.' When Mary Churchill was introduced to them their delight seemed complete. She was immediately invited to a dinner in her honour, at which the zouave band would play special melodies. Mary accepted conditionally for she was off to England the next day with her father and her return depended on the Election results.

Meanwhile, in the garden next door Stalin's personal bodyguard of officers, armed with tommy guns, crept through the flower-beds, and climbed the trees and tapped the chairs on which their Generalissimo might sit. There were armed Russians in the pantry and under the sink and behind the screens and bothering the cook and tripping over the toes of Churchill's own Scots Guards. Then Joe arrived, resplendent in white and gold, with a red stripe down his dragoon trousers, and a smile under the big moustache. This was Churchill's farewell dinner before flying to England to witness the Election results. I don't think any Russian doubted but that he had 'seen' to the Elections and arranged the result in advance. One of the English officers I knew had dined with the Russian general in charge of security and asked him frankly, what struck him about the British. He replied – 'I cannot understand why British generals and officers ignore their personal appearance, and have no sense of discipline or vanity. We have all had special suits made for this conference. As far as I can see none of you have bothered! Look at Marshal Montgomery in battle-dress and Marshal Alexander has been seen laughing and talking with a private soldier as if he were an equal. I myself have seen a British general arrive for a conference alone in a car and carry his own dispatch case. Doesn't he think of making people respect him?'

This was the only human Russian opinion I ever heard. We were cut off from their officers, those few who spoke French and were prepared to drink everyone under the table, never came to a French mess alone. They always kept in pairs who checked up on each other, so conversation remained stiff and stilted. The only question any Russian officer put to me in Germany was: 'Why are British soldiers allowed to walk on the pavements? Only officers should walk on the pavement and soldiers must walk on the road.'

The thousands of Tartar guards who surrounded Potsdam with their gleaming bayonets looked clean and well turned-out. The smartest were put to cordon Potsdam, whereas along the *autobahn* and all through the Russian zone, soldiers walked about in filthy, torn uniforms. By filthy, I mean they smelt as they passed one in the street. In fact the ordinary soldiers looked like bands of refugees who had trekked for months, sleeping in their clothes. By contrast, the girl traffic police were neatly turned-out in short pleated skirts, belted tunics and smart boots, and seemed efficient at their job, swirling round with coloured flags in each hand. If a car misunderstood and drove in the wrong direction the Russian Miss would pack the flags under her arm and shake her fist, a gesture whose meaning is plain in all countries.

On July 26th the 2nd Squadron of the 3rd Chasseurs, anxious to meet the most famous British armoured car regiment, gave a dinner for officers of the 11th Hussars, which took the entire day to prepare. Jeff de Baritault, the messing officer, disappeared at dawn in his armoured car to raid the neighbouring gardens for salads which Nizola demanded in order to *faire une bonne impression* on the English. Several kinds of tinned meats were begged borrowed or stolen and Nizola panted around with a large cookery book which he had carried throughout the campaign. Nizola was twenty-four, his two brothers had been killed in the war, and his old mother lived alone at Dijon. As soon as he could get demobilized he was going there to open a restaurant. 'The trouble is one needs money even for a café.' Having one English pound note I gave it to him as a beginning. But he made me write across it in large ink letters *'Bon souvenir de Berlin'*, and swore he would frame it.

Meanwhile the other officers were rushing about trying in vain to find some kind of alcohol for the dinner. They were in despair, for their English guests would not be able to intoxicate themselves with talk, like the French. At a late hour one of the lieutenants returned tired but triumphant, having made friends with a Russian OC Loot, from whom he had managed to procure a quantity of Greek wine. The only contribution I could make was to gather some wild flowers growing on a nearby rubbish heap and arrange them in an old tin as a table decoration. By the time the guests arrived, I was dazed and drooping. The news they brought (we had been too busy with preparations to listen to the wireless) was of Churchill's defeat. The French reaction was of amazement: 'But . . . but, aren't they pleased he won the war?'

However, the dinner proved a success and Colonel Guibert gave another the following week, for officers of both 11th and 8th Hussars.

In the meantime we had very little to eat in the mess and I set to, trying to procure cigarettes for our wistful troops who were always stopping me in the compound with:

'We have heard you are the new *assistante sociale* and have great pull with the British. Don't you think that *Monsieur le Général* Lyne would allow us to buy at a British canteen?'

Not smoking myself, it was hard to imagine the distress they were going through. However I drove a truck into the southern suburbs of Berlin and spent five hours trying to locate the American office dealing with rations. A colonel was charming but said it was impossible to step outside instructions. All cigarette rations to the French had ceased. I learnt how maddening and humiliating it can be to belong to a nation which has to ask for everything like a poor relation. Next day I started plodding from one British Headquarters to another. They all seemed to be in huge buildings miles apart and one was perpetually redirected to where one had just come from.

At last I tried General Lyne's headquarters and, to my surprise, I was ushered into the office of Lieutenant-Colonel Forster of the Northumberland Fusiliers, a friend whom I had last seen in Beirut when we dined and danced by the Mediterranean long before Sicily had been invaded. It was an equal surprise for him to find me marching into his Berlin office in French uniform. But as soon as he heard of the Frenchmen's plight he gave instructions that I could purchase one week's soap and cigarette rations at the NAAFI for them, and promised to take the matter up with the GOC. Elated, I got a truck and drove off to the NAAFI warehouse. The British soldiers there were darlings. They said: 'It's not right, it isn't. They ought to have their cigarettes like everyone else.' Next day every French soldier I met came up beaming to ask me to thank the English for their kindness. We might have got a weekly

arrangement, for General Lyne was favourable, but some senior
officer in HQ put his foot down and rocketed about the lot we
had got. It seemed to me more important to allow a cigarette
ration to 800 Frenchmen who were fighting troops, than to stuff
French politicians with huge dinners.

Whenever we could get transport we drove round the desolation that was Berlin. At first it was interesting but the long miles
of ruins and the processions of haggard, grey-faced civilians
pushing their belongings in handcarts grew more and more
depressing. Every day the bartering market in the Unter den
Linden increased. There, beside the Bradenburg Arch, against a
sombre drop-scene of burned buildings, blackened trees and
broken, bronze statues, the Berliners would come with their
oddments of jewellery, their cameras and films, their ornaments
and clothing, which they hoped to exchange for food or cigarettes. Cigarettes were now like gold, the basic currency.

I imagine the Americans must have done well out of this
marketing for their rations were liberal, whereas the British had
only just enough. It was maddening to be offered the camera one
had always longed to possess for two hundred cigarettes that one
hadn't got. 'Find some and come back in the afternoon,' the owner
would cry, and I cursed myself for not having stuffed my pockets
with tobacco in London!

We drove the French soldiers around Berlin in lorries to see
the bombing and they stared in silence, a remarkable achievement for Frenchmen. All that one of the drivers said to me was:
'You learn more from a look at Berlin than from any history
book.' And Berlin was in truth like a corpse, horrible but still
warm, the Nazi breath had only just left it, and in the sunshine it
had a kind of dramatic majesty. Those scenes must be printed
deep in our different memories, the desolate streets with hordes

of shabby Russians trekking in hay carts, their unkempt girls in oddments of uniform, snoring beside them; the well-dressed American soldiers swopping 'Camels' at the black markets that sprang up at every corner; the Desert Rats armed with rifles, marching in brisk couples in search of a cup of tea and a bun at the 'Winston Club', and eyeing, with pity, the bleak-faced women in the Russian zone doing forced labour of clearing away debris in buckets.

There were hardly any amusements for our troops till a couple of cinemas opened. One of these showed a documentary film composed of the best pictures taken in every action. It was called *True Glory*. I went with some Frenchmen, who kept saying: 'But where do we come in. There is no mention of what we did in the Vosges or Colmar – I suppose we are too stupid to take photographs of ourselves fighting. We must next time.'

Then suddenly the screen showed a scene taken in the deep snow of last January. The vocal commentator was muttering something about 'but the only girls we ever saw were these,' and there was an ambulance with two helmeted, jacketed, trousered figures brushing snow off the bonnet, and I remembered the girls telling me how they'd been stopped in a snowstorm by some camera men. It gave me a sudden twinge for one of the laughing faces was that of Lucette Lecoq. 'True Glory'? – so that was how I saw her last and no one could have guessed how lovely she was.

One evening I was left sitting in a jeep in the Kurfürstendamm, a street that had been lightly hit and among the Germans who walked by, at least twenty per cent appeared to be shell-shocked, mumbling to themselves or jerking queerly.

Seven or eight night clubs which had survived in this district were allowed to open between six and eight-thirty. None of them served alcohol or food but you paid a nominal 10 marks for a drink of syrup that too often included typhoid and was soon *verboten* to British troops.

I brought home a menu from the 'Piccadilly Club' which reads:

> 'It is allowed to sell the British troops only tea. Limonade and
> cooktales are for these troops not permitted.'
>   10% Law on drinks.
>   10% Service.

To the biggest of these haunts, 'The Femina', the richest Berliners came every evening because a plate of cucumber and potato could be ordered for about £2 – it was the only place where they could get anything to eat without points. The band was good and a selection of cabaret turns did their utmost between dances. On the evening I went there with the officers of the 9th Chasseurs and two American officers we procured a table from which we could see the rest of the hall which held us fascinated. Through the blue pall of smoke the faces of spectators were lit up by the garish dance-floor lights. British soldiers came with their pockets stuffed with beer bottles. Americans staggered in carrying tubs of something potent, and Russian officers brought their own vodka (which needs a very tough stomach lining).

The band syncopated its hungry utmost, a hideous Greek woman sang with abandon, and blondes in printed crêpe frocks offered favours for a bar of chocolate or tin of bully, while a screech of saxophones announced the first cabaret turn. A middle-aged couple whose clothes and shoes were ready for the dustbin waltzed around unsteadily. During their pirouettes I could study the long table across the floor where some dozen Russian officers were making a night of it! They had all moved to one side of the table to watch the dance and their fierce, high-cheek-boned, tight-skinned faces gleamed in the spotlight. They were all rather drunk and their eyes shone. They seemed spellbound by the ragged spangled dancers and, when the act ended to a thin applause produced by pity, one of the Russians rose unsteadily to his feet and tiptoed across the floor after the poor old girl in tinsel.

He was a lithe young Mongolian with Chinese eyes and yellow skin, and looked like a panther stalking its prey through the wilderness. Obviously, in his drunken state he thought no one could see him if he bent double. A roar of laughter went up from some Germans who understood Russian when he caught her by the wrist and spoke. His request was soon translated and passed from table to table. By this time his companions had gathered the idea that their brother officer was not being genteel and lured him back affectionately to their own table where he sat expressionless until the girl who introduced the acts in three languages through a microphone announced the next turn.

She was a pretty brunette who had spent too much of the evening clinging to an American officer who wanted someone to help drink up his whisky. She could hardly stand but, when the Tartar captain put his arm round her and gave her his own fixed ideas in Russian, she looked around in horror and as I was the only woman in uniform fled to me for protection. The situation was saved at this stage by a buxom girl in Russian uniform who came into the restaurant and strode up to the table of officers. Evidently she was a kind of army governess sent to collect this party and bring them home like good boys. Upon her protruding bosom dangled several shining medals. The Russians pulled themselves together and marched out in single file like children when nanny sweeps in on the party and says: 'Bed-time, no nonsense now.' Only the Mongolian lagged behind, staring longingly back at the dance floor, with the eyes of a smacked tiger.

A German comedian stepped forward and gave an impersonation of Goebbels giving his last speech (which was a crib of Churchill's: 'We'll fight on the beaches . . .') which was in such bad taste that no one smiled or clapped except the German tarts.

At eight-thirty the clubs all closed and we went out dazed into the sunlit street where crowds of painted prostitutes were accosting the soldiers. Then we drove home through ten miles of ruins silhouetted against the clear evening sky, holding our noses as we bumped through areas of particularly noisome smells.

Meanwhile, in the pleasant country that lay around our billets no Frenchman could go for a walk without being waylaid by some young woman. I alone, being a woman, could go for long walks without fear of amorous attack.

One evening I dined in an 8th Hussar Squadron mess and realized too late it was approaching the curfew hour of ten. A Major Firth offered to drive me the ten miles across Berlin to the French zone as speedily as possible but it was the darkest of nights and soon we were lost in the Russian zone. Inevitably a sentry stepped out in a dark street and shouted. We knew he'd shoot if we did not stop. He opened the door, shoved in a gleaming bayonet and gabbled in Russian. He was very Mongolian and we thought it best to be jauntily obedient. He signalled me to show my watch which I did drearily for the Russians had a habit of pocketing watches of any size (the bigger the better), but evidently he wanted me to tell the time which he could not read himself. He climbed in the car with the bare bayonet unpleasantly near and directed us to the nearest *Kommandatura*. The Russian zone was full of these places, open day and night, hung with red flags and decorated with red lights at night. At first I had thought they were Soviet troops cafés and peered in expecting to hear the sounds of balalaika, but they were bare offices with one table and one chair where a gloomy Russian sat day and night waiting for people to be marched in and flung into jail.

I knew Major Firth must be furious with me, for we were quite likely going to spend the night, if not in a cell, then sitting in this abysmal office under arrest, but he managed the show beautifully – made much of his badges of rank, offered cigarettes all round and bluffed without a trace of nervousness. The more high-handed you are with these people the more chance you have of escaping unpleasant experiences. A half-witted French soldier of the 1st Free French Division, returning from leave in North Africa got directed by mistake to the 1st Armoured Division, quartered in Berlin. He had been picked up in the Russian zone trying to hitch-hike his way and spent two weeks in a filthy prison. All his clothes and possessions were stolen by the Russians before they returned him to us in his underpants, too terrified to grumble.

When we had explained ourselves away, had shaken hands all round, and been redirected by more Tartar soldiers, who wore broad smiles in spite of the bayonets which were kept much too near, Major Firth refused to journey another yard towards the French zone. We made hell for leather back to his mess for fear of being arrested by an 11th Hussar patrol which, though less dangerous, would be more shaming. I was not popular by this time, but the Major went to a sofa and let me sleep in his camp bed and wear his pyjamas. In the morning his batman came in with a cup of tea. I was fast asleep on my face so he could only see the usual white pyjama jacket. He tapped me on the shoulders and said: 'Your morning tea, sir.' His face when I rolled over was delicious.

On 8 August Colonel Guibert and I were invited to dinner at the 8th Hussars Headquarters mess. We arrived simultaneously with a bundle of papers from England. The officers greeted us with cocktails and we strolled out on a balcony to look over the news together. Suddenly conversation died for huge headlines announced 'Atom Bomb'. At dinner the talk was of little else and someone quoted Clemenceau's remark about military progress in the last war 'the fire of Jupiter is in the hands of apes.'

Next morning one of our officers went up to a crowd of Germans gathered around the News sheet pinned up on a street notice-board and listened to their comments. There, in a street of ruined houses a grey-faced, ragged woman was reading the account of Hiroshima and saying: 'Aren't we *lucky* . . .'

The brief glamour of the Potsdam conference disappeared and rain made Berlin more dismal than ever. As well as feeling the plight of the people I noticed the thin starved horses and one grey morning I saw one fall dead in the road. The bleak ten-mile drive through the Russian zone we had to make every time we came to the centre of the city grew more and more depressing. No matter what incidents we passed it was out of the question to stop. One morning I saw a German woman try to cross the road. She was stopped by a Russian sentry. Perhaps she argued, for, as we drove past, he cracked her over the head with his rifle butt. Some civilians came and dragged her away. No one looked surprised or shocked. Driving back and forth through the Russian zone I began to feel it was a horrible, gloomy fate to be a human; better to be a wild animal living and fighting and dying in the jungle. The lives of wolves hunting in the snow have dignity and beauty compared to this. The people I had known, from my London charwoman to the desert Arabs, either had a belief or sought some belief. The Russians seemed devoid of any thirst for spiritual reality. We were curious about them, but nothing about us interested their officers or men, except our lack of snobbishness regarding army ranks.

In Russian, the adjectives red and beautiful are translated by the same word *Krasnyy*. They are certainly lavish with scarlet paint, so perhaps they think that colour poured on their tombstones and waved by their flags is beauty enough in the desolation of their impersonal lives.

On 11 August, hearing that my unit was on the Moselle, and not yet coming to Berlin, Colonel Guibert told me to rejoin. I boarded an American plane at Tempelhof Aerodrome (where Goering had his HQ, and where the vast underground factory of fighter planes had never been penetrated by a bomb). As the Dakota roared up into the air and made for Frankfurt the only other occupants, two American soldiers with a barrel of white wine, and a tin mug, asked cheerily: 'Want a drink to celebrate the news?' I'd been sitting in the rain all the morning waiting for the weather to clear so that the planes could go and knew nothing: 'What news?'

'Japan has asked for peace. *All* the Wars are over – Whoopee!'

35

White Wine on the Moselle

From Frankfurt, where the plane came down at 3 p.m., I hitch-hiked a hundred and fifty miles to Trèves. It took five different jeeps to cover the twenty odd miles to Mainz and there I stood on the Rhine bridge, waving a thumb westward, until a car stopped and an American voice answered: 'Sure, we're going right through to Trèves.' For three hours we drove through a romantic setting of Rhineland castles. Then dusk fell in the wooded mountains and the Moselle glinted below us. 'I crossed that damn river three times in combat – Moselle! – hell! . . .' said the American officer driving. Alamein for England's and Vosges for France's and Moselle for America's banners of memory!

As night fell they dropped me on the outskirts of Trèves and looking up and down the road in the hope of finding a divisional sign I suddenly saw that good chance had deposited me on the doorstep of the 1st Squadron of 3rd Chasseurs. I stepped into the mess and they laughed to hear I had left the 2nd Squadron at dawn and hitch-hiked all the 300 miles from Berlin since.

Next day I travelled on to the ambulance unit at Wittlich. The kindly British colonel who had given me a lift watched in amazement when the *ambulancières* ran out, saw me, shrieked and kissed me on both cheeks in their demonstrative fashion. They had been expecting to go to Berlin for a month and thought it very funny that I had proceeded on my own under Colonel Guibert, of whom everyone was terrified.

Our brigade was strewn over the Moselle country in small mediaeval villages. It was a picturesque background with castles and old winepresses and the famous grapes were ripening on every slope. There was nothing to do and very little to eat, but all the fragrant white wine one could drink. Boar and deer roamed in the forest, but it was forbidden to shoot them for they would have been exterminated in a week if the soldiers – who were only getting meat twice a week – were let loose. The *ambulancières* had even less work than anyone else for owing to petrol shortage they were never allowed to drive their ambulances unless a man was on the verge of death.

Wittlich was deluged with romance; Susanne Coignard, who had got engaged while crossing the Rhine, was the first to marry a 3rd Chasseur, and she was followed by little Mimi, whose good-looking husband of twenty-three was in the same squadron.

Our great friend, *Père* Condeau of the tank regiment, drove over to confess them before he was posted to Tibet, and they were married in the village church with all the armoured cars of his squadron lined up outside. Brigadier Gruss gave Mimi away and flung a party for her. The honeymoon was not exactly private, for the groom's squadron was billeted in Wittlich, two houses away from the *ambulancières*' mess. Neither Mimi nor Michael had a family in France. In fact they had nowhere to go, for all good hotels were requisitioned by the Americans as rest camps, etc., and food was short. As Mimi said in her practical way, 'even on a honeymoon you must eat.' So the brigade borrowed a charming cottage from some Germans and Mimi and Michael were able to spend a week together and yet go to their own messes for meals. Incidentally our German servants were as excited as anyone else over the preparations and kept tactlessly asking who was the next *Fräulein* to be married. I wondered if an English unit would not have found it – or rather made it – embarrassing to have a bridal couple in a squadron mess, but by this time I had been so long with the French that I accepted their customs, and it had been quite a shock to come up against rigid British ideas on the segregation of women.

On the day after my arrival at Wittlich, Genny and I were sent off to the artillery who were grouped at Monzel, an enchanting village on a high vine-covered ridge along the river. We lodged in the house of *Monsieur* le Curé and in his kitchen I found the most fascinating birds' nests taken from the woods around. They were woven of anti-radar silver tinsel which our bombers had dropped all over the countryside. Delighted little birds had used the metal threads to make nests of gleaming silver, interwoven with moss and horse-hair.

We had hardly gone to bed when a message arrived that we must both be up at six next morning with ironed skirts, polished boots, and our best white gloves, to parade at Wittlich where the brigade was holding a ceremonial review and decorations were to be presented. We got up by candle-light and were ready to leave, when another message came through that we must collect any artillery sick cases and bring them to the infirmary at Wittlich. The usual sick parade was at nine, so a number of furious, grumbling patients were roused from their beds and dumped at the infirmary. Then, breakfastless, we hurried to the parade ground outside the town. Solange, our commanding officer, ran up to look us over: 'Your noses are as shiny as your shoes,' she said, which was poor reward for getting up at midnight to use a last tin of Cherry Blossom. However, someone had powder and puff to hand. We two were the *enfants terribles* of the unit, always being reprimanded for not being *soignée*.

But we were presentable enough by the time we marched to our places with two other girls and some forty men who were to be decorated. The parade was held to commemorate the landing of the 1st Armoured Division near Marseilles the year before. Against the misty German hills the tank regiment was lined up with the zouaves band playing, bugles blowing, and banners flying. As the notes of the *Marseillaise* crashed forth, Brigadier Gruss arrived. Pals, who were not in the parade, sat about on armoured cars to clap and make a fuss and suddenly I realized that in all the brigade there was not a man I did not know and like, and how much their smiling faces meant (my Moroccan enemies were being sent back to their own country in weekly batches). When the parade was over, the general sent for the four *ambulancières* to stand beside him for the march past. We were told this day must be celebrated from beginning to end, we were to wear our *Croix de guerres* and white gloves and be congratulated all the *jour de fête* (just like the French First Communion Day).

Then we proceeded to the shelled church where a thanksgiving Mass was to be held, for apart from being Napoleon's birthday and the anniversary of the Marseilles landings, 15 August is the Assumption, which is a great feast in France. There was so much to celebrate we hardly knew if we were on our heads or our heels. *Le père* said Mass amidst broken, gilt-wood angels with the sky shining through the glassless windows of Wittlich Church, and his sermon was full of military fire. He described that day a year ago, the day of the great landing of French troops in their own country, and his zeal brought before our eyes the fleet of ships steaming landwards to disgorge tanks; the flash and roar of guns against a background of blue sea, blue sky and golden sunlit land.

'And as I watched the shells fall into the sea around us I knew that every miss was a miracle, the Virgin Mary was there amongst us and was deflecting them, pleased that on this day of her assumption we fought again on the soil of *la Belle* France.' 'Combined Ops' in the truest sense of the word!

From High Mass, Genny and I tore off to the zouaves luncheon fete, for Commandant Vallin (now a *député* and one of de Gaulle's staunchest adherents) was to come from Paris and celebrate with his battalion. Luckily the quality of the local wine enabled one to avoid headaches. We went for a gasping hour's walk along the vineyards before attending Brigadier Grass's fete, which was a *thé-dansant* with champagne instead of tea.

By eight that night I had drunk a toast with every friend in the division. We were now reminded we must drive back through the sunlit hills for a celebration dinner with the artillery and pick up on the way our unfortunate sick cases who had been sitting at the infirmary all day. They were very bad-tempered, 'What on earth is happening to the *ambulancières*.' Genny and I turned round with the crosses on our breasts and their petulance subsided.

'*Ah les nouvelles décorées* – did the general embrace you? *Bravo! Bravo!*'

During dinner I wanted to listen to the radio account of Japan's surrender but the French were not interested. We really could not send for more champagne or face one more toast.

36

All Change

The beauty of this hill country acted like a charm after the squalor of Berlin. We were posted in turn to the different regiments which gave us the chance to explore all the local forests and castles. The girls clamoured to be demobilized, yet we were all sad that the unit must soon break up. Genny and I went for long walks through the hot sunshine and cool showers which alternated all day giving the grapes their special flavour and wondered what we should do next in life, unlike the other girls who knew just what they wanted and were now getting married in most business-like fashion, just as they had always said they would when war ended.

Genny did not want to settle down. She had been brought up in Lorraine and had suffered bitterly under the German occupation. Her fiancé, whom she had known since childhood, had been killed near us in the Vosges and she was the type who would mourn for years. I think she half-hankered for death herself, and so the reconnaissance work with the Americans had fascinated her. Now at the age of twenty-five she found herself leading a life in which there was no danger and she began to fidget and plan to go to Morocco or Indo-China.

The soldiers were contented enough however. They had their own amusements, and although Frenchmen would not be seen walking beside a German woman, none of them slept alone. The docility of the handsome, golden-haired women of this part of Germany approached imbecility and seemed to extend through all classes. One day Colonel Harris, who ran the enormous Trèves UNNAA camp for Poles, had a new batch to be fumigated before being allowed contact with the others. The American sergeant in charge was standing, bellowing his head off.

'Come on all of you! Hurry up for God's sake! Come on! De-lousing!—Oh God! I've had a letter from my wife in my pocket for two hours and haven't had time to read it – get along there! Yes, all of you.' And the Poles who did not understand a word of English, streamed on accompanied by a stout German Frau, out for her morning's marketing! Twelve hours later, when she and her clothes, her parcels and innocent vegetables had been thoroughly decontaminated in every possible way, she explained who she was, and asked permission to send a message to her worried husband. She had just got caught in the throng and accepted decontamination without question.

There were a few, a very few, complaints of attempted rape. The French officers asked cynically how rape was possible when *elles se donnent*. However, we had one instance in Wittlich when several new native orderlies arrived from North Africa to work in the Infirmary. One of these unglamorous figures came straight from Algiers with the fixed idea that heroes of his type might take what woman they chose. He had been less than a week with the company when he went out at dusk and selected the local swimming champion, returning from the bathing pool! She beat him off, and arrived angrily at the brigade station to report the incident. She identified her assailant and he was seriously reprimanded and told he might suffer court-martial.

Next day he took a savage, if foolish, revenge, and beat her up. The swimming champion did not show much sense in continuing to bathe alone, and she suffered for it. She was carried in with both legs broken and two teeth knocked out. We were most embarrassed. Her aggressor did not reappear and was for three days posted as a deserter. Then we found him drowned in the pool. Few enquiries were made, for he was small loss to any army. Owing to red tape he had been dead a week, when I was ordered to drive him 80 miles to Metz to be buried. Genny volunteered to come also for it was her own country and she wanted to see friends. We left at five in the morning, and the coffin was loaded into my ambulance with four tough Moroccan stretcher-bearers to carry it. I asked why on earth the order had been given to leave at this hour. 'You'll soon know.' We drove off and the sun rose and lit the mists of the Moselle as we followed the river towards Luxembourg.

Genny wanted to stop in this picturesque city but the warmth of the sun was making the smell in the ambulance unbearable. We halted once to breakfast at 'GI Joe's' roadside canteen run by Americans with superb efficiency. Five big tents at wide intervals gave place for the largest convoy to feed without overcrowding. German POWs served hot coffee and sandwiches throughout the twenty-four hours. My Moroccans rubbed their eyes at the plates of bread, clean mugs, bins for rubbish, neat green lawns and general perfect organization.

Like a governess, leading a party of not very well-mannered children, I hurried them to the tent labelled 'Latrine', and explained what that word meant and what the trim green lawns were *not* intended for. They spared me further shame and jabbered about the luxury of the Americans all the way to Metz. It was now ten o'clock and the sun beat down on the jolting ambulance. Hard fighting had taken-place around Metz and the roads were execrable. The jolting aroused an appalling stench, yet if we slowed the pace insufficient draught blew through the windows and prolonged the agony.

Seeing groups of soldiers we yelled: 'Where is the military cemetery?' but they proved to be dazed Italians and Czechs, all newly attired by UNRAA in battle dress.

Creeping around the outskirts of the city the stomachs of my four coffin bearers also began to be queasy. They assured me they could not stand it much longer and I groaned for fear they might bring up their highly-caloried American breakfast. At last we reached the big cemetery where rows and rows of French soldiers lay under the warm green grass.

We flung open the doors and deposited the coffin with enormous haste in the morgue. But now the corporal in charge had to be fetched by two grave-diggers and papers signed and the number of the grave allotted. The old corporal shuffled up on a crutch and delved into the sheaf of papers we had brought from brigade HQ authorizing burial. All went according to plan until we discovered the impossibility of burying our late lamented with his feet to the East, for all the graves lay in a different part of the garden and their feet pointed away from Mecca.

'Couldn't you just turn him round?' I quavered.

'No! No! *Mademoiselle*, that would mean putting the head stone at his feet and would never do. No, you must take him to the civilian cemetery, where people can be buried all ways.'

Seeing it would be vain to argue with a self-important despot who had been king-pin of the cemetery for decades, we groaned, reloaded and drove off. Our next enquiries revealed the fact that Metz boasted several civilian cemeteries.

'Which shall we try?' asked Genny.

'Anywhere at all! Only quick! quick!'

The next morgue was littered with corpses and smelt worse than our ambulance. We dumped the coffin inside and I suggested flight, but Genny replied conscientiously: 'No, no, we must get the papers signed.'

A rollicking old Frenchman in a beret, evidently the cemetery caretaker, came out and greeted us affably: 'Why, of course, I can bury him any way you like. I have *boches* working for me and they will put him where you choose, as you choose.'

On the way home through Luxembourg we discussed the defunct. 'In any case,' I said, 'he broke the woman's legs; he was not much loss.' But the Moroccans defended him with their sublime simplicity: *'Non non,'* they insisted in pidgeon French, 'he was a nice type – *très calme comme nous.'*

But in spite of their limited intelligence and unlimited dishonesty I grew quite fond of several of these North African natives. Edmond de Pourtales' gloomy native batman had evinced no interest in the war whatever, expressionless, he witnessed aeroplanes, tanks and guns firing, he could push a car but could not be trusted to crank it. Then the day came in Alsace when Edmond had a bedroom with a wash basin of the type that is set in a cupboard, and tips up emptying its contents into a bucket beneath. For the first time Edmond saw his batman's face light up with happiness. Six times a day he carried up hot water, 'Don't you wish to wash your hands, *Mon Capitain*?' Then he tipped the basin, heard it splash, and opened the little wooden door – yes! just as he had thought, the bucket was full and he would carry it downstairs and empty it in the garden. At last there was something in life that he could understand.

It was September, when my ambulance was ordered to go to Paris with one of our girls who had broken her leg, and a zouave soldier, also in plaster.

All across France we were fascinated to see German soldiers at farm work – the old enemy in the old familiar uniform – ploughing!

In Paris we found the hospital and deposited our patients. Then we had to find billets. Knowing the discomfort in which the French Army allows its personnel to live, I was for trying to locate a British transit camp. I'd heard wonderful tales of a British transit hotel near the Madeleine, but it had been closed. We drove round and round the brilliantly lit Place de la Concorde. There were YMCA's and Salvation Army clubs, but not for French girls, and we had our wretched ambulance to park. It was ten at night and we'd not eaten since early breakfast, so it was in a very peevish state that we arrived at the Caserne Dupleix, the only barracks in Paris open to us for the night. Here a harassed but amiable officer showed us the barrack square where we might park the ambulance and sleep in it till 'drill began at 6 a.m.' How well I knew the form, the usual army form, which would necessitate getting out of the ambulance to the cries of a sergeant major and washing at an icy tap in front of fifty men.

The barracks concierge, a most charming old lady with great black tragic eyes, came down and invited us up to her room where we could heat our rations on the glimmer of gas. '*Mesdemoiselles*,' she spoke graciously – 'it is an honour to assist you. I know what you must have meant to our wounded. My own sons were both killed. We, the mothers, are grateful to you. I would invite you to spend the night but we are two as it is in this room.'

The OC now appeared and said that, although we were '*simple soldats*', he would make an exception and give us tickets for rooms in an officers' hotel near the Étoile. We could leave the ambulance here under guard. We had already covered our faces with cold cream. Without troubling to wipe it off we crammed our caps on, grabbed a tooth-brush in one hand and pyjamas in the other and hurried off to catch the last metro before midnight. As *militaires* we travelled free, which saved us standing in queues for tickets, and if glances were cast at our greased faces and odd baggage we were far too mutinous and irritable to care. It seemed this was the most interminable day on record.

There were hordes of people around the Arc de Triomphe, but none of them had heard of the hotel to which we had been allocated. At last we found it, a slatternly building that had five lavatories, not one of which worked. We were shown our room, all grubby red plush and with a creaky double bed in which I am sure we were the first moral couple ever to sleep. This was a typical French 'transit hotel', transit being a suitable adjective – for it certainly made you want to move somewhere else speedily. However, we found a tap of cold running water where we could get the day's grime off, and towards one in the morning we fell asleep.

There was only one pillow in the bed and soon we were quarrelling over it, not to put our heads on but to hide them under, in the futile hope of shutting out the din that rose from the street below. There was some kind of night club next door and at intervals various parties were chucked out. The noise was an international jabber. The whole street rang with cat-calls, shrill vituperations, the sound of drunken fist-fights and the most unbelievably loud and prolonged retching.

At eight we rose. It proved impossible to obtain a hot cup of coffee in this hotel or in any café, so we took the metro back to the Caserne Dupleix where we made *Nescafé* in the ambulance. The little officer hoped we'd had a good night and was sorry he could not repeat the favour of '*logements* in officers' quarters'. We said: 'Thank you very much, once is enough.' We had three

days to spend in Paris with jobs to be done which entailed
driving all over the city. It looked as if we would never be out
of the ambulance, driving it by day and sleeping in it by night.
Then I remembered that in Italy Elizabeth de Breteuil had
invited me to use her house in the rue de Bellechasse. But how
could one take an ambulance into a house? We drove there and
rang. Our hearts lifted: the exquisite eighteenth-century house
had been built around a courtyard and there, where the coaches
used to roll in, we could leave our vehicle. The concierge and
his wife, Marie, looked after us as though we were infants. The
countess was in Italy but we were given a guest room and slept
that night in linen sheets surrounded by beautiful old furniture.
We gave Marie our rations and she brought us breakfast in bed
on trays of lovely old silver. But though people in Paris might
still have their taffeta curtains and beautiful belongings, the
larder was a different matter. We discovered 'The Armoured
Corps', a restaurant, taken over by the French Army and run
exclusively for members of the armoured divisions. It was
splendidly organized and one got a really good lunch for 100
frs. (10s.).

We explored the famous shopping centres of Paris, whose
windows were full of ribbons and tasteful decorations, but there
was nothing one could buy except post-war perfume which did
not cling for five minutes.

The twenty-five *ambulancières* had subscribed £25 for a wedding
present for Mimi. In the end we bought her a sewing box, which
was the only object of good quality I had seen in any shop. The
shopkeeper, in whom we had confided, was pleasant enough, and
produced this box saying it had been in his shop for years – the
reason for its cheapness – No one wanted sewing boxes, they only
wanted make-up cases! 'Ah! *la vanité des femmes!* It seems to get

worse and worse! As our stomachs empty they paste more on their faces.'

When we returned to the Moselle, Jeanne de l'Espée told me I could be posted to an HQ in Paris and be demobilized from there. The final moment had come and I went around saying goodbye to the brigade.

The men of 'my tank' the Peronne II gave a lunch party for me. It was the last of the little feasts they had organized for their 'godmother' and as they now shared a cottage with another tank crew and had their own kitchen the fare should be good. They killed 'the rabbit' – a famous personage who had lived with them for weeks and it seemed rather awful to eat him. The countryside provided its wonderful wine. But it proved a doleful meal for it was not *au revoir*, it was *adieu*. Cycling back to Wittlich with the warm goodbyes of Peronne II ringing in my ears I realized that I meant something to these French people, that I was the only British girl they had ever known really well, and their affection had become precious to me.

This brigade was composed of Frenchmen of the type who do not come in contact with foreigners. They were in a way more restricted and conventional in their outlook than the more insular British, but we were intimately linked through experiences we had been through together. For good or for bad they judged me as typical of my race; and they had given me a wonderful comradeship. In the whole brigade, my only enemies were the lower-strata Algerians. There was not one Frenchman I ever disliked and the girls I loved. It was all over now and, pedalling back along the bumpy road to Wittlich in the warm sun of that German autumn I almost choked – it was too ridiculous, people weep at leaving school and when they get married . . . not at departing from a combat command!

It was terrible saying goodbye to the girls and then suddenly I was in a car bound for Metz to catch the midnight train to Paris.

I sat up all night with soldiers sleeping on my feet and babies crying on my lap. At seven we arrived, and I had the usual free metro tickets issued to me by the army. My kit-bag was filled with bottles of champagne, several for friends in Paris and several to take home. I lugged it down into the metro, for it was too heavy to carry on my shoulder. I had to change twice and by the time I struggled up into the street was pouring with sweat. I looked peevishly around for some coal-heaver on hire but only sleek and well-dressed citizens were hurrying by. Stopping every few yards I finally reached the rue de Bellechasse in a state of rage and exhaustion. As it is no fun being angry with oneself I rang up my friends and blamed them because I had thought of bringing them presents. Charlie de Breteuil appeared, and as two of the Champagne bottles were for him I could work off my temper, show him my bleeding fingers and wallow in martyred feelings. He invited me to go that evening to see 'what there was of smart Paris', and rushed out to buy a bunch of red roses (flowers in Paris were even more exorbitant than champagne).

After a hot bath I set out on the task of getting demobilized. This entailed hours of standing in queues, sitting in queues, being X-rayed in queues, and writing quadruplicate forms to explain why I possessed no long underpants to return to the army.

Marie, the concierge, admired me greatly. Having cleaned my army boots she brought them up, exclaiming at their weight. 'And *Mademoiselle* wears these and can lift her feet? Ah, how noble! *Que c'est beau, quel patriotisme.*'

In the evening I walked from the Chambre-Des-Deputés along the Seine, exquisite in the golden light, right up the Champs-Élysées to the Colony Club, the new fashionable meeting-place of that *beau monde,* the gilded rich world of Paris one heard so much about. Charlie had asked me to meet him there to gape at the expensive *demi-mondaines* of the city. Since the upheavals of our time, I'm not sure if the word *demi-mondaine* can still be used, for since every class and sphere in all worlds have gone up in fireworks it must be difficult to classify a woman as half in or out of any of them. However there was plenty to watch here, where the rich men of Paris sat with their mistresses. It was like some ridiculous dream, a scene roused from the half-forgotten world of six years ago, as if the ghost of a luxury liner had suddenly sailed into port and there were its millionaires still at play.

After a few days spent disentangling the various knots of red tape that bound me to the French Army I obtained permission to be flown to Ireland by the RAF. I had a sheaf of papers liberating me from French military discipline and the RAF proved most obliging. Luckily they did not bother to translate my permits in detail, for it might not have impressed them to learn that the French Army were allowing them to transport by 'every sort of aerial convenience' one, Anita Leslie, *soldat 2ème classe,* back to the Irish Free State.

In London I had a last task to accomplish. Monique, the sister of Solange de la Brosse our commanding officer, had been wounded at Marseilles when a shell had blown her right arm off as she unloaded her ambulance. Since then she had run a Red Cross transport unit for repatriating deported French civilians, had married a French officer, and was expecting a baby. She had often come over from her unit in Metz and had asked me to find some wool in England that her friends could knit into baby wear, for in the whole of France one could not buy a skein of real wool. But as a French *demobilisé* I found my London status was that of a couponless outcast and I could buy nothing.

However, I heard from an officer who had been on Churchill's staff that the prime minister's map-room was in the process of closing down. The great maps, which had for five years hung on the walls so that Winston could at any time of day or night stroll in to see happenings in every battle theatre, were being rolled up and tucked away, and the long strands of wool which had marked the advance of armies were no longer needed. I applied for the discarded fighting lines – they arrived in pink balls – pink wool of the best Churchillian quality! I posted it off to Monique and on my way home buying a newspaper whose front page told of guns blown up as scrap and million-pound submarines sunk to the Atlantic bottom – I reflected happily that little pink pants need never grow obsolete.

THE END

A NOTE ON THE AUTHOR

Anita Leslie (1914–1985), daughter of Shane Leslie (Sir John Randolph Leslie, 3rd Baronet) and first cousin once removed to Sir Winston Churchill, was a writer of memoir and biography. She joined the mechanized transport corps as a fully trained mechanic and ambulance driver during WWII, serving in Libya, Syria, Palestine, Italy, France and Germany. She wrote letters home from Hitler's office in the Reich Chancellery and took part in the Victory Parade in Berlin. In the latter part of the war she drove an ambulance for the Free French Forces, and was awarded the *Croix de guerre* in 1945 by General Charles de Gaulle.

Leslie later married Bill King and had two children. She published seventeen books, the last in 1985 – the year she died.

Index

Abbassia   34

Abdullah, Emir   62, 65–7, 69–70

African native pioneers   58

Aga Khan   53

Ahmed Sadikh Bey   33

Ain Sofar   73–5

Aix-en-Provence   117

Alanbrooke, General Lord   104, 274

Aleppo   42–3, 48, 50, 80–1, 84

Alexander the Great   70

Alexander, General Harold   68–70, 87–8, 96, 98, 101, 104–5, 269, 274, 279, 283

Alexandre (Russian servant)   77–8, 82

Alexandria   2, 22, 29, 60, 68, 74, 84, 92

Algiers   102, 141, 194, 300

Ali Khan, Prince   53, 57

Ali Khan, Princess   53

Alouites   42

Alsace

  Alsatians serving in German army   169–70

battle for Colmar

  pocket   171–2, 181, 190–6

dialect   143, 164

liberation of   140–50, 153–4

regional dress   202

wine   153

Altkirch   142–3, 146, 148, 150

American Field Service   130

American Red Cross girls   89, 96

Amet, Mme   127

Amies, Hardy   1

Amman   61, 65–6, 68

Amy, Professor   44–5

André, Jeanine   136, 152, 163–4, 194, 216

Anna (*ambulancière*)   156–7

Anzio   83, 89–90, 94, 100

appendicitis   228

Arab Legion   44, 48, 69

Arabic language   61–2

Ardennes   165, 169, 171, 180

Aries, Lieutenant   221

Armistice Commission   73

Arnhem, battle of   208–9

atom bombs   278, 292

al-Atrash, Asmahan   31–2, 49,
    72–6, 104
Attlee, Clement   274
Auchinleck, General Claude   22,
    33, 69
'Auld Lang Syne'   260

Baalbek   82
Baden   217
Barcelonnette   116
Baritault, Jeff de   284
Baruch, Bernard   19
Bastogne salient   171
Battle of Britain   9, 21
bazookas   154, 235, 242
BBC   115, 151, 169, 266
Bedouin   43, 48, 61–3, 65, 69
Beirut
    accommodation   45–6, 58–9,
        71–2, 77–8, 82–3
    riots and curfew   78–9
    St. George's Hotel   71–2
    servant problem   77–8
    submarine flotilla   77
    in summer   59–60
Bekaa Valley   41, 43, 58
Belfort   139, 143, 151,
    153–4, 174
Bellefond, Lieutenant Bernard
    de   217, 243, 248
Benghazi   22
Benishu, Captain   187
Berchtesgaden   251
Berlin   270, 272–94, 299
    fall of   234

Germania statue   276
Hotel Adlon   279
night clubs   287–90
Sedan Victory Column   276
Unter den Linden   274, 286
victory parade   274–6
Besançon   118–20, 174, 178
Béthouart,
    General Antoine   165–6, 172,
        182, 202
'Big Flap, the'   60
Bir Hakeim, battle of   60, 184
Black Forest   154, 215, 217
Blackfoot Indians   68
Blamey, General Thomas   30
Blount, Father   29–30
Boer War   18
boots, waterproof   128
Boraud, Isabelle   183
Bordel Millitaire de
    Campagne   175
Borea, Maxime   194
Brandenburg plain   272
Bremen   272
Brenner Pass   247, 252
Breteuil, Charles de   153, 158,
    213, 308–9
Breteuil, Elizabeth de   105–7, 306
Brosset, General Diégo-Charles-
    Joseph   54–5, 91, 96, 120, 153
Brunswick   271
Buchenwald concentration
    camp   262, 265
Budapest   166
Burgh, Rose   1

Burma 34
Byblos 82

Cairo
air crashes 26, 36
air raid 36
Citadel 26, 28, 36
letter home 28–9
Pyramids 20
Calais 176–7
Caledon, Lord 68
Caledon House 68–9
camels 44, 61–2
Campbell, General Jock 38; 276
Cape Town Highlanders 19
Capodichino airfield 94, 99
Capri 100
Caroline, Queen 271
Caserne Dupleix 304–5
Caserta 87, 102
Catroux, General Georges 30,
57, 80
Catroux, Mme 57
Cernay 195
Chad 15
Chalompey 196
Chambrey, Totote de 119–22
Charon, Mme 117
Château Beaufort 53
Château Hohrenderhubel 186
Chelsea Barracks 10
Chequers 208–10, 277
Cherwell, Professor Lord 278
Churchill, Mary 274, 277, 282
Churchill, Randolph 83

Churchill, Winston 1, 34, 69,
104–5, 171, 208–12, 251–2,
274–8, 282, 284,
290, 310
Churston, Lord 53
cigarettes 281, 285–6
Clark, General Mark 96, 101
Clemenceau, Georges 292
Coignard, Susanne 217–18, 220,
222, 231, 239–40, 245, 295
Collet, General 49
Colmar 151, 153, 171, 181–2,
189–90, 195–6, 200, 202,
211–12, 277–8, 287
Colony Club 308–9
concentration camps 199, 235,
262–6
Condeau, Father 125, 295
Congress of Vienna 103
Cooper, Lady Diana 106
Cornimont 129
Corsica 113
Coventry Blitz 19
Crete 19, 28–9
Croix de guerre 4, 82, 202–3,
297–8
Curie, Eve 103
Cyprus 82–3
Cyrenaica 21, 276
Czechoslovakia 69

dachshund, in Horb 222
Daily Mirror 43
d'Albiac, Air Marshal
John 101

Damascus 31, 39, 41–3, 48–9, 54, 62, 83–4
 'Street called Straight' 51
Dannemarie 179
Dautany, Captain 198
D-Day 96–7, 115
de Gaulle, General Charles 30, 120, 171, 202, 282, 298
de Salis, Colonel John 29
Deir ez-Zor 54–5
Deraa 31
desert gazelles 62
Desert Rats 21, 273–6, 287
Devers, General Jacob 182
Dijon 284
Djemal Pasha 23
Dog River 43
doughnuts 89, 135
Druzes 32, 42, 49, 53
du Boisrouvrey brothers 15
Dublin 206–7
Dunkirk 21
Dunsany, Lord 13–14
Durban 19
Durosoy, Colonel 158

Eastern Times 2, 40–3, 45–7, 49–50, 52–5, 71, 77–80, 83
 acquires new press 50
 Christmas party 46–7, 78–9
 continues as Ninth Army News 79
Eden, Anthony 209, 274, 277–9
Egyptian Agricultural Society 25
Egyptian Army 24

Eisenhower, General Dwight D. 96, 171, 181–2, 209
El Alamein, battle of 69, 274, 276, 294
Elijah, Prophet 56
ENSA 98
Ensisheim 193, 195

Farouk, King 24, 51
Fénelon, François 201
Ferrier, Denise 182
Firth, Major 290–1
Fitzpatrick Pasha 26
Florence 104
Foreign Legionnaires 218–20
Forster, Lieutenant-Colonel 285
Fortescue, Lilah 77–8, 83
Fougère, Captain 235, 246–7
Franken 164
Frankfurt 261, 269–70, 293–4
Frederick, Emperor 270
Frederick Schloss 270–1
Free French 31, 60, 120
Free French Air Force 13–15, 113
French, Major Stuart 273
French Army
 adopts arms of Colmar 277
 Arab conscription 203–4
 author joins 105–7
 and Berlin victory parade 276
 casualties 135
 Churchill and 210–12, 277–8
 cigarette ration 281, 285–6
 composition 119–20

enters Germany 215–17
enters Tyrol 243–4
and 'fraternization' 259
and German propaganda 230
prisoners taken 135
rate of advance 247–8
reaches Rhine 143
wine ration 280–1
French Resistance
  (Maquis) 114–17, 176–7
Freudenstadt 217
Frosinone 95
Fuller, Dean 132
Funny Folks Fudge 133

Galloway, Brigadier Sandy 101
Gaza 64
Gelis, Captain 247
general election (1945) 282, 284
Genny (*ambulancière*) 212–13,
  215, 217–20, 222–3, 228, 232,
  234, 236, 239, 245, 248, 251–3,
  255–6, 260–1, 267–8, 296,
  298–9, 301–3
George IV, King 271
George, King of Greece 42
George Cross 19
Gérardmer 145
Germersheim 252–60
Gestapo 115, 117
Geubwiller 199
Gillet, Captain 221
Gloucester, HRH Duke of 56–8
Glubb, Colonel John 48, 61, 65
Glubb, Mrs 66

Goddard, Paulette 84
Goebbels, Joseph 290
Goering, Hermann 293
Goff, Lieutenant-Colonel and
  Mrs 102
Goode, Joy 51
Gott, General William
  ('Strafer') 22, 38, 276
goums 107–9, 133, 175
Graziani, Marshal Rodolfo 21
Greece 22–3, 96
Gruss, General Adrein-Pierre-
  Raymond 165–6, 206, 212,
  230–1, 254, 295, 297–8
Guibert, Colonel 280–1, 284,
  291, 293, 295
Guillot, Dr 192–3, 221, 225,
  236–40
Gurkhas 98, 100

Haguenau 216
Haidar Pasha 70
Haifa 31, 56, 64
Hailtengen 239, 241–2
Hama 42, 48, 52
Hamilton, Lady 91
Harding, General 101
Harris, Colonel 300
Harth Forest 153, 196, 198–9
Haye, Captain 116–17
Heidelberg 259
Heidwiller wood 146, 150, 154
Heliopolis 21
Helmiah Camp 21
Himmler, Heinrich 244

Hitler, Adolf 210, 217, 256, 269, 274, 279–80
HMS *Formidable* 83
HMS *Pembroke* 275
HMS *Telemachus* 83
Hohenzollern, Princess 233
Homs 42, 48, 52
Horb 218–24, 228, 269
horses, cruelty to 96
Howah 62
Hugo, Victor 178
Husser, Lieutenant 144–9, 151–2, 185–7, 192–5, 218–26, 228–9, 231–2, 236–7, 243–7
and Russian patients 256–7

Illfurth 144, 147, 149
Indo-China 299
Indo-Chinese soldiers 178
Inniskilling Fusiliers 90, 96
Irish, the
temperament 18–19
welcome returning soldiers 207–8
Irish Free State 68, 269, 309
Iron Cross 269
Ismailis 53

Jabal al-Druze 31, 49, 73
Jaffa 64
Japanese surrender 293, 298
Jazira plain 54–5
Jeanne d'Arc, feast of 253
Jebel Sinjar 43
Jellicoe, George 82, 101–2

Jerome, Jennie 209
Jerusalem 30–2, 39, 50, 60, 63, 66, 73, 84
King David Hotel 30–1, 75
Jezebel 54, 56
Johannesburg 18
Juin, General Alphonse 101
Juni 53

Karlsruhe 252
Katena camp 43
Kennels, the 102–3
Keyserling, Hermann von 128
khamseen 27, 64
Khoury, Mme 46–7, 78
Khoury, President 46, 50, 78–9
Kiltelly, Lieutenant-Colonel 39
King, Bill 77, 83
Kingersheim 190, 193, 195
Kleber, Mme 124, 160–1, 187, 197, 202, 243
Koenig, General Marie-Pierre 55, 120
Koran 25
Krak des Chevaliers 53

la Brosse, Monique de 309–10
la Brosse, Solange de 213–15, 218, 250, 296
la Forcade, Commandant de 125
Lafftraak 145
Lake Bolsena 101
Lake Constance 229
Lake Trasimeno 100–1
Lampson, Sir Miles 34, 51

Lampson, Miranda 34–6, 51
Landau Divisional HQ 254–5
Landser 157, 162
Lansdowne, Charlie 83
Laporte, Lieutenant 246–7
Lattre de Tassigny, General Jean
    de 119–20, 143, 154, 171,
    181–2, 196, 214, 247, 250,
    276–7
Laval, Pierre 231, 233
Lawrence, T. E. 23, 25, 48
    The Seven Pillars of Wisdom 25
Laycock, General Robert 282
le Gentilhomme, General
    Paul 31
Leclerc, General Philippe 251
Lecoq, Lucette 3, 180, 190, 194,
    212, 214–15, 228, 237–40, 287
Lecoq, Odette 3, 212, 214–15,
    228, 237–40
Lecuyer, Captain 116
Lemnitzer, General Lyman 101
Leslie, Lady Leonie 2
Leslie, Lionel 97
Leslie, Marjorie 1–3
l'Espée, General Jean de 121
l'Espée, Jeanne de 3, 121–2,
    124–6, 130–3, 142, 152–3, 157,
    178–9, 187, 203, 213, 307
Le Thillot 145
'Lili Marlene' 90
Lloyd, Lord 10
London Blitz 9
Lutterbach 154
Luxembourg 301, 303

Lyne, General Lewis 276, 285–6
Lyon 118

McLeod, General Sir F. 104–5
Macmillan, Lady Dorothy 106
Madaba 61
Madagascar 19
Magdeburg 271
Mainz 294
Majid Arslan, Emir 79–80
Malouf, Mr 41
Mannerheim, Field-Marshal
    Carl 279
Mannheim 261, 281
Maquis, *see* French Resistance
Marie Antoinette, Queen 254
'La Marseillaise' 113, 165, 297
Marseilles 104, 113–18, 163, 297
    Resistance Movement 114–15
al-Masri, Aziz 23–6
Mechanized Transport Corps
    (MTC) 7–11
Metz 152, 301–2, 308–9
Milburn, General Frank 182
Mimi (*ambulancière*) 152, 202,
    218, 220–2, 231, 239–40, 245,
    295, 306
mistral 118
Monaghan 208
Monckton, Sir Walter 38, 50
Montbéliard 139
Monte Cassino 87, 89, 91–2, 94,
    97, 100, 102, 108, 251
Montgomery, General
    Bernard 22, 98, 274, 283

Monsabert, General Joseph de
    Goislard de 182
Monzel 296
Moran, Lord 278
Moreau, Captain 141–2
Moreau, Commandant 44, 51, 78
Moreau, Yvonne 141–2
Moroccans, with shaved
    heads 259
Morse, Rear Admiral 105
Mosque of Mohamed Ali 26
Mount Hermon 31
Moustafa (gardener) 59
Mulhouse 143–4, 151, 153,
    160–2, 179–83, 189–90, 193,
    195–7, 200–3, 211, 214, 265
Mussolini, Benito (Il Duce) 29,
    210, 244

Nahas, Mostafa 51
Naples 87–90, 94–5, 97, 105–7
Napoleon Bonaparte 211,
    235, 297
Narvik 14
Nejib (office boy) 50
Nelson, Admiral Horatio 91
Newall, Mrs 33
Nizola (cook) 280, 284
No Orchids for Miss
    Blandish 101
Nordhausen concentration
    camp 3, 261–5, 269
Norrie, General
    Willoughby 36–7
Notre Dame Cathedral 210

Obernai 215
Oberstaufen 246
O'Connor, General Richard 102
OGPU 277
O'Kane, Patsy 77–8, 82–3
Olivares, Sergeant Major 184
Oran 202, 204
Ostheim 214
Otto, Penelope 38

Paillot, Mme 137–9
Palestine 23, 30–1, 34
    Jewish population 63–5
Palmyra 44, 51, 54, 82
Pariante, Dr 184
Paris 69, 206, 210–11, 303–9
Patch, General Alexander 135
Patou 131
Patton, General George 171, 212,
    260
Paulette's rabbit 161–2
Pêche, Lieutenant 123, 240
Pennapiedimonte 98
Peronne tanks (I and II) 211, 307
Pétain, Marshal Philippe 3, 231,
    233–4, 244
Peter of Greece, Prince 38–9
Petra 61
Pforzheim 251
Poland 166, 170
Poles 92, 98, 102, 170, 235, 241,
    263–4, 300
Pope, Brigadier 36
Port-sur-Saône 135–9, 161
Potsdam 275–8, 281–3, 292

Pourtales, Edmond de 125, 213, 303

POWs
captured general 244
escaped 97–8
German 127–8, 217, 301
German/Russian 147–9
numbers of 247
padres taken prisoner 242–3
return to France 229
SS officers 254
surrendering Germans 230–1, 235–6
taken by *ambulancières* 228

Pozzuoli 107, 109
Pretoria 16–18
prostitutes 28–30, 202
Pyramids 20

Racy, Mr 41
Ramadan 65
Ranfurly, Hermione 102–3, 105
rape, attempted 234, 300
Ras El-Bar 76
Rastatt 217
rats 207
Ratzenveldt 244–5
Ravensburg 238
Red Cross 80–1, 84
Reinickendorf 277
Richard *Coeur de Lion* 53, 82–3
Roberts Heights Camp 17
Roehampton Convent 233
Rome, fall of 96–7
Romeo and Juliet 177

Rommel, General Erwin 60, 282
Romney marshes 208
Roosevelt, Franklin D., 209
Rosenveldt 225
Rosselli, Major 40–2, 49
Rothwell, Lieutenant-Colonel 206, 270–1
Rottweil 224–5
Ruck-Keene, Captain Philip 77, 83
Rupt 121
Ruskin, John 88
Russell, Brigadier 36
Russians 99, 227, 256–9, 265
in Berlin 272–3, 282–3, 287–93
German/Russian POWs 147–9

St. Dié 145
St. Paul 51
St. Stephen's Green 206–7
Salerno 83
Sauggart, murder of Lecoq sisters 237–40
Saulxures 127–34
Schmidt, Frau 164–8
Senegalese soldiers 79, 114, 203
Sergison-Brooke, General Sir T. 84, 91, 93
SHAEF, dissolution of 270
Sherman tanks 121, 144, 183–4, 192, 220, 223, 230, 253
Sicily 285
Sidon 53–4, 56

Siegfried Line 216

Siena 95, 101, 104, 108

Sigmaringen 231–5, 237

silk stockings 220, 269

Sitwell, Sacheverell 88

slave-workers, returning 255

Smuts, General Jan 17

snipers 129, 194

Soudre, General 123, 174, 202–3, 260

Soueida 49

South African Army 16–18

spahis 55, 153, 158, 199, 201–2

Spears, General Sir Edward 30, 80

Spears, Lady 80

Speyer Cathedral 260

SS

  and concentration camps 262, 264, 267

  officers taken prisoner 254

  shoot civilians 225, 241–2

SS *Arundel Castle* 1

SS *Empress of Britain* 12

SS *Nieuw Holland* 19–20

SS *Stirling Castle* 12

Stalin, Josef 282

Stalingrad, battle of 60, 249

Stanhope, Lady Hester 53–4

Stockach 229–30

storks 214

Storrs, Ronald 23

Strasbourg 151, 163, 165, 168, 171–2, 181, 199, 214

suicides 63

Sulemya 53

suntan, artificial 203

swallows 252–3

Tagsdorf 164

Tallal, Prince 66, 68

Tangiers 169

Taranto 87

Tatler 53

Tay (labrador) 68–9

Te Deum 260

Tel Aviv 64

Thiéfosse 123, 126

Times, The 224

Tito, Marshal 102–3

Tobruk 22, 29, 36, 60

Totora (boxer) 117

Transjordan Frontier Force 2, 39, 64–5, 69

Trèves 294, 300

Tripoli 41, 57

True Glory 287

tuberculosis 256–7, 267

Tunis 55

Tuttlingen 229

Ulm 235, 248

V weapons 262–5, 269

VADs, Scottish 81

Vallin, Commandant 144, 151, 164, 218, 230–1, 244–5, 298

VE Day 251

Victoria, Princess 270

Victoria, Queen 18, 270–1
Virtue in Tropical Lands
 (lecture) 9
Voltaire 280

WAAFs, executed 199
Wainman, Lieutenant-
 Colonel 274
Waldighoffen 142–3
Waldsee 243
Wasserman, Professor 63–4
Wattat (jockey and pilot) 54–5
Wauters, Jacques 266
Wavell, General Archibald 21–2,
 30, 33, 273, 276
Wavell, Pamela 2, 80
Westerham 209
Wilhelm II, Kaiser 271
Wilson, General Henry
 Maitland 30, 39, 42, 53, 57,
 72, 102, 274, 279

Wingate, Colonel Orde 33–4
Wittenheim 184, 192–3
Wittlich 294–8, 300, 307
Wolf Cubs 260
women
 Arab 62–3
 German 259–60
 and morality 155–6, 201–2
 Russian 227, 257–8, 273
 sentimentality and
  practicality 205
 snipers 129
Woolwich 66, 68

X-rays 105, 173, 176,
 178, 266, 308

Yugoslavs 98–9, 103, 232

Zassingen 168–9
Zenobia, Queen 44
Zerka oasis 61

GOING UNDERGROUND

D0347081

UNDERGROUND

MATTHEW TANNER

Navigator Guides Ltd
The Old Post Office, Swanton Novers
Melton Constable, Norfolk NR24 2AJ
postmaster@navigatorguides.com

Design concept by BK Design

ISBN 1-903872-03-0

A catalogue record for this book is available
from the British Library

Colour reproduction by
C3 Imaging Newcastle Ltd
Printed in Italy by
Printer Trento srl

Photo Credits
The Publishers would like to thank all those
organisations who supplied photographs and
© London Transport Museum for photographs
on pages i, ii/iii, 2/3, 24/25, 42/43, 66/67, 78/79,
92/93. ©The Natural History Museum,
Imperial War Museum, Guildhall
© Corporation of London, Design Museum ©
Jefferson Smith, National Gallery, Victoria and
Albert Museum, HMS Belfast, Queen Elizabeth
II Great Court © Phil Sayer, © Royal Academy of
Arts, The Royal Collection © 2000 Her Majesty
Queen Elizabeth 11, Tate Britain by Mark
Heathcote, ©The Wallace Collection by kind
permission of the Wallace Collection,
© Museum of London.

Acknowledgements
This publishers would like to thank Matthew
Tanner, Kinga Tommasi, Fay Franklin and Sarah
Gardner for their invaluable help in the
production of this book.

CONTENTS

Line by line | iv

Introduction | vii

The Underground map | xi

BAKERLOO LINE | 2

CENTRAL LINE | 24

CIRCLE LINE | 42

NORTHERN LINE | 66

PICCADILLY LINE | 78

VICTORIA LINE | 92

Directory | 101

Index of sights | 107

Index of food and drink | 108

CONTENTS

BAKERLOO LINE

LAMBETH NORTH
Imperial War Museum 4

WATERLOO
British Airways London Eye 6
FA Premier League Hall of Fame 6
Florence Nightingale Museum 7
Gabriel's Wharf 7
London Aquarium 8
The Museum of... 8
Namco Station 9
South Bank Arts Centre 9

CHARING CROSS
Institute of Contemporary Arts (ICA) 11
National Gallery 11
National Portrait Gallery 12
St Martin-in-the-Fields 13
Trafalgar Square 14

PICCADILLY CIRCUS
Berwick Street Market 15
Pepsi Trocadero 15
Rainforest Café 15
Rock Circus 16
Royal Academy of Arts 16
St James's Church Piccadilly 17

OXFORD CIRCUS
BBC Experience 18
Carnaby Street 19
Hamleys 19
Liberty's 19

REGENTS PARK
London Zoo 20
Regents Park 21

BAKER STREET
London Planetarium 22
Madame Tussaud's 22
Sherlock Holmes Museum 23

CENTRAL LINE

NOTTING HILL GATE
Portobello Market 26

LANCASTER GATE
London Toy and Model Museum 27

MARBLE ARCH
Hyde Park/Speaker's Corner 27

BOND STREET
Selfridges 28
Wallace Collection 28
Wigmore Hall 29

OXFORD CIRCUS
BBC Experience see p18
Carnaby Street see p19
Hamleys see p19
Liberty's see p19

TOTTENHAM COURT ROAD
British Museum 30

HOLBORN
Sir John Soane's Museum 32

CHANCERY LANE
Dr Johnson's House 33

ST PAUL'S
Museum of London 34
Old Bailey 34
St Paul's Cathedral 35

BANK
Bank of England Museum 36
Clockmakers' Company Museum 37
Guildhall 37

LIVERPOOL STREET
Brick Lane Market 39
Columbia Road Flower Market 39
Geffrye Museum 40
Petticoat Lane Market 40

CIRCLE LINE

SOUTH KENSINGTON
Conran Shop 44
Natural History Museum 44
Science Museum 46
Serpentine Gallery 47
Victoria and Albert Museum 47

SLOANE SQUARE
Carlyle's House 49
Chelsea Physic Garden 50

VICTORIA
Royal Mews see p95
Westminster Cathedral see p96

ST JAMES'S PARK
Buckingham Palace 52
London Transport Headquarters 52
St James's Park 52

WESTMINSTER
Cabinet War Rooms 53
Horse Guards 53
Houses of Parliament & Big Ben 54
Westminster Abbey 55

TEMPLE
Courtauld Gallery 56
Gilbert Collection 56
Prince Henry's Room 57

BLACKFRIARS
Tate Modern 57
Millennium Bridge 59

MONUMENT
The Monument 59

TOWER HILL
Tower Hill 60
Tower of London 60

LIVERPOOL STREET
Brick Lane Market see p39
Columbia Rd Flower Market see p39
Geffrye Museum see p40
Petticoat Lane see p40

BARBICAN
Barbican Centre 62

FARRINGDON
House of Detention 62

KINGS CROSS/ST PANCRAS
London Canal Museum 76

BAKER STREET
London Planetarium se p22
Madame Tussauds see p22
Sherlock Holmes Museum see p23

NOTTING HILL GATE
Portobello Market see p26

HIGH ST KENSINGTON
Albert Hall & Albert Monument 64
Kensington Palace 65

NORTHERN LINE

LONDON BRIDGE
Bramah Tea and Coffee Museum 68
Clink Prison Museum 68
Design Museum 69
Golden Hinde 69
HMS Belfast 70
London Dungeon 70
Old Operating Theatre and Herb
    Garrett 71
Shakespeare's Globe Theatre 72
Vinopolis, City of Wine 73
Winston Churchill's Britain at War 73

BANK
Bank of England Museum see p36
Clockmakers' Museum see p37
Guildhall see p37

ANGEL
Camden Passage 75

KINGS CROSS/ST PANCRAS
London Canal Museum 76

NORTHERN LINE
WEST END BRANCH

GOODGE STREET
Habitat 76
Heal's 76
Pollock's Toy Museum 77

CONTENTS

PICCADILLY LINE

SOUTH KENSINGTON
Conran Shop see p44
Natural History Museum see p44
Science Museum dee p46
Serpentine Gallery see p47
Victoria and Albert Museum see p47

KNIGHTSBRIGE
Harrods 79
Hyde Park Corner
The Wellington Museum 80

GREEN PARK
Faraday Museum see p97
Fortnum and Mason see p98
Green Park see p97
Ritz Hotel see p98

PICCADILLY CIRCUS
Berwick Street Market see p15
Pepsi Trocadero see p15
Rainforest Café see p15
Rock Circus see p15
Royal Academy of Arts see p16
St James's Church Piccadilly see p17

LEICESTER SQUARE
Chinatown 82
Half-price ticket booth 83
London Coliseum 83

COVENT GARDEN
Covent Garden Market and Piazza 85
Apple Market 85
Benjamin Pollock's Toy Shop 85
London Doll's House Company 86
London Transport Museum 86
Neal Street East 87
Neal's Yard Bakery 87
Neal's Yard Dairy 87
Royal Opera House 87
St Paul's Church 88
Stanley Gibbons International 88
The Kite Store 88
The Tea House 89
The Tintin Shop 89
The Wild Bunch 89
Theatre Museum 90

HOLBORN
Sir John Soane's Museum see p32
Russell Square
Dickens House Museum 91

KINGS CROSS/
ST PANCRAS
London Canal Museum see p76

VICTORIA LINE

PIMLICO
Tate Britain 94

VICTORIA
Royal Mews 95
Westminster Cathedral 95

GREEN PARK
Faraday Museum 97
Fortnum & Mason 97
Green Park 98
Ritz Hotel 98

OXFORD CIRCUS
BBC Experience see p18
Carnaby Street see p19
Hamleys see p19
Liberty's see p19

EUSTON
British Library 99

KING'S CROSS/ST
PANCRAS
London Canal Museum see p76

Discover Central London by tube

The tube makes London simple. Even for people who live here, the city can be a vast, frantic and bewildering place. Yet all of its sites, the pubs, restaurants and bars as well as the cinemas, theatres and endless shopping opportunities become easily accessible as soon as you venture underground. Exploring London by tube means not getting lost, avoiding the traffic jams, getting quickly to where you want to go and, with a Travelcard, roaming at will. Visitors who master the Underground are well on their way to mastering London.

The Underground is an historic achievement which has shaped the capital. This guide treats the network as an attraction in its own right. Taking the tube is an adventure. Down, down, down into the bowels of the earth, like Alice down the rabbit hole, you descend to the platform. First comes the rumble. Then the train emerges, lights gleaming, from the dark tunnel. You climb aboard, the doors close and you're off. Hey presto! Having popped down one hole you pop up another. As if by magic, you have been spirited to a different part of town.

Guide to the guide

This book is as easy to navigate as London is by tube. Each of the six sections is devoted to a single line: Bakerloo, Central, Circle, Northern, Piccadilly and Victoria. Taken together, these cover every major tube stop in Central London with something of interest close by. **Under each stop, the sites above ground are listed in alphabetical order and in the directory starting on p101 any nearby theatres, cinemas, restaurants, cafés, pubs bars and shops.**

Which line or route you take, however, is a matter of choice or convenience. If you have an attraction in mind, consult the contents on pages iv-vi to find the closest stop. Then look at the tube map at the front cover of this book to see the best way to get there. Alternatively, you may want to explore a single line. On the Central Line, for example, you could travel from east to west to visit the Bank of England Museum (Bank) and Sir John Soane's Museum (Holborn) in the morning, lunch at Simpson's of Chancery Lane (Holborn) and then on to the Wallace Collection (Bond Street) to spend an afternoon admiring French and Dutch masters. Or you might try a bit of line hopping and switch from the Central Line to the Bakerloo Line at Oxford Circus for a stroll through Regent's Park. Finally, if the weather is good, you could get back onto the Bakerloo Line and head for Gabriel's Wharf (Waterloo) to enjoy a pizza and a bottle of wine beside the river. Whatever you want to see or do in London, it's easy by tube. This guide provides a key.

Maps

As well as this guide, visitors should arm themselves with a good map of London. The Benson Mini Map covers the centre of town and is particularly clear and easy to use.

Tickets, Carnets and Travelcards

You can buy your tickets and carnets from any Underground station. One Day, Weekend and 7 Day Travelcards can also be purchased at London Travel Information Centres, National Rail Stations and local London Transport ticket outlets (many newsagents sell Travelcards). Under-5s travel free on London Underground. **Children aged 5–15** get concessionary rates (see below). **Please note these prices were valid when this book went to press in 2001**

Single fares
Zone 1
Adult £1.50   Child 60p
Zone 1 & 2
Adult £1.90   Child 80p

Carnet

A book of 10 single Underground tickets for use in Zone 1 only.
Adult £11.50   Child £5

One Day Travelcards

Valid for Zones 1 and 2 (tube, rail and bus) from 9.30 Mon–Fri and any time at the weekend or public holidays.

Zones 1 & 2

Adult £4.00   Child £2

All zones

Adult £4.90   Child £2

Weekend Travelcards

Cheaper by 25% than buying two One Day Travelcards.
Valid Sat and Sun and any two consecutive days during
public holidays.

Zones 1 & 2

Adult £6.00   Child £3

All zones

Adult £7.30   Child £3

Family Travelcards

One day tickets for up to two adults travelling with up to
four children. Groups need not be related but must travel
together at all times. Children aged 14–15 require a Child
Photocard (see below). Tickets valid from 9.30 Mon–Fri and
any time at the weekend or public holidays.

Zones 1 & 2

Adult £2.60   Child 80p

All zones

Adult £3.20   Child 80p

7 Day Travelcards

Valid any time for seven consecutive days (Photocard
required).

Zones 1 & 2

Adult £18.90   Child £7.70

All zones

Adult £36.40   Child £15.40

Photocards

Required when buying a Travelcard for seven days or
longer and by 14 and 15 year olds buying child-rate tickets.
Photocards are free. Take a passport-sized photo to any
Underground station, London Travel Information Centre of

local London Transport outlet. Child Photocards require proof of age and a completed application form (available at Photocard issuing points).

Lost property

Baker Street Underground Station

London Transport Lost Property Office

200 Baker Street, NW1

Tel: (recorded info) (020) 7486 2496

Open: Mon–Fri 9.30–2pm

Toilets

The following Zone 1 stations have toilets on site or nearby. You must have a valid ticket to use toilets in a Compulsory Ticket Area.

Baker Street

Farringdon

King's Cross/St Pancras

Liverpool Street

London Bridge

Marylebone

Paddington

Piccadilly Circus

South Kensington

Victoria

Waterloo

Travel Information

The following Zone 1 stations have a dedicated Travel Information Centre.

Euston

King's Cross/St Pancras

Liverpool Street

Oxford Circus

Paddington

Piccadilly Circus

St James's Park

Victoria

The Underground Map

The first all-inclusive map of the London Underground was published in 1906. With the routes traced over an ordinary map, it served its purpose up to a point but was difficult to understand and full of irrelevant information. Harry Beck, a 29-year-old unemployed engineering draughtsman, saw that it could be improved and, in his own time, sketched out in an exercise book the basis of what was to become a design classic.

Inspired by his work drawing electrical circuits, Beck's design broke with a traditional map format altogether and limited routes to horizontal, vertical and 45° degree diagonal lines. All surface detail, except for a simplified version of the River Thames, was omitted and each of the lines, though they had been colour-coded previously, was given a new distinctive colour to make the map easier to read, especially at night. Perhaps most importantly, he gave the central area (now Zone 1) a prominence out of all proportion to its actual size, as if seen through a convex lens, and shrank the outlying areas so that the entire network could be concentrated into a manageable format.

When Beck submitted his design to the publicity department of London Transport in 1931 it was rejected as too 'revolutionary'. No-one would understand it, he was told. Not to be put off, he returned a year later. This time he was more successful and a trial map was printed in 1933 with the words 'A new design for an old map. We should welcome your comments'. The travelling public took to it from the start and a version of the map has been in use ever since.

Sadly for Beck, he had signed away his copyright

for a pittance in 1937 and though he was unable to leave the map alone, refining and improving it to the point where it became an obsession, he never managed to capitalize on the brilliance of his design.

Since then, the map has been through a number of revisions (notably the vacuum flask shape for the Circle Line which was introduced in 1962) but it still clearly shows its debt to Beck with the

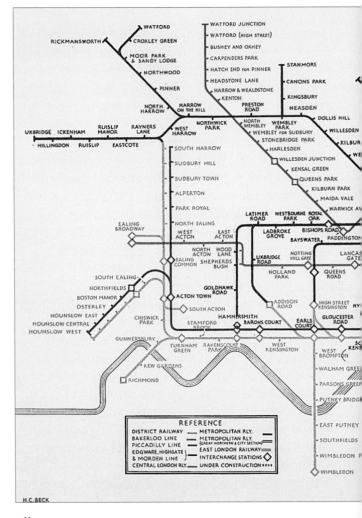

design proving itself flexible enough to accommodate many subsequent changes in the system. Though largely forgotten for many years, a room at the London Transport Museum (see p86) has now been named after Beck to honour the man who brought clarity and ease of use to the most complicated underground rail network in the world.

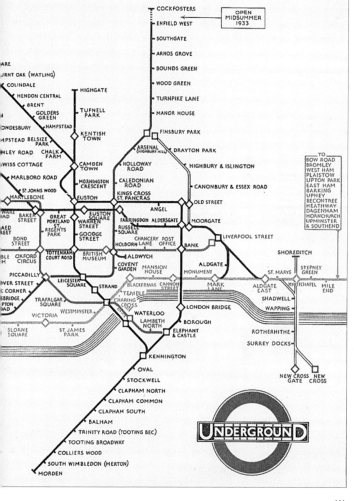

The Bakerloo Line, along with the Piccadilly and Northern Lines, was originally financed by an American, Charles Tyson Yerkes. Rumour has it that the idea for it originated from a few London businessmen who wanted to get to Lord's Cricket ground as quickly as possible. Whether this is true or not, there was obviously a far greater need and, when it opened on 10 March 1906, the Bakerloo Line carried 36,000 passengers on the first day.

LAMBETH NORTH

Imperial War Museum 4

WATERLOO

British Airways London Eye 6
FA Premier League Hall of Fame 6
Florence Nightingale Museum 7
Gabriel's Wharf 7
London Aquarium 8
The Museum of... 8
Namco Station 9
South Bank Arts Centre 9

CHARING CROSS

Institute of Contemporary Arts (ICA) 11
National Gallery 11
National Portrait Gallery 12
St Martin-in-the-Fields 13
Trafalgar Square 14

PICCADILLY CIRCUS

Berwick Street Market 15
Pepsi Trocadero 15
Rainforest Café 15
Rock Circus 16
Royal Academy of Arts 16
St James's Church Piccadilly 17

OXFORD CIRCUS

BBC Experience 18
Carnaby Street 19
Hamleys 19
Liberty's 19

REGENTS PARK

London Zoo 20
Regents Park 21

BAKER STREET

London Planetarium 22
Madame Tussaud's 22
Sherlock Holmes Museum 23

LAMBETH NORTH

Imperial War Museum

Lambeth Road, SE1
Tel: (020) 7416 5320
www.iwm.org.uk
Open: 10–6 daily
Adm: adult £5.20, child free, concs £4.20
(free for everyone after 4.30)

Considering some people's belief that war is insanity, it is appropriate enough that the Imperial War Museum should be housed in the former Bethlehem Royal Hospital, otherwise known as Bedlam, where the mad, the sad and the deranged were kept like caged animals during the 17th and 18th centuries for the amusement of the public who were allowed in free to snigger at the lunatics. These days the museum is one of the capital's best attractions with an incomparable collection of war memorabilia, a good shop and decent café.

The first sight you see is the massive 15-inch naval guns, weighing in at 100 tons each, which could propel a 1,925lb shell a distance of 18 1/4 miles. Enter the museum and there is a vast atrium where you can appreciate Mankind's wonderful ingenuity with large exhibits such as a restored Jagdpanther tank destroyer, a Supermarine Spitfire and a V2 rocket. Children, of course, love it all and happily step into the bowels of a cramped Halifax bomber or take on the role of a pilot in a flight simulator (extra payment required).

The basement area is devoted to the two World Wars. As you enter, you see a clock counting the number of those killed in all wars. On 31 December 1999 it passed the 100 million mark. As well as the massive collection of uniforms, weaponry, equipment and memorabilia are two 'experiences'. The Trench Experience lets you grope your way through a dingy (and smelly) trench during World War I. With the Blitz Experience you find yourself in a London street as fires rage and Hitler's doodlebugs give the city a pounding.

Secret War on the first floor attempts to explain the world of espionage and has lots of buttons to press (can you crack the 'Enigma' code?). On the second floor is the museum's art collection, including work by Henry Moore, John Singer Sargent and Stanley Spencer.

The newest and most moving exhibit is on the newly-built top two floors. The Holocaust Exhibition (free separate ticket required) charts the rise of Hitler and the Nazi party through to the horror of the Final Solution and its aftermath. This is gruelling stuff and not recommended for children under 14. The exhibition begins before the Nazis. Smiling faces peer out from family photos as you learn what life was like before 6 million Jews (a quarter of them children), not to mention gypsies, homosexuals and anyone else the Nazis didn't like, were exterminated. Large storyboards, film clips, interviews and photos tell all with great clarity. Yet it is the little things that really attract the attention: a child's tatty exercise book with notes on German racial superiority copied out in a neat hand, a faded yellow star, a rough hewn wooden clog worn by a Russian prisoner of war, a tiny, battered doll found in the arms of dead girl.

After the Holocaust Exhibition you may want to step outside where there is a Tibetan Peace Garden, opened by His Holiness, The Dalai Lama in May 1999.

food and drink

The Fire Station

150 Waterloo Road, SE1
Tel: (020) 7620 2226
Open: Mon-Sat 11-11,
Sun noon-10.30

One time fire station, now an incredibly popular pub with a restaurant at the back.

Brendan O'Grady's

67-69 Kennington Road, SE1
Tel: (020) 7928 5974
Open: Mon-Sat noon-11
Sun noon-10.30

An Irish pub through and through with Irish food, ale and music.

Babushka

173 Blackfriars Road, SE1
Tel: (020) 7928 3693
Open: Mon-Sat noon-midnight

One large bar with lounge area at back with a grand piano and enormous beer garden for barbecues. Very busy at weekend as pre-clubbers prepare for a long night at the nearby Ministry of Sound nearby.

WATERLOO

British Airways London Eye

Jubilee Gardens, SE1
Tel: (0870) 500 0600
www.ba-londoneye.com
Open: Apr–Oct 9am–dusk daily;
Nov–Mar 10–6 daily
Adm: adult £7.45, child £4.95
(under–5s free), concs £5.95

The British Airways London Eye is everything the Dome at Greenwich should have been but wasn't: simple, cheap and popular. A massive 443ft wheel, the Eye is genuinely impressive and has already become part of the skyline, notable not only for its size but for its circularity amid the swathe of surrounding square, oblong and rectangular buildings. Thirty-two capsules, each holding up to 25 people, take a gentle 30–minute round trip affording 25-mile views. On a clear day you can see as far as Heathrow airport and Windsor Castle. Think twice if you are at all afraid of heights: the clear capsules and the panoramic views can be daunting for anyone with even a hint of vertigo. Once you are in you can't get out! When it is hot the capsules can get very stuffy so take a drink.

FA Premier League Hall of Fame

County Hall, Riverside Building, Westminster Bridge Road, SE1
Tel: (0870) 848 8484
www.hall-of-fame.co.uk
Open: 10–6 daily (last entry 5pm)
Adm: adult £9.95, child £6.50 (under–5s free), concs £7.50

Opened in 1999, County Hall's FA Premier League Hall of Fame aims to tell football's story from the Middle Ages to the present day. The collection includes videos, photographs, waxworks and trophies, and also a number of kits donated by famous players such as Bobby Moore and Pele. As well as the obvious range of exhibits – medals, photos, programmes etc. – there is also a selection of more bizarre trivia including a Victorian shin pad, cigarette cards from the 1890s, a World War I trench football game and a copy of the original Subbutteo game then called 'Newfotty Table Soccer'.

Florence Nightingale Museum

St Thomas's Hospital, 2 Lambeth Palace Road, SE1
Tel: (020) 7620 0374
www.florence–nightingale.co.uk
Open: Mon–Fri 10–5 (last entry 4pm), Sat & Sun 11.30–4.30
(last entry 3.30)
Adm: adult £4.80, child & concs £3.60, family £10

Housed in St Thomas's Hospital, where Florence Nightingale founded the world's first school of nursing over a 100 years ago, this museum presents the indomitable woman at various stages in her life through personal artefacts, paintings, set-pieces, quotations and storyboards. There is correspondence and school books from her days as a privileged and well-educated girl, a little medicine chest taken to the Crimea, a set piece portraying the lady, lamp in hand, attending to the sick (in the background a man's leg is being amputated) and a recreation of one of the simply furnished rooms where she spent her later years campaigning tirelessly for medical reform and laying the foundations for modern nursing.

Gabriel's Wharf

A short walk east along the river from the South Bank (see p9) is Gabriel's Wharf, a homely selection of mini-shops, boutiques, restaurants and bars as well as sculpture, ceramics, fashion and jewellery workshops. Want a hand-knitted pair of designer baby booties? Or a futuristic lava lamp? This is the place. It is also a nice spot to sit out. Roughly hewn hobby horses (and other animals) are free for kids to play on and there is often some form of live musical entertainment on the bandstand.

London Aquarium

County Hall, Riverside Building, Westminster Bridge Road, SE1
Tel: (020) 7967 8000
www.londonaquarium.co.uk
Open: 10–6 daily (last entry 5pm)
Adm: adult £8.50, child and concs £5 (under-3s free), family £24,
wheelchair users free

It has not been open long but the Aquarium is already packing them in. Set over three levels, thousands of gobby eyed fish, sharks and eels are on display,

swimming in lazy circles round huge tanks, or ruminating, dead still, on the sandy bottom. Some are so well-camouflaged you can hardly see them at all. Arranged according to different oceans and water environments, the museum gestures towards modern ecological concerns with an exhibit devoted to the declining rainforest and another to the polluted River Thames. One of the biggest draws is the touch pool where, if you manage to squeeze past the excitable toddlers, you can stroke some of the more benign fish including a friendly giant ray. The sharks are also strangely hypnotic. With bleak, black eyes, they range the tanks as best they can, indifferent both to their fellow creatures in the water and the odd looking creatures staring in at them from the other side of the glass.

The Museum of...

Oxo Tower Wharf, Bargehouse Street, SE1
Tel: (020) 7928 1255
Open: Tue–Sun 11–6 (last entry 5.30pm)
Adm: free

This is a new kind of attraction: a versatile space which is turned into a completely different museum every 16 weeks. By this means the organizers hope to 'challenge the way we think about museums'. Forthcoming exhibitions for 2001 include the Museum of the Unknown and the Museum of the River Thames (phone for details).

Namco Station

County Hall, Riverside Building,
Westminster Bridge Road, SE1
Tel: (020) 7967 1066
Open: 10–midnight daily
Adm: free (pay to play)

Two floors of shoot-em-ups, driving simulators, space rides
and pixelated kick-boxers. This is heaven for gameplayers of
all ages. If you are not used to it, the bright lights and
frenzied bashing of buttons and tugging of levers can get a
bit much and the machines guzzle pound coins with a
ferocious appetite. But, if you like video games, Namco
Station is fun so long as the money holds out.

South Bank Arts Centre

South Bank, SE1
Tel: (020) 7928 6143 www.sbc.org.uk

This riverside arts complex includes the Hayward Gallery, Royal
Festival Hall, Royal National Theatre and the National Film Theatre
(NFT). It also houses MOMI (The Museum of the Moving Image)
which is closed until 2003 for refurbishment.
The whole area is currently undergoing a
face-lift (part of the beautification of the
south side of the river) but this is still an
invigorating place to come, day or night. You
can sit outside the NFT and sip a cool beer, sift
through the second-hand books and prints
on sale under the bridge, stroll along the river
towards Gabriel's Wharf (you may see a fire-
eater or juggling comedian) or watch the
skateboarders and rollerbladers fall over as
they hop about trying out new tricks.

And this is all before you enter a single
building. The Royal Festival Hall looks better
on the inside than it does on the outside.
Large and airy, with a good bar, bookshop and café, this is one of
the top venues for classical music in the country. It also hosts
occasional free exhibitions. The NFT does a good line in classic
screenings with a children's matinee at the weekend. The
Hayward is an art exhibition space and puts on big name shows
throughout the year while the Royal National Theatre is actually
three theatres – catering for everything from large-scale
razzmatazz to worthy drama and razor-edged fringe.

9

Hayward Gallery

Belvedere Road, South Bank Centre, SE1
Tel: (020) 7960 4242
Open: 10–6 daily, until 8 on Wed & Thur
Adm: varies (phone for details)

National Film Theatre

South Bank, SE1
Tel: (020) 7928 3232

Royal Festival Hall

South Bank, SE1
Tel: (020) 7960 4242
Open: (box office) 10–9 daily

Royal National Theatre

South Bank, SE1
Tel: (020) 7452 3000
Open: (box office) 10–8 daily

food and drink

Gourmet Pizza Company

Unit 20
Gabriel's Wharf
South Bank, SE1
Tel: (020) 7928 3188
Open: Mon–Sat noon–10.45,
Sun noon–10.30

Superior pizzas with views.

Oxo Tower

Barge House Street, SE1
Tel: (020) 7803 3888
Open: Mon-Sat noon–3 & 6–11.30,
Sun noon-3.30 & 6.30-10.30

Upmarket modern European
restaurant boasting one of the
most spectacular views in London.

The People's Palace

Royal Festival Hall
4th Floor
South Bank Centre, SE1
Tel: (020) 7928 9999
Open: daily noon–3, 5.30–10.50

Pricey modern cooking with
magnificent river views.

Auberge

1 Sandell Street, SE1
Tel: (020) 7633 0610
Open: Mon–Fri 11am–midnight,
Sat noon–11

Quiet café bar. Good line in
Belgian beer.

Doggett's Coat and Badge

1 Blackfriars Bridge,
Blackfriars Road, SE1
Tel: (020) 7633 9057
Open: Mon-Sat noon–3, Sun
7–10.30

Good beer and river views. Worth
a walk along the river.

Studio Six

Gabriel's Wharf, SE1
Tel: (020) 7928 6243
Open: Mon–Sat noon–11, Sun
noon–10.30

Plenty of outside seating. Food
also available.

CHARING CROSS

Institute of Contemporary Arts (ICA)

The Mall, SW1
Tel: (020) 7873 0062
www.ica.org.uk
Open: (box office) noon–9.30 daily
Adm: varies

Just down the road from Buckingham Palace and the heart of the British establishment, the ICA was opened in 1948 as a challenge to the conservatism of the major galleries. Arch modernists Henry Moore and Pablo Picasso were first exhibited in London here, as was Damien Hirst (he of the embalmed floating animals). Plenty of avant-garde dance and the odd film screening are also reasons to visit, as is the trendy bar-cum-café. It's a good place for celebrity spotting too!

National Gallery

Trafalgar Square, WC2
Tel: (020) 7747 2885
www.nationalgallery.org.uk
Open: Mon, Tue, Thur–Sun 10–6, Wed 10–9
Adm: free

The National Gallery's collection began in 1824 when the government paid £57,000 to buy up 38 pictures from a recently deceased merchant, John Julius Angerstein. Included in this original scoop was work by Raphael, Rembrandt and Van Dyck. In the Victorian era, as England grew rich on the proceeds of the Industrial Revolution, the gallery engaged in numerous buying sprees. Even today it has some £2 million a year to spend. The results are staggering, with examples of virtually every major school of Western European art from the 13th to the early 20th centuries displayed in four colour-coded wings.

The oldest work is now kept in the newly-built Sainsbury Wing (1260–1510) as is the excellent shop and one of two Micro Galleries where you can explore the museum's collection without budging an inch and print out your own tour. You can also pick up a useful CD gallery guide at the top of the stairs to talk you round. The guide is free though it is a brazen visitor who refuses to pay the requested £4 contribution. Most people head for Rooms 51, 56 and 60 in the Sainsbury Wing to take in, respectively, work by Leonardo da Vinci, Van Eyck and Raphael.

You can't hope to appreciate the whole gallery in a day and it does little harm to leave out the West Wing (1510–1600) altogether. There are only 10 rooms and the paintings look a little samey, though the Tintorettos and Titians in Room 7 are worth visiting if you can spare the time. Instead, head straight through to the North Wing (1600–1700) where painting seems to shift up a gear. Here you'll see the dreamy harbour scenes of Lorraine (contrasted with two works by Turner in Room 15), the quiet calm of the Dutch interiors, especially the Vermeers, in Room 16 and Samuel van Hoogstraat's ingenious peepshow in Room 17. Rembrandt's highly detailed and expressive self-portraits (Room 23) and Ruben's exuberant biblical scenes (Room 29), as well as the characterful portraits of Velazquez (Room 30), are also not to be missed.

If you were congratulating yourself on visiting on such a quiet day, wait until you reach the East Wing (1700–1900), and Rooms 43–45 in particular which contain work by the Impressionists including Renoir, Monet, Van Gogh and Cezanne. It is difficult to appreciate these famous paintings (amongst them Van Gogh's *Sunflowers*, Seurat's *Bathers at Asnières* and Monet's *Water Lilies*) while being jostled and prodded by hordes of school children and students. Far better to head for Room 34 to squint at Turner's *Rain, Steam and Speed* and Room 38 for the opulent barge and street scenes of Canaletto and return to see the Impressionists when the museum has emptied out.

National Portrait Gallery

2 St Martin's Place, WC2
Tel: (020) 7306 0055
www.npg.org.uk
Open: Mon–Sat 10–6, Sun noon–6
Adm: free

In 1856, when the NPG was founded to celebrate Britain's heroes, you had to be royalty or high up in government to hang on the walls. Today you need only be a celebrity. A poet, a pop star, a journalist, even a cook or footballer are worthy subjects. The sitter rather than the art is the point and consequently not all of the paintings are first rate. But it hardly matters as you trace the history of England through the faces of its movers and shakers.

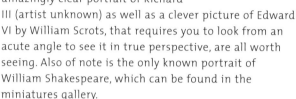

The collection now begins in the spruce new Ondaatje Wing with the Tudors. Holbein's vivid sketch of Henrys VII and VIII, the amazingly clear portrait of Richard III (artist unknown) as well as a clever picture of Edward VI by William Scrots, that requires you to look from an acute angle to see it in true perspective, are all worth seeing. Also of note is the only known portrait of William Shakespeare, which can be found in the miniatures gallery.

The current royals are now on the first floor landing (Room 33). Look out, too, for Bryan Organ's youthful representation of Diana, Princess of Wales, painted before the cracks began to appear in her marriage (Room 36).

The new Balcony Gallery leads you into the 20th century and includes photos of the Beatles, George Best and Julie Christie. On the first floor, where the bulk of 20th-century portraits are to be found, you might also bump into cook Delia Smith surrounded by pans, David Beckham (before the haircut) or a shapely but decidedly yellow Darcy Bussell, gracefully dancing on points.

St Martin–in–the–Fields

Trafalgar Square, WC2
Tel: (020) 7930 1862
www.stmartin–in–the–fields.org
Open: 8–6.30 daily
Adm: free

As the traffic grinds constantly past, it is hard to imagine that this used to be 'in the fields'. Though a church has stood here since the 13th century, the present building was finished in 1726. Designed by James Gibbs, it is the oldest building in the square. Inside, richly ornate woodwork and plaster remind one that this is the Queen's parish church (a Royal Box stands to the left of the gallery). Lunchtime and evening recitals keep the visitor numbers up while down in the crypt are the London Brass Rubbing Centre and a busy, atmospheric café.

food and drink

The Criterion

224 Piccadilly, W1
Tel: (020) 930 0488
Open: Mon–Sat noon–2.30 &
6–11.30, Sun 6–10.30

The food is excellent here and the room, all glamour and gold, is worth a visit for its own sake.

Café Fish

39 Panton Street, SW1
Tel: (020) 930 3999
Open: Mon–Fri noon–3 &
5.30–11.30, Sat noon–11.30,
Sun noon–10.30

Bustling bistro-type fish restaurant serving everything from kedgeree to fish and chips.

Café in the Crypt

St Martin-in-the-Fields, WC2
Tel: (020) 7839 4342
Open: Mon–Sat 10–8, Sun
noon–8 (hot food noon–3.15 &
5–7.30)

Cavernous café in the bowels of the church. Escape from the heat or warm up with a bowl of home-made soup.

Trafalgar Square

Trafalgar Square is the centre of London from which all distances from the capital are measured. Begun some 170 years ago, it was laid on the site of the king's mews (all the king's horses were once lodged here). The original plans were drawn up by the architect John Nash who hoped to create a huge open space to glorify the country's sea power. Unfortunately he fell from grace before his scheme could come to fruition and today the square is a busy, noisy, somewhat characterless place. Even so, it remains popular and its natural incline (from north to south) makes it possible to gaze down the imposing thoroughfares which lead to Westminster (Whitehall), Buckingham Palace (the Mall) and the Thames (Northumberland Ave).

People come to see Nelson's Column, all 171ft of it, that commemorates Britain's most famous sailor who lost his life beating the combined Franco-Prussian fleet in 1805. Kids like it here because they can clamber onto Edwin Landseer's enormous bronze lions to have their photograph taken. They also enjoy dipping their hands in the fountains (built in 1845) which gurgle into life at 10 o'clock every morning.

Each year at Christmastime people gather to sing carols round a tree donated by the Norwegians in thanks for Britain's help during World War II. A week or so later it is party time as thousands pile in to wait for the chimes of Big Ben to ring in the New Year.

PICCADILLY CIRCUS

Berwick Street Market

Berwick Street, W1
Open: Mon–Sat 8–6

Londoners were first introduced to the delights of the pineapple here in 1890. The market is still one of the best places to come for fruit and veg. Most is sold fairly cheaply and, as it often teeters on the edge of being over-ripe, is consequently perfect to eat straight away or a little later as part of a picnic. The stall holders are part of the fun, clamouring for your custom and barking out ribald innuendo regarding their produce. On either side of the market are a number of old-fashioned fabric shops (good for exotica and zebra print), a couple of greasy spoon cafés, some trendy hairdressing salons, a delicatessen and a clutch of second-hand record shops. At number 93 is a branch of Simply Sausages while Bar Du Marché across the road will provide you with ice-cold beers, good wine by the glass or bottle and reasonably priced, well cooked food.

Pepsi Trocadero

1 Piccadilly Circus, W1
Tel: (020) 7734 2777
Open: 10am–midnight daily
Adm: varies (see below)
Restricted wheelchair access

At the Trocadero you will find six floors of video games, virtual reality rides, pool tables, putting and bumper cars, as well as numerous burger bars and a cyber café. All this is set in a futuristic, if somewhat dowdy, environment known as Funland. If you haven't eaten for a while, try the Pepsi Max drop ride (£3) where you plummet 130ft (six floors) in a little under two seconds. For an additional £3 you can have your photo taken as you fall.

Rainforest Café

20 Shaftesbury Avenue, W1
Tel: (020) 7434 3111
Open: Mon–Thur noon–10.30, Fri noon–11.30, Sat 11.30–11.30, Sun 11.30–10.30

People queue to get in here. The food is pure Americana: burgers, fries, waffles, gloopy milkshakes and ice-cream sundaes. And very tasty it is too. You gobble it up amid cascading waterfalls, dense Amazonian foliage and a host of robotic forest animals including parakeets, chimps and snakes. Every so often there's even lightening and a thunderstorm overhead. The menu is on the pricey side but the surroundings make for a memorable visit. Kids will love it.

Rock Circus

London Pavilion, 1 Piccadilly Circus, W1
Tel: (020) 7734 7203
Open: Mon, Wed, Thur, Sun 11–9, Fri & Sat 11–10
Adm: adult £8.25, child £6.25, concs £7.25

Madame Tussaud's revamped Rock Circus is unashamedly a collection for musically-minded children. Set over three floors of the London Pavilion, the exhibition sings and dances its way through the history of pop using animatronic characters, stage sets, dioramas and hi-tech, multimedia experiences. There's a treasure chest of priceless memorabilia including Elvis's shirt, Elton John's platform shoes, Roy Orbison's guitar and the Beatles' suits from *A Hard Day's Night*. The excitement increases as you get a chance to become stars yourself, hanging around at a backstage party attended by Elvis, Jarvis Cocker and Bono. The highlight is the Revolving Show (staged in Europe's biggest revolving auditorium) where you can enjoy a parade of music–making from Aretha Franklin to ZZ Top at top volume via individual infrared headsets.

Royal Academy of Arts

Burlington House, Piccadilly, W1
Tel: (020) 7300 5959
www.royalacademy.org.uk
Open: 10–6 daily (Fri till 8.30)
Adm: depends on the exhibition

The Royal Academy's Palladian building was completed in 1720 as the private home for the third Earl of Burlington. It remained a private residence until 1854 when it was bought by the government to house the Royal Academy of Arts. The brainchild of Sir Joshua Reynolds (whose statue, brush and palette in hand, stands in the courtyard), it was the country's first ever school of art. These days the RA is better known for its temporary exhibitions (forthcoming shows for 2001 include Botticelli's Drawing and Rembrandt's Women). The other big draw is the Summer Exhibition which attracts huge numbers between

May and August. The difference with this exhibition is that all of the art has been submitted by the artists themselves (some famous, some unknown). The works are then looked at by a panel of judges. About 1,500 paintings and sculptures are accepted for the show. Thousands more fail to get past the committee. The RA also has a small permanent exhibition which shows paintings from many of its most famous members including Reynolds, Gainsborough, Constable and Turner. The café serves good coffee and even better cakes. The shop is a safe bet for souvenirs and presents.

St James's Church Piccadilly

197 Piccadilly, W1
Tel: (020) 7734 4511
Open: 8–7 daily
Adm: free

Although Christopher Wren worked on many of London's churches, patching them up after the Great Fire of London in 1666, St James's Piccadilly is the only one which he built from scratch. It proved to be one of his favourites, 'I think it may be found beautiful and convenient' the great architect later wrote. After the bustle and noise of Piccadilly, the church is a restful place. The free lunchtime recitals are also a good reason to visit, as is the flea market (Wed–Sun), antiques market (Tues) and the vegetarian café/restaurant in the annexe.

food and drink

Bar Du Marché

19 Berwick Street, W1
Tel: (020) 7734 4606
Open: Mon–Sat noon–11
(closed Sun)

Popular after-work spot with genuinely French staff, cold beers, decent wines and good food.

Planet Hollywood

13 Coventy Street, W1
Tel: (020) 7734 6220
Open: Mon–Sat 11.30am–1.30am,
Sun 11.30am-12.30am

Burgers and fries, milkshakes, the lot! Plus Hollywood memorabilia and a gift shop.

food and drink

Fortnum & Mason
Fountain Room

181 Piccadilly, W1
Tel: (020) 7734 8040
Open: Mon–Sat 7.30am–11pm

Elegant tea room housed in the shop's basement.

Ritz Hotel

150 Piccadilly, W1
Tel: (020) 7493 8181

If you can afford it, tea at the Ritz is a holiday memory to be savoured. Also open for lunch, dinner and breakfast.

TGI Fridays

25-29 Coventry Street, W1
Tel: (020) 7839 6262
Open: noon–midnight daily

Lively child-friendly Tex-Mex diner. The staff not only serve you but can perform magic and juggling acts too.

Blue Posts

22 Berwick Street, W1
Tel: (020) 7437 5000
Open: Mon–Sat noon–3,
Sun 7–10.30

Traditional, unspoilt British boozer. Many of the market stall holders come here after work.

OXFORD CIRCUS

BBC Experience

Broadcasting House, Portland Place, W1
Tel: (0870) 603 0304
www.bbc.co.uk/experience
Open: Mon 11–6, Tue–Sun 10–6 (last tour 4.30 daily)
Adm: (by tour only) adult £6.95, child £4.95, concs £5.95,
family £19.95

Opened in 1997 to celebrate the BBC's 75th birthday, the BBC Experience is a mixture of history and interactive fun. You can learn about the organization's story of success from the early days of boffins in white coats through to the digital explosion of the late-20th century and beyond. Interesting though this is, the real fun is to be had in he interactive section where you can try your hand at reading the news, forecasting the weather or directing your own episode of the London soap opera, EastEnders. Admission also includes a tour of the building and a look at the collection of early Marconi radio equipment. There is, of course, a café and plenty of purchasing opportunities in the well-stocked souvenir shop.

Carnaby Street

Gone are the days when you might have seen anyone famous shopping on Carnaby Street though you might see the odd pop star or two in nearby Newburgh Street which has a batch of severely trendy clothing shops. Being pedestrianized, however, it is a pleasant place to sit outside and though the Carnabetian Army has long since upped sticks and moved elsewhere, there are one or two shops worth a browse including Shelleys (at number 44) for streetsmart boots and shoes and Storm (number 21) for designer watches. Numbers 47 and 47a Carnaby Street have been protected by Westminster Council, which has decreed that no-one can use these buildings for anything but tailoring.

Hamleys

188 Regent Street, W1
Tel: (020) 7734 3161
Open: Mon–Wed & Fri 10–7, Thur 10–8, Sat 9.30–7, Sun noon–6

More than a shop, Hamleys is a tourist attraction in its own right. As soon as you walk through the doors you realize you're in for something special as demonstrators, standing on small plinths, buzz you with low-flying planes, blow extra large bubbles or construct miniature masterpieces from balloons. Set over six floors, with a video arcade and café in the basement, you can easily spend half a day here trying out the latest toys and games, fiddling with the *Lego* and racing the *Scalextrix* cars at top speed round a mini Brands Hatch. The kids may like it too.

Liberty's

214–220 Regent Street, W1
Tel: (020) 7734 1234
Open: Mon–Wed 10–6.30, Thur till 8, Fri & Sat till 7

One of London's most famous department stores, Liberty's began in the 19th century as an outlet for the Arts and Crafts movement selling, amongst other things, silks, fabrics and wallpaper designed by the poet and craftsman William Morris. The fake Tudor exterior and rich wooden panelling inside, together with the warren–like layout full of inviting nooks and crannies, make it a fun place to shop. The women's fashion, jewellery and accessories are especially good (though expensive), as is the kitchenware. On the top floor you can still buy good quality Arts and Crafts furniture.

food and drink

Nico Central

35 Gt Portland Street, W1
Tel: (020) 7436 8846
Open: Mon–Fri 10–3, 6–10.30,
Sat 10–3 (closed Sun)

Good French food. On the pricey side but set menus are a cheaper option.

Patisserie Valerie

66 Portland Place, W1
Tel: (020) 7631 0467
Open: Mon–Sat 8–6

Heavenly gateaux, tarts and pastries.

Pizza Express

4-5 Langham Place, W1
Tel: (020) 580 3700
Open: 11.30–midnight

Better-than-average pizza chain.

RK Stanley's

6 Little Portland Street, W1
Tel: (020) 7462 0099
Open: Mon–Sat noon–11

Good value sausage restaurant. Kids eat for free on Saturdays.

Villandry

170 Gt Portland Street, W1
Tel: (020) 7631 3131
Open: Mon–Sat noon–3, 7–10.30,
Sun noon–3

Impressive food hall with its own café and dining room.

Bonbonnierre

36 Great Marlborough Street, W1
Tel: (020) 7408 0648
Open: Mon-Sat 7–7

One of the last of a dying breed of family run Italian cafés to be found in Soho. The coffee isn't great but the mixed grills and pasta dishes go down a treat.

The Lexington

45 Lexington Street, W1
Tel: (020) 7434 3401
Open: Mon–Fri 12.30–2,
Mon–Sat 6.30–11

Reasonably priced modern European food with a jazz pianist in the evenings.

Dover Castle

43 Weymouth Mews, W1
Tel: (020) 7580 4412
Open: Mon–Fri 11.30am–11pm,
Sat noon–11

Inviting little pub, tucked away in a mews.

REGENT'S PARK

London Zoo

Regent's Park, NW1
Tel: (020) 7722 3333
www.londonzoo.co.uk/londonzoo
Open: Nov–Mar 10–4 daily; Apr–Oct 10–5 daily
Adm: adult £9, child £7 (under–3s free), concs £8

The word 'zoo' comes from an abbreviation for the Zoological Society of London which was founded in 1826 and opened its gardens to the public two years later. Britain, then a major colonial power, was importing animals from around the globe and, for the majority of people, it was their first sighting of such mythic beasts as alligators, elephants, giraffes, kangaroos and panda bears. The zoo fell out of favour in the late 1980s and early '90s as environmental concerns kept people away, but the attraction has since made a valiant comeback and transformed its image from animal prison to animal sanctuary.

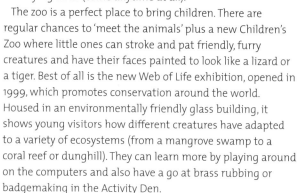

Among the highlights are the curvaceous penguin pool (come at feeding time), the elephant and rhino pavilion (come when its time for their daily bath) and the aviary full of free-flying birds (come anytime at all).

The zoo is a perfect place to bring children. There are regular chances to 'meet the animals' plus a new Children's Zoo where little ones can stroke and pat friendly, furry creatures and have their faces painted to look like a lizard or a tiger. Best of all is the new Web of Life exhibition, opened in 1999, which promotes conservation around the world. Housed in an environmentally friendly glass building, it shows young visitors how different creatures have adapted to a variety of ecosystems (from a mangrove swamp to a coral reef or dunghill). They can learn more by playing around on the computers and also have a go at brass rubbing or badgemaking in the Activity Den.

Regent's Park

Tel: (020) 7486 7905
Open: 5am to dusk daily
Adm: free

Originally part of Middlesex Forest and then a royal hunting ground, Regent's Park was laid out over 11 years from 1817–28 by the architect John Nash. One of London's neatest parks, its rose gardens within the inner circle are pristine with beds of colourful flowers that bloom in profusion throughout the summer. There's plenty to do here with a boating lake (also home to herons and black swans), playgrounds, a bandstand for music and an open air theatre which has both evening and daytime performances. A café next to the theatre provides sandwiches, crisps, teas, coffees and cold drinks.

BAKER STREET

London Planetarium

Marylebone Road, NW1
Tel: (020) 7935 6861
www.madame-tussauds.com
Open: June–Aug 10.20–5 daily; Sept–May Mon–Fri 12.20–5, Sat & Sun 10.20–5
Adm: adult £6.30, child £4.20 (under–5s free), concs £4.85; combined ticket with Madame Tussaud's: adult £12.95, child £8.50 (under–5s free), concs £9.80

Right next door to Madame Tussaud's (see below), the Planetarium takes you on a celestial journey through our solar system. Sit down in a comfy chair, stare up at the dome shaped ceiling and, hey presto!, you find yourself on a 'Planetary Quest', journeying past comets, planets and moons, asteroid belts and exploding supernovas. After the show you can visit the Planetarium's museum. Here there are waxworks of pioneering astronauts Neil Armstrong and Buzz Aldrin, live satellite broadcasts from space and a machine to gauge how much you'd weigh if you were on the moon.

Madame Tussaud's

Marylebone Road, NW1
Tel: (020) 7935 6861
www.madame-tussauds.com
Open: May–Sept 10–5.30 daily; Oct–Jun Mon–Fri 10–5.30, Sat & Sun 9.30–5.30
Adm: adult £10.50, child £7 (under–5s free), concs £8; combined ticket with London Planetarium: adult £12.95, child £8.50 (under-5s free), concs £9.80

Love it or hate it, the popularity of Madame Tussaud's is undeniable, as you soon realize when you visit and find yourself standing in a queue for well over an hour. This is the country's third most visited tourist attraction, topped only by the British Museum and the National Gallery. Its popularity is in part due, without doubt, to the famous name of Tussaud. Then there is the chance to have a photo of yourself taken beside Madonna or Arnold Schwarzenegger, which is always a giggle.

Underlying all, however, is the spookiness of the lifelike waxwork effigies. They chilled the hearts of visitors back in 1802 when Madame Tussaud, a former drawing

mistress of King Louis XVI's children, came to England fleeing the French Revolution with her own collection of death masks. And though their power is today less intense, there is still something threatening about the lifeless dummies which holds an unfathomable fascination. They won't suddenly come alive of course – or perhaps they just might.

Madame Tussaud's has several sections. At a garden party you can rub shoulders with celebrities such as Linford Christie and Pierce Brosnan (dressed as 007) who mingle with the other guests. In the main hall you come face to face with monarchs, politicians, dictators, writers and assorted pop stars. Down in the basement is the Chamber of Horrors where the lifeless eyes of such monsters as Dr Crippen and Jack the Ripper stare back at you, unapologetic. Finally, the Spirit of London carries you in a London taxi through 400 years of history beginning in Elizabethan times and ending in the present day with a grinning, saluting effigy of comedian Benny Hill.

Sherlock Holmes Museum

221b Baker Street, NW1
Tel: (020) 7935 8866
www.sherlock-holmes.co.uk
Open: 9.30–6 daily
Adm: adult £6, child £3.50
No disabled facilities

You know as soon as you get out at Baker Street that you're in Sherlock Holmes' territory by the statue which stands outside the station. At 221b (actually it's number 239) is the home of the fictional sleuth, where you are greeted by a Victorian policeman and escorted round the house by Holmes's maid, Mrs Hudson. Created according to hints and descriptions from the stories of Conan Doyle, the rooms look wonderfully Victorian, comfy and close, and contain, of course, the detective's famous magnifying glass, pipe and deerstalker hat. For serious fans, a shop across the roads sells Sherlock-related memorabilia, mugs, hats, playing cards, videos of film adaptations (you name it) and, of course, the books themselves.

CENTRAL LINE

'Yesterday the crowds swayed and surged to get on to the trains. It was a cosmopolitan throng. Nearly every civilized nation under the sun was represented among the humanity that was struggling to experience London's latest sensation.' So ran the *Daily Mail*, reporting on the opening of the Central Line in 1900. The new line was a success from the start, carrying 84,500 passengers on its first day. It soon became known as the 'Twopenny Tube' because of its affordable fare of 2d (just under a penny) for a ride from Shepherd's Bush to Bank. The carriages were of a new design and pulled by rather heavy electric motors which caused some residents living above ground to complain that their houses shook when the trains passed underneath.

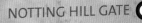

NOTTING HILL GATE ⦿
Portobello Market 26

LANCASTER GATE ⦿
London Toy and Model Museum 27

MARBLE ARCH ⦿
Hyde Park/Speaker's Corner 27

BOND STREET ⦿
Selfridges 28
Wallace Collection 28
Wigmore Hall 29

OXFORD CIRCUS ⦿
BBC Experience see p18
Carnaby Street see p19
Hamleys see p19
Liberty's see p19'

TOTTENHAM COURT ROAD ⦿
British Museum 30

HOLBORN ⦿
Sir John Soane's Museum 32

CHANCERY LANE ⦿
Dr Johnson's House 33

ST PAUL'S ⦿
Museum of London 34
Old Bailey 34
St Paul's Cathedral 35

BANK ⦿
Bank of England Museum 36
Clockmakers' Company Museum 37
Guildhall 37

LIVERPOOL STREET ⦿
Brick Lane Market 39
Columbia Road Flower Market 39
Geffrye Musuem 40
Petticoat Lane Market 40

NOTTING HILL GATE

Portobello Market

Portobello Road
Chepstow Villas–Elgin Crescent
www.portobelloroad.co.uk
Open: Sat 4am–6pm (antiques); Fri 7–4, Sat 8–5, Sun 9–4 (clothes
and bric-à-brac); Thur 11–6 (organic produce market); Mon–Wed
8–6, Thur 9–1, Fri & Sat 7–7 (general market)

When the sun is shining, a Saturday morning spent
rummaging along Portobello Road is hard to beat. And

even if it is raining, there is something
so vibrant about this area that it can
hardly fail to lift the spirits. In reality
Portobello is several markets joined
top-to-tail. They stretch for over a mile
– begin at the Notting Hill end. Here
you find antiques, rugs, paintings
(some even genuine) and high prices.
Walk further down and you are in a
bustling fruit and vegetable market:
traders piling their stalls high with
cauliflowers and cabbage rub
shoulders with purveyors of yams and
coconuts. On this stretch you can take advantage of the
trendy cafés and pubs lining the sides of the road.
Further on still, under the Westway flyover, Portobello
transforms itself once again to become London's best
bric-à-brac market with all manner of collectibles
including antique radios, china, glass and toys as well as
groovy clothes and CDs galore.

food and drink

Books for Cooks

1 Blenheim Crescent, W11
Tel: (020) 7221 1992
Open: Mon–Sat 9.30–6

A bit of an oddity. A book shop
with a restaurant where you can
try out some of the recipes from
the volumes on sale.

Pharmacy

150 Notting Hill Gate, W11
Tel: (020) 7221 2442
Open: Mon–Thur noon–3pm,
6–1am (2am Fri & Sat,
10.30pm Sun)

Designed by the controversial
young artist Damien Hirst, this
fun and lively restaurant looks like
a chemist and has even been
mistaken for one.

food and drink

Sausage and Mash Café

268 Portobello Road, W10
Tel: (020) 8968 8898
Open: Tue-Sun 11–10

Top-notch bangers and mash. All kinds of delicious flavours.

Le Prince Bonaparte

80 Chepstow Place W2
Tel: (020) 7313 9491
Open: Wed-Mon noon–11, Tue 5.30-11pm

Gastropub serving modern European cuisine to the rhythms of techno music.

LANCASTER GATE

London Toy and Model Museum

21–23 Craven Hill, W2
Tel: (020) 7706 8000
Open: Mon–Sat 10–5.30
Adm: adult £5.50, child & concs £3.50, under-4s free

One of the city's less well known attractions, the London Toy and Model Museum is a delight, with five floors of exhibits dating from 1850 through to the present. Dolls and dolls' houses, train sets, antique teddy bears and toy cars as well as intricate models including a working coal mine and fairground will fascinate children. For the technically minded, there is the latest in computer games in the Whatever Next? gallery while those who hanker for simpler pleasures may enjoy the carousel, miniature train ride and tearoom in the museum's pretty garden.

MARBLE ARCH

Hyde Park/Speaker's Corner

Hyde Park
Tel: (020) 7298 2100
Open: 5am–midnight daily
Adm: free

Hyde Park was once Henry VIII's private hunting ground and was not even open to the public until the 17th century. The city got its first ever street lighting here when William III hung 300 lamps along Rotten Row to deter robbers (Rotten Row comes from the French 'route de roi' meaning king's way). In the 18th century people came here to settle disputes by duel and, in 1730, the L-shaped Serpentine lake was created by Queen Caroline

27

when she had the underground Westbourne River dammed. These days the park is like London's lung, a calm, green breathing space in the city centre. You can go boating on the Serpentine, swim at the Lido, snooze away the afternoon in a striped deckchair (£1) and, unlike some other parks, play about on the grass as much as you wish.

Since 1872, some barmy Londoners have let off steam at Speaker's Corner on Sunday afternoons. Anyone can say what they want here and, standing on a makeshift platform, attempt to rally walkers to their cause (be it Jesus Christ, Karl Marx or the medicinal benefits of bananas), providing they can make themselves heard above the din from the traffic on Park Lane.

BOND STREET

Selfridges

400 Oxford Street, W1
Tel: (020) 7629 1234
Open: Mon–Sat 9.30–6, Thur till 8pm

After Harrods, the best store in London. This bastion of London retailing has recently been overhauled and is looking fairly nifty. It still has one of London's best food halls as well as an enormous and sweet-smelling cosmetics department. On the ground floor you there is a good selection of designer gear including clobber by Ted Baker, Diesel, Oasis, Warehouse, Red or Dead and Karen Millen. Selfridges promises your money back if you find the same article cheaper elsewhere.

Wallace Collection

Hertford House, Manchester Square, W1
Tel: (020) 7935 0687
www.the-wallace-collection.org.uk
Open: Mon–Sat 10–5, Sun 2–5
Adm: free

Assembled by four successive Marquesses of Hertford and the 4th Marquess's illegitimate son, Sir Richard Wallace, this collection occupies 25 galleries in the former family home at the top of Manchester Square. A 10-minute walk from Bond Street, you will rarely find throngs of visitors, which makes it all the more pleasant to saunter round this stunning 18th-century mansion house. Many of the 5,470 items on display are paintings including Frans Hals' *Laughing Cavalier* and masterpieces by Canaletto, Rubens, Rembrandt and Velasquez.

Besides these, there are some choice pieces of furniture, Sèvres porcelain and, on the ground floor, a huge collection of armour including a terrifying-looking war harness for man and horse from South Germany c. 1475–85. Despite the formal setting, the Wallace Collection is actually rather child-friendly. A year-round Wheely Cart offers the wherewithal for various activities and the Collection also organizes imaginative workshops for kids during the holidays, such as designing doll's dresses, armour handling and art classes with established artists (phone ahead for

details). A recent refit by architect Rick Mather (responsible for the current South Bank improvements) has added four new galleries and a study centre on the lower ground floor plus an all-weather sculpture garden and café.

Wigmore Hall

36 Wigmaker Street, W1
Tel: (020) 7935 2141
Open: (box office) Apr–Oct Mon–Sat 10–8.30, Sun 10.30–8;
Nov–Mar Mon–Sat 10–8, Sun 10.30–5
Tickets: £5–£35

This was built in 1901 for a German piano manufacturer, Friedrich Bechstein, only to be confiscated as enemy property during World War I. Since it opened as Wigmaker Hall in 1917 the delightful auditorium, excellent acoustics and intimate setting has attracted top-class solo performers. Ticket prices are low (for London) with Monday lunchtime performances (recorded for transmission on BBC Radio 3) being especially good value.

food and drink

Sofra

1 St Christopher's Place, W1
Tel: (020) 7224 4080
Open: noon–11.45 daily

Authentic Turkish restaurant tucked away in a little square. Friendly staff. Terrace in fine weather.

Spighetta

43 Blandford St, W1
Tel: (020) 7486 7340
Open: Mon–Sat noon–2.30,
6.30–10.30, Sun 6.30–10.30

Superior pizzas and a fine range of Italian dishes in rustic-looking surroundings.

food and drink

De Gustibus

53 Blandford St, W1
Tel: (020) 7486 6608
Open: Mon–Fri 7–4.30, Sat 9–3

Traditional bakery. Good for coffee, cakes and snacks.

William Wallace

44 Blandford St, W1
Tel: (020) 7935 5963
Open: Mon–Sat 11–11, Sun noon–10.30

Scottish pub. Small dining room and terrace for superior pub meals.

OXFORD CIRCUS (See Bakerloo Line)

BBC Experience see p18
Carnaby Street see p19
Hamleys see p19
Liberty's see p19

TOTTENHAM COURT ROAD

British Museum

Great Russell Street, WC1
Tel: (020) 7636 1555
Tel (020) 7323 8783 (recorded info)
Tel: (020) 7636 7384 (recorded info for disabled visitors)
www.british-museum.ac.uk
Open: Mon–Sat 10–5, Sun noon–6
Adm: free (donation appreciated)

The British Museum is the country's most visited tourist attraction, a treasure house with 100 galleries, and some of mankind's greatest relics. You'd need a week to fully appreciate the sheer volume of stuff to be found here and unless you are fascinated by countless examples of Greek coinage, Roman pots, Native American beadwork, Medieval European headgear or Bronze-Age tools it is as well to miss out much of what the collection has to offer and head direct for what is likely to be of most interest.

By far the most popular exhibits are the dead people. The Ancient Egyptian Galleries (Rooms 62–66) have mummies galore as well as a menagerie of their companions including mummified cats, fish and livestock. Lindow Man in Room 50 also has a strange fascination. This leathery looking Briton was ritually slain, perhaps as a sacrifice, in the 1st century AD and lay perfectly preserved in a Cheshire peat marsh until he was uncovered by archaeologists in 1984.

Also not to be missed are the Elgin Marbles (Room 8), the frieze reliefs from the Parthenon in Athens which, depending on whom you believe, were either rescued or stolen by Lord Elgin, British Ambassador to the Ottoman Empire, in 1802. Carved in about 440BC to decorate Athena's temple on the Acropolis, they depict a festival to commemorate Athena's birthday which includes a grand procession of chariots, musicians, pitcher bearers, sacrificial victims and beautiful women as well as the gods Hermes and Dionysus.

The British Museum's other famous exhibits include the Rosetta Stone (Room 25) inscribed with the same decree in three languages which allowed Egyptian hieroglyphics to be deciphered for the first time, and the Sutton Hoo Treasure (Room 41), a jewel-encrusted collection of swords, helmets, bowls and buckles from Europe. Next to this is Room 44 where you will find a fabulous collection of clocks and watches. The room is filled with the ticks and chimes of myriad timepieces including a mechanical gold ship c. 1585 and a French-made Congreve Rolling Ball Timepiece (1810–40) which uses a steel ball, travelling in a groove across a metal plate, to measure the passing of the minutes.

Following the removal of the British Library to Euston, the British Museum is undergoing a massive reshaping which will see a glass-topped Great Court, designed by Norman Foster to be London's first covered square, and the opening of the spectacular domed reading room to the public for the first time in 150 years. The massive King's Library, built between 1823 and 1827, was long used for storing some of the British Library's collection. This has also been opened up and will, if all goes well, be devoted to a new display on learning and discovery by the end of 2001.

food and drink

Pizza Express

30 Coptic Street, WC1
Tel: (020) 7636 3232
Open: noon–11.30 daily

Extremely elegant branch of this superior pizza chain.

Townhouse Brasserie

24 Coptic Street, WC1
Tel: (020) 7636 2731
Open: Mon–Fri noon–11, Sat 3–11, Sun 10–6

Rather sophisticated Modern French eatery upstairs with a special children's eating area in the basement.

Wagamama

4a Streatham Street, WC1
Tel: (020) 323 9223
Open: Mon–Sat noon–11, Sun noon–10

One of the first of the new breed of noodle restaurants. Diners share long benches and tuck into large stir fries and big bowls of soupy noodle dishes.

The Lamb

Lamb's Conduit Street, WC1
Tel: (020) 7405 0713
Open: Mon–Sat 11–11, Sun noon–4, 7–10.30

A little way from the British Museum but worth the walk for the fine beers and the ornate, hinged glass panels which separate the staff from the public.

Truckles of Pied Bull Yard

Off Bury Place, WC1
Tel: (020) 7404 5338
Open: Mon–Fri 11–10, Sat 11.30–3

Wine bar with two floors and a paved courtyard. Good wines, reasonable food.

HOLBORN

Sir John Soane's Museum

12–14 Lincoln's Inn Fields, WC2
Tel: (020) 7405 2107 www.soane.org
Open: Tue–Sat 10–5 (6–9pm first Tue of every month)
Adm: free (donations appreciated)

Sir John Soane (1753–1837), architect of the Bank of England, was one of this country's great eccentrics as well as being one of the finest architects of his age. In his later years, he bought up three houses on Lincoln's Inn Fields and transformed them into an extraordinary treasure trove, full of nooks and crannies, for his huge collection of paintings, sculpture, and assorted curiosities including Christopher Wren's watch and a monument to his wife's dog. Among the highlights are Hogarth's *Rake's Progress* in the picture room (note the hinged walls) and the sarcophagus of the Egyptian Pharaoh Seti I, but it is the house itself which is the star of the show. Odd angles, sudden drops, mysterious little rooms, domed skylights, and craftily placed mirrors and windows make exploring this museum a delightful, though disorientating, experience.

CHANCERY LANE

Dr Johnson's House

17 Gough Square (off Fleet Street), EC4
Tel: (020) 7353 3745
www.drjh.dircon.co.uk
Open: May–Sept Mon–Sat 11–5.30; Oct–Apr Mon–Sat 11–5
Adm: adult £3, 10s–18s £1 (under-10s free), concs £2

This 17th-century house was home to
Doctor Samuel Johnson, lexicographer,
author, critic and wit, from 1748 to 1759.
His *Dictionary* of 1755, still interesting for
the vigour and humour of its definitions
(lexicographer=a writer of dictionaries, a
harmless drudge), was mostly written
here in the attic room where the good
Doctor perched on a three-legged stool
and barked orders at his six clerks. Not
much in the house actually belonged to
Johnson but the re-created rooms
manage to convey a good impression of
what life was like at a time when literary

London was coming of age and Johnson and his pals
(including such luminaries as Joshua Reynolds, Oliver
Goldsmith, David Garrick and Edmund Burke) caroused till
morning discussing philosophy, art, religion, politics and the
relative merits of London's brothels.

food and drink

Ye Old Cheshire Cheese

Wine Office Court,
15 Fleet Street, EC4
Tel: (020) 7353 6170
Open: Mon–Fri 11–11

This historic pub, with its ancient
beams, was once the favourite
watering hole of Dr Johnson and
his biographer James Boswell.

Cittie of York

22 High Holborn, WC1
Tel: (020) 7242 7670
Open: Mon–Fri 11–11

This pub's main claim to fame is
that it boasts the longest bar in
London. Cosy booths make it a
good place for quiet winter drinks.

Ye Olde Mitre

1 Ely Court (off Ely Place), EC1
Tel: (020) 7405 4751
Open: Mon–Fri 11–11

Hidden away down a little alley,
this 16th–century inn, with its
blackened beams and yellowing
walls, is a genuine throwback.

ST PAUL'S

Museum of London

150 London Wall, EC2
Tel: (020) 7600 3699
Tel: (020) 7600 0807 (recorded info)
www.museumoflondon.org.uk
Open: Mon–Sat 10–5.30, Sun noon–5.50
Adm: (tickets valid for one year) adult £5, child free, concs £3
(admission free after 4.30pm)

Named by the London Tourist Board as the Best Large Attraction of the Year (1999) this imaginative museum opened in 1976 to tell the story of London from prehistoric times to the present day using a mixture of models (including a Viking ship, the Great Fire and a modern terraced street), artefacts and historical documents. Some of the museum's most lively displays take the form of reconstructions which include a Newgate prison cell, a 16th-century grocer's shop, a Victorian pub and a World War II bedroom with a protective cage known as a Morrison shelter. If you can't make it to the Lord Mayor's Show (second Saturday in November), you can get a good look at the richly decorated State Coach which is parked here the other 364 days of the year.

Old Bailey

Corner of Newgate Street and Old Bailey, EC4
Tel: (020) 7248 3277
Open: Mon–Fri 10.30–1, 2–4
(Guided Tours Tue, Fri, Sat 11am, 2pm)
Adm: free (no under-14s, 14s–16s accompanied by adult)

The Old Bailey – actually the Central Criminal Court – is built on the site of the notorious Newgate Prison where prisoners were left to rot (literally) in dark, stinking, underground dungeons. The prison was finally demolished in 1902 and the courts which took its place were named after the alley which runs off Newgate Street. Look out for the copper dome topped by a bronze figure of justice which overlooks the place where the condemned were publicly hanged until 1868. Part of the building, including the entrance, was rebuilt after bomb damage was sustained in World War II. Inside, the Old Hall with its high domed ceiling, extolling the virtues of Art, Truth, Justice and Work, is one of the most beautiful to be found anywhere in London. These courts (some 20 in all) deal with serious crime only and have handled some of the country's most famous modern trials including Oscar Wilde (1895), Dr Crippen (1910) and William 'Lord Haw-Haw' Joyce (1945). The public can attend current trials in one of the public galleries (join the queue outside for admittance).

St Paul's Cathedral

St Paul's Churchyard, EC4
Tel: (020) 7236 4128
www.stpaulslondon.anglican.org
Open: Mon–Sat 8.30–4
Adm: (cathedral, crypt and gallery) adult £5, child £2.50, concs £4
No wheelchair access to galleries

St Paul's Cathedral is the masterpiece of Sir Christopher Wren and was completed in 1710, following 35 years of building and

planning and 44 years after the Great Fire had destroyed the old St Paul's which stood on this site. Wren had already been commissioned to repair the Norman building when he got the chance to start afresh. Besides the sheer scale of the project, Wren's chief headache was getting his ideas approved. His first plan (known as the New Model) never made it past the drawing board. His second (the Great Model) is on display in the crypt.

This 20ft oak replica was rejected outright by the project's commissioners whereupon the frustrated architect is said to have burst into tears. It was only when Wren agreed to have a spire rather than an expensive dome that his third plan, known as the Warrant Design, was finally accepted. This was agreed with the fortunate coda that he could 'make some variations rather ornamental than essential, as from time to time he should see proper'. In the end, Wren changed quite a lot and reverted to many of his original ideas – including putting the dome back on top!

At the heart of the City's money-making square mile, it is perhaps not surprising (though a little disappointing) that you have to pay to get in. Despite this, it is worth it just to stand under the dazzlingly ornate dome and look up. From here you can make you way up the 627 steps past the Whispering Gallery (where providing it is quiet enough you can hear someone whisper 107 feet away), the Stone Gallery (encircling the outside of the dome) and the Outer Golden Gallery (providing one of the best views to be had in the city). Look west and you see the British Telecom Tower (formally the Post Office Tower), look northwest for the Old Bailey, look south for the Tate Modern, east for Canary Wharf and towards the river for the turrets of Tower Bridge.

Back on the ground, there are a number of important memorials including, in the south choir aisle, one to the poet John Donne, who was Dean of the old St Paul's for the last 10 years of his life and a memorial to Wren himself, directly under the dome, which bears the inscription (in Latin): 'Reader, if you seek his monument, look around you'. In the crypt, apart from the shop and child–friendly restaurant, you can find a black sarcophagus (made from the mast of a vanquished French flagship) containing the remains of the British naval hero Admiral Nelson who died at the Battle of Trafalgar in 1805 and was pickled in alcohol before his final journey home.

food and drink

Café Rouge

Hillgate House,
Limeburner Lane, EC4
Tel: (020) 7329 1234
Open: Mon–Fri 10am–10.30pm

Despite being dwarfed by a huge, black office block opposite, this is a jolly branch of the reliable French café chain. Child-friendly.

The Place Below

St Mary-le-Bow, Cheapside, EC2
Tel: (020) 7329 0789
Open: Mon–Fri 7.30am–2.30pm

Award-winning self-service vegetarian restaurant in a church crypt. Very popular.

BANK

Bank of England Museum

Threadneedle Street, EC2
Tel: (020) 7601 5545
Open: Mon–Fri 10–5
Adm: free

The Bank of England Museum traces the history of this venerable institution, known affectionately as 'the Old Lady of Threadneedle Street', which manages the national debt, issues banknotes, sets interest rates and keeps the country's gold locked up safe and sound. The first room you enter is a reconstruction of the bank's Stock Office, designed by Sir John Soane (see page 32) in 1793, where mannequins of clerks and

customers in period costume go about their daily business amid the mahogany counter tops and oak ledger rests. Other rooms elaborate on the history of the bank, its architecture, its survival during the Gordon Riots of 1780, the war years and the modern stock exchange. Interactive screens, bickering animatronic replicas of Charles James Fox and William Pitt, and the tantalising display of solid gold bars (worth some £75,000 each) in the 1930s Rotunda make this a surprisingly enjoyable place to visit.

Clockmakers' Company Museum

The Clockroom
Guildhall Library, Aldermanbury, EC2
Tel: (020) 7332 1868
Open: Mon–Fri 9.30–4.45
Adm: free

The Clockmakers' Company was founded by Royal Charter in 1631 and controlled the quality of the products, supervised the training of apprentice clockmakers and involved itself in various charities. The Clockmakers' Collection, begun in 1814, is the oldest such collection in the world and includes 600 English and European watches, 30 clocks and 15 marine timekeepers, together with a number of rare horological portraits. Among the prize exhibits are John Harrison's 5th Marine timekeeper which finally made it possible for ships to chart their exact position while at sea (chronicled in Dava Sobel's *Longitude*), the pocket chronometer worn by George Vancouver when he took possession in 1792 of the island which now bears his name, and the watch worn by Sir Edmund Hillary during his ascent of Everest in 1953.

Guildhall

Off Gresham Street, EC2
Tel: (020) 7606 3030
Open: daily 9–5
Adm: free

The Guildhall dates back to the 15th century and is the City of London's historic heart. In the Middle Ages the guilds were hugely powerful, lording it even over the monarchy because of the massive amounts of money they generated. Today the

building's role is purely ceremonial and it is used for the annual election of the Lord Mayor of London, just as it has been for the last 800 years. Partly damaged during the Great Fire in 1666 and bomb damaged during World War Two, it nevertheless remains, in essence, intact. The 152-foot-long Old Hall is especially worth visiting to see the colourfully ornate banners of the 12 Great Livery Companies – Mercers, Grocers, Drapers, Fishmongers, Goldsmiths, Skinners, Merchant Taylors, Haberdashers, Salters, Ironmongers, Vintners and Clothworkers – which decorate the walls. Next to each banner is the coat of arms and motto of the respective company. Gog and Magog, the mythical giants who founded ancient Albion, are perched in the west gallery where they glower down on all who dare to enter.

food and drink

Jamaica Wine House

St Michael's Alley (off Cornhill), EC3
Tel: (020) 7626 9496
Open: Mon–Fri 11–11

Once the favourite of London's rum merchants, there is little in this low-key pub to remind you of the 21st (or even the 20th) century.

Old Dr Butler's Head

2 Mason's Avenue (between Coleman Street & Basinghall Street), EC2
Tel: (020) 7606 3504
Open: Mon–Fri 11–11

This old London boozer was built, in 1610 by William Butler, physician to King James I. It was burnt down in the Great Fire and subsequently rebuilt. Avoid lunchtimes if you don't like crowds.

Silks & Spice

Temple Court,
11 Queen Victoria Street, EC4
Tel: (020) 7248 7878
Open: Mon–Thurs 11–11,
Fri 11am -2am

Small Thai/Malaysian curry house with music and dancing until 2am on Friday nights.

Simpson's Tavern

38 1-2 Cornhill, EC3
Tel: (020) 7626 9985
Open: Mo--Fri 11–11

This chophouse tries to take you back to what dining was like 200 years ago, with steak and kidney pies, chops and steamed puddings.

LIVERPOOL STREET

Brick Lane Market

Brick Lane (north of railway bridge), Bethnal Green Road, Cygnet Street, Grimsby Street, Sclater Street E1; Bacon Street, Cheshire Street, E2
Open: Sun 7–1

In the 16th century they used to make bricks here. These days, during the week, Brick Lane is alive with cheap Indian restaurants, stores selling brightly-coloured saris or Indian sweets and small-scale textile factories. On Sunday mornings, however, it becomes one of London's busiest markets, attracting a wide variety of Londoners who come early looking for bric-à-brac, clothes, food and all manner of junk. It's fairly scruffy but fun to poke about in, especially among the more established covered stalls halfway down. Brick Lane is not as cheap as it once was but there

is still the chance, unlike at Portobello Market, that you may pick up a genuine antique for pounds if not pennies.

Columbia Road Flower Market

Columbia Road (between Gosset Street & the Royal Oak pub), E2
Open: Sun 8am–1pm

On Sundays the flower market heaves so be prepared to jostle and fight your way along. It's worth approaching from the west so that you can make your way eventually to the best cafés. The flowers and plants are good quality and extremely cheap and even if you don't buy any, the combined scent of freesias, carnations, roses, lilies and daffodils is enough to make you dizzy. Lining the street, the little Victorian shops sell pretty pots and household knick-knacks, while some have become welcoming cafés where you can get a steaming cappuccino and a fresh croissant to keep you going 'til lunch. Two of the best shops are The Pot Centre which sells a full range of terracotta pots at very resonable prices and Idonia Van der Bijl a gift shop which specialises in hand-made products from both the UK and abroad.

Geffrye Museum

Kingsland Road, E2
Tel: (020) 7739 9893
Tel: (020) 7739 8543
www.geffrye-museum.org.uk
Open: Tue–Sat 10–5, Sun noon–5
Adm: free

The Geffrye Museum is a stiff walk from Liverpool Street and it is better to hop on a 149 or 242 bus from outside the tube to save your legs. Set in a row of former almshouses it takes you on a journey through 400 years of English interiors from 17th-century heavy oak furniture and panelling through to post war utility and beyond. On the way you get a glimpse of past times and tastes: an elegant Neoclassical interior from the Georgian period modelled on the town house of a wealthy London gent; a wallpaper-lined Regency drawing room with a decorative white marble fireplace; the opulence of a middle class Victorian parlour with heavy rugs and gaslight; the war-time austerity of government approved products and drawn black-out curtains, and a zany 1950's-style room decked out for a party. A new wing provides space to move the story along into the 21st century, while a walled herb garden, shop and café offer the chance to rest up before heading back to the tube.

Petticoat Lane Market

Middlesex Street, EC1
Open: Sun 9–2

Don't look for Petticoat Lane on the map. It isn't there and hasn't existed since 1830 when the Victorians decided to change its name for reasons of delicacy. You won't see too many petticoats either. What you will see are stalls piled with shirts, socks, coats, jeans, underwear and hats. If you are after a good quality leather jacket at a rock-bottom price, head for the top end of the market near Aldgate East tube. It's not all clothes here and the crammed streets running off the main drag throw up all kinds of bric-à-brac, furniture, jewellery, cycles, books, CDs and assorted junk. (A word of caution: not everything you find here has been honestly acquired.) Petticoat Lane is at the heart of what was once the city's rag trade. Predominantly Jewish, there are still plenty of shops and stalls selling bagels and salt-beef sandwiches if you are feeling peckish.

food and drink

Bagel Bakery

159 Brick Lane, E1
Tel: (020) 7729 0616
Open: daily 24 hours

This famous bagel shop is open 24 hours a day and serves piping hot, freshly baked bagels with delicious fillings. Salmon and cream cheese is a firm favourite with most of the regulars.

Moshi Moshi Sushi

Unit 24 Liverpool St Station
(Platform 1) EC2
Tel: (020) 7247 3227

Open: Mon–Fri 11.30–9

Sushi bar housed in what looks like a goldfish bowl suspended above the platforms at Liverpool Street Station. Packed with City workers for their lunch hour.

Dirty Dick's

202 Bishopsgate, EC2
Tel: (020) 7283 5888
Open: Mon–Fri 11–11

This cheery cellar bar was built in 1870. It is named after Nathaniel Bentley who lived in a house on this site and who refused ever to wash again after his fiancée died on the eve of their wedding in 1787.

George

Great Eastern Hotel
Liverpool Street, EC2
Tel: (020) 7618 7300
Open: Mon–Sat 11–11, Sun noon–10

Leaded windows, wooden panelling and chandliers are the setting for 'school dinner' food.

UNDERGROUND

CIRCLE LINE

A committee of the House of Lords was advising as early as 1863 that London needed an 'inner circuit' to connect the capital's main-line termini which were either built or already planned. With this in mind, the Metropolitan Line sought and gained permission to extend its line eastwards round the City and, in the other direction, from Paddington to Brompton (now South Kensington). At the same time, a new company, the Metropolitan District, was formed to link Brompton up to the City. The Circle Line opened gradually, section by section, beginning in 1868, but it was not until 1884 that it became possible to travel the entire way round the circuit.

SOUTH KENSINGTON

Conran Shop 44
Natural History Museum 44
Science Museum 46
Serpentine Gallery 47
Victoria and Albert Museum 47

SLOANE SQUARE

Carlyle's House 49
Chelsea Physic Garden 50

VICTORIA

Royal Mews see p95
Westminster Cathedral see p96

ST JAMES'S PARK

Buckingham Palace 51
London Transport Headquarters 52
St James's Park 52

WESTMINSTER

Cabinet War Rooms 53
Horse Guards 53
Houses of Parliament & Big Ben 54
Westminster Abbey 55

TEMPLE

Courtauld Gallery 56
Gilbert Collection 56
Prince Henry's Room 57

BLACKFRIARS

Tate Modern 57
Millennium Bridge 59

MONUMENT

The Monument 59

TOWER HILL

Tower Hill 60
Tower of London 60

LIVERPOOL STREET

Brick Lane Market see p39
Columbia Road Flower Market see p39
Geffrye Museum see p40
Petticoat Lane see p40

BARBICAN

Barbican Centre 62

FARRINGDON

House of Detention 62

KINGS CROSS/ ST PANCRAS

London Canal Museum see p76

BAKER STREET

London Planetarium see p22
Madame Tussauds see p22
Sherlock Holmes Museum see p23

NOTTING HILL GATE

Portobello Market see p26

HIGH ST KENSINGTON

Albert Hall & Albert Monument 64
Kensington Palace 65

SOUTH KENSINGTON

Conran Shop

Michelin House, 81 Fulham Road, SW3
Tel: (020) 7589 7401
www.conran.co.uk
Open: Mon, Tue, Fri 10–6, Wed & Thur 10–7,
Sat 10–6.30, Sun noon–6

Sir Terence Conran opened Habitat in the 1960s and almost single-handedly transformed the British interior overnight with his range of simple, affordable and well-designed household goods. The Conran shop is an up-market version of the same thing with high quality furniture, lighting, kitchenware, soft furnishings and other accessories to give your home a dash of style. Even if you don't wish to buy anything, it is worth going just to see Michelin House, a witty Art Noveau palace designed by the French architect F. Espinasse as an advert for the Michelin tyre company. Note the corners of the building, capped with the bulbous stacks of 'tyres' which light up to form the torso of the Michelin Man. On the top floor is a swanky restaurant (see p49).

Natural History Museum

Cromwell Road, SW7
Tel: (020) 7942 5000
www.nhm.ac.uk
Open: Mon–Sat 10–5.50, Sun 11–5.50
Adm: adult £6.50, child (16 and under) free, concs £3.50, family £16
(free for everyone after 4.30 Mon–Fri and after 5 Sat, Sun &
Bank Holidays)

This museum was opened in 1881 after it became evident that the British Museum was too small to contain the nation's everexpanding collection of natural history specimens. Today, with a staggering 68 million plants, animals, fossils, rocks and minerals, the Natural History Museum is itself bursting at the seams. The Gothic extravagance of the main façade is the work of architect Alfred Waterhouse, who wanted to inspire visitors to look afresh at the wonders of creation. Though the exhibits are aimed mostly at children (with enough activity sheets, quizzes and trails to keep kids amused for hours), few visitors will leave without a sense of awe at the rich complexity of our planet.

The museum is split into Earth Galleries and Life Galleries. The Life Galleries contain what is probably the most popular exhibit of all – the Dinosaurs. You first encounter one of these creatures in the main hall where a huge 150-ft skeleton of a plant-eating diplodocus greets visitors as they enter. This massive room contains some of the museum's treasures including the diminutive frame of a tiny humanoid ape brought to England in 1698, a 225-million-year-old tree trunk and an egg laid by the extinct Madagascan elephant bird which is 200 times the size of a chicken's egg. The rest of the dinosaurs can be found in Room 21 where the highlight is an animatronic display in which three ferocious Deinonychus tear strips of flesh from an unfortunate Tenontosauraus which 'unwisely strayed from its herd'. The mammals begin in Room 23. Here you encounter animals of every description. Some, like the stuffed 5-inch-long pink armadillo are real. Others, such as the massive blue

whale which dominates Room 24, are fake. There is much to see, but try to make time for are the hands-on Human Biology section (Room 22), the imaginative Ecology exhibit (Room 32) which looks at the many threats to biodiversity on our planet and Creepy Crawlies (Room 33) where you can find out how many bugs share your home.

The Earth Galleries have had a fair bit of cash thrown at them and it shows. The stunning vaulted glass entrance has a central escalator which takes you up through the earth's inner core to The Power Within where you can stand in a Japanese supermarket as it gets shaken by a massive earthquake. In Restless Surface you learn what makes the winds blow and the tides turn, while From the Beginning examines how life began and ends by asking some chilling questions about the planet's future. The final 'must-see' is Earth's Treasury (Room 64). Here, under subdued lighting, precious stones twinkle and glitter in their cases. Look out for the sample of Alexandrite – a rare gem which changes colour according to whether it is under natural or artificial light.

Science Museum

Exhibition Road, SW7
Tel: (020) 7942 4454
www.sciencemuseum.org.uk
Open: 10–6 daily
Adm: adult £6.50, child free, concs £3.50 (free for everyone after
4.30 Mon–Fri and after 5 Sat, Sun & Bank Holidays)

With the opening of the new £48-million Wellcome Wing, the Science Museum has launched itself into the 21st century. Set over four floors and bathed in futuristic blue light, state-of-the-art exhibits and multimedia offer bags of hands-on fun and interactivity. The ground floor has regularly changing exhibits based around what's hot in the world of science, plus an IMAX film theatre with a screen as high as five double-decker buses. Would-be Flash Gordons can take a trip to Mars or join the crew aboard the Comet Interceptor before exploring the other floors which cover human identity, the impact of digital technology and the ways in which science may shape our future.

Though impressive, the new wing feels rather sterile when compared to the older parts of the museum which, with a natty new café and handy interactive screens to help navigate the five floors, is looking better than ever. All the old favourites are here including the traditional push-me-pull-you buttons and levers, pops, bangs and whizzes and the impressive hardware.

Making the Modern World is a new organization of old exhibits, covering the period 1750–2000 and includes Stephenson's Rocket, a Model-T Ford, a V2 missile and the Apollo 10 command module. Next you come to Space, where you can find out about the space race and the future of stellar exploration and have a go at designing your own rocket using a computer. From here, head down the stairs to the basement where The Secret Life of the Home takes a humorous look at domestic gizmos and gadget from vacuum cleaners and washing machines to WCs, fridges and heaters. The rest of the basement is given over to activities for younger children and provides a good opportunity for pram-weary little ones to crawl about.

There is far too much to see in a single day so it is worth planning your visit. You can do this in Synopsis (by the main entrance) which has an overview of the museum and also contains some of its most treasured exhibits. Among the other attractions which should not be missed are: Challenge of Materials (1st floor) – an interactive-rich exhibit exploring the uses and production of manmade products; Flight (3rd floor) – an aviator's dream with all manner of planes, rockets and engines including a Spitfire, a Messerschmitt and a Doodlebug; and Flight Lab (3rd floor) – a hands-on gallery looking at how aircraft fly, which includes a nausea-inducing flight simulator (for which there is an additional charge).

Before heading for the shop, make time, if you haven't already seen it or didn't take it in, for the 1903 Harle Syke mill engine on the ground floor. This pillar-box-red monster could power 1,700 looms in its day. Two engineers are now permanently on hand to keep it running and answer visitors' questions. It never goes above quarter speed for fear of shaking the building to its foundations.

Serpentine Gallery

Kensington Gardens (near Albert Memorial)
Tel: (020) 7402 6075
www.serpentinegallery.org
Open: 10–6 daily
Adm: free

This small, bright pavilion was once a popular tearoom and now mounts several first-class exhibitions of modern art a year. The shows are often a little off-the-wall but always worth a visit, especially as it is free to get in. The building looks out through french windows onto the lake, home to countless ducks and dotted with rowing boats during the summer. An open-air café a little way along from the gallery serves non-alcoholic drinks and light snacks. The tiny birds are so tame here that they will eat out of your hand. Should you wish to stretch your legs you can walk round the lake, over the Serpentine Bridge (built in 1826 by George Rennie) and cross over into Hyde Park.

Victoria and Albert Museum

Cromwell Road, SW7
Tel: (020) 7938 8500
www.vam.ac.uk
Open: 10–5.45 daily (Wed late view 6.30–9.30 – seasonal, phone for details)
Adm: adult £5, under-18s free, disabled/helpers free, concs £3 (free for everyone after 4.30)
Wheelchair access: (use Exhibition Road entrance or call Tel: (020) 7938 8638 to book an escort in advance

Though originally intended as the permanent version of the 1851 Great Exhibition, the V&A is now a vast collection of stuff loosely assembled under the heading of Decorative Arts. This includes all manner of art, design and sculpture from around the world: silverware, armour, tapestries, plaster casts, wrought-iron work, furniture, clothes, textiles, household items, posters, photographs, toys, household appliances.... Much of it could easily be reorganized and sent off to other London museums and galleries. The seven huge Raphael Cartoons might look better in the National Gallery. The compact collection of musical instruments would probably be happier down the road at the Royal College of Music. And so on. Nevertheless, this huge, eclectic, sprawling, pick-'n'-mix

of a museum, once defined by a former director as an 'extremely capacious handbag', makes a virtue of its variety and never fails to satisfy whether you are visiting it for the first or the hundredth time.

Though you are handed a map at the main entrance, you may just as well set off in any direction and see where you finish up. With 7 miles of corridors and 145 galleries, visitors are bound to stumble upon something of interest. Nevertheless, some of the highlights of the V&A are worth seeking out before you are completely exhausted. Plaster Casts (Level A, Rooms 46a–b) has recreations of some of the world's most famous (and biggest) sculptures including Michelangelo's David and Moses and the colossal Trajan's Column from Rome. The 20th-century gallery (Level B, Rooms 70–74 & 103–6) concentrates on household design (look out for Salvador Dali's sofa in the shape of Mae West's lips) but also includes toys, textiles and modern graphics. Also don't miss the new Glass Gallery (Level C, Room 131) where 4,000 years of glassware is reflected into infinity in a room lined with huge mirrors, or the European Dress Collection (Level A, Room 45) with fashions from the 17th and 18th centuries (including wigs, hats, shoes and gloves), through to Dior's 'New Look' and on to the latest items to hit the catwalks including clothes by Vivienne Westwood and Jean Muir.

Some of the rooms, such as the Morris, Gamble and Poynter rooms (which house a popular café), are worth visiting for their own sakes. The Morris Room, decked out with ornate tilework designed by William Morris, takes as its theme nature and greenery and is especially stunning.

The V&A is one of those museums which improves on a second visit. The late view on Wednesdays lets you explore until 10pm while on Sundays the New Restaurant, situated near the Exhibition Road entrance, is a popular spot to enjoy a traditional English roast (£11.50). Activities for children and families, as well as varied talks and workshops, take place throughout the year (pick up a leaflet or phone ahead for details).

food and drink

Bibendum

Michelin House
81 Fulham Road, SW3
Tel: (020) 7581 5817
Open: (lunch) Mon–Fri
noon–2.30, Sat & Sun 12.30–3pm,
(dinner) Mon–Sat 7–11.30,
Sun 7–10.30

One of London's most trendy dining places. A little on the pricey side but you are paying for top chefs and a classic Art Noveau venue in which to dine. An experience to remember.

Daquise

20 Thurloe Street, SW7
Tel: (020) 7589 6117
Open: 11.30–11 daily

Just yards from the tube station, a café serving large portions of traditional Polish food: sausage with sauerkraut, stuffed cabbage, strong coffee and cakes.

Cactus Blue

86 Fulham Road, SW3
Tel: (020) 7823 7858
Open: (brunch) Sat & Sun
noon–4, (dinner) Mon–Sat
5.30–11.45, Sun 5.30–11

American southwestern food. The tequila and beer flows freely to combat the hot and spicy food served in this hip Tex-Mex eatery.

Greenfields Café

13 Exhibition Road, SW7
Tel: (020) 7584 1396
Open: Mon–Fri 7–7, Sat & Sun
10–6

A good stop-off for snacks and sandwiches. You can squeeze inside for soup and warm bread if it's cold. Tasty salads and outside seating if it's sunny.

SLOANE SQUARE

Carlyle's House

24 Cheyne Row, SW3
Tel: (020) 7352 7087
Open: Apr–Oct Wed–Sun 11–5
Adm: adult £3.50, child £1.75

Thomas Carlyle, the 'sage of Chelsea', was the Scottish author of two best-selling historical works, *The French Revolution* and *Frederick the Great* (now all but forgotten) and the founder of The London Library in St James's Square. He moved with his wife, the tempestuous poet Jane Carlyle, to this house in 1834 and the couple became a part of literary London with Charles Dickens, William Makepeace Thackery, Alfred Tennyson and George Eliot as regular visitors. The red-brick Queen Anne house has been kept virtually intact and, since 1930, has been in the care of the National Trust. With its rich Victorian colours, oil lamps, original fireplaces and decoupage screens, the house conjures up a strong sense of the period, as well as providing a vivid portrait of the couple who lived beneath its roof.

Chelsea Physic Garden

66 Royal Hospital Road (entrance in Swan Walk), SW3
Tel: (020) 7352 5646
www.cpgarden.demon.co.uk
Open: Apr–Oct Wed noon–5, Sun 2–6
Adm: adult £4, child £2

A wonderful walled garden with unusual trees, plants, herbs and seeds. Founded in 1676 by the Apothecaries' Company, it predates Kew by a century and was London's first botanical garden. It was responsible for cultivating some of England's original cedar trees in the late 17th-century and, in the 1730s, sent the first cotton seed to the southern states of the USA to help establish the cotton industry there. Among the highlights are the world's first-ever rock garden (1772), made from stone taken from the Tower of London, and a 30ft-high olive tree which once produced seven pounds of olives in a season. In the middle is a statue of Sir Hans Sloane, physician to Queen Anne and George II, who developed the garden in the 18th century and whose collection of art and antiquities formed the nucleus of the British Museum after his death in 1753.

food and drink

Orange Brewery

37 Pimlico Road, SW1
Tel: (020) 7730 5984
Open: Mon–Sat 11–11, Sun
noon–10.30

An 18th-century pub with its own brewery on site. Traditional pub food such as meat pies flavoured with beer and huge (24oz) Cumberland sausages.

The Albert

52 Victoria Street, SW1
Tel: (020) 8222 5577
Open: Mon–Sat 11–11, Sun
11–10.30

Victoriana reigns, with antique gas lamps, burnished wood and authentic prints about the perils of alcohol on the walls.

VICTORIA (See Victoria Line)

Royal Mews see p95
Wesminster Cathedral see p96

ST JAMES'S PARK

Buckingham Palace

The Mall, SW1
Tel: (020) 7839 1377
www.royal.gov.uk
Open: Aug–Sep 9.30–4.15 daily
Adm: adult £10.50, child £5 (under-5s free), concs £8

Buckingham Palace is something of a newcomer in terms of royal residences. The original building was erected in 1703 for the Duke of Buckingham. George III rather liked it, and bought it in 1762, renaming it the King's House. His spendthrift son George IV tried to turn it into a palace, then knocked it down and hired the architect John Nash who produced a grand plan for a vast three-sided building with a triumphal arch (the Marble Arch which now sits at the top of Park Lane). Parliament, dismayed at the mounting cost, sacked Nash after George died in 1830 and the work was handed over to a plodding but efficient architect Edward Blore, who finished the job as cheaply as he could. The final result was a disaster with stinking lavatories, windows that wouldn't open, bells that wouldn't ring and doors that wouldn't shut. Despite condemning it as a 'disgrace to the country' Queen Victoria made it her home following her accession in 1837 and it has been the monarch's official residence ever since.

Eighteen rooms of the State Apartments are now on show to

the public during August and September, when the Queen goes on holiday. These include the Throne Room (with pink and yellow his'n'hers thrones), the State Dining Room (for official banquets) and the Music Room (where Princess Diana allegedly tap danced, while Elton John played the piano). The 155-ft Picture Gallery has hundreds of paintings crammed on to its walls including works by Poussin, Claude Lorrain, Frans Hals and Rubens. Tour passes are on sale from 9am at the ticket office on Constitution Hill. Alternatively, you can pay in advance by credit card over the phone.

London Transport Headquarters

55 Broadway
Tel: (020) 7222 1234
www.londontransport.co.uk
Open: 24 hours

Built on top of St James's Park Station and opened in 1930, Broadway was the imposing headquarters for Underground Electronic Railways Limited and remains London Transport's head office. The 13-storey building was designed in such a way that every room had natural light. Its architect, Charles Holden, was responsible for many of the modernistic Piccadilly Line extensions such as Southgate and Cockfosters (Zones 4 & 5). Look out for the twin sculptures on the exterior depicting 'Day' and 'Night' by Sir Jacob Epstein. A Travel Information Centre is located on the ground floor.

St James's Park

The Mall, SW1
Tel: (020) 7930 1793
Open: dawn–dusk, daily
Adm: free

Built on top of a former leper colony, St James's is now the most picturesque park in the city, with tall trees, a graceful stretch of water and fine views of Buckingham Palace. In the 17th century the park had several aviaries and today its lake is home to over 20 different kinds of bird including ducks, geese and pelicans. A playground (with sandpit) and a tearoom make this a good stopping-off point if you have children. At night, coloured spotlights across the waters makes the views even more magical.

food and drink

Goring Hotel

15 Beeston Place, SW1
Tel: (020) 7396 9000
Open: 12.30–2.30, 6–10 daily

For a special treat, visit the swanky dining room of this hotel, which is open to non-residents. Half-portions available for children. Dress smartish.

PizzaExpress

154 Victoria Street, SW1
Tel: (020) 828 1477
Open: 11.30–midnight daily

Trusty chain with crusty pizzas, tasty salads and gooey puddings. Child-friendly.

WESTMINSTER

Cabinet War Rooms

Clive Steps, King Charles Street, SW1
Tel: (020) 7930 6961
www.iwm.org.uk
Open: Apr–Sep 9.30–6, Oct–Mar 10–6 daily
Adm: adult £4.80, child £3.50, concs £2.20

These cramped, claustrophobic, bombproof rooms have remained largely unchanged since the final years of World War II when they were the nerve centre for the British war effort. The Cabinet Room looks set for a tense meeting, pins chart the direction of the Allied campaign in the Map Room, the Telephone Room's hot line is ready for an urgent call to the White House and, in Winston Churchill's bedroom, a nightshirt is laid out and a chamber pot sits under the bed. In the Prime Minister's office (a former broom cupboard) you can still see the desk at which Churchill sat when he told a war-weary nation that this was to be their finest hour.

Horse Guards

Whitehall
On guard: 10–4 daily

It's a picture postcard sight of London: sombre, motionless, in scarlet tunics with swords hanging down and topped off with bearskin hats, the Household Cavalry are supposed to protect London's palaces but, in reality, are more of a tourist attraction than anything else. The Changing of the Guard, when three officers and 40 soldiers of the Foot Guards march from Wellington Barracks to Buckingham Palace, takes place every morning between April and August at 11.27 on the dot and on alternate days from September to March at the same time. If you can squeeze in, get a front row view from outside Buckingham Palace. Otherwise, outside Wellington Barracks on Birdcage Walk (running alongside St James's Park) offers a good vantage point. A small museum devoted to the uniforms, weapons and history of these illustrious regiments can also be found at the barracks on Birdcage Walk.

Houses of Parliament and Big Ben

Parliament Square, SW1
Tel: (020) 7219 4272 (Commons info)
Tel: (020) 7219 3107 (Lords info)
www.parliament.uk
Open: (House of Commons Visitors) Gallery) Mon & Tue from 2.30,
Wed 9.30–2, Thur 11.30–7.30, Fri 9.30–3; (House of Lords Visitors'
Gallery) Mon–Wed from 2.30–10 Thur from 3–10 Fri from 9.30–3
Adm: free

The Palace of Westminster was established in the 11th century by Edward the Confessor and became Parliament's official home in 1532 when Henry VIII decided to decamp to

Whitehall. Following a fire in 1834, all that remains of this original complex are Westminster Hall and the Jewel Tower (see below). The present building is the work of architects Charles Barry and Augustus Pugin whose grandiose Gothic masterpiece was selected from among 97 other designs submitted after the fire. The 320-ft high Clock Tower was not completed until 1858

and contains the 13-ton bell known as Big Ben. The famous chimes, known around the globe via the BBC World Service, come on the hour and quarter-hour. The distinctive throaty bong is actually the result of a large crack which appeared when the bell was being installed. Depending on who you believe, Big Ben is either named after Sir Benjamin Hill, the stout commissioner of works who oversaw construction of the present building, or Benjamin Caunt, a heavyweight champion boxer who ran a pub a few hundred yards from here in St Martin's Lane. To find out more, visit the Jewel Tower, Abingdon St, SW1 (at the opposite end of Parliament from Big Ben). Built in 1356 to house Edward III's jewels, this building is a survivor from the medieval Palace and now contains a special exhibition on the 'History of Parliament: Past and Present'.

It isn't easy for members of the public to get a look inside this enormous building (which has two miles of corridors, 1,100 rooms, 100 staircases, 11 courtyards and eight bars) but, if you are prepared to queue up, you can watch a debate from the Visitors' Gallery (the queue for the Lords is generally shorter). For a more comprehensive tour, visitors should apply to their MP or embassy at least two months in advance.

Westminster Abbey

Dean's Yard, SW1
Tel: (020) 7222 5152
www.westminster-abbey.org
Open: Mon–Fri 9.30–4.45 (last entry 3.45), Sat 9–2.45
(last entry 1.45)
Adm: adult £5, child (under 16) £2, concs £3, family ticket £10

Westminster Abbey is the most ancient of London's great churches. Nearly every British monarch has been crowned here and many of them, including Edward the Confessor, Henry III, Edward I, Henry VII, Elizabeth I, Charles II, William III, Anne and George II, are buried here, too. Recently it was made famous by the funeral of Princess Diana. It is surprising that visitors can get in at all as the abbey is crowded, almost to overflowing, with statues, monuments plaques and dedications which add up to a history of the nation. Among the most visited spots are memorials to the Battle of Britain (dedicated in 1947) and the Tomb of the Unknown

Warrior, where an anonymous World War I soldier is buried, in memory of fallen soldiers from both world wars. In Statesman's Aisle you can find prime ministers galore including Palmerston, Gladstone and Disraeli while in Poet's Corner there are dedications to the country's literary men and women including Geoffrey Chaucer, Samuel Johnson and Alfred Tennyson (who are buried here), William Shakespeare, Jane Austen and

William Wordsworth (who are not) and Ben Jonson (who is buried upright). The world of science and engineering is represented by memorials to, among others, Sir Isaac Newton, James Watt and Michael Faraday. Surprisingly, there is only one painter: the virtually unknown Godfrey Kneller, court painter to Charles II, whose dying words, 'By God, I will not be buried in Westminster Abbey', appear to have been totally ignored. For an additional charge (£1 with main entrance ticket), the Abbey's museum is worth visiting, if only to see the armour worn by Henry V when he defeated the French at the Battle of Agincourt in 1415.

TEMPLE

Courtauld Gallery

Somerset House, Strand, WC2
Tel: (020) 7848 2526
www.courtauld.ac.uk
Open: Mon–Sat 10–6, Sun noon–6
Adm: adult £4, child free, concs £3; combined ticket with Gilbert Collection £7, concs £5

This Georgian building was erected in the 1770s after the first Somerset House, built for the Duke of Somerset in the mid-16th century, was knocked down. For a long time it was used to house public records but more recently has been turned over to two great collections of art and its courtyard cleared to make a way for a fine piazza with fountains, a café and the occasional performance of classical music. The chief attraction is the Courtauld Institute, which has a stunning collection of Impressionist and Post-Impressionist paintings including works by Manet, Monet, Gauguin, Pissarro, Renoir, Van Gogh, Cézanne and Modigliani. The collection also includes 32 works by Rubens, a Botticelli Trinity and gouaches by Rouault.

Gilbert Collection

Somerset House, Strand, WC2
Tel: (020) 7240 4080
www.gilbert-collection.org.uk
Open: Open: Mon–Sat 10–6, Sun noon–6
Adm: adult £4, child free, concs £3; combined ticket with Courtauld Gallery £7, concs £5

The Gilbert Collection once belonged to Londoner Arthur Gilbert, and comprises 800 pieces including gold snuff boxes, Italian *pietra dura* mosaics and European silverware. An informative audio guide is included in the price of admission.

Prince Henry's Room

17 Fleet Street, EC4
Tel: (020) 7936 4004
Open: Mon–Sat 11–2
Adm: free

Little of London remains which predates the Great Fire of 1666. This is one of the notable exceptions. The best way to get here from Temple is to walk a little way down the Embankment, cross at the lights, and turn left into The Temple. A pleasant walk through the Inns of Court brings you out on Fleet Street. A Jacobean half-timbered house, Prince Henry's Room was built in 1611 to honour Henry, James I's eldest son, who had just become the Prince of Wales. The original panelling and plaster ceiling (bearing the letters P.H.) are still intact, and the room is now used to house a collection of memorabilia devoted to the 17th-century diarist Samuel Pepys which includes various extracts from his diary, household objects and a pair of his spectacles.

Tate Modern

25 Sumnor Street, SE1
Tel: (020) 7887 8000
www.tate.org.uk
Open: Sun–Thur 10–6, Fri & Sat 10–10
Adm: free

Almost overnight, modern art became acceptable when the Tate Modern opened its doors in 2000. Visit the old Tate (now Tate Britain) up the river at Pimlico and it seems empty. At the Tate Modern you can hardly move for people.

Designed by Sir Giles Gilbert Scott as a power station in 1947, the building was converted by the Swiss architects Herzog & de Meuron who constructed a two-storey glass 'lightbeam' to flood the main turbine hall with natural light. Additional light comes via the illuminated bay windows on the 3rd and 5th floors which offer a spectacular view of the hall below.

The Tate Modern has 100,000 sq ft in which to display its collection of modern international art from the 19th century to the present day, including works by Bacon, Dali, Duchamp, Freud, Hockney, Matisse, Picasso, Pollock, Rothko, Spencer and Warhol. Breaking with tradition, the Tate has arranged its galleries thematically rather than chronologically. Umbrella topics trace links and resonances between artists who might otherwise seem to have little in common. So, for example, in Landscape/Matter/Form (3rd floor) you can find Claude Monet's 19th-century *Water-Lilies* next to Richard Long's 20th-century mud paintings to highlight both artists' similar sense of immersion in landscape. Much of the work on show, such as Marcel Duchamp's *Fountain* (actually a urinal) and Carl André's *Equivalent Viii* (a pile of bricks), questions our very notions of what art is. Peter Fischli and David Weiss, for instance, have constructed what for all the world looks like an unfinished room, waiting for paintings to be hung. You could easily walk right past. Yet every object here has been hand-carved from polyurethane foam and painted by hand. Up on the 5th floor in History/Memory/Society the Fluxus collective invite us to see everything as art except for the work found in museums. In the same room, you have the chance to try your hand at a game of Fluxipingpong using impossible bats – one bat has a large hole, another a tin can attached to it which sends the ball zipping off in every direction but the one you intended (bring your own ball).

There is far too much to see in a single day. To help get the most from your visit, audio guides can be picked up from a variety of information points (children's versions available) and cost only £1. Should the vastness of the building become daunting, lightweight collapsible stools are on hand free of charge to take round with you. There are are plenty of comfy sofas as well as two restaurants and a café.

On the ground floor, the Tate's gift shop has not missed a trick and sells every conceivable kind of merchandise. Tate pens, mugs T-shirts and umbrellas go like hot cakes. So do the Tate rubic cubes decorated with works by concept artists Gilbert and George and the Tate stationery box in the shape of the Bankside building which includes a magnetic 'lightbeam' lid plus pencils, stickers and paper clips. Best of all are the Tate coat hooks, originally designed for Homebase by the sculptor Antony Gormley.

The Millennium Bridge

This beautiful walkway, designed by Norman Foster, Anthony Caro and Ove Arup, was supposed to lead the way across the river from the Tate to St Paul's. However it shook from side to side so violently on its first day under the weight of human traffic that it is closed indefinitely for modifications.

food and drink

Shepherd's

Marsham Court
Tel: (020) 7834 9552
Open: Mon–Fri noon–3, 6.30–11

Traditional English food at reasonable prices.

The Black Friar

174 Queen Victoria Street, EC4
Tel: (020) 7236 5650
Open: Mon–Fri 11–11

Arts and Crafts interior with mother of pearl, wood carvings, stained glass and marble pillars.

MONUMENT

The Monument

Monument Street, EC3
Tel: (020) 7626 2717
Open: 10–5.40 daily
Adm: adult £1.50, child 50p (under-5s free)
No disabled access

On 2 September 1666, in the early hours of the morning, a fire broke out at Farynor's bakery in Pudding Lane. It was a windy night and sparks soon set fire to the nearby Star Inn and, from there, spread through the entire neighbourhood. By morning London Bridge and 300 houses were ablaze. Four days later, when the fire was finally put under control, 13,200 houses, 44 livery halls and 87 churches (including the old St Paul's – see p.35) had gone up in smoke. Amazingly, only 18 people perished in the fire. The Monument, designed by Sir Christopher Wren, and topped by a flaming bronze urn, commemorates these events. At 202ft – being the exact distance from here to the bakery on Pudding Lane – it was the world's tallest isolated stone column when it was erected in 1671. A stiff climb (311 steps) takes you to the viewing gallery at the top where you get a fine view of rooftop London, only partially spoiled by the characterless office buildings crowding round.

TOWER HILL

Tower Bridge Experience

Tel: (020) 7378 1928
www.towerbridge.org.uk
Open: Mar–Oct Mon– Sat 9–5, Sun 10–5; Nov–Feb
Mon & Sun 10–4, Tue–Sat 9–4
Adm: adult £6.25, child & concs £4.25 (under-5s free), family ticket
(2+2) £18.25

Tower Bridge, famous for its enormous bascules (arms) which rise to let riverborne traffic pass underneath, is nowhere near as old it looks. Mock-Gothic in appearance, it is in fact Portland stone constructed round a steel frame, an innovation when it was unveiled in 1894. Though a little pricey, the tour is worth it as you find yourself taken back in time by Harry Stoner, an animatronic construction worker. Interactive displays and the occasional appearance of the ghost of Horace Jones, the bridge's architect who died before the work was complete, only add to the fun. The tour takes you up to the elevated walkways which run along the top, offering a grand view up and down the river, and ends in the engine room where you can see the gleaming steam pumps used to lift the decks until 1976. Though the bridge is not raised as often as it once was, the bascules still rise at least once a day. To find out precisely when Tel: (020) 7378 7700.

Tower of London

Tower Hill, EC3
Tel: (020) 7709 0765
www.tower-of-london.com
Open: Mar–Oct Mon–Sat 9–5, Sun 10–5; Nov–Feb Tue–Sat 9–4,
Sun–Mon 10–4
Adm: adult £10.50, child £6.90, concs £7.90, family (2+2) £31
Very limited wheelchair access, Tel: (020) 7403 1115 for
access guide

Having just invaded England, William the Conqueror needed somewhere secure to protect him from disaffected English rebels and so erected the 15-ft thick walls of the White Tower. This impregnable fortress was further strengthened by successive monarchs, to include two additional towers, outer walls and a moat (now dry). As well as keeping people out, the Tower has proved equally useful at keeping them in. Among the victims brought here through Traitor's Gate were Anne Boleyn, Katherine Howard, Lady Jane Grey, Sir Thomas More, Sir Walter Raleigh and Guy Fawkes. Some of these were executed on Tower Green where the squawking ravens are all that remain of the menagerie introduced by Henry III that included lions, leopards, a polar bear (kept on a chain so it could fish in the Thames) and an elephant. Though the animals were moved to London Zoo in 1834, the Tower is still home to the Queen's Crown Jewels. You can see these, glittering behind bulletproof glass, by stepping onto a moving walkway which takes you past at a gentle pace. Among the priceless collection of baubles are the Royal Sceptre, the Imperial State Crown (which includes 2,800 diamonds and the Black Prince's ruby, reputedly worn by Henry V at the Battle of Agincourt), and the 530-carat Cullinan stone, the world's largest cut diamond. Though you can take a spooky subterranean ride on the Tower Hill Pageant, the best way to learn more about this medieval fortress is to take a free tour. These leave every half hour from the Middle Tower and are conducted by one of the 38 resident Yeoman Warders. A fact-packed walk round the principal sights, they have the additional benefit of allowing you to talk personally to one of the famous Beefeaters (so-called because of their daily 2lb ration of meat) who have been faithfully guarding the Tower since 1458.

food and drink

Café Spice Namaste

16 Prescot Street, E1
Tel: (020) 7488 9242
Open: Mon–Fri noon–3,
6.15–10.30, Sat 6.30–10

Innovative Indian restaurant in a former Victorian law court. Home-made Indian pickles can be bought to take home. Tends to fill up with City types in the week.

Dicken's Inn

St Katherine's Way, E1
Tel: (020) 7488 2208
Open: Mon–Sat noon–3, 6.30–11,
Sun noon–3

Moved to its present location on wheels. Large pub with flower-festooned balconies and decent food. Child-friendly.

LIVERPOOL STREET (See Central line)

Brick Lane Market see p39
Columbia Road Flower Market see p39
Geffrye Museum see p40
Petticoat Lane see p40

BARBICAN

Barbican Centre

Silk Street, The Barbican, EC2
Tel: (020) 7368 4141
www.barbican.org.uk
Open: (box office) 9–8 daily
Tickets: £6–30

Though Columbus might have discovered America without a compass he'd have had his work cut out navigating the Barbican. This entire area suffered heavy wartime bombing which reduced it to rubble. It took 20 years of rebuilding and, when it was finally unveiled in 1982, people almost immediately complained that they couldn't find their way about. Despite the hasty addition of yellow lines on the walkways and improved signposting it is only the most seasoned visitor who doesn't get lost at some point. But this is partly because there's so much here. Home to the Royal Shakespeare Company, the London Symphony Orchestra, the English Chamber Orchestra and the Guildhall School of Music and Drama, it also has three cinemas, an art gallery, several bars and a couple of restaurants, not to mention the shops, residential high-rise flats and the underground car-park. Londoners don't really like the Barbican – it's grey, ugly and windswept. But they come for the quality of the performances (dance, theatre, music), the world-class exhibitions and, during the summer, the terrace with its pond and benches which becomes a popular drinking spot, especially when a jazz band is giving one of the frequent free concerts.

FARRINGDON

House of Detention

Clerkenwell Close, EC1
Tel: (020) 7253 9494
Open: 10–6 daily (last entry 5.15)
Adm: adult £4, child £2.50, concs £3, family ticket £10

A prison has stood on this site since 1616. Famous inmates have included the highwaymen Jack Sheppard and Dick Turpin. At its peak in the late 1800s, when you could be locked up for begging, attempting suicide or even minor cases of theft, it received some 10,000 prisoners a year. Today all that remains are the dingy, damp and dark underground passages. The spooky cells at the end give some idea of the awful conditions the prisoners had to endure, as does the collection of torture implements on display that were designed to tear the throats, smash the thumbs and pull out the tongues of the unfortunate inmates.

food and drink

Ask Pizza

103 St John Street, EC1
Tel: (020) 7253 0323
Open: Mon–Fri noon–11, Sat &
Sun noon–10.30

Family-friendly pizza restaurant, similar in style and price to PizzaExpress. Half-portions available.

Quality Chop House

94 Farringdon Road, EC1
Tel: (020) 7837 5093
Open: Mon–Fri noon–3,
6.30–11.30 (closed Sat lunch)

Converted from a former 19th-century working men's club, this moderately priced restaurant now serves posh versions of fish cakes, bangers & mash and egg & chips. Delicious.

St John

26 St John Street, EC1
Tel: (020) 7251 0848
Open: Mon–Fri noon–3, 6–11
(closed Sat lunch)

Meat, meat, meat and more meat, served in a former smokehouse. Child-friendly.

Bleeding Heart

Bleeding Heart Yard (off Greville
Street), EC1
Tel: (020) 7242 8238
Open: Mon–Fri noon–11

Recently restored to look as it would have in 1746. Popular wine bar with a small, and rather smart, dining area.

The Eagle

159 Farringdon Road, EC1
Tel: (020) 7837 1353
Open: Mon–Sat noon–11,
Sun noon–5

One of the first gastropubs in London and still incredibly popular. Good value Mediterranean food. Order at the bar.

Jerusalem Tavern

55 Britton Street, EC1
Tel: (020) 7490 4281
Open: Mon–Fri 9am–11pm

Tiny Georgian parlour with original fires, cosy cubicles and great beer. Often crowded.

KING'S CROSS/ST PANCRAS
(See Northern line)
London Canal Museum see p76

BAKER STREET (See Bakerloo Line)
London Planetarium see p22
Madame Tussaud's see p22
Sherlock Holmes Museum see p23

NOTTING HILL GATE (See Central Line)
Portobello Market see p26

HIGH STREET KENSINGTON

Albert Hall and Albert Memorial

Kensington Gore, SW7
Tel: (020) 7589 8212
Open: (box office) 9–9 daily
Tickets: £3–£150

Prince Albert, the beloved husband of Queen Victoria
from 1840 until his death from typhoid fever in 1861, is
memorialized in two buildings which stand facing each
other across Kensington Gore. The domed, circular Albert
Hall is one of the grandest Victorian buildings in London.
It can seat 8,000 in the auditorium and was paid for by
public donation. Additional capital was raised by selling
1,300 of the seats at £100 each for every first night
performance for 999 years. These days the hall is in
constant use for concerts from pop to classical, the odd
tennis match and, most famously, for the Proms, a series
of classical music concerts held each summer. Short for
Promenades, the concerts were originally held in the
open air and, even today, some of the audience stand or
sit on the floor. On the last night of the Proms (early
September) the orchestra belts out nationalistic
melodies and the excitable audience sings along as loud
as they can.

The Albert Memorial was erected by Queen Victoria to
honour her husband. During World War II the gilding on
the statue was removed for fear of attracting enemy
bombs but has been lovingly replaced following a recent
£14-million renovation. Designed by George Gilbert Scott,
it is 175ft high with a stone canopy protecting the 14-ft
statue of Albert from the elements.

Kensington Palace

The State Apartments, Kensington Gardens, W8
Tel: (020) 7937 9561
www.hrp.org.uk
Open: 10–4 daily
Adm: adult £9.50, child £7.10, concs £7.70, family ticket £29.10

This palace was favoured as the royal residence until George III decided to move to Buckingham House. It was Queen Victoria's birthplace in 1819 and, more recently, was the refuge of Princess Diana following the breakdown of her marriage to Prince Charles. Princess Diana's private apartments are not open to the public but you can visit the palace for tours of the State Apartments, including the King's Gallery (look out for the painted episodes of Homer's *Odyssey* on the ceiling) and the room where Queen Victoria was baptised. You also get to see the royal dress collection which includes the flamboyant coronation garb of George IV and the sober costume worn by Queen Victoria at her coronation in 1837.

food and drink

Wódka

12 St Alban's Grove, W8
Tel: (020) 7937 6513
Open: Mon–Fri 12.30–2.30, 7–11.15

Modern Polish food and probably the purest vodka to be found in the capital. Moderately priced. Reservations essential.

Wagamama

26–24 Kensington High St, W8
Tel: (020) 7376 1717
Open: Mon–Sat noon–11, Sun 12.30–10

Eat noodles and stir fries at wooden benches and tables in canteen-style surroundings. Simple and healthy. Reasonably priced.

Windsor Castle

114 Campden Hill Road, W8
Tel: (020) 7352 7572
Open: Mon–Sat noon–11, Sun noon–10.30

Three bars and a pretty walled garden with good pub food and a relaxed atmosphere.

LONDON BRIDGE

Bramah Tea and Coffee Museum 68
Clink Prison Museum 68
Design Museum 69
Golden Hinde 69
HMS Belfast 70
London Dungeon 70
Old Operating Theatre and Herb Garrett 71
Shakespeare's Globe Theatre 72
Vinopolis, City of Wine 73
Winston Churchill's Britain at War 73

NORTHERN LINE
CITY BRANCH

In 1890 the City and South London Railway (renamed the Northern Line in 1937) opened the world's first deep-level electric railway which ran from the City and under the river to Stockwell. This line, along with what are now the Bakerloo and Piccadilly lines, was financed by an American entrepreneur, Charles Tyson Yerkes, who had made his fortune building a rapid transit system for Chicago. On these early trains entry and exit was by way of gates, which were opened and closed by gatemen who also announced the station at each stop. The little trains could seat fewer than 100 passengers and were dimly lit by electric lights which flickered on and off with fluctuations in the current. Each carriage had high-backed seating and frosted windows out of which nothing could be seen, and it was not long before they became known as 'padded cells' by the people who travelled in them.

BANK

Bank of England Museum see p36
Clockmakers' Company Museum see p37
Guildhall see p37

ANGEL

Camden Passage 75

KINGS CROSS/ ST PANCRAS

London Canal Museum 76

WEST END BRANCH

GOODGE STREET

Habitat 76
Heal's 76
Pollock's Toy Museum 77

LONDON BRIDGE

Bramah Tea & Coffee Museum

1 Maguire Street, Butler's Wharf, SE1
Tel: (020) 7378 0222
www.bramahmuseum.co.uk
Open: 10–6 daily
Adm: adult £4, child and concs £3, family (2+4) £10

Edward Bramah, a one-time tea taster and commodity broker, set up this museum in the 1990s to show off his extraordinary collection of coffee-makers and teapots. They come in wonderful colours, shapes and sizes from fire-breathing dragons and ghouls to hedgehogs, petrol pumps and rosy-cheeked policemen. Besides the pots and other related bric-à-brac, the museum traces an engaging path through the history of tea and coffee-drinking in this country, from the arrival of the coffee bean in 1640 to the rise of coffee shops as unofficial centres for trade (Lloyd's of London began life as a coffee house) and the origins of the tea break as a sacrosanct English ritual. There is an airy café where you can sample a good range of teas and coffees, including the museum's own blends.

Clink Prison Museum

1 Clink Street, SE1
Tel: (020) 7403 6515
www.clink.co.uk
Open: 10–6 daily
Adm: adult & child £4, concs £3, family £9
No disabled access

If you've ever wondered where the expression 'in the clink' (meaning to be in prison) comes from then all will soon be revealed. Housed on the site of the Bishop of Winchester's own private jail where, in the Middle Ages, the good bishop locked away anyone who dared challenge him or his various extortion rackets, the Clink's exhibition attempts to convey some of the horrors of medieval prison life on Bankside. The museum feels a little tired but it's difficult, of course, to truly portray the suffering of the poor unfortunates who were variously thrown into holes and left to rot, tied in chairs to be tortured with pincers and hot pokers, or thrown into vats of boiling oil. Amazingly, despite the barbaric treatment, prisoners were expected to pay their own way here. They even had to fork out for their own ball and chain.

Design Museum

Butler's Wharf, Shad Thames, SE1
Tel: (020) 7403 6933
www.designmuseum.org
Open: 11.30–6 daily
Adm: adult £5.50, child & concs £4, under-5s free

It's not often you can walk round a museum and recognise exhibits behind the glass that you may have once owned and perhaps still do. The brainchild of style guru Sir Terence Conran, the Design Museum presents everyday items such as radios and televisions, washing machines, cameras and vacuum-cleaners as objects to be studied and valued. Not all could be described as classics but, when set side by side, you begin to look at each in a new way and perhaps start to appreciate how revolutionary such mundane items as, say, the anglepoise lamp truly are. The first floor of the museum is set apart for state-of-the-art design (just how small can a camera get?) as well as housing a temporary exhibition space where you might see anything from 1930's British furniture to an exhibition dedicated to Dr Marten's footwear. At the shop you can pick up your very own design classic (a period phone or a Dyson vacuum perhaps?) and get a coffee at the adjoining café – served, of course, in an ultra-stylish mug with equally fashionable cakes and pastries.

The Golden Hinde

St Mary Overie Dock, Cathedral Street, SE1
Tel: (020) 7403 0123
www.goldenhinde.co.uk
Open: 10–6 daily but call in advance
Adm: adult £2.50, child £1.75, concs £2.10
Overnight Living History Experience: £30 per person plus £10 deposit (no children under 6)
No disabled access

This full-size reconstruction of Sir Francis Drake's flagship, in which he became the first Englishman to circumnavigate the globe in 1580, has had quite a history of its own, sailing some 100,000 miles in its capacity as a floating museum since it was built in 1973. Now permanently moored in London, it is staffed by a jolly crew of knowledgeable actors in Elizabethan costume who will show you round all five decks and frighten the kids with tales of swashbuckling adventure and incredible feats of endurance on the high seas. If anybody wants to get a real feel for what life might have been like aboard a 16-century vessel, they can spend the night here on a Living History Experience, in which they assume the role of a crew member, carry out routine ship maintenance, dine on Elizabethan food and sleep in a cabin below decks.

HMS Belfast

Morgan's Lane, off Tooley Street, SE1
Tel: (020) 7940 6328
www.hmsbelfast.org.uk
Open: Mar–Oct 10–6 daily (last entry 5.15), Nov–Feb 10–5 daily
(last entry 4.15)
Adm: adult £5, under-16s free, concs £3.90

This 11,500-ton, 656ft battleship was one of the most powerful cruisers the Royal Navy ever built and remained an integral part of the fleet from 1938 to the end of the Korean

war in 1953. In that time it saw service during the D-Day landings and the decisive 1944 invasion of Normandy. Since 1971 it has been permanently moored in somewhat calmer waters and has become a spectacular floating museum. It isn't to everyone's tastes but war buffs and children will enjoy exploring the seven decks, which include the boiler and engine rooms, mess halls, punishments cells, operation rooms and the massive gun turrets. As an offshoot of the Imperial War Museum (see p4), the ship is also used to explore the history of the Royal Navy from 1914 to the present day.

London Dungeon

Tooley Street, SE1
Tel: (020) 7403 7221
www.dungeon.com
Open: Oct–Mar 10–5 daily, April–Sept 10–5.30 daily
Adm: adult £9.95, child (under 14) £6.50, concs £6.50–£8.50

An orgy of gore, if ever there was one. Some of the displays are a little creaky but the London Dungeon continues to pack in the crowds so must be doing something right. Basically, if it's horrid, it's here: dark and dingy arches resound with piteous screams and wailing as waxwork figures are subjected to unspeakable torture on the rack; Anne Boleyn delivers her 1536 speech before being decapitated; a human

is sacrificed by druids at Stonehenge, and Queen Boadicea hacks a Roman foot soldier to death. A new exhibit, 'Firestorm! 1666', is devoted to the Great Fire of London but the highlight (if you can call it that) is the Jack the Ripper Experience in which visitors are taken back in time to a foggy Victorian London where they are led by costumed actors through the East End on a search for this infamous murderer. Because of its content, the museum is not suitable for very young children or for anyone of a nervous disposition.

Old Operating Theatre and Herb Garrett

9a St Thomas Street, SE1
Tel: (020) 7955 4791
Open: 10–4 daily
Adm: adult £2.90, child £1.50 (under-8s free), concs £2, family ticket (2+2) £7.25
No disabled access

Surgery before antiseptics or anaesthetics was no joke, as you'll discover if you visit this museum. The tower once belonged to St Thomas's, which was founded as a hospital on this site in the 12th century. Most of the old buildings were demolished after the hospital was moved to Lambeth in 1862 but the tower remained, bricked up and forgotten. Then, in 1958, it was discovered by an historian, Raymond Russell, who crawled through a hole in the belfry to find a 19th-century operating theatre untouched by human hand for nearly a century. Restored in 1968, it is now a fascinating if disturbing museum which explores a period of surgery that saw patients blindfolded and gagged and held down by rops on a wooden table with a box of sawdust underneath to catch the blood. And these were the lucky ones!

Next door you can recover your senses in the Herb Garrett which tells the history of herbal medicine during the same period.

Shakespeare's Globe

Bear Gardens, Bankside,
New Globe Wall, Southwark, SE1
Tel: (020) 7401 9919
www.shakespeares-globe.org
Open: May–Sept 9–12.30pm daily, Oct–April 10–5 daily, for
performance times call in advance
Museum adm: adult £7.50, child £5 (under-5s free), concs £6,
family ticket (2+3) £23
Limited wheelchair access
Tickets: £5–25

Many of Shakespeare's plays, including *Romeo and Juliet*, *King Lear* and *Macbeth*, were first performed on Bankside at the famous O-shaped theatre that stood a few hundred feet away from the present reconstruction. The original theatre burnt down when a spark from a stage cannon set fire to the

roof during a performance of Henry VIII but, some 400 years later, the new Globe has been built using traditional methods and materials and is as close to the original as possible except for the addition of a few modern safety features (such as sprinklers). The performances of the plays, too, aim to be authentic. A huge stage pokes out into an unseated area, open to the elements, with room for 500 standing (known as groundlings) who may, at any time, get an authentic drenching if it starts to rain. For a little more comfort, seating is provided by wooden benches in three half-timbered circular galleries. The Elizabethan audiences were a rowdy lot. Mostly drunk, they were determined to enjoy the show, and would cheer for the goodies, hiss at the baddies and pitch rotten food at the stage (and each other) if they were displeased with the performance. Modern audiences should resist the temptation to launch a hamburger at Lady Macbeth, but booing, cat-calls and general merriment are still very much part of the fun.

The theatre is just a part of the complex which also includes an extensive exhibition (open all year round) on Shakespeare and his times, a fascinating look at how the Globe was rebuilt and a lively guided tour round the auditorium. If you visit only one theatre in London, make it this one.

Vinopolis, City of Wine

1 Bank End, SE1
Tel: (0870) 444 4777
www.vinopolis.co.uk
Open: 10–5 daily (last entry 4.30pm)
Adm: adult £11.50, child £4.50, concs £10.50

Opened in July 1999 in a complex of beautifully converted brick-vaulted cellars and railway arches, Vinopolis gives you the chance to tour the world's wine regions on the banks of the Thames. There are imaginative multimedia presentations for each section – for example, you can 'tour' the Tuscan wine villages aboard a (stationary) Vespa. Adult tickets include vouchers for five wine tastings, chosen from regional tables, and experts are on hand for occasional tutored tastings. At the end of the tour you can visit a wine warehouse to pick up a few select vintages (now that you know which are the good ones) and the wine shop to pick up natty corkscrews, wine racks, books and other wine-related paraphernalia. There's also an art gallery, good restaurant, wine bar, and a wine school.

Winston Churchill's Britain at War Experience

64–66 Tooley Street, SE1
Tel: (020) 7403 3171
www.britain-at-war.co.uk
Open: April–Sep 10–5.30 daily (last entry 5pm), Oct–Mar 10–4.30 daily (last entry 4pm)
Adm: adult £5.95, child (under 16) £2.95 (under-3s free), concs £3.95, family £14, wheelchair users free

This isn't a patch on the Imperial War Museum (see p4) or the Cabinet War Rooms (see p53) but it's still worth a visit, especially for children. Here, to a backdrop of archive footage, and accompanied by radio broadcasts and the rousing tunes of Vera Lynn, you can find out a little of what life was like during World War II. Seek shelter in an Underground station during an air raid. Pick your way through a darkened bomb site (with sirens wailing and spotlights searching the sky). The museum has a good collection of memorabilia (books, clothes, newspapers etc) as well as an admirable hands-on approach which encourages children to try on period costumes and gas masks to give them an additional sense of life in London during the Blitz.

food and drink

Old Thameside Inn

Pickford's Wharf, Clink Street, SE1
Tel: (020) 7403 4243
Open: Mon–Sat 11–11, Sun
noon–10.30

Good spot to sit out and watch the ships roll by. Reasonable, if somewhat unadventurous, bar food.

Anchor Bankside

34 Park Street, SE1
Tel: (020) 7407 1577
Open: Mon–Sat 11–11, Sun
noon–10.30

Extremely old riverside pub (Dr Johnson wrote part of his famous dictionary here). Eccentrically shaped rooms, good beer. Can get very busy.

The Horniman

Morgan Lane, SE1
Tel: (020) 7407 3611
Open: Mon–Sat 11–11, Sun
noon–10.30

Part of Hay's Galleria shopping complex. No seats outside but you can take your drinks out and lean against the wall.

Cynthia's Cyberbar

4 Tooley Street, SE1
Tel: (020) 7403 6777
Open: Mon–Wed noon–1am,
Thur–Sat noon–3am, Sun
noon–10.30pm

Futuristic but with a homey feel. The cocktails, including such favourites as Alien Vomit and Martian Blood, are mixed by two huge robots called Cynthia and Rastus.

The George Inn

77 Borough High Street, SE1
Tel: (020) 7407 2056
Open: Mon–Sat 11–11, Sun
noon–10.30

One of London's oldest pubs with a labyrinth of interconnecting bars and a courtyard where you can see morris dancing and open-air theatricals during the summer.

Fina Estampa

150 Tooley St, SE1
Tel: (020) 7403 1342
Open: Mon–Fri noon–2.30,
6.30–10.30, Sat & Sun 6.30–10.30

London's only Peruvian restaurant, strangely situated in the heart of Ye Olde London.

Globe Café

Tel: (020) 7902 1576
Open: 10am–15mins before end
of last performance

Rather posh but a good selection of snacks.

Globe Restaurant

Tel: (020) 7928 9444
Open: noon–2.30 & 5.30–11pm

Great Thameside views. Tasty dishes with the accent on grills.

fish!

Cathedral Street, SE1
Tel: (020) 7836 3236
Open: (lunch) Mon–Sat
11.30–3pm, (dinner)
Mon–Sat 5.30–11

Next to Borough Market, this restaurant is housed in an impressive glass structure. Inside, it's friendly, with good quality fish cooked to order. Child-friendly.

BANK (See Central Line)

Bank of England Museum see p36
Clockmakers' Company Museum see p37
Guildhall see p37

ANGEL

Camden Passage

Camden Passage, off Islington High Street, N1
Open: Wed & Sat 8.30–3

One of London's more genteel markets, 350 stallholders lay out their wares here twice a week and join the permanent dealers, many of whom have been here since the 1960s. You'll find everything from pretty knick-knacks and trinkets to antique dolls and Bakelite radios, glassware, paintings, costumes and rugs. You name it! It's all fairly picturesque and there are a numerous pubs and restaurants nearby to rest up after a hard morning's rummaging.

food and drink

The King's Head

115 Upper Street, N1
Tel: (020) 7226 0364
Open: Open: Mon–Sat noon–11,
Sun noon–10.30

A theatre pub with good bar food and the quaint affectation of charging for drinks using the pre-decimal system of pounds, shillings and pence.

Casale Franco

134–7 Upper Street, N1
Tel: (020) 7226 8994
Open: (lunch) Sat noon–9, Sun noon–3; (dinner) Tue–Sun 6–11 (Sun last orders 9pm)

The long queues attest to the tastiness and good value of the spicy Italian dishes and crusty pizzas served in this lively north-London restaurant.

Dôme

341 Upper Street, N1
Tel: (020) 7226 3414
Open: 8.30–10.30 daily

One of a chain of French-style bistros serving beers, wines and spirits, good strong coffee and tasty French cuisine.

Upper Street Fish Shop

324 Upper Street, N1
Tel: (020) 7359 1401
Open: (lunch) Tue–Fri noon–2.15, Sat noon–3; (dinner) Mon–Thur 6–10.15, Fri & Sat 5.30–10.15

Reasonably priced and fresh. Traditional fish in batter or more imaginative dishes such as tempura or deep-fried mussels. The puddings are a real treat.

KING'S CROSS/ST PANCRAS

London Canal Museum

12–13 New Wharf Road, N1
Tel: (020) 7713 0836
www.canalmuseum.org.uk
Open: Tue–Sun 10–4.30
Adm: adult £2.50, child £1.25 (under-8s free)
Partial disabled facilities (phone ahead)

During Britain's Industrial Revolution it was canal boats which brought the materials and products from the mechanised north into London to be used in the capital or sold abroad. The warehouse which now houses this museum was built used in the 1850s by one Carlo Gatti, an Italian-speaking Swiss immigrant who made his pile importing ice from Norway. Here you can learn about Gatti's story, take a peek into the huge ice wells where the blocks of ice were stored, explore restored canal boats and get some idea of the kind of lives led by the canal workers (adults and children) who scratched a tough living ferrying cargo in and out of the capital.

GOODGE STREET

The only tube stop on the West End branch of the Northern Line not covered by other lines in this guide, Goodge Street is worth stopping at for three reasons.

Habitat

196 Tottenham Court Road, W1
Tel: (020) 7631 3880
www.habitat.net
Open: Mon–Wed 10–6, Thur 10–8, Fri 10–6.30, Sat 9.30–6.30,
Sun noon–6

The flagship store of affordable good taste was opened by Sir Terence Conran in the 1960s. Upstairs you'll find sofas, chairs and kitchens. Downstairs lighting, kitchen and bathroom accessories, beds and office equipment. It also has a nice café.

Heal's

196 Tottenham Court Road, W1
Tel: (020) 7636 1666
Open: Mon–Wed 10–6, Thur 10–8, Fri 10–6.30, Sat 9.30–6.30,
Sun noon–6

This is one of the oldest furniture stores in London. Though a little pricier than Habitat next door, it is perhaps worth the extra money for the distinct edge it offers in style and quality.

Pollock's Toy Museum

1 Scala Street, W1
Tel: (020) 7636 3452
www.pollocks.cwc.net
Open: Mon–Sat 10–5
Adm: adult £3, child £1.50 (under-3s free)

Benjamin Pollock was one of London's leading manufacturers of toys. Though he specialised in miniature stage sets, this museum (set in two interlinked 18th-century houses) is crammed to the rafters with all kinds of fun: tin toys, board games, puppets, dolls and dolls' houses, Eastern European folk toys, and teddy bears of all vintages. The museum also has its own shop where you can pick up reproduction toy theatres made from wood and card for children (or their parents) to assemble. The shop also sells a seemingly unlimited amount of stocking fillers.

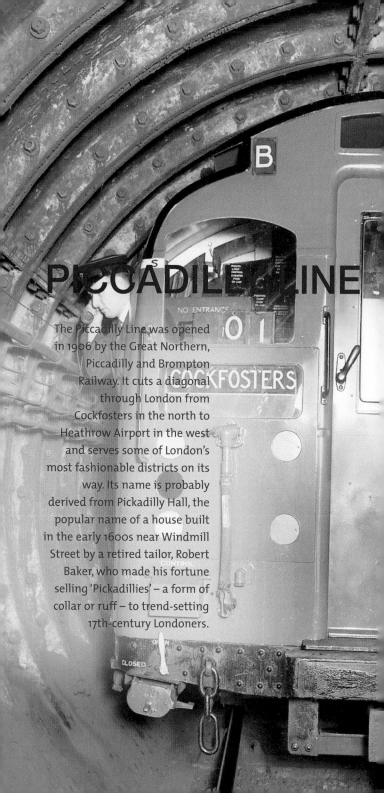

PICCADILLY LINE

The Piccadilly Line was opened in 1906 by the Great Northern, Piccadilly and Brompton Railway. It cuts a diagonal through London from Cockfosters in the north to Heathrow Airport in the west and serves some of London's most fashionable districts on its way. Its name is probably derived from Pickadilly Hall, the popular name of a house built in the early 1600s near Windmill Street by a retired tailor, Robert Baker, who made his fortune selling 'Pickadillies' – a form of collar or ruff – to trend-setting 17th-century Londoners.

SOUTH KENSINGTON

Conran Shop see p44
Natural History Museum see p44
Science Museum see p46
Serpentine Gallery see p47
Victoria and Albert Museum see p47

KNIGHTSBRIDGE

Harrods 80

HYDE PARK CORNER

Aspley House, The Wellington Museum 81

GREEN PARK

Faraday Museum see p97
Fortnum and Mason see p97
Green Park see p97
Ritz Hotel see p98

PICCADILLY CIRCUS

Berwick Street Market see p15
Pepsi Trocadero see p15
Rainforest Café see p15
Rock Circus see p15
Royal Academy of Arts see p16
St James's Church Piccadilly see p17

LEICESTER SQUARE

Chinatown 83
Half-price Ticket Booth 84
London Coliseum 84

COVENT GARDEN

Covent Garden Market and Piazza 85
Apple Market 85
Benjamin Pollock's Toy Shop 85
London Doll's House Company 86
London Transport Museum 86
Neal Street East 87
Neal's Yard Bakery 87
Neal's Yard Dairy 87
Royal Opera House 87
St Paul's Church 88
Stanley Gibbons International 88
The Kite Store 88
The Tea House 89
The Tintin Shop 89
The Wild Bunch 89
Theatre Museum 90

HOLBORN

Sir John Soane's Museum see p32

RUSSELL SQUARE

Dickens House Museum 91

KINGS CROSS/ST PANCRAS

London Canal Museum see p76

SOUTH KENSINGTON
(See Circle Line)

Conran Shop see p44

Natural History Museum see p44

Science Museum see p46

Serpentine Gallery see p47

Victoria and Albert Museum see p47

KNIGHTSBRIDGE

Harrods

87 Brompton Road, SW1
Tel: (020) 7730 1234
Open: Mon, Tue, Sat 10–6, Wed–Fri 10–7

Founded by Henry Charles Harrod, a tea merchant from Eastcheap, in 1849, this mecca for shoppers is now owned by Mohammed Al Fayed, whose son Dodi died in the same car crash as Princess Diana in 1997. You could spend the whole day here quite happily. The pet department is particularly good and usually proves a hit with children (time was you could order any animal in the world from here – even an elephant). The toy department, too, on the 4th floor will keep children amused for hours. If you're feeling peckish, the adjacent Planet Harrods, with its gloopy shakes and burgers, is a good stopping-off point. Don't miss the food halls (all seven of them) where the extravagance of the food displays is rivalled only by the lustre of the Edwardian Art Noveau tiling. At any time of the year, Harrods is one of London's big attractions but in the run up to Christmas every shop window becomes a pantomime in miniature and the food halls are piled high with festive treats. The famous sale in January is something of a tradition with people queuing all night to join the ritual stampede for top-quality bargains. While not as exclusive as it once was, Harrods may still refuse entry to those sporting large backpacks or unseemingly tight leggings.

food and drink

Gloriette Patisserie

128 Brompton Road, SW3
Tel: (020) 7589 4750
Open: Mon–Sat 7–7, Sun 9–6

Sticky Austrian cakes and sweets, salads and sandwiches. Good coffee. Child-friendly.

Pizza on the Park

11 Knightsbridge, SW1
Tel: (020) 7235 5273
Open: Mon–Fri 8am–midnight,
Sat & Sun 9am–10pm

Good quality pizza with a view over the park. A little on the pricey side but tasty nevertheless.

Planet Harrods

Tel: (020) 7730 1234
Open: Mon–Sat 10–6 (Thur till 7)

Next to the toys on the 4th floor. Chips, burgers and triple-thick shakes.

Bunch of Grapes

207 Brompton Road, SW3
Tel: (020) 7589 4944
Open: Mon–Sat 11–11, Sun
noon–10.30

Traditional London boozer with good beer and reasonable bar food.

HYDE PARK CORNER

Apsley House, The Wellington Museum

149 Piccadilly, W1
Tel: (020) 7499 5676
Open: Tue–Sun 11–5
Adm: adult £4.50, concs £3, under-18s free

As a reward for finishing off Napoleon at the Battle of Waterloo in 1815, the Duke of Wellington was given this house at 149 Piccadilly. Though delighted with his gift, he was less impressed with the address and promptly dubbed it Number One, London. A lover of art, Wellington amassed a sizeable collection during his stay here, from 1817 until his death in 1852, which included many paintings and precious objects given to him by influential figures, as well as various spoils of war. Wellington's descendants still live here but 10 rooms have been restored and are now open to the public. Paintings by great masters (Goya, Rubens, Velázquez etc), silver and gold plate and priceless porcelain are on show, as is the unmissable Canova: an 11ft statue of a nude Napoleon Bonaparte which towers over the grand staircase.

GREEN PARK (See Victoria Line)

Faraday Museum see p97
Fortnum and Mason see p97
Green Park see p97
Ritz Hotel see p98

PICCADILLY CIRCUS
(See Bakerloo Line)

Berwick Street Market see p15

Pepsi Trocadero see p15

Rainforest Café see p15

Rock Circus see p15

Royal Academy of Arts see p16

St James's Church Piccadilly see p17

food and drink

Andrew Edmunds

46 Lexington Street, W1
Tel: (020) 7437 5708
Open: (lunch) Mon–Fri 12.30–3,
Sat & Sun 1–3, (dinner) Mon–Sat
6–10.45, Sun 6–10.30

For a real culinary treat in cosy and unpretentious surroundings. Excellent, simple dishes and a good wine list. Very small and can get a little crowded.

Kula Kula

76 Brewer Street, W1
Tel: (020) 7734 7316
Open: Mon–Sat 5–10

Sushi on a conveyor belt. Cheap and no-nonsense.

Alfred

245 Shaftesbury Avenue, WC2
Tel: (020) 7240 2566
Open: Mon–Sat noon–4,
6–midnight, Sun noon–6

Reasonably priced and beautifully presented modern British cuisine.

Pollo

20 Old Compton Street, W1
Tel: (020) 7734 5917
Open: noon–midnight daily

Budget priced pasta. If you don't fancy Chinese food you may like to head for Pollo, one of the best known cheap eats in town. A little rough and ready, but family-run and friendly.

Patisserie Valerie

44 Old Compton Street, W1
Tel: (020) 7437 3466
Open: Mon–Fri 8–8, Sat 8–7, Sun
9.30–6

Just a glance at the window display is enough to entice half of London into this famous café which has been serving delicious pastries, flans and cakes since the 1920s.

St James Tavern

45 Great Windmill Street, W1
Tel: (020) 7437 5009
Open: Mon–Sat 11am–1am, Sun
noon–10.30

Late-opening Soho pub. Decorated with hand-painted tiles depicting scenes from Shakespeare.

LEICESTER SQUARE

Chinatown

Gerrard Street, Lisle Street, WC2

In the 1950s, the area round Gerrard Street and Lisle Street was fairly run down and, attracted by the cheap rents, many Chinese people from Hong Kong made it their home. Now known as Chinatown, there are a handful of Chinese supermarkets, herbalists and opticians. Since the 1970s, Gerrard Street has been pedestrianized and has oriental-looking street lamps and telephone boxes with pagoda-like tops. London's Chinatown is extremely compact and there isn't a great deal to see. The best time to visit is during the noisy Chinese New Year Festival (towards the end of January). Then, the area is brightly decorated with paper lanterns. Stalls sell Chinese crafts and food and a parade of dancing dragons, accompanied by firecrackers and music, slithers down the street. Whatever time of year, this is the best place to sample the delights of Chinese cookery. Here are four restaurants worth visiting.

Golden Harvest

17 Lisle Street, WC2

Tel: (020) 7287 3822

Open: noon–2.45am daily

Budget-priced and excellent with some wonderful seafood dishes.

Harbour City

46 Gerrard Street, W1

Tel: (020) 7439 7859

Open: Mon–Sat noon–11.30, Sun 11–11

Classic steamed *dim sum* (Chinese dumplings) and delicious house specialities from this superior Cantonese diner. Reasonably priced.

Fung Shing

15 Lisle Street, WC2

Tel: (020) 7437 1539

Open: noon–11.30 daily

Recently refurbished, one of Chinatown's best-known restaurants is now looking better than ever. A little pricey but worth it.

Mr Kong

21 Lisle Street, WC2

Tel: (020) 7437 7341

Open: noon–3am daily

A little crowded, but an enticing menu at reasonable prices.

Half-price Ticket Booth

Clocktower Building, Leicester Square, WC2

You can get disounted entry for the majority of the West End shows here for as little as half-price (plus £2 charge). Tickets are sold on a first-come, first-served basis, on the day of performance, from noon for matinées, 2.30–5.30 for evening performances. No phone bookings – you have to queue and wait your turn. Avoid the ticket touts who are hoping to rip off unsuspecting tourists.

London Coliseum (ENO)

St Martin's Lane, WC2
Tel: (020) 7632 8300
www.eno.org
Open: (box office) 24 hours daily
Tickets: £2.50–£55

The Coliseum was built in 1904 (it was the first theatre in England to have a revolving stage) and is now home to the English National Opera (ENO). You can see spectacular productions of the more accessible operas here (*The Magic Flute, Carmen* etc) as well as innovative new productions. It's easy to follow the plot as all of the productions are in English (there are often also subtitles on a big board above the stage). In line with the ENO's policy of making opera available to everyone, you can queue for same-day seats which go on sale at 10am and cost as little as £2.50. Same-day tickets can also be obtained by phone from 2.30pm onwards.

food and drink

Capital Radio Café

20/30 Leicester Square, W1
Tel: (020) 7484 8888
Open: Mon–Sat
11.45am–midnight, Sun noon–11

American style food (hamburgers, fries etc) in a bright, cheerful atmosphere with DJs supplying the sounds from a central booth. Child-friendly.

Photographer's Gallery Café

5 Great Newport Street, WC1
Tel: (020) 7831 1772
Open: Mon–Sat 11–5.30,
Sun noon–5.30

Kill two birds with a single stone. Eat a healthy salad for lunch and take in an exhibition of photography at the same time.

French House

49 Dean Street, W1
Tel: (020) 7437 2799
Open: Mon–Sat noon–11, Sun noon–10.30

The French Resistance convened here during World War II; in the 1960s it was the haunt of writers and artists and even today attracts its fair share of the literati. If you're feeling rich, visit the classy dining room upstairs.

COVENT GARDEN

Covent Garden Market and Piazza

In the 18th century you came to
Covent Garden for a good time. The
happy mix of market stalls, gambling
dens, coffee houses, Turkish baths,
brothels and rowdy taverns attracted
literary types such as Henry Fielding,
Alexander Pope, Richard Sheridan and
James Boswell who came, looking no
doubt for inspiration.In the 19th
century it became London's wholesale
fruit and vegetable market famous as
the setting for *My Fair Lady*. In 1974
the market moved out to Vauxhall
and the central market was dark and
deserted until 1980, when it reopened
in its present guise as a respectable,
pedestrianised piazza with shops,
stalls, some decent museums and

plenty of places to eat and sit out. Now the streets around
it are also filled with trendy shops and eateries. Covent
Garden is the best place to see London's street entertainers
where they perform on the predestianised road leading
from the tube and also in the main Piazza, the cobbled area
in front of St Paul's Church. At weekends large crowds
gather to watch jugglers, fire-eaters, mime artists and other
entertainers perform, often heckled by onlookers on the
balcony of the Punch and Judy pub. Here are some of the
best places in Covent Garden.

Apple Market

North Hall
Tel: (020) 7836 9136
Open: Mon 9–7, Tue–Sun 10.30–7

Crafts and clothes, antiques (Tues-Sun), bric-a-brac (Mon).

Benjamin Pollock's Toy Shop

44 The Market, Covent Garden, WC2
Tel: (020) 7379 7866
Open: Mon–Sat 10.30–6, Sun noon–5

Old-fashioned toys and teddies.

London Doll's House Company

29 Covent Garden Market, WC2
Tel: (020) 7240 8681
Open: Mon–Sat 10.30–7, Sun noon–5

Dolls and their houses and every kind of accessory from repro Victorian models to the ultra-modern.

London Transport Museum

Covent Garden Piazza, WC2
Tel: (020) 7379 6344
www.ltmuseum.co.uk
Open: Mon–Thur, Sat & Sun 10–6, Fri 11–6
Adm: adult £5.50, child and concs £2.95 (under-5s free),
*   family £13.95*

Housed in Covent Garden's former Flower Market, the London Transport Museum is every transport buff's dream, with an unrivalled collection of horse-drawn trams, buses, trolley cars and tube carriages dating from the 1830s to the present day. The museum succeeds very well in managing to conjure up the romance of London Transport. The coaches and buses, such as Thomas Tilling's 1875 'knifeboard' (London's first double-decker) have been beautifully restored and you can step inside later examples, such as the Routemaster bus (introduced in the 1950s) to appreciate the craftsmanship of these early vehicles. The piped sound effects of clip-clopping horses, early film footage and mannequins of passengers in period costume all help to summon up a feel for the times.

The making of the Underground is well documented. There are early carriages in which you can sit, special exhibits on tunnelling, tickets and station design and biographies of the movers and shakers in London Underground's history. The Frank Pick Gallery is named after the Managing Director of London Underground who, as Commercial Manager, was responsible for introducing a forward-looking visual sense to the company. Here you can see examples of graphics employed by London Underground including the blue and red roundel, the Johnston typeface and the specially commissioned posters. The Harry

Beck Gallery tells some of the story of London Underground's famous map (see page v).

The museum is extremely child-friendly with plenty of screens to touch and 15 hands-on zones which children can work their way round, punching a special ticket at each point, while learning about London Transport as they go. In addition they can try their hand at driving a tube train (this is fun for adults too), take a ride in the Fun Bus (under-5s only) and play with computers in the Fast Forward section which looks at the future of transport in London. Costumed actors, including a horse-dung collector (1,000 tons of dung were deposited each day when horses worked for London Transport), a First World War bus cleaner and a 1930s tram driver, are on hand to give visitors the benefit of their years of experience.

The shop is one of London's best museum outlets and has what is probably the largest collection of transport-related books and magazines to be found anywhere in the capital. Here, you can also pick up posters, mugs, ties, socks, videos, mouse mats and so on. For the real enthusiast, why not take home a sturdy cushion covered in genuine Underground seating fabric?

Neal Street East

5 Neal Street, WC2
Tel: (020) 7240 0135
Open: Mon–Wed 11–7, Thur–Sat 10–7.30, Sun noon–6

Oriental goods galore: clothes, cooking utensils, furniture.

Neal's Yard Bakery

6 Neal's Yard, WC2
Tel: (020) 7836 5199
Open: Mon–Sat 9–7, Sun 10–5

Organic cakes, savouries and wholefoods.

Neal's Yard Dairy

17 Shorts Gardens, WC2
Tel: (020) 7379 7646
Open: Mon–Sat 9–7, Sun 10–5

Traditional British farmhouse cheeses, many of which are matured on the premises.

Royal Opera House

Bow Street, WC2
Tel: (020) 7304 4000
Open: (box office) Mon–Sat 10–8
Tickets: £6–£150

The first two theatres on this site burnt down (1808 and 1856). The third, designed by architect Edward Barry (whose father was responsible for the Houses of Parliament) has recently reopened after an extensive, expensive and much publicised period of refurbishment. The Royal Opera House is also home to the Royal Ballet and is doing its best to justify the huge cost of rebuilding with a new policy of easy access which includes tours, exhibitions, cheaper tickets and free lunchtime concerts. In addition, you do not now need to buy an opera ticket to visit the ROH's new bar and restaurant or to sit out on the sunny terrace which overlooks Covent Garden's Piazza.

St Paul's Church

Bedford Street, WC2
Tel: (020) 7836 5221
Open: Tue–Fri 9.30–4.30
Adm: free

Built by Inigo Jones and completed in 1633, this barn-like church was one of the few buildings still standing after the Great Fire of London in 1666. In the heart of Theatreland, St Paul's is known as the actors' church and has memorials to a number of screen legends including Charlie Chaplin, Noel Coward and Vivien Leigh. The outside portico, usually taken up by street entertainers, is where Eliza Dolittle first met Professor 'Enry 'Iggins in George Bernard Shaw's *Pygmalion* (which later became the musical *My Fair Lady*).

Stanley Gibbon's International

399 The Strand, WC2
Tel: (020) 7836 8444
Open: Mon–Fri 8.30–6, Sat 9–5.30

Founded in 1856, this is a magnet for stamp collectors around the globe with (literally) millions of stamps (literally) on sale.

The Kite Store

48 Neal Street, WC2
Tel: (020) 7836 1666
Open: Mon–Wed & Fri 10–6, Thur 10–7

From traditional kites to the latest hi-tech stunt models, this shop has them all.

The Tea House

15a Neal Street, WC2
Tel: (020) 7240 7539
Open: Mon–Wed & Sat 10–7, Thur 10–7.30, Fri 10.30–7, Sun noon–6

A temple to tea with a huge range of blends and teapots.

The Tintin Shop

34 Floral Street, WC2
Tel: (020) 7836 1131
Open: Mon–Sat 10–6

An outlet solely devoted to the famous Belgian boy-detective and his pals.

The Wild Bunch

17 Earlham Street, WC2
Tel: (020) 7497 1200
Open: Mon–Sat 10–7.30

Echoing Covent Garden's floral past, any number of quality and unusual blooms and bunches. Friendly staff.

food and drink

Food for Thought

31 Neal Street, WC2
Tel: (020) 7836 0239
Open: Mon–Sat noon-8.15
Sun noon-4

This tiny Covent Garden institution offers possibly the best vegetarian food in London.

Belgo Centraal

50 Earlham St, WC2
Tel: (020) 7813 2233
Open: Mon–Sat noon–11.30, Sun 10–10.30

A short walk from the opera, the show continues with staff dressed in monk's habits serving mussels and fries . Good choice of beers. Reasonably priced.

Hammock Café

186 Drury Lane, WC2
Tel: (020) 7404 7808
Open: Mon–Sat 9–8

Cheerful café serving tasty Brazilian food.

Rock 'n' Sole Plaice

47 Endell Street, WC2
Tel: (020) 7836 3785
Open: Mon–Sat 11.30–10, Sun 11.30–9

This place has been open since 1871. Top quality fish and chips.

Calabash

Africa Centre, 8 King Street, WC2
Tel: (020) 7836 1976
Open: Mon–Fri 12.30–3, 6–11

African dishes (couscous, grilled chicken, meaty stews), served in the welcoming atmosphere of the Africa Centre's basement. Child friendly.

food and drink

Thai Pot

1 Bedfordbury, WC2
Tel: (020) 7379 4580
Open: (lunch) Mon–Fri noon–3,
(dinner) Mon–Sat 5.30–11.15

Airy classical-looking décor with subtle Thai standards on the menu.

Maxwell's

8–9 James Street, WC2
Tel: (020) 7836 0303
Open: Mon–Sat 10–midnight,
Sun 10–11.30

Child-friendly with kids' menus, high chairs and welcoming staff. Outside seating for good views of street performers.

PizzaExpress

9 Bow Street, WC2
Tel: (020) 7240 3443
Open: noon–midnight daily

As ever, good pizzas at reasonable prices are provided by this top-quality chain. Child-friendly.

Maggiore's Classic Italian Kitchen

17–21 Tavistock Street, WC2
Tel: (020) 7379 9696
Open: Mon–Sat noon–3.45,
5–11.45, Sun noon–3.45, 5–10.45

Tasty pizza and pasta. Under-12s eat for free (one adult per child).

Freedom Brewing Company

41 Earlham Street, WC2
Tel: (020) 7240 0606
Open: Mon–Sat 11–11, Sun
noon–10.30

Basement bar which brews its own beer. Good food too.

Lamb & Flag

33 Rose Street, WC2
Tel: (020) 7497 9504
Open: Mon–Thur 11–11, Fri & Sat
11–10.45, Sun noon–10.30

Tucked away in a little alley, this 17th-century pub was once nicknamed 'The Bucket of Blood' (the upstairs was used for bareknuckle boxing). These days it's a little calmer.

Theatre Museum

Tavistock Street (entrance off Russell Street), WC2
Tel: (020) 7836 7891
Open: Tue–Sun 10–6
Adm: adult £4.50, concs £2.50, under-16s free

A must for anyone interested in the stage, this little museum reviews the history of the English theatre from the opening of Britain's first playhouse (in 1576) through to the rise of the National Theatre and beyond. Special exhibitions are devoted to such topics as English pantomime or *Hamlet* through the ages and there is also a collection of memorabilia including costumes, props used by famous actors, countless playbills and posters and early drafts of well-known plays. The museum is engagingly hands-on with makeup and costume workshops to attend which give children and adults alike the chance to dress up. Fancy yourself as a werewolf? Or Snow White? The museum is somewhat disorganized and cluttered so the lively guided tour by a professional actor which takes place, free of any additional charge (at 11.30am, 2pm, 3pm), is highly recommended.

HOLBORN (See Central Line)

Sir John Soane's Museum see p32

RUSSELL SQUARE

Dickens House Museum

48 Doughty Street, WC1
Tel: (020) 7405 2127
www.dickensmuseum.com
Open: Mon–Sat 10–5
Adm: adult £4, child £2, concs £3, family £9

In the summer, Charles Dickens' favourite flowers, red geraniums, are planted in window boxes to decorate this Georgian house which was the English novelist's home from 1837 to 1839. During that time the prolific young writer polished off the last six monthly instalments of the *Pickwick Papers* and wrote and published *Oliver Twist* and *Nicholas Nickleby*. Most of the

rooms contain an abundance of portraits, letters and memorabilia including the quill pen Dickens used when composing his last unfinished novel, a turquoise engagement ring he presented to his wife in 1836, the tall desk where at which he wrote his novels (standing up), a monogrammed silver nail clipper and the bars from the Marshalsea Prison where his father was once jailed for non-payment of debt.

KING'S CROSS/ST PANCRAS
(See Northern Line)

London Canal Museum see p76

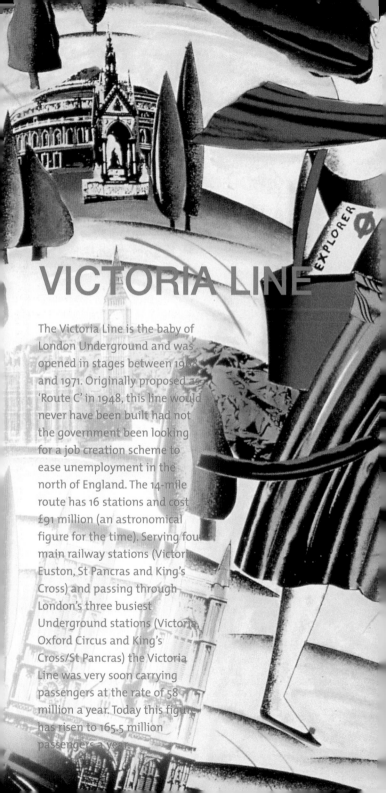

VICTORIA LINE

The Victoria Line is the baby of
London Underground and was
opened in stages between 1968
and 1971. Originally proposed as
'Route C' in 1948, this line would
never have been built had not
the government been looking
for a job creation scheme to
ease unemployment in the
north of England. The 14-mile
route has 16 stations and cost
£91 million (an astronomical
figure for the time). Serving four
main railway stations (Victoria,
Euston, St Pancras and King's
Cross) and passing through
London's three busiest
Underground stations (Victoria,
Oxford Circus and King's
Cross/St Pancras) the Victoria
Line was very soon carrying
passengers at the rate of 58
million a year. Today this figure
has risen to 165.5 million
passengers a year.

PIMLICO

Tate Britain 94

VICTORIA

Royal Mews 95
Westminster Cathedral 95

GREEN PARK

Faraday Museum 97
Fortnum & Mason 97
Green Park 98
Ritz Hotel 98

OXFORD CIRCUS

BBC Experience see p18
Carnaby Street see p19
Hamleys see p19
Liberty's see p19

EUSTON

British Library 99

KING'S CROSS/ST PANCRAS

London Canal Museum see p76

PIMLICO

Tate Britain

Millbank, SW1
Tel: (020) 7887 8000
www.tate.org.uk
Open: 10–5.30 daily
Adm: free

The Tate Gallery was opened in 1897, funded by Sir Henry Tate whose fortune was secure when he purchased the patent for a device which could manufacture sugar lumps. For years, all but 15 per cent of this national collection was locked away in vaults but, thanks to the opening of Tate Modern (see pages 57–58), the space problem has largely been resolved. With a new-found purpose, The Tate Gallery has been given a new name and been freed up to devote itself solely to British art. It is also (for the first time in many years) wonderfully quiet as most of the crowds have gone to Bankside to look at the new collection. Now, before the crowds come back, is a good time to visit.

Taking the cue from its younger sibling, the Tate Britain is currently organizing its collection according to themes rather than a chronology. Literature and Fantasy includes the work of the visionary artist William Blake as well as displaying famous Pre-Raphaelite works such as Sir John Everett Millais' *Ophelia* (1851–2) and *The Lady of Shallot* (1888) by John William Waterhouse. Be sure, also, not to miss Stanley Spencer's wonderful depiction of *St Francis and the Birds* (1935). Public and Private explores visions of the city and has Canaletto's glittering *View of London* (1749) placed alongside L.S. Lowry's bleaker *Industrial Landscape* (1955) as well as taking a look at home life (Jonathan Leaman's Dutch inspired *A Jan Steen Kitchen* – 1995–6 – is rather fun) and the portrait as a genre (look out for Peter Blake's *Self-Portrait with Badges* – 1961). Home & Abroad includes many of the war artists such as Paul Nash and John Singer Sargent as well as having a room devoted to British artists' impressions of foreign countries. Finally, Artists and Models focuses, among other things, on self-portraits and the nude, with an entire room given over to the colourful and inventive early work of David Hockney.

Though there are Constables and Gainsboroughs aplenty to admire, it is well worth saving enough energy for The Clore Gallery extension which houses a vast collection of paintings by J.M.W. Turner. It is difficult, now, to appreciate now just how influential this son of a London barber was, yet his freedom in capturing effects of weather and light, in works such as *Steamer in a Snowstorm* (1842), predate Impressionism by over 30 years.

Just as before, there are still plenty of things for children to do at the Tate. The ever-popular Art Trolley is wheeled out for fun and games on Sundays between noon and 5pm and every day during the holidays, while the new Tate Trails, with a variety of drawing and looking activities, offer kids a fun way to explore the museum on their own.

Though the area is short on decent places to eat, the Tate's restaurant offers a quality menu with main courses starting at around £15. For a cheaper alternative, the café has a good selection of salads, sandwiches and hot meals as well as cakes, coffees, teas and cold drinks.

VICTORIA

Royal Mews

Buckingham Palace Road, SW1
Tel: (020) 7733 2331
www.royal.gov.uk
Open: Aug–Sep Mon–Thur 10.30–4.30 (last admission 4pm),
Oct–July Mon–Thur noon–4 (last admission 3.30pm)
Adm: adult £4.30, child £2.10, concs £3.30, family ticket £10.70
Call in advance for disabled access

Children will love the Royal Mews for the glitter and chintz of the royal carriages which are kept here for state occasions. Among the many vehicles to be found here are Queen Victoria's Irish Coach, reserved for the State Opening of Parliament, and the Glass State Coach, built in 1910, for royal weddings. The gilded State Coach, commissioned by George III, is for coronation ceremonies. The Mews is also used to stable Her Majesty's thoroughbred horses which, with tiled walls and gleaming horse brasses, are kept in some luxury. But they need all the rest they can get – it takes eight of these mighty beasts to pull the gold and jewel-encrusted State Coach.

Westminster Cathedral

Victoria Street, SW1
Tel: (020) 7798 9055
www.westminstercathedral.org.uk
Open: Mon–Fri & Sun 7–7, Sat 8–7
Adm: free

Westminster Cathedral, the premier place of worship for British Roman Catholics, was completed in 1903 though some of the decoration work on the interior has yet to be undertaken. The neo-Byzantine excess of architect John Francis Bentley make this immense building (356ft long and 156ft wide) hard to miss. And nor would you want to. The green marble columns (cut from the same stone as Istanbul's 6th-century St Sophia), the mosaics (fashioned from over 100 different kinds of marble) and Eric Gill's much admired statues of the 14 Stations of the Cross (1914–18) are all worthy of note. So, too is the organ, which is unique in Britain for having a dual control system allowing it to be played from either end of the cathedral.

food and drink

Jenny Lo's Tea House

14 Eccleston Street, SW1
Tel: (020) 7259 0399
Open: Mon–Fri 11.30–3, 6–10, Sat noon–3, 6–10

Unfussy noodle bar.

Marché Mövenpick

Portland House,
Bressenden Place, SW1
Tel: (020) 7630 1733
Open: Mon–Sat 9–11, Sun 11–9

Swiss fast food. Healthy, fun with bright décor and a bar in the shape of a ship. Watch out for the sharks' heads on the walls! Child-friendly.

Seafresh

80–81 Wilton Rd, SW1
Tel: (020) 7828 0747
Open: Mon–Sat noon–10

Huge portions of up-market fish & chips in a restaurant cheerfully decorated with nets and shells. Grilled fish also available.

food and drink

Boisdale

15 Eccleston Street, SW1
Tel: (020) 7730 6922
Open: Mon–Fri noon–2.30,
Mon–Sat 7–11

Quite a rarity: a Scottish
restaurant. Good selection of
whisky (some rare vintages go for
as much as £100 a shot).

Chimes

26 Churton Street, SW1
Tel: (020) 7821 7456
Open: noon–3, 6–10.15 daily

A little way from the Cathedral.
Wonderfully old-fashioned and
authentic English food.

GREEN PARK

Faraday Museum

Royal Institution
21 Albemarle Street, W1
Tel: (020) 7409 2992
Open: Mon–Fri 9–5
Adm: £1

Michael Faraday, the impoverished son of a country
blacksmith, received little formal education and was
apprenticed to a bookbinder at the age of 14. During this
time he took the opportunity to read some of the books
brought in for rebinding. One article on electricity in an
edition of the *Encyclopaedia Britannica* particularly
fascinated him. Using old bottles and bits of rough wood
he began to carry out his own experiments. From these
humble beginnings the young lad went on to became
one of the greatest scientists of the 19th century and
famous for a wide range of achievements, most notably
the invention of the first electric motor and dynamo. You
can get a better understanding of Faraday's work by
visiting this little museum, which includes parts of his
original laboratory, in the basement of the
Royal Institution.

Fortnum & Mason

181 Piccadilly, W1
Tel: (020) 7734 8040
Open: Mon–Sat 9.30–6

On the opposite side of Green Park to Buckingham Palace,
this luxury food shop is where the Queen gets most of
her groceries. Founded by Charles Fortnum (one of

George III's footmen) and his partner John Mason in the 1770s, it is today a London institution. It's all terribly English and a little unreal with pristine packaging and equally immaculate staff. Most people come for the food halls on the ground floor which rival those of Harrods in Knightsbridge (see p80). Afternoon tea at Fortnum & Mason's upstairs Fountain room is served Mon–Sat between 3 and 5.30pm. Prices start at £13.50 per head.

Green Park

Open: dawn–dusk daily

This area was enclosed by Henry VIII and turned into a Royal Park by Charles II. It is not one of the capital's most interesting open spaces but, with acres of well-tended lawns, shady plane and lime trees, comfortable cast-iron benches and quaint old gas lamps, it is a nice enough place to relax. Green Park was originally a leper's burial ground and as a mark of respect for the dead below, no flowers are planted here. Nevertheless, come Spring, a profusion of daffodils pop up and turn it into a green park with yellow spots.

Ritz Hotel

150 Piccadilly, W1
Tel: (020) 7493 8181
Tea: 2–6 daily
Price: £27 per head

Though you have to be fairly wealthy (rooms start at £345 per night) to stay at this historic hotel which was opened in 1906, afternoon tea is somewhat more affordable and has become an institution. At £27 per head it is still rather steep but the grandeur of the venue, the politeness of the staff and the sight of the cakes, sandwiches and scones piled high on silver platters make it an experience few are likely to forget. It is a popular treat and you will need to book well in advance (at least three months for a weekend). Also, remember to dress smartly – jacket and tie are compulsor for men..

food and drink

Al Hamra

31–33 Shepherd Market, W1
Tel: (020) 7493 1954
Open: noon–midnight daily

Swanky Lebanese restaurant. A little pricey but the food is spicy and delicious.

Sofra

18 Shepherd Street, W1
Tel: (020) 7493 3320
Open: Daily noon–midnight

Middle Eastern fare. Fresh food. Prompt service. Delicious mezze dishes, grills and casseroles.

Tamarind

20 Queen Street, W1
Tel: (020) 7629 3561
Open: (lunch) Mon–Fri noon–3, Sun noon–2.30, (dinner) Mon–Sat 6–11.30, Sun 6–10.30

On the pricey side but one of the best Indian restaurants to be found in London. A treat.

OXFORD CIRCUS (see Bakerloo Line)

BBC Experience see p18

Carnaby Street see p19

Hamleys see p19

Liberty's see p19

EUSTON

British Library

96 Euston Road, NW1
Tel: (020) 7412 7332
www.bl.uk
Open: Mon, Wed, Thur, Fri 9.30–6, Tue 9.30–8, Sat 9.30–5, Sun 11–5
Adm: free (donations welcome)

Until 1998 the British Library was part of the British Museum (see pages 30-31) and most of it wasn't open to the public. Now, in a brand new building, there is far greater access. Containing some 18 million volumes, this is one of the biggest libraries in the world. You can admire the library's vast stamp collection or listen to part of its sound archive via a 1950's Wurlitzer-style jukebox on the upper ground floor but the best place to head for is the Treasures of the British Library. Here you can see such historic items as the beautifully illuminated Lindisfarne Gospels (c. 700), one of the four surviving copies of the Magna Carta (1215) and the first ever printed bible, known as the Gutenberg Bible (1455). In addition there is an illuminated version of Chaucer's *Canterbury Tales*, Shakespeare's First Folio (the first collected

edition of Shakespeare's plays), and literary works, in their own handwriting, by the likes of Ben Jonson, Andrew Marvell, Jane Austen, Charles Dickens, George Eliot and Virgina Woolf. More up-to-date exhibits include some of the original Beatles' lyrics to songs such as 'Ticket to Ride' and 'Michelle', written on bits of scrap paper and envelopes. Also don't miss the interactive Workshop of Words, Sound and Images which traces the story of print and book production from the earliest written documents through to modern digital printing (on Saturdays from 11am onwards there are free demonstrations of bookbinding, calligraphy and printing). The imposing six-storey tower, next to the café/restaurant, houses a 65,000-volume collection which once belonged to George III.

KINGS CROSS/ST PANCRAS
(see Northern Line)

London Canal Museum see p76

This selected listing of entertainment and shopping is given alphabetically by tube station name.

Baker Street

CINEMAS

Screen on Baker Street
96 Baker Street, W1
020 7935 2772

ACCESSORIES

K Accessories
73 York Street, W1
020 7724 3337

HATS

Philip Somerville
38 Chiltern Street, W1
020 7224 1517
www.cityscan.co.uk/philip
somerville

Barbican

CINEMAS

Barbican Centre
Silk Street, EC2
020 7382 7000

THEATRES

RSC The Barbican
(and The Pit)
Barbican, EC2
020 7638 8891

Bayswater

CINEMAS

UCI Whiteleys
2nd Floor, Whiteleys
Shopping Centre,
Queensway, W2
08700 102030

Bond Street

ACCESSORIES (MEN)

Ermenegildo Zegna
37-38 New Bond Street, W1
020 7518 2700
www.zegnaermengildo.com

ANTIQUES

Grays Antique Market
58 Davies Street, W1
020 7629 7034
www.graysantiques.com

Grays in the Mew
1-7 Davies Mews, W1
020 7629 7034
www.graysantiques.com

DEPARTMENT STORES

Debenhams
334-348 Oxford Street, W1
020 7580 3000
www.debenhams.com

Fenwick
63 New Bond Street, W1
020 7629 9161

Selfridges
400 Oxford Street, W1
020 7629 1234
www.selfridges.co.uk

DESIGNER FASHION

Burberry
21-23 New Bond Street, W1
020 7839 5222

Calvin Klein
53-55 New Bond Street, W1
020 7491 9656

Chanel
173 New Bond Street, W1
020 7499 0005

Gianni Versace
34-36 Old Bond Street, W1
020 7499 1862
www.gianniversace.com

Louis Vuitton
17-18 New Bond Street, W1
020 7399 4050
www. vuitton.com

Miu Miu
123 New Bond Street, W1
020 7409 0900

Tommy Hilfige
51 New Bond Street, W1
020 7290 9688
www.tommy.com

Vivienne Westwood
6 Davies Street, W1
020 7629 3757

Yves Saint Laurent
137 New Bond Street, W1
020 7493 1800

Jane & Dada
12 St Christopher's Place, W1
020 7487 4484

FASHION (MEN)

Browns
23-27 South Molton Street, W1
020 7514 0000
www.brownsfashion.com

SHOES

Russell & Bromley
24-25 New Bond Street, W1
020 7629 6903
www.russellandbromley.co.uk

Charing Cross

CINEMAS

CA Cinema 1 & 2
Nash House, The Mall, SW1
020 7930 3647

THEATRES

Adelphi Theatre
Strand, WC2
020 7344 0055

Lyceum Theatre
Wellington Street, WC2
0870 243 9000

Savoy Theatre
Strand, WC2
020 7836 8888

Whitehall Theatre
Whitehall, SW1
020 7369 1735

Covent Garden

THEATRES

Aldwych Theatre
The Aldwych, WC2
0870 400 0805

Cambridge Theatre
Earlham Street, WC2
020 7494 5080

Drury Lane Theatre Royal
Catherine Street, WC2
0207 494 5000

New London
Drury Lane, WC2
020 7405 0072

Strand Theatre
Aldwych, WC2
020 7930 8800

ANTIQUES, CRAFTS

Jubilee Market
Jubilee Hall, off
Southampton Street, WC2

CRAFTS

Apple Market, The Piazza,
Covent Garden, W1

DESIGNER FASHION

Paul Smith
40-44 Floral Street, WC2
020 7379 7133
www.paulsmith.co.uk

FASHION

Blu Nauta
69-76 Long Acre, WC2
020 7240 1018

Diesel
43 Earlham Street, WC2
020 7497 5543
www.diesel.com

Dockers
Unit 8, North Piazza, Covent
Garden, WC2
020 7240 7908
www.dockers.com

Gap
30-31 Long Acre, WC2
020 7379 0779
www.gap.com

Kookai
Unit 13, The Piazza,
Covent Garden, WC2
020 7379 1318
www.kookai.fr

Mambo
Thomas Neal Centre,
37 Earlham Street, WC2
020 7379 6066
www.mambo.com.au

Mango
8-12 Neal Street, WC2
020 7240 6099
www.mango.es

Mexx
112-115 Long Acre, WC2
020 7761 0600
www.mexx.com

Monsoon
3 James Street, WC2
020 7379 3623
www.monsoon.co.uk

Next
19-20 Long Acre, WC2
020 7836 1516
www.next.co.uk

O'Neill
9-15 Neal Street, WC2
020 7836 7686
www.oneilleurope.com

Oasis
13 James Street, WC2
020 7240 7445
www.oasis-stores.com

Question Air
38 Floral Street, WC2
020 7836 8220

Ted Baker
1-4 Langley Court WC2
020 7497 8862
www.tedbaker.co.uk

Warehouse
24 Long Acre, WC2
020 7240 8242
www.zoom.co.uk

FASHION (MEN)

Blazer
117B Long Acre, WC2
020 7379 0456
www.mossbros.co.uk

FASHION (SPORT)

Quiksilver
Thomas Neal Centre,
37 Earlham Street, WC2
020 7836 5371
www.quiksilver.com

OUTDOOR PURSUITS

Field & Trek
42 Maiden Lane, WC2
020 7379 3793
www.field-trek.co.uk

Karrimor Store
3 Southampton Street,
WC2
020 7497 0716

YHA Adventure Shop
14 Southampton Street,
WC2
020 7836 8541
www. yha.adventure.co.uk

SHOES

Bertie
25 Long Acre, WC2
020 7836 7223

Birkenstock
37 Neal Street, WC2
020 7240 2783
www.birkenstock.co.uk

**Dr Marten Department
Store**
1-4 King Street, WC2
020 7497 1460
www.drmartens.com

LK Bennett
130 Long Acre, WC2
020 7379 1710
www.lkbennett.com

Natural Shoe Store
21 Neal Street, WC2
020 7836 5254
www.naturesho.com

Sole Trader
72 Neal Street, WC2
020 7836 6777
www.sole-trader.co.uk

Edgware Road

ANTIQUES

Alfie's Antique Market
13-25 Church Street, NW8
020 7723 6066

Goodge Street

FURNITURE

Habitat
196 Tottenham Court Road,
020 7631 3880
www.habitat.net

Heals
196 Tottenham Court Road
020 7636 1666

INTERNET CAFÉ

Cyberia
39 Whitfield Street, W1
020 7681 4200
www.cyberiacafe.net

STATIONERY

Paperchase
213 Tottenham Court Road,
W1
020 7467 6200

Green Park

CINEMAS

Curzon Mayfair
38 Curzon Street, W1
020 7465 8865

ACCESSORIES

Georgina von Etzdorf
1-2 Burlington Arcade, W1
020 7409 7789
www.gve.co.uk

DEPARTMENT STORE

Fortnum & Mason
181 Piccadilly, W1
020 7734 8040
www.fortnumandmason.co.uk

DESIGNER FASHION

Gianni Versace
34-36 Old Bond Street, W1
020 7499 1862
www.gianniversace.com

Holland & Holland
31-33 Bruton Street, W1
020 7499 4411

Prada
15-16 Old Bond Street, W1
020 7647 5000
www.prada.com

Ralph Lauren
1 New Bond Street, W1
020 7535 4600
www.ralphlauren.com

Yves Saint Laurent
137 New Bond Street, W1
020 7493 1800
www.yslonline.com

FASHION

Favourbrook
8 Piccadilly Arcade, W1
020 7491 2331
www.favourbrook.com

FASHION (MEN)

Alfred Dunhill
48 Jermyn Street, W1
020 7290 8606

JEWELLERY

Cartier
175-176 New Bond Street, W1
020 7493 6962
www.cartier.com

Mikimoto
179 New Bond Street, W1
020 7629 5300

Tiffany & Co
25 Old Bond Street, W1
020 7409 2790
www.tiffany.com

High Street Kensington

CINEMAS

Odeon Kensington
High Street Kensington, W8
0870 5050 007

ACCESSORIES

Urban Outfitters
36-38 Kensington High Street, W8
020 7761 1001

FASHION

Benetton
129 Kensington High Street, W8
020 7937 3034
www.benetton.com

Kaliko
42 Kensington High Street, W8
020 7937 5845

OUTDOOR PURSUITS

Snow & Rock
188 Kensington High Street, W8
020 7937 0872

SHOES

Atticus
14 Kensington Church Street, W8
020 7376 0059

Holborn

BOOKS

Books etc
263 High Holborn, WC1
020 7404 0261

OUTDOOR PURSUITS

Black's
10-11 Holborn, EC1
020 7404 5681

Hyde Park Corner

CINEMAS

Curzon Mayfair
38 Curzon Street, W1
020 7465 8865

Knightsbridge

ACCESSORIES

La Joya
24 Cheval Place, SW7
020 7823 8066

DEPARTMENT STORE

Harrods
87-135 Brompton Road, SW1
020 7730 1234
www.harrods.com

Harvey Nichols
109-125 Knightsbridge, SW1
020 7235 5000

DESIGNER FASHION

Christian Dior
31 Sloane Street, SW1
020 7235 1357

Gucci
17-18 Sloane Street, SW1
020 7235 6707
www.gucci.com

Hermès
179 Sloane Street, SW1
020 7823 1014

Iceberg
10 Sloane Street, SW1
020 7259 6657

FASHION

Belinda Robertson
4 West Halkin Street, SW1
020 7235 0519
www.belindarobertson.co.uk

M-A-G
20 Beauchamp Place, SW3
020 7591 0552
www.m-a-g.com

pallant...
The Pantechnicon, 19A Motcomb St, SW1
020 7259 6046

Shi Cashmere
30 Lowndes Street, SW1
020 7235 3829

Violet
11 Pont Street, SW1
020 7259 5966

FASHION (SPORT)

Lacoste
20 Brompton Road, SW3
020 7225 2861
www.lacoste.com

SHOES

Annello & Davide
47 Beauchamp Place, SW3
020 7225 2468
www.handmadeshoes.co.uk

Pied à Terre
3 Sloane Street, SW1
020 7235 0564
www.piedaterrre.co.uk

UNDERWEAR

Rigby & Peller
2 Hans Road, SW3
020 7589 9293
www.rigbyandpeller.com

Leicester Square

CINEMAS

Curzon Soho
93-107 Shaftesbury Avenue, W1
020 7439 4805

Empire
Leicester Square, WC2
020 7437 1234

Metro
11 Rupert Street, W1
020 7437 0757

Odeon Mezzanine
Leicester Square, WC2
0870 5050 007

Odeon Wardour Street
Swiss Centre, WC2
0870 5050 007

Odeon West End
Leicester Square, WC2
0870 5050 007

Prince Charles
Leicester Place, WC2
020 7734 9127

UGC Trocadero
Trocadero, WC2
0870 907 0716

Warner Village West End
Leicester Square, WC2
020 437 3848

Odeon Leicester Square
Leicester Square, WC2
0870 5050 007

THEATRES

Albery Theatre
St Martin's Lane, WC2
020 7399 1740

Arts Theatre
6-7 Great Newport Street, WC2
020 7836 3334

Duke of York's
St Martin's Lane, WC2
020 7369 1791

Garrick Theatre
Charing Cross Road, WC2
020 7494 5085

New Ambassadors
West Street, WC2
020 7836 6111

Palace Theatre
Shaftesbury Avenue, W1
020 7434 0909

Phoenix Theatre
Charing Cross Road, WC2
020 7369 1733

Queen's Theatre
Shaftesbury Avenue, W1
020 7494 5040

DIRECTORY

St Martin's
West Street, WC2
020 7836 1443

Wymondhams Theatre
Charing Cross Road, WC2
020 7369 1736

FASHION

Johanna Hehir
42 Monmouth Street, WC2
020 7240 1227
www.johanna-hehir.com

O'Neill
9-15 Neal Street, WC2
020 7836 7686
www.oneilleurope.com

SHOES

LK Bennett
130 Long Acre, WC2
020 7379 1710
www.lkbennett.com

Marble Arch

DEPARTMENT STORE

Selfridges
400 Oxford Street
020 7629 1234
www.selfridges.co.uk

Marks & Spencer
458 Oxford Street, W1
020 7935 7954
www.marks-and-spencer.co.uk

Clarks Shop
476 Oxford Street, W1
020 7629 9609
www.clarks.co.uk

Moorgate

CINEMAS

Barbican Centre
Silk Street, EC2
020 7382 7000

THEATRES

RSC The Barbican (and The Pit)
Barbican, EC2
020 7638 8891

Notting Hill Gate

CINEMAS

Electric Cinema, The
191 Portobello Road, W11
020 7229 8688

Notting Hill Coronet
Notting Hill Gate, W11
020 7727 6705

FASHION

APC
40 Ledbury Road, W11
020 7229 4933
www.apc.fr

Siola
25 Kensington Park Road, W11
020 7727 8888

Wall
1 Denbigh Road, W11
020 7243 4623

INTERNET CAFÉ

BuzzBar at Portobello Gold
95-97 Portobello Road, W11
020 7460 4906
www.portobellogold.com

SHOES

Issues, A Natural Shoe Store
181 Westbourne Grove, W11
020 7727 1122

Oxford Circus

THEATRES

London Palladium
Argyll Street, W1
020 7494 5020

DEPARTMENT STORE

Debenhams
334-348 Oxford Street, W1
020 7580 3000
www.debenhams.com

Dickins & Jones
224-244 Regent Street, W1
020 7734 7070
www.houseoffraser.co.uk

John Lewis
278-306 Oxford Street, W1
020 7629 7711
www.johnlewis.co.uk

Liberty
210-220 Regent Street, W1
020 7734 1234
www.liberty-of-london.com

DESIGNER FASHION

Alexander McQueen
47 Conduit Street, W1
020 7734 2340
www.alexandermcqueen.co.uk

ELECTRONICS

Dixons
88 Oxford Street, W1
020 7636 8511
www.dixons.com

FASHION

Beau Monde
43 Lexington Street, W1
020 7734 6563
www.beaumonde.uk.com

Burberry
21-23 New Bond Street, W1
020 7839 5222

Episode
59 Brompton Road, SW3

020 7589 5724
www.episode.co.uk

French Connection
249-251 Regent Street, W1
020 7493 3124
www.frenchconnection.com

Jaeger
200-206 Regent Street, W1
020 7200 4000
www.coats-viyella.com

Jane Norman
262 Oxford Street, W1
020 7499 7454
www.janenorman.co.uk

Karen Millen
262-264 Regent Street, W1
020 7287 6158

Laura Ashley
256-258 Regent Street, W1
020 7437 9760
www.lauraashley.com

Mash
73 Oxford Street, W1
020 7434 9609

Pineal Eye
49 Broadwick Street, W1
020 7434 2567

Racing Green
195 Regent Street, W1
020 7437 4300
www.racinggreen.co.uk

Souvenir
17 Lexington Street, W1
020 7287 9877

Wallis
215-217 Oxford Street, W1
020 7437 0076
www.zoom.co.uk

INTERNET CAFÉ

Interc@fé
23-25 Great Portland Street
020 7631 0063
www.intercafe.co.uk/frontpage

JEWELLERY

Mappin & Webb
170 Regent Street, W1
020 7734 3801
www.mappin-and-webb.co.uk

MUSIC

HMV
150 Oxford Street, W1
020 7631 3423
www.hmv.co.uk

SHOES

Church's Shoes
201 Regent Street, W1
020 7734 2438
www.churchshoes.com

SPORTSWEAR

Nike Town
236 Oxford Street, W1
020 7612 0800
www.nike.com

Piccadilly Circus

CINEMAS

ABC Piccadilly
Piccadilly, W1
020 7287 3561

Curzon Soho
93-107 Shaftesbury Avenue,
W1
020 7439 4805

Empire
Leicester Square, WC2
020 7437 1234

ICA Cinema 1 & 2
Nash House,
The Mall, SW1
020 7930 3647

Metro
11 Rupert Street, W1
020 7437 0757

Odeon Panton Street
Panton Street, SW1
0870 5050 007

Odeon Wardour Street
Swiss Centre, WC2
0870 5050 007

Plaza
Lower Regent Street, W1
0990 888990

Prince Charles
Leicester Place, WC2
020 7734 9127

UGC Haymarket
62-65 Haymarket, W1
0870 907 0712

UGC Trocadero
Trocadero, WC2
0870 907 0716

THEATRES

Lyric Shaftesbury
Shaftesbury Avenue, W1
020 7494 5045

Apollo Shaftesbury
Shaftesbury Avenue, W1
020 7494 5070

Comedy Theatre
Panton Street, SW1
020 7369 1731

Criterion Theatre
Piccadilly Circus, WC2
020 7413 1437

Gielgud Theatre
Shaftesbury Avenue, W1
020 7494 5065

Haymarket Theatre Royal
Haymarket, SW1
020 7930 8800

Her Majesty's
Haymarket, SW1
020 7494 5400

Piccadilly Theatre
Denman Street, W1
020 7389 1734

BOOKS

Hatchards
187 Piccadilly, W1
020 7439 9921
www.hatchards.co.uk

Waterstone's
203-206 Piccadilly, W1
020 7851 2400
www.waterstones.co.uk

DEPARTMENT STORE

Fortnum & Mason
181 Piccadilly, W1
020 7734 8040
www.fortnumandmason.co.uk

DESIGNER FASHION

Alexander McQueen
47 Conduit Street, W1
020 7734 2340
www.alexandermcqueen.co.uk

Moschino
28-29 Conduit Street, W1
020 7318 0555
www.moschino.it

FASHION

Aquascutum
100 Regent Street, W1
020 7675 8200
www.aquascutum.co.uk

Austin Reed
103-113 Regent Street, W1
020 7734 6789
www.austinreed.co.uk

Episode
59 Brompton Road, SW3
020 7589 5724
www.episode.co.uk

Levi's Store
174-176 Regent Street, W1
020 7439 2014
www.eu.levi.com

FASHION (MEN)

Gieves & Hawkes
Savile Row, W1
020 7434 2001
www.gievesandhawkes.com

HATS (MEN)

Bates the Hatter
21A Jermyn Street, SW1
020 7734 2722
www.bates-hats.co.uk

INTERNET CAFÉ

Global Café
15 Golden Square, W1
020 7287 2242
www.globalcafe.net

Webshack
15 Dean Street, W1
020 7439 8000
www.webshack-cafe.com

JEWELLERY

Richard Ogden
28 Burlington Arcade, W1
020 7493 9136
www.richardogden.com

MUSIC

Tower Records
1 Piccadilly Circus, W1
020 7439 2500
www.towerrecords.co.uk

UNDERWEAR

Ann Summers
79 Wardour Street, W1
020 7434 2475
www.annsummers.com

Queensway

CINEMAS

UCI Whiteleys
2nd Floor, Whiteleys
Shopping Centre,
Queensway, W2
08700 102030

Russell Square

CINEMAS

Renoir
Brunswick Street, WC1
020 7837 8402

Sloane Square

CINEMAS

Chelsea Cinema
Kings Road, SW3
020 7351 3742

UGC Chelsea
279 Kings Road, SW3
0870 907 0710

THEATRES

Royal Court Theatre (both
Upstairs and Downstairs)
Sloane Square, SW1
020 7565 5000

ANTIQUES

Antiquarius
131-141 Kings Road, SW3
020 7351 5353

**Bourbon-Hanby Antiques
Centre**
151 Sydney Street, SW3
020 7352 2106

www.antiques.uk.co.uk/bourbon-hanby

BAGS

Anya Hindmarch
15-17 Pont Street, SW1
020 7838 9177
www.anyahindmarch.com

Lulu Guiness
3 Ellis Street, SW1
020 7823 4828
www.luluguiness.com

FASHION

Brora
344 King's Road, SW3
020 7352 3697
www.brora.co.uk

East
105 King's Road, SW3
020 7376 3161

Hobbs
84-88 King's Road, SW3
020 7581 2914

Jackpot & Cottonfield
106-108 King's Road, SW3
020 7838 0759

Violet
11 Pont Street, SW1
020 7259 5966

FASHION (MEN)

Hackett
137-138 Sloane Street, SW1
020 7730 3331
www.hackett.co.uk

HATS

Philip Treacy
69 Elizabeth Street, SW1
020 7824 8787
www.philiptreacy.com

UNDERWEAR

La Perla
163 Sloane Street, SW1
020 7245 0527
www.laperla.com

South Kensington

CINEMAS

UGC Fulham Road
142 Fulham Road, SW10
0870 907 0711

BOOKS

Pan Bookshop
158 Fulham Road, SW10
020 7373 4997

DESIGNER FASHION

Betsey Johnson
106 Draycott Avenue, SW3
020 7591 0005
www.betseyjohnson.com

FASHION

Agnès B
111 Fulham Road, SW3
020 7225 3477
www.agnesb.fr

Tokio
309 Brompton Road, SW3
020 7823 7310

FURNITURE

Conran Shop, The
Michelin House,
81 Fulham Road, SW3
020 7589 7401
www.conran.co.uk

SHOES

Annello & Davide
47 Beauchamp Place, SW3
020 7225 2468
www.handmadeshoes.co.uk

Tottenham Court Road

CINEMAS

ABC Shaftesbury Avenue
Shaftesbury Avennue, W1
0870 5050 007

Odeon
Tottenham Court Road, W1
0870 5050 007

THEATRES

Dominion Theatre
Tottenham Court Road, W1
0870 607 7460

BOOKS

Blackwells
100 Charing Cross Road,
WC2
020 7292 5100
www.bookshop.blackwell.co.uk

Borders Books & Music
120 Charing Cross Road,
WC2
020 7379 6838
www.borders.com

Foyles
113-119 Charing Cross Road,
WC2
020 7437 5660

ELECTRONICS

Apple Centre
78 New Oxford Street, WC1
020 7692 9990
www.square2.co.uk

Dixons
88 Oxford Street, W1
020 7636 8511
www.dixons.com

Shasonic
42 Tottenham Court Road, W1
020 7323 0333

FASHION

Morgan
7 Oxford Street, W1
020 7437 2768
www.morgan.fr

MUSIC

Virgin Megastore
14-16 Oxford Street, W1
020 7631 1234

PHOTOGRAPHY

Jessop
63-69 New Oxford Street,
WC1
020 7240 6077
www.jessop.co.uk

SHOES

Shoe Express
72-74 Oxford Street, W1
020 7436 8791

Victoria

THEATRES

Apollo Victoria
Wilton Road, SW1
0870 400 0870

INTERNET CAFÉ

Caté Internet
22-24 Buckingham Place
Road, SW1
020 7233 5786
www.cafeinternet.co.uk

EasyEverything
Wilton Road, SW1
020 7233 8456
www.easyeverything.com

Waterloo

CINEMAS

BFI London Imax Cinema
South Bank, Waterloo, SE1
020 7902 1234

THEATRES

National Theatre, Cottesloe
South Bank, SE1
020 7452 3000

National Theatre, Lyttelton
South Bank, SE1
020 7452 3000

National Theatre, Olivier
South Bank, SE1
020 7452 3000

OUTDOOR PURSUITS

Evans Cycles
77-81 The Cut, SE1
020 7928 4785
www.evanscycles.com

Index of Sights

Albert Hall & Albert
    Monument, 64
Apple Market, 85
Aspley House, The
    Wellington Museum, 81

Bank of England Museum,
    36
Barbican Centre, 62
BBC Experience, 18
Benjamin Pollock's Toy
    Museum, 85
Berwick Street Market, 15
Bramah Tea and Coffee
    Museum, 68
Brick Lane Market, 39
British Airways London Eye,
    6
British Library, 99
British Museum, 30
Buckingham Palace, 51

Cabinet War Rooms, 53
Camden Passage, 75
Carlyle's House, 49
Carnaby Street, 19
Chelsea Physic Garden, 50
Chinatown, 83
Clink Prison Museum, 68
Clockmakers' Company
    Museum, 37
Columbia Road Flower
    Market, 39
Conran Shop, 44
Courtauld Gallery, 56
Covent Garden Market and
    Piazza, 85

Design Museum, 69
Dickens House Museum, 91
Dr Johnson's House, 33

FA Premier League Hall of
    Fame, 6
Faraday Museum, 97
Florence Nightingale
    Museum, 7
Food and drink (see
    separate index)
Fortnum & Mason, 98

Gabriel's Wharf, 7
Geffrye Musuem, 40
Gilbert Collection, 56
Golden Hinde, The, 69
Green Park, 97
Guildhall, 37

Habitat, 76
Half-price Ticket Booth, 84
Hamleys, 19
Harrods, 80
Hayward Gallery, 10
Heal's, 76

HMS Belfast, 70
Horse Guards, 53
House of Detention, 62
Houses of Parliament & Big
    Ben, 54
Hyde Park/Speaker's Corner,
    27

Imperial War Museum, 4
Institute of Contemporary
    Arts (ICA), 11

Kensington Palace, 65
Kite Store, The, 86

Liberty's, 19
London Aquarium, 8
London Canal Museum, 76
London Coliseum, 84
London Doll's House
    Company, 86
London Dungeon, 70
London Planetarium, 22
London Toy and Model
    Museum, 27
London Transport
    Headquarters, 51
London Transport
    Museum, 87
London Zoo, 20

Madame Tussaud's, 22
Millennium Bridge, 59
Monument, The, 59
Museum of London, 34
Museum of... The, 8

Namco Station, 9
National Film Theatre, 10
National Gallery, 11
National Portrait Gallery, 12
Natural History Museum,
    44
Neal Street East, 86
Neal's Yard Bakery, 86
Neal's Yard Dairy, 34

Old Bailey, 34
Old Operating Theatre and
    Herb Garrett, 71

Pepsi Trocadero, 17
Petticoat Lane, 40
Portobello Market, 26
Pollock's Toy Museum, 77
Prince Henry's Room, 57

Rainforest Café, 15
Regents Park, 21
Ritz Hotel, 98
Rock Circus, 15
Royal Academy of Arts, 16
Royal Festival Hall, 10
Royal Mews, 95
Royal National Theatre, 10
Royal Opera House, 88

Science Museum, 46
Selfridges, 28
Serpentine Gallery, 47
Shakespeare's Globe
    Theatre, 72
Sherlock Holmes Museum,
    23
Sir John Soane's Museum,
    32
South Bank Arts Centre, 9
St James's Church Piccadilly,
    17
St James's Park, 52
St Martin-in-the-Fields, 13
St Paul's Cathedral, 35
St Paul's Church, 89
Stanley Gibbons
    International, 86

Tate Britain, 94
Tate Modern, 57
Tea House, The, 86
Theatre Museum, 90
Tintin Shop, The, 87
Tower Hill, 60
Tower of London, 60
Trafalgar Square, 14

Victoria and Albert
    Museum, 47
Vinopolis, City of Wine, 73

Wallace Collection, 28
Westminster Abbey, 55
Westminster Cathedral, 95
Wigmore Hall, 29
Wild Bunch, The, 87
Winston Churchill's Britain
    at War, 73

INDEX

Index of food and drink

Al Hamra, 99
Albert, The, 51
Alfred, 82
Anchor Bankside, 74
Andrew Edmunds, 82
Ask Pizza, 63
Auberge, 10

Babushka, 5
Bagel Bakery, 41
Bar Du Marché, 17
Belgo Centraal, 89
Bibendum, 49
Black Friar, The, 59
Bleeding Heart, 63
Blue Posts, 18
Boisdale, 97
Bonbonnierre, 20
Books for Cooks, 26
Brendan O'Gradys 5
Bunch of Grapes, 81

Cactus Blue, 49
Café Fish, 14
Café in the Crypt, 14
Café Rouge, 36
Café Spice Namaste, 61
Calabash, 89
Capital Radio Café, 84
Casale Franco, 75
Chimes, 97
Cittie of York, 33
Criterion, The, 14
Cynthia's Cyberbar, 74

Daquise, 49
De Gustibus, 30
Dicken's Inn, 61
Dirty Dick's, 41
Doggett's Coat and Badge, 10
Dôme, 75
Dover Castle, 20

Eagle, The, 63

Fina Estampa, 74
Fire Station, The, 5
fish!, 74
Food for Thought, 89
Fortnum & Mason Fountain
   Room, 18
Freedom Brewing Company,
   90
French House, 84
Fung Shing, 83

George, 41
George Inn, The, 74
Globe Café, 74
Globe Restaurant, 74
Gloriette Patisserie, 81
Golden Harvest, 83
Goring Hotel, 53
Gourmet Pizza Company, 10
Greenfields Café, 49

Hammock Café, 89
Harbour City, 83
Horniman, The, 74

Jamaica Wine House, 38
Jenny Lo's Tea House, 96
Jerusalem Tavern, 63

King's Head, The, 75
Kula Kula, 82

Lamb & Flag, 90
Lamb, The, 32
Le Prince Bonaparte, 27
Lexington, The, 20

**Maggiore's Classic Italian
   Kitchen, 90**
Marché Mövenpick, 96
Maxwell's, 90
Moshi Moshi Sushi, 41
Mr Kong, 84

Nico Central, 20

Old Dr Butler's Head, 38
Old Thameside Inn, 74
Orange Brewery, 51
Oxo Tower, 10

Patisserie Valerie, 82
People's Palace, The, 10
Pharmacy, 26
Photographer's Gallery Café,
   84
Pizza on the Park, 81
PizzaExpress (Bow Street,
   WC2), 90
PizzaExpress (Coptic Street,
   WC1), 32
PizzaExpress (Langham
   Place, W1), 20
PizzaExpress (Victoria
   Street, SW1), 53
Place Below, The, 36
Planet Harrods, 81
Planet Hollywood, 17
Pollo, 82

Quality Chop House, 63

Ritz Hotel, 18
RK Stanley's, 20
Rock 'n' Sole Plaice, 89

Sausage and Mash Café, 27
Seafresh, 96
Shepherd's, 59
Silks & Spice, 38
Simpson's Tavern, 38
Sofra, 29
Sofra, 99
Spighetta, 29
St James Tavern, 82
St John, 63
Studio Six, 10

Tamarind, 99
TGI Fridays, 18, 89
Thai Pot, 90
Townhouse Brasserie, 32
Truckles of Pied Bull Yard, 32

Upper Street Fish Shop, 75

Villandry, 20

Wagamama, 32
Wagamama, 65
William Wallace, 30
Windsor Castle, 65
Wódka, 65

Ye Old Cheshire Cheese, 33
Ye Olde Mitre, 33